CHURCH
Family
WORSHIP

Church Pastoral Aid Society
and Jubilate Hymns

Editor: Michael Perry

Hodder & Stoughton
LONDON SYDNEY AUCKLAND TORONTO

Also from Jubilate Hymns, published by
Hodder and Stoughton

Hymns for Today's Church
Carols for Today

Available from the Church Pastoral Aid Society
and Jubilate Hymns

Church Family Worship Source Book
Supplementary carol sheets

British Library Cataloguing in Publication Data

Church family worship.
  1. Family – Religious life   2. Liturgies
  3. Public worship
  I. Perry, Michael
  264   BV200

  ISBN Hbk 0 340 40548 1
       Pbk 0 340 39395 5

Editor
Michael Perry

Editorial Team
Richard Bewes and Paul Simmonds (Prayers)
Patrick Goodland (Free Church Worship)
Kenneth Habershon (Bible Readings)
David Peacock (Songs)
Richard Cattley, George Lihou,
Clifford Roseweir, Noël Tredinnick
Norman Warren

Consultant Editor
Michael Baughen, Bishop of Chester

CHURCH FAMILY WORSHIP
Introduction

Family Services have rapidly become a most viable and effective provision for worship in the community. Practices vary. In some churches, family services are quite different from any other event: once a month and at festivals the whole Christian family meets together. In other churches, worship begins and/or ends like this on most Sundays. Such services meet a special need where traditional fixed forms are inappropriate and standard books of hymns or songs inadequate. This need is for reverent simplicity, intelligent informality, and *substance* – for all ages.

What is the content of Church Family Worship?

As you see from a glance, the book contains currently popular traditional and modern music material, along with additional items which look to the future. There are responsive prayers with trigger phrases (versicles) which involve the whole congregation. New Testament creeds deepen the doctrinal content of thematic sections. Cross-referencing and a biblical index make easier the selection of prayers and music.

How may Church Family Worship be used?

Church Family Worship is a resource of a special kind. As a service book, it is flexible in its four modes of use.

1: Choose a standard format from the front – for instance, Morning or Evening Worship drawn from The Alternative Service Book 1980, supplement this with hymns, songs and prayers from the rest of the book – all accessible by number.

2: Select a theme or seasonal service and use one or more of the book's thirty thematic sections to provide all you need within the compass of a few pages.

3: Use the short service at the back – confession, creed, Lord's Prayer, prayers for the nation and the sick – and supplement with, say, a responsive psalm, a thanksgiving, hymns, songs, etc.

4: Creatively choose material from all over the book, adding perhaps 'minister's prayers' from the service-leader's section.

How was the content of Church Family Worship chosen?

Everything in the book has been tried. We are grateful for the advice of the experts whose help is acknowledged in section 41, and to the hundreds of other clergy and ministers who gave us the benefit of experience with their own family worship by submitting recommendations and contributions. We are grateful too for the statistical and textual input of an interdenominational spread of sources – from the Church of England diocesan liturgical committees to the Baptist's 'Mainstream' organisation. This has given the book a very broad base. Finally, we acknowledge our debt to our predecessor, CPAS's 'Family Worship', and to the members of the various liturgical commissions.

We commend this book to the English-speaking churches in the hope that it may become a vehicle of worship to delight and satisfy the church family wherever it is. Our aim above all is that services with integrity and direction may honour and glorify God, who must ever be the subject and the object of our prayer and praise:

'To him be glory in the church and in Christ Jesus throughout all generations for ever and ever. Amen.'

CHURCH FAMILY WORSHIP
Order of Contents

(References in brackets are to
corresponding themes of the Lectionary)

1 Morning or Evening Worship

drawn from The Alternative
Service Book 1980

1 (24) **Stand**. This introduction may be
said:

We have come together
    as the family of God
in our Father's presence
to offer him praise and thanksgiving,
to hear and receive his holy word,
to bring before him
    the needs of the world,
to ask his forgiveness of our sins,
and to seek his grace,
that through his Son Jesus Christ
we may give ourselves to his service.

2 (25) A sentence of Scripture may be said
and a hymn may be sung.

3 (26) This sentence may be said:

If we say we have no sin,
we deceive ourselves,
and the truth is not in us.
If we confess our sins,
God is faithful and just,
and will forgive us our sins,
and cleanse us
    from all unrighteousness.

1 John 1.8–9

4 (27) The minister may say:

Let us confess our sins to almighty
God:

5 (28)

**Almighty God, our heavenly Father,
we have sinned against you
    and against our fellow men,
in thought and word and deed,
through negligence,
    through weakness,**

**through our own deliberate fault.
We are truly sorry
and repent of all our sins.
For the sake of your Son Jesus Christ,
    who died for us,
forgive us all that is past;
and grant that we may serve you
    in newness of life
to the glory of your name. Amen.**

Or

**Almighty God, our heavenly Father,
we have sinned against you,
through our own fault,
in thought and word and deed,
and in what we have left undone.
For your Son our Lord Jesus Christ's
    sake,
forgive us all that is past;
and grant that we may serve you
    in newness of life
to the glory of your name. Amen.**

(See also ASB alternative confession at 417)

6 (29) Absolution:

Almighty God, who forgives all who
truly repent, have mercy upon *you*,
pardon and deliver *you* from all *your*
sins, confirm and strengthen *you* in all
goodness, and keep *you* in life eternal;
through Jesus Christ our Lord. **Amen.**

8 (31) Stand:

O Lord, open our lips;
**and our mouth shall proclaim
    your praise.**

Let us worship the Lord:
all praise to his name.

**Glory to the Father, and to the Son,
and to the Holy Spirit:
as it was in the beginning, is now,
and shall be for ever. Amen.**

9–15 (32–38)
Psalm(s)

Reading(s) ending:

This is the word of the Lord:
thanks be to God.

Canticle(s)

16 (39) The Apostles' Creed

**I believe in God, the Father almighty,
creator of heaven and earth.
I believe in Jesus Christ, his only Son,
our Lord.
He was conceived by the power
of the Holy Spirit
and born of the Virgin Mary.
He suffered under Pontius Pilate,
was crucified, died, and was buried.
He descended to the dead.
On the third day he rose again.
He ascended into heaven,
and is seated at the right hand
of the Father.
He will come again to judge the living
and the dead.**

**I believe in the Holy Spirit,
the holy catholic Church,
the communion of saints,
the forgiveness of sins,
the resurrection of the body,
and the life everlasting. Amen.**

17 (40) The minister may say:

Lord, have mercy upon us.
Christ, have mercy upon us.
Lord, have mercy upon us.

18 (41)

**Our Father in heaven,
hallowed be your name,
your kingdom come,
your will be done,
on earth as in heaven.
Give us today our daily bread.
Forgive us our sins
as we forgive those
who sin against us.
Lead us not into temptation
but deliver us from evil.**

**For the kingdom, the power,
and the glory are yours
now and for ever. Amen.**

19 (42) These versicles and responses may
be said:

Show us your mercy, O Lord;
and grant us your salvation.

O Lord, save the Queen;
and teach her counsellors wisdom.

Let your priests be clothed with righteousness;
and let your servants shout for joy.

O Lord, make your ways known upon
the earth;
**let all nations acknowledge
your saving power.**
Give your people the blessing of peace;
**and let your glory be over
all the world.**
Make our hearts clean, O God;
and renew a right spirit within us.

20 (43) The prayer ('collect') of the day/
theme is said.

22 At Morning Prayer one of these prayers
('collects') is said:

Almighty and everlasting Father,
we thank you
that you have brought us safely
to the beginning of this day.
Keep us from falling into sin
or running into danger;
order us in all our doings;
and guide us to do always
what is right in your eyes;
through Jesus Christ our Lord. **Amen.**

Or

Eternal God and Father,
you create us by your power
and redeem us by your love:
guide and strengthen us
by your Spirit,
that we may give ourselves
in love and service
to one another and to you;
through Jesus Christ our Lord. **Amen.**

45 At Evening Prayer this prayer ('collect')
is said:

Lighten our darkness,
Lord, we pray;
and in your mercy defend us
from all perils and dangers
of this night;
for the love of your only Son,
our Saviour Jesus Christ. **Amen.**

23 (46) Here may be read the State Prayers,
occasional prayers and thanksgivings, or
other forms of prayer. A sermon may be
preached, hymns may be sung, and the
service may end with a blessing.

2 The Order for Holy Communion Rite A

from The Alternative Service Book 1980

THE PREPARATION

1 At the entry of the ministers an appropriate sentence may be used; and a hymn, a canticle, or a psalm may be sung.

2 The president welcomes the people using these or other appropriate words:

The Lord be with you:
and also with you.

Or

The Lord is here:
his Spirit is with us.

Or, Easter Day to Pentecost:

Alleluia! Christ is risen:
he is risen indeed. Alleluia!

3 This prayer may be said:

**Almighty God,
to whom all hearts are open,
all desires known,
and from whom no secrets are hidden:
cleanse the thoughts of our hearts
by the inspiration of your Holy Spirit,
that we may perfectly love you,
and worthily magnify
        your holy name;
through Christ our Lord. Amen.**

4–8
PRAYERS OF PENITENCE

4 The prayers of penitence may be said here, or after section 23; if they are said here, sections 6–8 are always used. Alternative confessions may be used.

5 The commandments (number 127) or the following summary of the law may be said:

Our Lord Jesus Christ said: The first commandment is this: 'Hear, O Israel, the Lord our God is the only Lord. You shall love the Lord your God with all your heart, with all your soul, with all your mind, and with all your strength.' The second is this: 'Love your neighbour as yourself.' There is no other commandment greater than these.
Amen. Lord, have mercy.

6,7 The minister invites the congregation to confess their sins in these or other suitable words:

God so loved the world that he gave his only Son Jesus Christ to save us from our sins, to be our advocate in heaven, and to bring us to eternal life.

Let us confess our sins, in penitence and faith, firmly resolved to keep God's commandments and to live in love and peace with all men:

**Almighty God, our heavenly Father,
we have sinned against you
and against our fellow men,
in thought and word and deed,
through negligence,
        through weakness,
through our own deliberate fault.
We are truly sorry
and repent of all our sins.
For the sake of your Son Jesus Christ,
        who died for us,
forgive us all that is past;
and grant that we may serve you
        in newness of life
to the glory of your name. Amen.**

Or

**Almighty God, our heavenly Father,
we have sinned against you,
through our own fault,
in thought and word and deed,
and in what we have left undone.
For your Son our Lord Jesus Christ's
        sake,
forgive us all that is past;**

and grant that we may serve you
    in newness of life
to the glory of your name. Amen.

(See also ASB alternative confession at 417)

8 President:

Almighty God, who forgives all who
truly repent, have mercy upon *you*,
pardon and deliver *you* from all *your*
sins, confirm and strengthen *you* in all
goodness, and keep *you* in life eternal;
through Jesus Christ our Lord. **Amen.**

9
KYRIE ELEISON

Lord, have mercy.
Lord, have mercy.

Christ, have mercy.
Christ, have mercy.

Lord, have mercy.
Lord, have mercy.

10
GLORIA IN EXCELSIS

**Glory to God in the highest,
and peace to his people on earth.**

**Lord God, heavenly King,
almighty God and Father,
we worship you, we give you thanks,
we praise you for your glory.**

**Lord Jesus Christ,
    only Son of the Father,
Lord God, Lamb of God,
you take away the sin of the world:
have mercy on us;
you are seated at the right hand
    of the Father:
receive our prayer.**

**For you alone are the Holy One,
you alone are the Lord,
you alone are the Most High,
Jesus Christ,**

with the Holy Spirit,
in the glory of God the Father. Amen.

11 The president says the collect.

THE MINISTRY OF THE WORD

12 Either two or three readings from scripture follow, the last of which is always the
Gospel.

13 Sit: Old Testament Reading. At the end
may be said:
This is the word of the Lord:
thanks be to God.

14 A psalm may be used (see section 46).

15 Sit: New Testament Reading (Epistle).
At the end may be said:
This is the word of the Lord:
thanks be to God.

16 A canticle, a hymn, or a psalm may be
used.

17 Stand: The Gospel. When it is
announced:
Glory to Christ our Saviour.

At the end:
This is the Gospel of Christ:
praise to Christ our Lord.

18 Sit: The Sermon

19 Stand: The Nicene Creed is said on Sundays and other Holy Days, and may be said
on other days:
**We believe in one God,
the Father, the almighty,
maker of heaven and earth,
of all that is,
seen and unseen.**

**We believe in one Lord, Jesus Christ,
the only Son of God,
eternally begotten of the Father,
God from God, Light from Light,**

true God from true God,
begotten, not made,
of one Being with the Father.
Through him all things were made.
For us and for our salvation
he came down from heaven;
by the power of the Holy Spirit
he became incarnate of the Virgin
    Mary, and was made man.
For our sake he was crucified
    under Pontius Pilate;
he suffered death and was buried.

On the third day he rose again
in accordance with the Scriptures;
he ascended into heaven
and is seated at the right hand
    of the Father.
He will come again in glory
to judge the living and the dead,
and his kingdom will have no end.

We believe in the Holy Spirit,
the Lord, the giver of life,
who proceeds from the Father
    and the Son.
With the Father and the Son
    he is worshipped and glorified.
He has spoken through the Prophets.

We believe in one holy catholic
    and apostolic Church.
We acknowledge one baptism
    for the forgiveness of sins.
We look for the resurrection
    of the dead,
and the life of the world to come.
Amen.

20–21
THE INTERCESSION

20, 21 Intercessions and thanksgivings are
led by the president, or by others. The form
below or other suitable words, may be used
(for example number 694). This form may
be used (a) with the insertion of specific
subjects between the paragraphs; (b) as a
continuous whole with or without brief biddings. Not all paragraphs need be used on
every occasion. Individual names may be
added at the places indicated. This response may be used before or after each
paragraph:

Lord, in your mercy
hear our prayer.

Let us pray for the Church and for the
world, and let us thank God for his
goodness:

Almighty God, our heavenly Father, you
promised through your Son Jesus Christ to
hear us when we pray in faith.

Strengthen N our bishop and all your
Church in the service of Christ; that those
who confess your name may be united in
your truth, live together in your love, and
reveal your glory in the world.

Bless and guide Elizabeth our Queen; give
wisdom to all in authority; and direct this
and every nation in the ways of justice and
of peace; that we may honour one another,
and seek the common good.

Give grace to us, our families and friends,
and to all our neighbours; that we may
serve Christ in one another, and love as he
loves us.

Comfort and heal all those who suffer
in body, mind, or spirit . . .; give them
courage and hope in their troubles; and
bring them the joy of your salvation.

Hear us as we remember those who have
died in the faith of Christ . . .; according to
your promises, grant us with them a share
in your eternal kingdom.

Rejoicing in the fellowship of (N and of) all
your saints, we commend ourselves and all
Christian people to your unfailing love.

Merciful Father,
accept these prayers
for the sake of your Son,
our Saviour Jesus Christ. Amen.

23–28 The prayers of penitence (sections
5–8) are said here if not used previously.
Sentences may be found at number 693.

PRAYER OF HUMBLE ACCESS

One of these prayers may be said:

We do not presume
to come to this your table,
merciful Lord,
trusting in our own righteousness,
but in your manifold and great
mercies.
We are not worthy
so much as to gather up the crumbs
under your table.
But you are the same Lord
whose nature is always to have mercy.
Grant us therefore, gracious Lord,
so to eat the flesh of your dear son
Jesus Christ
and to drink his blood,
that we may evermore dwell in him
and he in us. Amen.

Or

Most merciful Lord,
your love compels us to come in.
Our hands were unclean,
our hearts were unprepared;
we were not fit
even to eat the crumbs
from under your table.
But you, Lord,
are the God of our salvation,
and share your bread with sinners.
So cleanse and feed us
with the precious body and blood
of your Son,
that he may live in us and we in him;
and that we, with the whole company
of Christ,
may sit and eat in your kingdom.
Amen.

THE MINISTRY OF THE
SACRAMENT

THE PEACE

Stand: The president says either of the following or other suitable words:

Christ is our peace. He has reconciled us to God in one body by the cross. We meet in his name and share his peace.

Or

We are the Body of Christ. In the one Spirit we were all baptised into one body. Let us then pursue all that makes for peace and builds up our common life.

He then says:

The peace of the Lord be always with you:
and also with you.

31 The president may say:

Let us offer one another a sign of peace.

and all may exchange a sign of peace.

THE PREPARATION OF THE GIFTS

32 The bread and wine are placed on the holy table.

33 The president may praise God for his gifts in appropriate words to which all respond:

Blessed be God for ever.

34 The offerings of the people may be collected and presented. These words may be used:

Yours, Lord, is the greatness,
the power,
the glory, the splendour,
and the majesty;
for everything in heaven and on earth
is yours.
All things come from you,
and of your own do we give you.

35 At the preparation of the gifts a hymn may be sung.

Holy Communion A/9

THE EUCHARISTIC PRAYER

The Taking of the Bread and Cup and the Giving of Thanks:

36, 37 The president takes the bread and cup into his hands and replaces them on the holy table. The president uses one of the four Eucharistic Prayers which follow (see also page 17).

38 First Eucharistic Prayer:

The Lord be with you:
and also with you.

Or

The Lord is here:
his Spirit is with us.

Lift up your hearts:
we lift them to the Lord.

Let us give thanks to the Lord our God:
it is right to give him thanks
and praise.

It is indeed right, it is our duty and our joy, at all times and in all places to give you thanks and praise, holy Father, heavenly King, almighty and eternal God, through Jesus Christ your only Son our Lord.

For he is your living Word; through him you have created all things from the beginning, and formed us in your own image.

Through him you have freed us from the slavery of sin, giving him to be born as man and to die upon the cross; you raised him from the dead and exalted him to your right hand on high.

Through him you have sent upon us your holy and life-giving Spirit, and made us a people for your own possession.

Proper Preface, when appropriate.

Continues page 12, column 1

39 Second Eucharistic Prayer:

The Lord be with you:
and also with you.

Or

The Lord is here:
his Spirit is with us.

Lift up your hearts:
we lift them to the Lord.

Let us give thanks to the Lord our God:
it is right to give him thanks
and praise.

It is indeed right, it is our duty and our joy, at all times and in all places to give you thanks and praise, holy Father, heavenly King, almighty and eternal God, through Jesus Christ your only Son our Lord.

The following may be omitted if a Proper Preface is used:

For he is your living Word; through him you have created all things from the beginning, and formed us in your own image.

Through him you have freed us from the slavery of sin, giving him to be born as man and to die upon the cross; you raised him from the dead and exalted him to your right hand on high.

Through him you have sent upon us your holy and life-giving Spirit, and made us a people for your own possession.

Proper Preface, when appropriate.

Continues page 12, column 2

40 Third Eucharistic Prayer:

The Lord be with you:
and also with you.

Or

The Lord is here:
his Spirit is with us.

Lift up your hearts:
we lift them to the Lord.

Let us give thanks to the Lord our God:
**it is right to give him thanks
    and praise.**

Father, we give you thanks and praise through your beloved Son Jesus Christ, your living Word through whom you have created all things;

Who was sent by you, in your great goodness, to be our Saviour; by the power of the Holy Spirit he took flesh and, as your Son, born of the blessed Virgin, was seen on earth and went about among us;

He opened wide his arms for us on the cross; he put an end to death by dying for us and revealed the resurrection by rising to new life; so he fulfilled your will and won for you a holy people.

Proper Preface, when appropriate.

Therefore with angels and archangels, and with all the company of heaven, we proclaim your great and glorious name, for ever praising you and saying:
**Holy, holy, holy Lord,
God of power and might,
heaven and earth
    are full of your glory.
Hosanna in the highest.**

Continues page 13, column 1

41 Fourth Eucharistic Prayer:

The Lord be with you:
and also with you.

Or

The Lord is here:
his Spirit is with us.

Lift up your hearts:
we lift them to the Lord.

Let us give thanks to the Lord our God:
**it is right to give him thanks
    and praise.**

It is indeed right, it is our duty and our joy, at all times and in all places to give you thanks and praise, holy Father, heavenly King, almighty and eternal God, creator of heaven and earth, through Jesus Christ our Lord:

Proper Preface, when appropriate. The following is used when no Proper Preface is provided:

For he is the true high priest, who has loosed us from our sins and has made us to be a royal priesthood to you, our God and Father.

Therefore with angels and archangels, and with all the company of heaven, we proclaim your great and glorious name, for ever praising you and saying:
**Holy, holy, holy Lord,
God of power and might,
heaven and earth
    are full of your glory.
Hosanna in the highest.**

This Anthem may also be used:

**Blessed is he who comes
    in the name of the Lord;
hosanna in the highest.**

Continues page 13, column 2

Holy Communion A/11

Therefore with angels and archangels, and with all the company of heaven, we proclaim your great and glorious name, for ever praising you and saying:
Holy, holy, holy Lord,
God of power and might,
heaven and earth
    are full of your glory.
Hosanna in the highest.

This Anthem may also be used:
Blessed is he who comes
    in the name of the Lord;
hosanna in the highest.

Accept our praises, heavenly Father, through your Son our Saviour Jesus Christ; and as we follow his example and obey his command, grant that by the power of your Holy Spirit these gifts of bread and wine may be to us his body and his blood;

Who in the same night that he was betrayed, took bread and gave you thanks; he broke it and gave it to his disciples, saying, 'Take, eat; this is my body which is given for you; do this in remembrance of me.' In the same way, after supper he took the cup and gave you thanks; he gave it to them, saying, 'Drink this, all of you; this is my blood of the new covenant, which is shed for you and for many for the forgiveness of sins. Do this, as often as you drink it, in remembrance of me.'

Christ has died,
Christ is risen,
Christ will come again.

Therefore, heavenly Father, we remember his offering of himself made once for all upon the cross, and proclaim his mighty resurrection and glorious ascension. As we look for his coming in glory, we celebrate with this bread and this cup his one perfect sacrifice.

Continues page 14, column 1

Therefore with angels and archangels, and with all the company of heaven, we proclaim your great and glorious name, for ever praising you and saying:
Holy, holy, holy Lord,
God of power and might,
heaven and earth
    are full of your glory.
Hosanna in the highest.

This Anthem may also be used:
Blessed is he who comes
    in the name of the Lord;
hosanna in the highest.

Hear us, heavenly Father, through Jesus Christ your Son our Lord, through him accept our sacrifice of praise; and grant that by the power of your Holy Spirit these gifts of bread and wine may be to us his body and his blood;

Who in the same night that he was betrayed, took bread and gave you thanks; he broke it and gave it to his disciples, saying, 'Take, eat; this is my body which is given for you; do this in remembrance of me.' In the same way, after supper he took the cup and gave you thanks; he gave it to them, saying, 'Drink this, all of you; this is my blood of the new covenant, which is shed for you and for many for the forgiveness of sins. Do this, as often as you drink it, in remembrance of me.'

Christ has died,
Christ is risen,
Christ will come again.

Therefore, Lord and heavenly Father, having in remembrance his death once for all upon the cross, his resurrection from the dead, and his ascension into heaven, and looking for the coming of his kingdom, we make with this bread and this cup the memorial of Christ your Son our Lord.

Continues page 14, column 2

This Anthem may also be used:
Blessed is he who comes
in the name of the Lord;
hosanna in the highest.

Lord, you are holy indeed, the source of all holiness; grant that, by the power of your Holy Spirit, and according to your holy will, these your gifts of bread and wine may be to us the body and blood of our Lord Jesus Christ;

Who in the same night that he was betrayed, took bread and gave you thanks; he broke it and gave it to his disciples, saying, 'Take, eat; this is my body which is given for you; do this in remembrance of me.' In the same way, after supper he took the cup and gave you thanks; he gave it to them, saying, 'Drink this, all of you; this is my blood of the new covenant, which is shed for you and for many for the forgiveness of sins. Do this, as often as you drink it, in remembrance of me.'

Christ has died,
Christ is risen,
Christ will come again.

And so, Father, calling to mind his death on the cross, his perfect sacrifice made once for the sins of all, rejoicing at his mighty resurrection and glorious ascension, and looking for his coming in glory, we celebrate this memorial of our redemption;

We thank you for counting us worthy to stand in your presence and serve you; we bring before you this bread and this cup;

We pray you to accept this our duty and service, a spiritual sacrifice of praise and thanksgiving;

Continues page 15, column 1

All glory to you, our heavenly Father: in your tender mercy you gave your only Son Jesus Christ to suffer death upon the cross for our redemption; he made there a full atonement for the sins of the whole world, offering once for all his one sacrifice of himself; he instituted, and in his holy gospel commanded us to continue, a perpetual memory of his precious death until he comes again.

Hear us, merciful Father, we humbly pray, and grant that by the power of your Holy Spirit we who receive these gifts of your creation, this bread and this wine, according to your Son our Saviour Jesus Christ's holy institution, in remembrance of the death that he suffered, may be partakers of his most blessed body and blood;

Who in the same night that he was betrayed, took bread and gave you thanks; he broke it and gave it to his disciples, saying, 'Take, eat; this is my body which is given for you; do this in remembrance of me.' In the same way, after supper he took the cup and gave you thanks; he gave it to them, saying,

'Drink this, all of you; this is my blood of the new covenant, which is shed for you and for many for the forgiveness of sins. Do this, as often as you drink it, in remembrance of me.'

Christ has died,
Christ is risen,
Christ will come again.

Therefore, Lord and heavenly Father, in remembrance of the precious death and passion, the mighty resurrection and glorious ascension of your dear Son Jesus Christ, we offer you through him this sacrifice of praise and thanksgiving.

Continues page 15, column 2

Holy Communion A/13

Accept through him, our great high priest, this our sacrifice of thanks and praise; and as we eat and drink these holy gifts in the presence of your divine majesty, renew us by your Spirit, inspire us with your love, and unite us in the body of your Son, Jesus Christ our Lord.

Through him, and with him, and in him, by the power of the Holy Spirit, with all who stand before you in earth and heaven, we worship you, Father almighty, in songs of everlasting praise:
**Blessing and honour
    and glory and power
be yours for ever and ever. Amen.**

Silence may be kept.

Continues below (section 42)

Accept through him this offering of our duty and service; and as we eat and drink these holy gifts in the presence of your divine majesty, fill us with your grace and heavenly blessing; nourish us with the body and blood of your Son, that we may grow into his likeness and, made one by your Spirit, become a living temple to your glory.

Through Jesus Christ our Lord, by whom, and with whom, and in whom, in the unity of the Holy Spirit, all honour and glory be yours, almighty Father, from all who stand before you in earth and heaven, now and for ever.
Amen.

Silence may be kept.

Continues column 1 (section 42)

42–49
THE COMMUNION

The Breaking of the Bread and the Giving of the Bread and Cup

42 The Lord's Prayer is said either as follows or in its traditional form. President:
As our Saviour taught us, so we pray.
**Our Father in heaven,
hallowed be your name,
your kingdom come,
your will be done,
on earth as in heaven.
Give us today our daily bread.
Forgive us our sins
as we forgive those
    who sin against us.
Lead us not into temptation
but deliver us from evil.**

**For the kingdom, the power,
    and the glory are yours
now and for ever. Amen.**

43 The president breaks the consecrated bread, saying:
We break this bread to share in the body of Christ:
though we are many, we are one body, because we all share in one bread.

44 Either here or during the distribution one of the following Anthems may be said:
**Lamb of God,
you take away the sins of the world:
have mercy on us.**

**Lamb of God,
you take away the sins of the world:
have mercy on us.**

**Lamb of God,
you take away the sins of the world:
grant us peace.**

Send the Holy Spirit on your people and gather into one in your kingdom all who share this one bread and one cup, so that we, in the company of all the saints, may praise and glorify you for ever, through him from whom all good things come, Jesus Christ our Lord;

By whom, and with whom, and in whom, in the unity of the Holy Spirit, all honour and glory be yours, almighty Father, for ever and ever. **Amen.**

Grant that by his merits and death, and through faith in his blood, we and all your Church may receive forgiveness of our sins and all other benefits of his passion. Although we are unworthy, through our many sins, to offer you any sacrifice, yet we pray that you will accept this, the duty and service that we owe; do not weigh our merits, but pardon our offences, and fill us all who share in this holy communion with your grace and heavenly blessing.

Through Jesus Christ our Lord, by whom, and with whom, and in whom, in the unity of the Holy Spirit, all honour and glory be yours, almighty Father, now and for ever. **Amen.**

Silence may be kept.

Silence may be kept.

Continues page 14, column 1 (section 42)

Continues page 14, column 1 (section 42)

Or

Jesus, Lamb of God:
 have mercy on us.
Jesus, bearer of our sins:
 have mercy on us.
Jesus, redeemer of the world:
 give us your peace.

45 Before the distribution the president says:

Draw near with faith. Receive the body of our Lord Jesus Christ which he gave for you, and his blood which he shed for you. Eat and drink in remembrance that he died for you, and feed on him in your hearts by faith with thanksgiving.

One of the following sentences may also be said:

Jesus is the Lamb of God who takes

away the sins of the world. Happy are those who are called to his supper.
Lord, I am not worthy to receive you,
but only say the word,
 and I shall be healed.

Or

The gifts of God for the people of God.
Jesus Christ is holy,
Jesus Christ is Lord,
to the glory of God the Father.

Or, Easter Day to Pentecost:

Alleluia! Christ our Passover is sacrificed for us.
Alleluia! Let us keep the feast.

Holy Communion A/15

46 The president and people receive the communion. At the distribution the minister says to each communicant:

The body of Christ keep you in eternal life.
The blood of Christ keep you in eternal life.

Or

The body of Christ.
The blood of Christ.

The communicant replies each time **Amen**, and then receives.

47 During the distribution hymns and anthems may be sung.

48 If either or both of the consecrated elements be likely to prove insufficient, the president himself returns to the holy table and adds more, saying these words: Father, giving thanks over the bread and the cup according to the institution of your Son Jesus Christ, who said, Take, eat; this is my body (*and/or* Drink this; this is my blood), we pray that this bread/wine also may be to us his body/blood, to be received in remembrance of him.

49 Any consecrated bread and wine which is not required for purposes of communion is consumed at the end of the distribution or after the service.

AFTER COMMUNION

50 An appropriate sentence may be said and a hymn may be sung.

51, 52 Either or both of the following prayers or other suitable prayers are said:

Father of all,
we give you thanks and praise,
that when we were still far off
you met us in your Son
       and brought us home.
Dying and living,
he declared your love,
gave us grace,

and opened the gate of glory.
May we who share Christ's body
live his risen life;
we who drink his cup
bring life to others;
we whom the Spirit lights
give light to the world.
Keep us firm
in the hope you have set before us,
so we and all your children
       shall be free,
and the whole earth
live to praise your name;
through Christ our Lord. **Amen.**

53 Or

Almighty God,
we thank you for feeding us
with the body and blood of your Son
       Jesus Christ.
Through him we offer you our souls
       and bodies
to be a living sacrifice.
Send us out
in the power of your Spirit
to live and work
to your praise and glory. Amen.

54–56
THE DISMISSAL

54 The president may say this or an alternative blessing:

The peace of God, which passes all understanding, keep your hearts and minds in the knowledge and love of God, and of his Son Jesus Christ our Lord; and the blessing of God almighty, the Father, the Son, and the Holy Spirit, be among you, and remain with you always. **Amen.**

55 President:
Go in peace to love and serve the Lord.
In the name of Christ. Amen.

Or

Go in the peace of Christ.
Thanks be to God.

From Easter Day to Pentecost 'Alleluia! Alleluia!' may be added after both the versicle and the response.

56 The ministers and people depart.

ALTERNATIVE EUCHARISTIC PRAYER: 'A EUCHARISTIC PRAYER FOR USE WITH THE SICK'
from Holy Communion Rite A Appendices The Alternative Service Book 1980, page 171

The Lord be with you:
and also with you.

Or

The Lord is here:
his Spirit is with us.

Lift up your hearts:
we lift them to the Lord.

Let us give thanks to the Lord our God:
**it is right to give him thanks
    and praise.**

It is indeed right, it is our duty and our joy, to give you thanks, holy Father, through Jesus Christ our Lord.

Through him you have created us in your image; through him you have freed us from sin and death; through him you have made us your own people by the gift of the Holy Spirit.

Hear us, Father, through Christ your Son our Lord, and grant that by the power of your Holy Spirit these gifts of bread and wine may be to us his body and his blood;

Who in the same night that he was betrayed, took bread and gave you thanks; he broke it and gave it to his disciples, saying, 'Take, eat; this is my body which is given for you; do this in remembrance of me.'

In the same way, after supper he took the cup and gave you thanks; he gave it to them, saying, 'Drink this, all of you; this is my blood of the new covenant, which is shed for you and for many for the forgiveness of sins. Do this, as often as you drink it, in remembrance of me.'

Therefore, Father, proclaiming his saving death and resurrection and looking for his coming in glory, we celebrate with this bread and this cup his one perfect sacrifice.

Accept through him, our great high priest, this our sacrifice of thanks and praise; and grant that we who eat this bread and drink this cup may be renewed by your Spirit and grow into his likeness;

Through Jesus Christ our Lord, by whom, and with whom, and in whom, all honour and glory be yours, Father, now and for ever. **Amen.**

NOTES
Notes for the use of Holy Communion Rite A are to be found in section 40 (For the Minister), and on pages 115–118 of the Alternative Service Book 1980.

3 The Baptism of Children

at Holy Communion or at Morning or Evening Worship from The Alternative Service Book 1980.

42, 43
THE DUTIES OF PARENTS AND GODPARENTS

42 The priest says:

Children who are too young to profess the Christian faith are baptised on the understanding that they are brought up as Christians within the family of the Church.

As they grow up, they need the help and encouragement of that family, so that they learn to be faithful in public worship and private prayer, to live by trust in God, and come to confirmation.

Parents and godparents, the *children* whom you have brought for baptism *depend* chiefly on you for the help and encouragement *they need*. Are you willing to give it to *them* by your prayers, by your example, and by your teaching?

Parents and godparents:
I am willing.

43 And if the *child* is old enough to understand, the priest speaks to *him* in these or similar words:

N, when you are baptised, you become *a member* of a new family. God takes you for his own *child*, and all Christian people will be your brothers and sisters.

46 This prayer may be said:

We thank God therefore for our baptism to life in Christ, and we pray for *these children (N)* and say together:

Heavenly Father, in your love
you have called us to know you,
led us to trust you,
and bound our life with yours.
Surround *these children* with your love;
protect *them* from evil;
fill *them* with your Holy Spirit;
and receive *them*
into the family of your Church;
that *they* may walk with us
in the way of Christ
and grow in the knowledge
of your love. Amen.

47–51
THE DECISION

The parents and godparents stand, and the priest says to them:

Those who bring children to be baptised must affirm their allegiance to Christ and their rejection of all that is evil. It is your duty to bring up *these children* to fight against evil and to follow Christ.

(48)

Therefore I ask these questions which you must answer for yourselves and for *these children:*

Do you turn to Christ?
I turn to Christ.

Do you repent of your sins?
I repent of my sins.

Do you renounce evil?
I renounce evil.

49 Either here or at section 56 the priest makes the sign of the cross on the forehead of each child, saying to each:

I sign you with the cross, the sign of Christ.

After the signing of each or all:

Do not be ashamed to confess the faith of Christ crucified.

Fight valiantly
under the banner of Christ
against sin, the world, and the devil,
and continue his faithful *soldiers*
     and *servants*
to the end of your *lives.*

50 Priest:

May almighty God deliver you from the powers of darkness, and lead you in the light and obedience of Christ. **Amen.**

51 A hymn or psalm may be sung.

52–57
THE BAPTISM

52 The priest stands before the water of baptism and says:

Praise God who made heaven and earth,
who keeps his promise for ever.

Almighty God, whose Son Jesus Christ was baptised in the river Jordan: we thank you for the gift of water to cleanse us and revive us; we thank you that through the waters of the Red Sea, you led your people out of slavery to freedom in the promised land; we thank you that through the deep waters of death you brought your Son, and raised him to life in triumph. Bless this water, that your *servants* who *are* washed in it may be made one with Christ in his death and in his resurrection, to be cleansed and delivered from all sin. Send your Holy Spirit upon *them* to bring *them* to new birth in the family of your Church, and raise *them* with Christ to full and eternal life. For all might, majesty, authority, and power are yours, now and for ever. **Amen.**

53 The priest says to the parents and god-parents:

You have brought *these children* to baptism. You must now declare before God and his Church the Christian faith into which *they are* to be baptised, and in which you will help *them* to grow. You must answer for yourselves and for *these children.*

Do you believe and trust in God the Father, who made the world?
I believe and trust in him.

Do you believe and trust in his Son Jesus Christ, who redeemed mankind?
I believe and trust in him.

Do you believe and trust in his Holy Spirit, who gives life to the people of God?
I believe and trust in him.

54 The priest turns to the congregation and says:

This is the faith of the Church.
This is our faith.
We believe and trust in one God,
Father, Son, and Holy Spirit.

55 The parents and godparents being present with each child, the priest baptises *him.* He dips *him* in the water or pours water on *him,* addressing *him* by name:

N, I baptise you in the name of the Father, and of the Son, and of the Holy Spirit.

And each one of *his* sponsors answers:
Amen.

56 The priest makes the sign of the cross on the forehead of each child if he has not already done so, saying to each:

I sign you with the cross, the sign of Christ.

After the signing of each or all:

Do not be ashamed to confess the faith of Christ crucified.   →

Fight valiantly
under the banner of Christ
against sin, the world, and the devil,
and continue his faithful *soldiers*
and *servants*
to the end of your *lives.*

57 The priest or other person may give to a parent or godparent for each child a lighted candle, saying to each:

Receive this light.

And when a candle has been given to each one:

This is to show that you have passed from darkness to light.
Shine as a light in the world
to the glory of God the Father.

58
THE WELCOME

58 The priest and the congregation, representing the whole Church, welcome the newly baptised:

God has received you by baptism into his Church.
We welcome you
into the Lord's Family.
We are members together
of the body of Christ;
we are children
of the same heavenly Father;
we are inheritors together
of the kingdom of God.
We welcome you.

It is customary in some churches to present a Bible or New Testament at this point.

Full notes for guidance in the ordering of this service are set out on pages 241, 242 of The Alternative Service Book 1980. The service of Baptism when not in the context of another service may be found there on pages 243 following.

The Renewal of Baptismal Vows on Various Occasions
From The Alternative Service Book 1980

94 At Easter the minister says:

As we celebrate again the resurrection of our Lord Jesus Christ from the dead, we remember that through the paschal mystery we have died and been buried with him in baptism, so that we may rise with him to a new life within the family of his Church. Now that we have completed our observance of Lent, we renew the promises made at our baptism, affirming our allegiance to Christ, and our rejection of all that is evil.

95 On other occasions the minister says:

In our baptism we died with Christ and were buried with him, so that we might rise with him to a new life within the family of his Church. Today we renew the promises made at our baptism, affirming our allegiance to Christ, and our rejection of all that is evil.

96
Therefore I ask these questions:
Do you turn to Christ?
I turn to Christ.

Do you repent of your sins?
I repent of my sins.

Do you renounce evil?
I renounce evil.

97 The minister says:

And now I ask you to make the profession of Christian faith into which you were baptised, and in which you live and grow.

Do you believe and trust in God the
Father, who made the world?
I believe and trust in him.

Do you believe and trust in his Son
Jesus Christ, who redeemed mankind?
I believe and trust in him.

Do you believe and trust in his Holy
Spirit, who gives life to the people of
God?
I believe and trust in him.

98 The minister says:
This is the faith of the Church.
This is our faith.
We believe and trust in one God,
Father, Son, and Holy Spirit.

99 The minister says one or more of these
prayers:

100
Almighty God, we thank you for our
fellowship in the household of faith
with all those who have been baptised
in your name. Keep us faithful to our
baptism, and so make us ready for that
day when the whole creation shall be
made perfect in your Son, our Saviour
Jesus Christ. **Amen.**

101
Almighty God, whose Holy Spirit
equips the Church with a rich variety of
gifts; grant that we may use them to
bear witness to Christ by lives built on
faith and love. Make us ready to live his
Gospel and eager to do his will, that we
may share with all your Church in the
joys of eternal life; through Jesus Christ
our Lord. **Amen.**

102
Lord, make us
instruments of your peace.
Where there is hatred, let us sow love;
where there is injury,
let there be pardon;
where there is discord, union;
where there is doubt, faith;
where there is despair, hope;
where there is darkness, light;
where there is sadness, joy;
for your mercy
and for your truth's sake. Amen.

103
Lord Jesus, we thank you
for all the benefits
you have won for us,
for all the pains and insults
you have borne for us.
Most merciful redeemer,
friend and brother,
may we know you more clearly,
love you more dearly,
and follow you more nearly,
day by day. Amen.

104
Eternal God,
you have declared in Christ
the completion
of your purpose of love.
May we live by faith, walk in hope,
and be renewed in love,
until the world reflects your glory,
and you are all in all.
Even so; come, Lord Jesus. Amen.

Notes for guidance in the use of this service are
set out on page 275 of The Alternative Service
Book 1980.

4 Thanksgiving for a Child

drawn from Thanksgiving for the Birth of a Child, and Thanksgiving after Adoption in The Alternative Service Book 1980

1 (17) Minister:

Let us thank God that in his goodness he has given you *this son/daughter:*

God our Father,
maker of all that is living,
we praise you
for the wonder and joy of creation.
We thank you from our hearts
for the life of *this child,*
*for a safe delivery,
and for the privilege of parenthood.
Accept our thanks and praise
through Jesus Christ our Lord. **Amen.**

2 (18) The parents of the *child* may say together:

God our Father,
in giving us *this child*
you have shown us your love.
Help us to be trustworthy parents.
Make us patient and understanding,
that our *child* may always be sure
  of our love
and grow up to be happy
  and responsible;
through Jesus Christ our Lord. **Amen.**

3 (19) The following versicles and responses are said, or Psalm 100 (see numbers 96, 367, 443, 787), or a hymn may be sung.

My soul proclaims the greatness of the Lord,
my spirit rejoices in God my saviour.

Glory and honour and power are yours by right, O Lord our God;
**for you created all things,
and by your will
  they have their being.**

Holy, holy, holy is God the sovereign Lord of all,
**who is, and who was,
  and who is to come.**

Great and marvellous are your deeds, O Lord God,
**just and true are your ways,
O King of the ages.**

Praise our God, all you his servants,
**you that fear him,
  both great and small.**

His mercy rests on those who fear him,
now and for countless ages. Amen.

4 (20) Minister:

Hear these words from the Gospel according to St Mark: They brought children for Jesus to touch. The disciples rebuked them, but when Jesus saw this he was indignant and said to them, 'Let the children come to me; do not try to stop them; for the kingdom of God belongs to such as these. I tell you, whoever does not accept the kingdom of God like a child will never enter it.' And he put his arms round them, laid his hands upon them, and blessed them.   Mark 10.13–16

(21) The minister may give a copy of one of the gospels to the parents, saying:

This book contains the Good News of God's love. Read it, for it tells how you and your family can share in eternal life, through repentance and faith in Jesus Christ.

---

* Note: this phrase is not appropriate to Thanksgiving after Adoption

22/Thanksgiving for a Child

6 (22)

Jesus taught us to call God our Father,
and so in faith and trust we say:
Our Father in heaven,
hallowed be your name,
your kingdom come,
your will be done,
on earth as in heaven.
Give us today our daily bread.
Forgive us our sins
as we forgive those
who sin against us.
Lead us not into temptation
but deliver us from evil.

For the kingdom, the power,
and the glory are yours
now and for ever. Amen.

7 (23) Minister:

Almighty God, look with favour on *this child*; grant that, being nourished with all goodness, *he* may grow in discipline and grace until *he comes* to the fullness of faith; through Jesus Christ our Lord. **Amen.**

24–25 (Thanksgiving after Adoption):

God, whose nature is
always to have mercy,
look down with love
on the natural father and mother
of *this child*;
keep them in your good providence,
and give them your peace
in their hearts;
through Jesus Christ our Lord. **Amen.**

The members of the family then say together:

We receive *this child* into our family
with thanksgiving and joy.
Through the love of God
we receive *him*;

with the love of God
we will care for *him*;
by the love of God we will guide *him*;
and in the love of God
may we all abide for ever. **Amen.**

---

9 (26) Minister:

Heavenly Father, whose blessed Son shared at Nazareth the life of an earthly home: bless the *home* of *this child*, and help all *the family* to live together in your love. Teach them to serve you and each other, and make them always ready to show your love to those in need; for the sake of Jesus Christ our Lord. **Amen.**

Other prayers may follow here. This prayer may be said by all:

14 (27)

God our Father,
we pray for *this child*,
that in due time
he **may be received by baptism**
into the family of your Church,
and become *an inheritor*
of your kingdom;
through Jesus Christ our Lord. Amen.

15 (28) The minister ends the service with one of these blessings:

The Lord bless you and watch over you, the Lord make his face shine upon you and be gracious to you, the Lord look kindly on you and give you peace; and the blessing of God almighty, the Father, the Son, and the Holy Spirit, be among you and remain with you always. **Amen.**

Or →

The love of the Lord Jesus draw you to himself, the power of the Lord Jesus strengthen you in his service, the joy of the Lord Jesus fill your hearts; and the blessing of God almighty, the Father, the Son, and the Holy Spirit, be among you and remain with you always. **Amen.**

Full notes for the use of these services are to be found on page 212 of The Alternative Service Book 1980.

5 A Covenant Service
in the Free Church Tradition.

'This is the covenant that I will make with the house of Israel after that time,' declares the Lord. 'I will put my law in their minds and write it on their hearts. I will be their God, and they will be my people.'

Jeremiah 31.33

THE COVENANT

In an eternal covenant with Abraham, God called into being a people through whom the world would be blessed. God, through Moses, chose Israel to be a holy nation, to walk before him and to keep his laws. Jeremiah anticipated a new covenant requiring individual knowledge of God, and the obedience of faith. Our Lord Jesus Christ, by his incarnation, death and resurrection has brought God's new covenant to all who are made one with him by grace through faith.

We who are called by his name, are pledged to live no more for ourselves, but for him; to obey his commandments and to bear witness of his salvation to the ends of the earth.

**As a company of men and women
who have received Christ as saviour
and by grace become God's children,
we here and now
    dedicate ourselves to him;
we desire to renew our commitment
as a church of Jesus Christ,
indwelt by the Holy Spirit,
united to walk worthily
    of our profession,
set apart to proclaim his word,
to observe his commandments,
and by God's grace to work
    according to his will
for the salvation of others
and the well-being of his world.
Amen.**

→

AT A COVENANT SERVICE
In free church use this service is preceded by a reading and usually by a sermon, and followed by The Lord's Supper. It is not authorised for Church of England use, but the prayers may be suitable for general purposes.

Hymns, Psalms, Songs and Prayers
See sections:

Readings

THE PROMISE

Lord God, holy Father, since you have called us through Christ to share in this gracious Covenant, we take upon ourselves afresh the yoke of obedience. And, for love of you, we engage ourselves in the task of making you known to our neighbours and serving them in your name: we are no longer our own, but yours.

I am no longer my own, but yours,
send me where you will,
rank me with whom you will;
let me be employed for you,
or laid aside for you;
exalted for you,
or brought low for you;
let me be full, let me be empty;
let me have all things,
let me have nothing:
Freely and wholeheartedly
I yield my life and all I possess
to your pleasure and disposal. Amen.

Father, we dedicate ourselves
to serve you faithfully
and to follow Christ,
to face the future with him,
seeking his special purpose
    for our lives.
Send us out now to work
    and to witness
freely, gratefully and hopefully,
in the power of the Holy Spirit,
and for the honour and glory
    of your Son,
Jesus Christ our Lord. Amen.

6 At a Baptism/ Thanksgiving for a Child

Jesus said to his disciples, 'If you want to come with me, you must forget self, carry your cross and follow me.'

Matthew 16.24

1

PRAISE
Give thanks to God, for he is good;
his love endures for ever.

Let those whom the Lord has redeemed repeat these words of praise:
**O thank the Lord for his love
and the wonderful things he has done!
Amen.**

from Psalm 107

4 This is the covenant of grace –
God to the nations shows his love;
people of every tribe and race,
born by his Spirit from above.

5 This is the badge we proudly wear:
washed by our God,
        the Three-in-One;
welcomed in fellowship, we share
hope of eternal life begun.

© Michael Saward/Jubilate Hymns

2

Fulda, Duke Street
Hymns for Today's Church 16, 526(i)

1 This is the truth which we proclaim,
God makes a promise firm and sure;
marked by this sign
        made in his name,
here, for our sickness,
        God's own cure.

2 This is the grave in which we lie:
pierced to the heart
        by sin's sharp sword,
risen with Christ, to self we die,
and live to praise our reigning Lord.

3 This is the sacrament of birth:
sealed by a Saviour's death for sin,
trust in his mercy, all on earth,
open your hearts and let him in!

3

CONFESSION
Let us confess our sins to God.

If we say that we have no sin, we deceive ourselves, and the truth is not in us:
**If we confess our sins,
God will keep his promise
and do what is right –
he will forgive us our sins
and cleanse us
        from every kind of wrong.**

**Father, have mercy on us
through Jesus Christ our Lord. Amen.**

from 1 John 1†

At a Baptism (1–3)

4

PSALM
Praise the Lord:

You servants of the Lord, praise his name:
**Let the name of the Lord be praised,
both now and for evermore.**

From the rising of the sun to the place where it sets:
the name of the Lord be praised!

The Lord is exalted above the earth:
his glory over the heavens.

Who is like the Lord our God?
He is throned in the heights above.

Yet he bends down:
yet he stoops to look at our world.

He raises the poor from the dust:
and lifts the needy from their sorrow.

He honours the childless wife in her home:
**he makes her happy,
        the mother of children.**

Praise the Lord. **Amen.**

Psalm 113

5 Oakley
   Jesus Praise 147

CANTICLE

1 To God's loving-kindness
        we commit you:
    the Lord bless your life
        and make you strong –
    may the praises of God,
    the Father and the Son
    and the Spirit – Three-in-One,
    be your song.

2 To God's holy favour
        we commend you:

the Lord hear your prayers
        and show his face –
    and the mercy of God,
    the Father and the Son
    and the Spirit – Three-in-One,
    bring you grace.

3 To God's great protection
        we entrust you:
    the Lord take your hand
        and give you peace –
    let the blessing of God,
    the Father and the Son
    and the Spirit – Three-in-One,
    never cease!

from Numbers 6
© Michael Perry/Jubilate Hymns

6 The King is among us
   Mission Praise 222

1 The King is among us,
        his Spirit is here:
    let's draw near and worship,
    let songs fill the air!

2 He looks down upon us,
        delight in his face,
    enjoying his children's love,
    enthralled by our praise.

3 For each child is special,
        accepted and loved –
    a love-gift from Jesus
    to his Father above.

4 And now he is giving
        his gifts to us all;
    for no one is worthless
    and each one is called.

5 The Spirit's anointing
        on all flesh comes down,
    and we shall be channels
    for works like his own:

(4–6) At a Baptism

6 We come now believing
  your promise of power,
 for we are your people
  and this is your hour.

7 The King is among us,
  his Spirit is here:
 let's draw near and worship,
  let songs fill the air!

7 Jesus loves Kristi
  Fresh Sounds 83

Jesus, Jesus loves _____* –
  yes, he does, yes, he does;
Jesus, Jesus loves _____* –
  yes, he does, yes, he does:
And he wants _____*
  to love him too.

(*Name to be supplied here, or use 'me', 'you'.)

8 The light of Christ
  Mission Praise 223

  The light of Christ
  has come into the world,
  the light of Christ
  has come into the world.

1 We all must be born again
   to see the kingdom of God;
  the water and the Spirit bring
   new life in God's love.
  The light of Christ . . .

2 God gave up his only Son
   out of love for the world,
  so that all those who believe in him
   will live for ever.
  The light of Christ . . .

3 The light of God has come to us
   so that we might have salvation;
  from the darkness of our sins
   we walk
   into glory with Christ Jesus.
  The light of Christ . . .

9

CREED

Do you believe and trust in God the
Father, who made the world?
We believe and trust in him.

Do you believe and trust in his Son
Jesus Christ, who redeemed mankind?
We believe and trust in him.

Do you believe and trust in his Holy
Spirit, who gives life to the people of
God?
We believe and trust in him.

This is the faith of the Church.
This is our faith.
We believe and trust in one God:
Father, Son, and Holy Spirit. Amen. †

10 Quem pastores laudavere
  Hymns for Today's Church 277

1 Father, in your presence kneeling,
  all our heart's desire revealing,
  to your love, in faith appealing,
   for our children, Lord, we pray.

2 Grant us wisdom so to train them
  that no mortal evil stain them –
  young for Jesus
   we would gain them:
   for our children, Lord, we pray.

At a Baptism (7–10)

3 Keep them onward,
  upward pressing,
courage, self-control possessing;
bravely Christ their king confessing:
  for our children, Lord, we pray.

4 Strengthen them
  for high endeavour –
to your will unfaithful never,
God and neighbour serving ever:
  for our children, Lord, we pray.

5 Lord, on life's adventure
  guide them,
in your secret presence hide them;
to your love we now confide them:
  for our children, Lord, we pray.

Copyright controlled†

11 North Coates
Hymns for Today's Church 384

1 Father, now behold us
  and this child, we pray:
in your love enfold us,
  wash our sins away.

2 Christ's eternal blessing
  for this life we claim:
faith, by ours, professing;
  signed in Jesus' name.

3 By the Spirit tended,
  childhood grow to youth,
from all ill defended,
  full of grace and truth.

4 God of all creation,
  stoop from heaven's throne,
and by Christ's salvation
  make this child your own!

© Timothy Dudley-Smith

12

INTERCESSION
We pray that *N* may bear fruit as a
new branch of the Vine which is Jesus
Christ:

May the spirit of the Lord
  rest upon *him*:
the spirit of wisdom
  and understanding,
the spirit of counsel and power,
the spirit of knowledge
  and the fear of the Lord;
may *he* delight in the Lord. **Amen.**

from Isaiah 11

13

THANKSGIVING

We praise you,
O God and Father
  of our Lord Jesus Christ,
that in your great mercy
you have given us new birth
into a living hope
through the resurrection
  of Jesus Christ from the dead,
and into an inheritance
that can never perish, spoil or fade –
kept in heaven for us,
who through faith
are shielded by God's power
until the coming of the salvation
that is ready to be revealed
  in the last time:
in this we greatly rejoice. **Amen.**

from 1 Peter 1

14 England's Lane
Hymns for Today's Church 298(i)

1 Welcome to Christ's family,
  fellow-member with us all!
God who beckons you today
  down the years your name will call.

(11–14) At a Baptism

Christle Lord
    makes all things new:
in his name we welcome you!

2 Welcome to Christ's army now,
    soldier, servant to the end:
    God the Spirit strengthens you
    as with evil you contend.
    Christ the Lord . . .

3 Welcome to the Lord's own school:
    life and love from him we learn –
    giver of the golden rule,
    teacher, friend to whom we turn.
    Christ the Lord . . .

4 Welcome as a branch new-grown,
    added here with faith and prayer,

joined with us to Christ the Vine,
watched and watered with due care.
    Christ the Lord . . .

5 Welcome to Christ's body here
    and in many a scattered place:
    Christian people far and near
    serve the Lord of every race.
    Christ the Lord . . .

6 Welcome!
    All Christ's wealth is yours,
    riches vast beyond compare;
    we are Christ's inheritors
    and his heavenly kingdom share.
    Christ the Lord . . .

© David Mowbray/Jubilate Hymns

AT A BAPTISM/THANKSGIVING
Other items appropriate to this theme

Hymns

Faithful Shepherd, feed me	571
Glorious things of you are spoken	183
Guide me, O my great Redeemer	129
Lead us, heavenly Father, lead us	111
May the grace of Christ our saviour	504
May the mind of Christ my saviour	452
My faithful shepherd is the Lord	560
Soldiers of Christ, arise	529
Take my life and let it be	151
The king of love my shepherd is	27
The Lord my shepherd	137

Songs

All the way, all the way	207
Bind us together, Lord	119
Christ in me is to live	140
Cleanse me from my sin, Lord	225
He's got the whole world	189
O Holy Spirit, breathe on me	316

Psalm Version (sung)

I love you, O Lord, you alone (Psalm 18)	248

Psalm Version (spoken)

Happy are those who (Psalm 40)	136

Prayers

There is one God and Father (Creed)	426
We are risen with Christ (Easter Greeting)	240
Lord God almighty, grant your people (Collect)	545
O God our Father (For a Spirit of Caring)	455
Heavenly Father, we thank you	430

Readings

Saved Through the Flood –
    Genesis 7.17–23 (or 7.17–8.5)
Saved Through the Red Sea –
    Exodus 14.19–31
The Cleansing of Naaman –
    2 Kings 5.1–15a
Take up Your Cross –
    Matthew 16.24–27
Born from Water and the Spirit –
    John 3.1–8
Baptism at Philippi – Acts 16.25–34

(See also Minister's Section 682–690.
The Lord's Prayer is printed inside the
back cover.)

7 At Holy Communion

Whenever you eat this bread and drink this cup, you proclaim the Lord's death until he comes.

1 Corinthians 11.26

15

PRAISE

Let us give thanks to the Lord for his unfailing love
**and the wonderful things
he has done for us.**

He satisfies the thirsty
**and fills the hungry with good things.
Amen.**

from Psalm 107

4 And thus with joy
        we meet our Lord;
his presence, always near,
is in such friendship better known:
we see and praise him here.

5 Together met, together bound,
we'll go our different ways;
and as his people in the world
we'll live and speak his praise.

Brian Wren
© Oxford University Press

16 University
Hymns for Today's Church 408 (i)

1 I come with joy to meet my Lord,
forgiven, loved, and free;
in awe and wonder to recall
his life laid down for me.

2 I come with Christians far and near
to find, as all are fed,
the new community of love
in Christ's communion bread.

3 As Christ breaks bread
        and bids us share,
each proud division ends;
the love that made us,
        makes us one,
and strangers now are friends.

17 Orientis Partibus
Hymns for Today's Church 472

1 See the feast our God prepares;
all who hunger, come to dine!
Jesus with his people shares
richest food and finest wine.

2 Here he suddenly removes
prisoners' shame
        and mourners' grief;
here the wanderers whom he loves
find their rest and their relief.

3 Now our tears are wiped away,
now for ever death undone;
he who rose on Easter Day
ends our darkness like the sun.

(15–17) At Holy Communion

4 Christ our God! With joy acclaim
all the glories of our king.
Christ the Lord! We love his name:
every tongue, his praises sing!

from Isaiah 25
© Christopher Idle/Jubilate Hymns

18

FOR PURITY

Almighty God,
you see into our hearts
and you know our minds;
we cannot hide our secrets from you:
cleanse our thoughts and our desires
by the power of your Holy Spirit,
that we may love you perfectly
and worship you acceptably;
through Jesus Christ our Lord. **Amen.**

†

19

RESPONSES

Blessed are the poor in spirit:
for theirs is the kingdom of heaven.

Blessed are those who hunger and
thirst for righteousness:
for they will be filled.

Praise the Lord:
The Lord's name be praised! Amen.

from Matthew 5

20

ACT OF DEDICATION

What can I offer the Lord for all his
goodness to me?
**I will bring a wine-offering
to the Lord,
to thank him for saving me.**

In the assembly of his people:
I will give him what I have promised.

I will give you a sacrifice of thanksgiving:
and offer my prayer to you.

In the assembly of all your people:
I will give you what I have promised.

Praise the Lord:
the Lord's name be praised. Amen.

from Psalm 116

21

CONFESSION

**Almighty God,
Father of our Lord Jesus Christ,
maker and judge of all:
we confess the sins
which again and again
    we have so hurtfully committed
against you, our God and king.
By right you are angry
    and displeased at us.
We sincerely repent
and are truly sorry
for the wrong things
    we have done –
their memory is painful
and more than we can bear.
Have mercy on us,
    most merciful Father;
for Jesus' sake forgive us
    all that is past,
and renew our lives from this day
that we may serve you and please you,
and bring honour and glory
    to your name;
through Jesus Christ our Lord. Amen.**

†

after the Book of Common Prayer
Confession at Holy Communion

At Holy Communion (18–21)

22

FOR MERCY (CONFESSION)

Lord God, have mercy on us,
according to your steadfast love;
and in your abundant mercy,
blot out our transgressions:
cleanse us from our sin,
create in us a clean heart and life,
and continually renew
a right spirit within us. Amen.

from Psalm 51

23

COMMANDMENTS (CONFESSION)

Jesus said: Love the Lord your God with all your heart and with all your soul and with all your mind and with all your strength; and love your neighbour as yourself.

Lord, we have broken
your commandments:
forgive us, and help us to obey;
for your name's sake. Amen.

from Mark 12

24 Ode to Joy
Hymns for Today's Church 581

GLORIA . . .

1 Glory be to God in heaven,
peace to those who love him well;
on the earth let all his people
speak his grace, his wonders tell:
Lord, we praise you for your glory,
mighty Father, heaven's king;
hear our joyful adoration
and accept the thanks we bring.

2 Only Son of God the Father,
Lamb who takes our sin away,
now with him in triumph seated –

for your mercy, Lord, we pray:
Jesus Christ, most high and holy,
Saviour, you are God alone
in the glory of the Father
with the Spirit: Three-in-One!

from Gloria in Excelsis
© Michael Perry/Jubilate Hymns

25 Land of hope
Church Family Worship Source Book

GLORIA . . .

1 Glory in the highest
to the God of heaven!
Peace to all your people
through the earth be given!
Mighty God and Father,
thanks and praise we bring,
singing Alleluia
to our heavenly king;
singing Alleluia
to our heavenly king.

2 Jesus Christ is risen,
God the Father's Son!
With the Holy Spirit,
you are Lord alone!
Lamb once killed for sinners,
all our guilt to bear,
show us now your mercy,
now receive our prayer;
show us now your mercy,
now receive our prayer.

3 Christ the world's true Saviour,
high and holy one,
seated now and reigning
from your Father's throne:
Lord and God, we praise you!
Highest heaven adores:
in the Father's glory,
all the praise be yours;
in the Father's glory,
all the praise be yours!

from Gloria in Excelsis
© Christopher Idle/Jubilate Hymns

(22–25) At Holy Communion

26

PSALM

I love the Lord because he heard my voice:
**the Lord in mercy listened
to my prayers.**

Because the Lord has turned his ear to me:
I'll call on him as long as I shall live.

The cords of death entangled me around:
the horrors of the grave came over me.

But then I called upon the Lord my God:
**I said to him,
'O Lord, I beg you, save!'**

The Lord our God is merciful and good:
**the Lord protects
the simple-hearted ones.**

The Lord saved me from death and stopped my tears:
**he saved me from defeat
and picked me up.**

And so I walk before him all my days:
**and live to love and praise his holy
name.**

What shall I give the Lord for all his grace?
**I'll take his saving cup,
and pay my vows.**

Within the congregation of his saints:
I'll offer him my sacrifice of praise.

Praise the Lord: **Amen. Amen.**

from Psalm 116

27
Dominus regit me or The Followers
Hymns for Today's Church 44

PSALM

1 The king of love my shepherd is,
whose goodness fails me never;
I nothing lack if I am his
and he is mine for ever.

2 Where streams of living water flow
a ransomed soul, he leads me;
and where the fertile pastures grow,
with food from heaven feeds me.

3 Perverse and foolish I have strayed,
but in his love he sought me;
and on his shoulder gently laid,
and home, rejoicing, brought me.

4 In death's dark vale I fear no ill
with you, dear Lord, beside me;
your rod and staff my comfort still,
your cross before to guide me.

5 You spread a banquet in my sight
of love beyond all knowing;
and O the gladness and delight
from your pure chalice flowing!

6 And so
through all the length of days
your goodness fails me never;
Good Shepherd,
may I sing your praise
within your house for ever!

from Psalm 23
H W Baker (1821–1877)
© in this version Jubilee Hymns

28
O taste and see
Songs of Fellowship 3   461

PSALM

O taste and see that the Lord is good:
how blessed is the man
who hides himself in him!

At Holy Communion (26–28)

I sought the Lord
and he answered me,
and set me free from all my fears.
I will give thanks to him,
for he is good,
his steadfast love to me will never end.

from Psalm 34
Phil Rogers
© Thankyou Music†

29 Calypso Praise
Hymns for Today's Church 414

1 Let us talents and tongues employ,
reaching out with a shout of joy:
bread is broken, the wine is poured,
Christ is spoken
and seen and heard.
Jesus lives again,
earth can breathe again,
pass the Word around:
loaves abound!

2 Christ is able to make us one,
at the table he sets the tone,
teaching people to live to bless,
love in word and in deed express.
Jesus lives again . . .

3 Jesus calls us in, sends us out
bearing fruit in a world of doubt,
gives us love to tell, bread to share:
God Emmanuel, everywhere.
Jesus lives again . . .

Fred Kaan
© Stainer and Bell Limited†

30 One shall tell another
Songs of Fellowship 2   274

1 One shall tell another,
and he shall tell his friends;
husbands, wives and children
shall come following on.
From house to house in families
shall more be gathered in;

and lights will shine in every street,
so warm and welcoming.
Come on in
and taste the new wine,
the wine of the kingdom,
the wine of the kingdom of God
here is healing and forgiveness,
the wine of the kingdom,
the wine of the kingdom of God.

2 Compassion of the Father
is ready now to flow;
through acts of love and mercy
we must let it show.
He turns now from his anger
to show a smiling face,
and longs
that we should stand beneath
the fountain of his grace.
Come on in . . .

3 He longs to do much more than
our faith has yet allowed,
to thrill us and surprise us
with his sovereign power.
Where darkness has been darkest,
the brightest light will shine;
his invitation comes to us –
it's yours and it is mine.
Come on in . . .

Graham Kendrick
© Thankyou Music†

31

CREED
Let us affirm our faith in God:

**We believe and trust
in God the Father
who made the world.**

**We believe and trust
in his Son Jesus Christ,
who redeemed mankind.**

(29–31) At Holy Communion

We believe and trust
in his Holy Spirit,
who gives life to the people of God.

We believe and trust in one God:
Father, Son, and Holy Spirit. Amen. †

32

DEDICATION

Lord Jesus Christ,
we give ourselves into your hands.
Grant us grace to see you,
to know your way,
to feel you near.
Find us now in the quiet,
and hold us fast
in the haste of the day;
for your glory's sake. **Amen.**　　†

33 The Canticle of the Gift
　　　 Jesus Praise 99

O what a gift!
What a wonderful gift! –
who can tell the wonders
of the Lord?
Let us open our eyes
and our ears
and our hearts –
it is Christ the Lord, it is he!

1 In the stillness of the night,
when the world was asleep,
the almighty Word leapt out;
he came to Mary, he came to us –
Christ came to the land of Galilee,
Christ our Lord and our king!
O what a gift . . .

2 On the night before he died
it was Passover night,
and he gathered his friends
together;

he broke the bread,
he blessed the wine –
it was the gift of his love and his life,
Christ our Lord and our king!
O what a gift . . .

3 On the hill of Calvary
while the world held its breath,
it was there for us all to see;
God gave his Son, his only Son,
for the love of you and me:
Christ our Lord and our king!
O what a gift . . .

4 It was early on that morning
when the guards were asleep,
back to life came he:
he conquered death,
he conquered sin –
but victory he gave to you and me,
Christ our Lord and our king!
O what a gift . . .

5 Some day with the saints
we will come before our Father,
and then we will shout
and dance and sing
for in our midst for our eyes to see
will be Christ our Lord
and our king,
Christ our Lord and our king!
O what a gift . . .

Pat Uhl Howard
© American Catholic Press†

34 Selfless love, Christmas Carol
　　　 Hymns for Today's Church 405, 88(ii)

1 He gave his life in selfless love,
for sinful man he came;
he had no stain of sin himself
but bore our guilt and shame:
he took the cup of pain and death,
his blood was freely shed;
we see his body on the cross,
we share the living bread.

At Holy Communion (32–34)

2 He did not come to call the good
    but sinners to repent;
  it was the lame, the deaf, the blind
    for whom his life was spent:
  to heal the sick, to find the lost –
    it was for such he came,
  and round his table all may come
    to praise his holy name.

3 They heard him call
    his Father's name –
  then 'Finished!' was his cry;
  like them we have forsaken him
    and left him there to die:
  the sins that crucified him then
    are sins his blood has cured;
  the love that bound him to a cross
    our freedom has ensured.

4 His body broken once for us
    is glorious now above;
  the cup of blessing we receive,
    a sharing of his love:
  as in his presence we partake,
    his dying we proclaim
  until the hour of majesty
    when Jesus comes again.

                © Christopher Porteous/Jubilate Hymns

35 Passion Chorale, Crüger
        Hymns for Today's Church 139, 190

1 We come as guests invited
    when Jesus bids us dine,
  his friends on earth united
    to share the bread and wine;
  the bread of life is broken,
    the wine is freely poured
  for us, in solemn token
    of Christ our dying Lord.

2 We eat and drink, receiving
    from Christ the grace we need,
  and in our hearts believing
    on him by faith we feed;

with wonder and thanksgiving
  for love that knows no end,
we find in Jesus living
  our ever-present friend.

3 One bread is ours for sharing,
    one single fruitful vine,
  our fellowship declaring
    renewed in bread and wine –
  renewed, sustained and given
    by token, sign and word,
  the pledge and seal of heaven,
    the love of Christ our Lord.

                © Timothy Dudley-Smith

36

ASCRIPTION

Lord God, may you be praised for ever
and ever:
**You are great and powerful,
glorious, splendid and majestic;
everything in heaven and earth
    is yours
and you are king,
supreme ruler over all;
all riches and wealth come from you;
you rule everything
by your strength and power;
and you are able to make anyone
    great and strong:
now, our God, we give you thanks
and praise your glorious name. Amen.**

                From 1 Chronicles 29

37

AN INVITATION

Come to this table, not because you are
strong, but because you are weak;
come, not because any goodness of
your own gives you a right to come, but

because you need mercy and help;
come, because you love the Lord a little
and would like to love him more; come,
not because you are worthy to
approach him, but because he died for
sinners; come, because he loved you
and gave himself for you:

Your death, O Lord,
**   we commemorate,**
your resurrection we proclaim,
your coming again in glory
**   we anticipate:**
glory to you, living saviour and Lord!
Amen.   †

Or 38

PRAYER OF APPROACH

Jesus,
we come to this your table
not because we are strong,
but because we are weak;
not because any goodness of our own
gives us the right to come,
but because we need your mercy
    and your help;
not because of anything
    we have achieved,
but because you died for sinners.

Glory be to you,
our living saviour and Lord. Amen. †

39 Take this bread
Spirit of Praise 1   172

1 Take this bread I give to you,
    and as you do, remember me:
    this bread is my body
    broken just for you –
    take it, eat it;
    each time you do,
        remember me, remember me,
        remember me, remember me.

2 Take this cup I fill for you,
    and as you do, remember me:
    this cup is the new covenant
    I'm making with you:
    take it, drink it:
    each time you do,
        remember me . . .

3 Take this love I've given you,
    and as you do,
        remember me, remember me,
        remember me.

from 1 Corinthians 11
Barry McGuire
© Sparrow Song/Cherry Lane Music Limited†

40 Broken for me
Jesus Praise 134

    Broken for me, broken for you,
    the body of Jesus broken for you.

1 He offered his body,
        he poured out his soul,
    Jesus was broken
        that we might be whole:
    Broken for me . . .

2 Come to my table and with me dine,
    eat of my bread
        and drink of my wine:
    Broken for me . . .

3 This is my body given for you,
    eat it remembering I died for you:
    Broken for me . . .

4 This is my blood I shed for you,
    for your forgiveness,
        making you new:
    Broken for me . . .

Janet Lunt
© Mustard Seed Music†

At Holy Communion (38–40)

41

DIALOGUE

The Lord be with you:
and also with you.

Or

The Lord is here:
his Spirit is with us.

Lift up your hearts:
we lift them to the Lord.

Let us give thanks to the Lord our God:
**it is right to give him
thanks and praise.**

42

THE WORDS OF INSTITUTION

Our Lord Jesus Christ,
in the same night that he was
betrayed,
took bread,
and when he had given thanks
he broke it and said,
'This is my body, which is for you;
do this to remember me.'

In the same way, after supper
he took the cup, saying,
'This cup is the new covenant
in my blood;
do this, whenever you drink it,
to remember me.'

(For whenever you eat this bread
and drink this cup,
you proclaim the Lord's death
until he comes.) **Amen.**

from 1 Corinthians 11

43

SENTENCES
At the breaking of the bread:

Jesus said, 'I am the bread of life: those who come to me will never grow hungry, and those who believe in me will never be thirsty.'
**'Lord, give us this bread for ever.'
Amen.**

At the taking of the wine:

Jesus said, 'I am the true vine . . . remain in me, and I will remain in you.'
Amen.

from John 6 and 15

Or 44

SENTENCES
At the breaking of the bread:

Jesus said, 'I have eagerly desired to eat this passover with you before I suffer; for I tell you, I will not eat it again until it finds fulfilment in the kingdom of God.'
'Do this in memory of me.' **Amen.**

At the taking of the wine:

Jesus said, 'I tell you the truth, I will not drink again of the fruit of the vine until that day when I drink it anew in the kingdom of God.'
'Take this and share it among you.'
Amen.

from Luke 22 and Mark 14

(41–44) At Holy Communion

45 Worthy is the Lamb
Mission Praise 280

1 Worthy is the Lamb,
   worthy . . .
   worthy . . .
   worthy . . .

2 Holy is the Lamb . . .

3 Precious is the Lamb . . .

4 Praises to the Lamb . . .

5 Glory to the Lamb . . .

6 Jesus is our Lamb . . .

from Revelation 5
Copyright controlled†

46 Cross of Jesus
Hymns for Today's Church 403

1 For the bread
      which you have broken,
   for the wine
      which you have poured,
   for the words
      which you have spoken,
   now we give you thanks, O Lord.

2 By these pledges that you love us,
   by your gift of peace restored,
   by your call to heaven above us,
   consecrate our lives, O Lord:

3 In your service, Lord, defend us,
   help us to obey your word;
   in the world to which you send us
   let your kingdom come, O Lord!

L F Benson (1855–1930)

47 Thaxted
Hymns for Today's Church 36

1 O God beyond all praising,
      we worship you today
   and sing the love amazing
      that songs cannot repay;
   for we can only wonder
      at every gift you send,
   at blessings without number
      and mercies without end:
   we lift our hearts before you
      and wait upon your word,
   we honour and adore you,
      our great and mighty Lord.

2 Then hear, O gracious Saviour,
      accept the love we bring,
   that we who know your favour
      may serve you as our king;
   and whether our tomorrows
      be filled with good or ill,
   we'll triumph through our sorrows
      and rise to bless you still:
   to marvel at your beauty
      and glory in your ways,
   and make a joyful duty
      our sacrifice of praise.

© Michael Perry/Jubilate Hymns

At Holy Communion (45–47)

AT HOLY COMMUNION
Other items appropriate to this theme

Hymns

Lord Jesus Christ, you have come
to us   390

Speak, Lord, in the stillness   174

Canticle

Jesus, Saviour of the world   356

Songs

Abba, Father   399

Father, we adore you   191

Father, we love you   336

Here he comes   57

Jesus, name above all names   226

There is a redeemer   228

Worthy, O worthy   296

Prayers

Jesus, you come to live among us
(Act of Praise)   597

The Ten Commandments   127

Jesus' commandment   149

We do not presume   page 9

Most merciful Lord   page 9
(Prayers of Humble Access)

Family Communion Prayer   785

Readings

The Lord's Supper –
Matthew 26.26–30; Mark 14.22–26;
Luke 22.14–20;
1 Corinthians 11.23–25

Its Meaning, John 6.53–58

Its Forerunners, Exodus 12.12–14;
Exodus 16.31–36; Exodus 24.6–11

(See also Palm Sunday, Good Friday
and Easter sections 200–263, and Minister's Section 691–701, 785. The Lord's
Prayer is printed inside the back cover.)

At Holy Communion (Other items)

8 At Local Festivals/ For the Peace of the World

Be of one mind, live in peace. And the God of love and peace will be with you.

2 Corinthians 13.11

48

PRAISE

Let the people praise you, O God;
let all the people praise you!

Let your ways be known on earth;
your saving power in all the world!
Amen.

from Psalm 67

49 Luckington
Hymns for Today's Church 342(i)

1 Let all the world
    in every corner sing,
      'My God and King!'
The heavens are not too high,
his praise may thither fly;
the earth is not too low,
his praises there may grow:
let all the world in every corner sing,
    'My God and King!'

2 Let all the world
    in every corner sing,
      'My God and King!'
The church with psalms
    must shout –
no door can keep them out;
but above all, the heart
must bear the longest part:
let all the world in every corner sing,
    'My God and King!'

G Herbert (1593–1632)

50 St Anne
Hymns for Today's Church 37

1 O God, our help in ages past,
our hope for years to come,
our shelter from the stormy blast,
and our eternal home:

2 Beneath the shadow of your throne
your people live secure;
sufficient is your arm alone,
and our defence is sure.

3 Before the hills in order stood,
or earth from darkness came,
from everlasting you are God,
to endless years the same.

4 A thousand ages in your sight
are like an evening gone;
short as the watch
    that ends the night,
before the rising sun.

5 Time, like an ever-rolling stream,
will bear us all away;
we pass forgotten, as a dream
dies with the dawning day.

6 O God, our help in ages past,
our hope for years to come:
be our defence while life shall last,
and our eternal home!

from Psalm 90
I Watts (1674–1748)
© in this version Jubilate Hymns

At Local Festivals (48–50)

51

CONFESSION

Lord God, our maker and our redeemer, this is your world and we are your people: come among us and save us.

Where we have wilfully misused your gifts of creation, be merciful, Lord:
forgive us and help us.

Where we have seen the ill-treatment of others and have not gone to their aid, be merciful, Lord:
forgive us and help us.

Where we have condoned the lie in our society, and failed to achieve justice or compassion, be merciful, Lord:
forgive us and help us.

Where we have heard for ourselves the good news of Christ, but have not shared it with our generation nor taught it to our children, be merciful, Lord:
forgive us and help us.

Where we have not loved you with all our heart, nor our neighbours as ourselves, be merciful, Lord:
forgive us and help us.

**O God,
forgive us for our lack of love,
and in your mercy make us
what you would have us be,
through Jesus Christ our Lord. Amen.**

✝

52

ACT OF REMEMBRANCE
(See Minister's Section, number 702)

They shall grow not old,
as we who are left grow old:
age shall not weary them,
nor the years condemn:

at the going down of the sun
and in the morning
we will remember them:
we will remember them. ✝

53

PSALM

I was glad when they said to me:
let us go to the house of the Lord!

Pray for the peace of Jerusalem:
**may those who love our land
be blessed.**

May there be peace in your homes:
and safety for our families.

For the sake of those we love we say:
Let there be peace! Amen.

from Psalm 122

54 Jerusalem
Hymns for Today's Church 336

PSALM

1 Bring to the Lord a glad new song,
children of grace, extol your king;
worship and praise to God belong –
to instruments of music, sing!
Let those be warned
    who spurn his name;
nations and kings, attend his word;
God's justice shall bring (*all)
    tyrants shame:
let every creature praise the Lord!

2 Praise him
    within these hallowed walls,
praise him
    beneath the dome of heaven;
by cymbals' sounds
    and trumpets' calls
let praises fit for God be given:
with strings and brass
    and wind rejoice –

(51–54) At Local Festivals

then, join his praise with full accord
all living things
with breath and voice:
let every creature praise the Lord!

(*Omit when using HTC accompaniment)

faith on the earth,
and from his holy place
he comes in glory,
the righteous saviour.

56 Orientis Partibus
Hymns for Today's Church 472

CANTICLE

1 Bless the Lord, our fathers' God,
bless the name of heaven's king;
bless him in his holy place,
tell his praise, his glories sing.

2 Bless the Lord who reigns on high
throned between the cherubim;
bless the Lord
who knows the depths,
show his praise and worship him.

3 Bless the Lord for evermore;
bless the Holy Trinity:
bless the Father, Spirit, Son,
sing his praise eternally!

55 Sine Nomine
Hymns for Today's Church 567

PSALM

1 When this land knew
God's gracious love outpoured,
guilt was removed
and captive lives restored;
then was drawn back
the anger of the Lord,
his people pardoned
by sovereign favour.

2 But now where wrong
so flagrantly has trod,
will he for ever punish with his rod?
Once more revive us!
Give us life, O God!
Give joy for anguish –
for wrath, salvation.

3 O let me hear
God's word of sweet command:
peace to his saints,
salvation is at hand;
peace to his people,
glory in our land
for those who fear him,
who turn and worship.

4 That day draws near
when truth will join with grace,
justice and peace
will meet in love's embrace;

57 Robed in majesty
Cry Hosanna 134

Here he comes robed in majesty,
'King of the Jews',
living with power among us:
he's won the victory over death!

1 Come behold the king,
Jesus, risen Son,
offering his life to us all;
come receive his life of sacrifice,
come take his flesh and his blood.
And God sends down love
Here he comes . . .

At Local Festivals (55–57)

2 Come behold the life,
    Spirit of the Lord,
offering his power to us all,
as at Pentecost when the Spirit drew
the ones whom Jesus loved,
    and God sent down fire.
Here he comes robed in majesty,
'King of the Jews',
living with power among us:
he's won the victory over death!

3 Come among us now,
    Jesus, risen Lord,
offering the grace for unity!
Christ is in our midst;
we're open to the fullness of his life,
    and God sends down power.
Here he comes . . .

Maggie Durran
© Celebration/Thankyou Music†

58 Let there be love
Mission Praise 137

Let there be love shared among us,
    let there be love in our eyes;
may now your love sweep this nation,
    cause us, O Lord, to arise:
give us a fresh understanding
    of brotherly love that is real;
let there be love shared among us,
    let there be love!

David Bilbrough
© Thankyou Music†

59 The Lord is a great and mighty king
Mission Praise 224

The Lord
    is a great and mighty king,
just and gentle with everything;
so with happiness we sing,
and let his praises ring.

1 We are his voice, we his song:
    let us praise him all day long –
        Alleluia!
    The Lord is . . .

2 We are his body here on earth;
    from above he gave us birth –
        Alleluia!
    The Lord is . . .

3 For our Lord we will stand,
    sent by him to every land –
        Alleluia!
    The Lord is . . .

4 The Lord our God is One,
    Father, Spirit and the Son –
        Alleluia!
    The Lord is . . .

Diane Davis
© GIA Publications Incorporated†

60

CREED

Do you believe in God the Father?
**We believe and trust
    in God the Father,
who made the world.**

Do you believe in God the Son?
**We believe and trust
    in his Son Jesus Christ
who redeemed mankind.**

Do you believe in the Holy Spirit?
**We believe and trust
    in the Holy Spirit,
who gives life to the people of God.**

**We believe and trust in one God:
Father, Son, and Holy Spirit. Amen.** †

(58–60) At Local Festivals

61

THEME PRAYER (COLLECT)

Almighty God,
you have taught us through your Son
that love is the fulfilling of the law.
Grant that we may love you
    with our whole heart
and our neighbours as ourselves;
through Jesus Christ our Lord. **Amen.**

Pentecost 16, ASB

62 Rhuddlan
Hymns for Today's Church 329

1 Judge eternal, throned in splendour,
    Lord of lords and King of kings,
    with your living fire of judgement
    purge this realm of bitter things;
    comfort all its wide dominion
    with the healing of your wings.

2 Weary people still are longing
    for the hour that brings release,
    and the city's crowded clamour
    cries aloud for sin to cease;
    and the countryside and woodlands
    plead in silence for their peace.

3 Crown, O Lord,
        your own endeavour,
    cleave our darkness
        with your sword,
    cheer the faint and feed the hungry
    with the richness of your word;
    cleanse the body of this nation
    through the glory of the Lord.

H S Holland (1847–1918)
© in this version Jubilee Hymns

63

FOR OUR NATIONAL LEADERS

Almighty God,
we pray for our Queen
and all leaders of our country,
that they may govern us
    wisely and well;
we pray for one another,
that we may live and work together
in love, mutual understanding
    and peace,
through Jesus Christ our Lord. **Amen.**

†

64

FOR OUR *VILLAGE/TOWN/CITY*

Heavenly Father,
we thank you for our *village/town/city*,
and for every person who lives here.
Help us to care more
    for our community,
to share your love,
and to stand for your truth:
through Jesus Christ our Lord. **Amen.**

†

65

FOR VISION AND STRENGTH

O God our Father, who in Jesus came to
bring good news to the poor, sight to
the blind, freedom to the oppressed,
and salvation to your people:

Inspire us to care for each other like
brothers and like sisters: Father, by
your grace,
help us to love one another.   →

At Local Festivals (61–65)

Send us out to relieve the poor and rescue the oppressed: Father, by your grace,
help us to love one another.

Prepare us to tell the world the good news of your saving love: Father, by your grace,
help us to love one another.

O God,
make us one in heart and mind,
in the spirit of service,
and in the faith
of Jesus Christ our Lord. Amen. †

66

ASCRIPTION

Glory be to you, O God,
Father, Son, and Holy Spirit –
you have power, wisdom and majesty:
receive from us
honour, glory, worship and blessing.
Great and marvellous are your works,
just and true are your ways:
blessing and honour
　　and glory and power
be to him who reigns upon the throne,
and to the Lamb,
through the one eternal Spirit,
now and for ever. **Amen.**

from Revelation 15

67 St Cecilia
Hymns for Today's Church 334

1 Your kingdom come, O God!
　your rule, O Christ, begin;
　break with your iron rod
　the tyrannies of sin.

2 Where is your reign of peace
　and purity and love?
　When shall all hatred cease
　as in the realms above?

3 When comes the promised time,
　the end of strife and war;
　when lust, oppression, crime
　and greed shall be no more?

4 O Lord our God, arise
　and come in your great might!
　revive our longing eyes
　which languish for your sight.

5 Men scorn your sacred name
　and wolves devour your fold;
　by many deeds of shame
　we learn that love grows cold.

6 On nations near and far
　thick darkness gathers yet:
　arise, O Morning Star,
　arise and never set!

L Hensley (1824–1905)

68 National Anthem
Hymns for Today's Church 592

God save our gracious Queen,
long live our noble Queen,
　God save the Queen!
Send her victorious,
happy and glorious,
long to reign over us:
　God save the Queen!

Unknown

69

ACCLAMATION

Lord God of our fathers,
may you be praised for ever and ever!

You are great and powerful, glorious, splendid and majestic: Lord God of our fathers,
may you be praised for ever and ever!

(66–69) At Local Festivals

Everything in heaven and earth is yours, and you are king, supreme ruler over all: Lord God of our fathers,
may you be praised for ever and ever!

All riches and wealth come from you; you rule everything by your strength and power: Lord God of our fathers,
may you be praised for ever and ever!

**Now, our God,
we give you thanks,
and praise your glorious name;
through Jesus Christ our Lord. Amen.**

from 1 Chronicles 29

70 Tallis' Canon
Hymns for Today's Church 586

Praise God
    from whom all blessings flow,
in heaven above and earth below;
one God, three persons, we adore –
to him be praise for evermore!

after T Ken (1637–1710)
© in this version Jubilate Hymns

---

9 New Year/ Thanksgiving for the Old Year

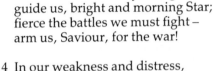

Forgetting what is behind and reaching for what is ahead, I press on towards the goal to win the prize for which God has called me heavenwards in Christ Jesus.

Philippians 3.13,14

Anyone in Christ is a new creation; the old has gone, the new has come!

2 Corinthians 5.17

71

PRAISE

We give you thanks, O God;
we give you thanks.

We proclaim how great you are,
**and tell of the wonderful things
    you have done. Amen.**

from Psalm 75

3 Dark the future – let your light
   guide us, bright and morning Star;
   fierce the battles we must fight –
   arm us, Saviour, for the war!

4 In our weakness and distress,
   be our Rock, O Lord, we pray;
   in the pathless wilderness,
   be our true and living Way.

5 Keep us faithful, keep us pure,
   keep us evermore your own;
   help, O help us to endure,
   make us fit to wear the crown!

H Downton (1818–1885)
© in this version Jubilate Hymns

72 Culbach
Hymns for Today's Church 258

1 For your mercy and your grace
   faithful through another year,
   hear our song of thankfulness,
   Saviour and Redeemer, hear.

2 All our sins on you we cast,
   you, our perfect Sacrifice;
   and, forgetting what is past,
   press towards our glorious prize.

73 Dedication
Hymns for Today's Church 257

1 Father, let us dedicate
       all this year to you,
   for the service small or great
       you would have us do;
   not from any painful thing
       freedom can we claim,
   but in all, that we may bring
       glory to your name.

(71–73) New Year

2 Can a child presume to choose
      where or how to live?
can a Father's love refuse
      all the best to give?
More you give us every day
      than we dare to claim,
and our grateful voices say,
      'Glory to your name!'

3 If you call us to a cross
      and its shadows come
turning all our gain to loss,
      shrouding heart and home,
let us think how your dear Son
      to his triumph came,
then through pain and tears
      pray on,
      'Glory to your name!'

4 If in mercy you prepare
      joyful years ahead,
if through days serene and fair
      peaceful paths we tread;
then, whatever life may bring,
      let our lips proclaim
and our glad hearts ever sing,
      'Glory to your name!'

L Tuttiett (1825–1897)
© in this version Jubilate Hymns

74

CONFESSION
We look to God for forgiveness, knowing that in this last year we have often grieved him through our failures and sins:

Where we have not cared enough for you:
forgive us, O God.

Where we have not cared enough for your world:
forgive us, O God.

Where we have been content with ourselves as we are:
forgive us, O God.

**Give us the will and the power
to live in the Spirit of Jesus;
now and always. Amen.** †

75

PSALM*

^A Give thanks to God, for he is good:
his love shall last for ever!

^B Give thanks to him, the God of gods:
his love shall last for ever!

^C Give thanks to him, the Lord of lords:
his love shall last for ever!

^A For God alone works miracles:
his love shall last for ever!

^B The skies were made at his command:
his love shall last for ever!

^C He spread the seas upon the earth:
his love shall last for ever!

^A He made the stars to shine at night:
his love shall last for ever!

^B He made the sun to shine by day:
his love shall last for ever!

^C He brought us out from slavery:
his love shall last for ever!

^A He leads us onward by his grace:
his love shall last for ever!

^B He saves us from our enemies:
his love shall last for ever!

^C Give thanks to God, for he is good:
his love shall last for ever!

from Psalm 136

(* The congregation/choir may divide at A, B and C – all say the refrain)

PSALM/CANTICLE

1 O come let us sing to the Lord,
let us worship the rock of salvation,
and enter his presence with praise –
with thanksgiving
and great jubilation!

2 The Lord is our maker and king,
he is mighty, the God of creation;
the earth and the oceans are his,
and the people
of each race and nation.

3 O come let us fall at his feet,
let us call him our Lord
and our master;
for we are the sheep of his hand,
ever kept by his power
from disaster.

4 Today let us heed what he says,
and not harden our hearts
by complaining
like those who rebelled at his word,
in the desert
his goodness disdaining.

5 They tried him and tested his love,
and rejected the word
he had spoken;
their hearts they had turned
from his ways,
and his excellent law
they had broken.

6 The Lord in his anger declared:
'They shall never inherit
my blessing!'
Let us not be stubborn, O Lord,
but obey you,
your great name confessing.

from Psalm 95 (*Venite*)
J E Seddon (1915–1983)
© Mrs M Seddon/Jubilate Hymns

PSALM

1 God is our strength and refuge,
our present help in trouble;
and we therefore will not fear,
though the earth should change!
Though mountains
shake and tremble,
though swirling floods are raging,
God the Lord of hosts
is with us evermore!

2 There is a flowing river,
within God's holy city;
God is in the midst of her –
she shall not be moved!
God's help is swiftly given,
thrones vanish at his presence –
God the Lord of hosts
is with us evermore!

3 Come, see the works of our maker,
learn of his deeds all-powerful;
wars will cease across the world
when he shatters the spear!
Be still and know your creator,
uplift him in the nations –
God the Lord of hosts
is with us evermore!

from Psalm 46
© Richard Bewes/Jubilate Hymns

PSALM

1 Take heart and praise our God;
rejoice and clap your hands –
his power our foe subdued,
his mercy ever stands:
let trumpets sound
and people sing,
the Lord through all the earth
is King!

2 Take heart, but sing with fear
  exalt his worthy name;
  with mind alert and clear
  now celebrate his fame:
    let trumpets sound . . .

3 Take heart for future days,
  for tasks as yet unknown –
  the God whose name we praise
  is seated on the throne:
    let trumpets sound . . .

4 Take heart and trust in God
  the Father and the Son –
  God is our strength and shield,
  his Spirit guides us on:
    let trumpets sound . . .

from Psalm 47
© David Mowbray/Jubilate Hymns

79 Because your love
Mission Praise 19

1 Because your love is better than life,
  with my lips I will glorify you:
    I will praise you as long as I live;
    in your name I lift my hands.

2 Because your Son has given me life,
  with my lips I will glorify you:
    I will praise you . . .

3 Because your Spirit is filling my life,
  with my lips I will glorify you:
    I will praise you . . .

4 Because your love is better than life,
  with my lips I will glorify you:
    I will praise you . . .

Phil Potter
© Thankyou Music†

80 Bless the Lord
Mission Praise 26

Bless the Lord, O my soul,
  bless the Lord, O my soul,
and all that is within me
  bless his holy name;
bless the Lord . . .

King of kings (for ever and ever),
Lord of lords (for ever and ever),
King of kings (for ever and ever),
King of kings and Lord of lords.

Bless the Lord . . .

Bless the Lord . . .

from Psalm 103
Copyright controlled†

81 I will sing about your love
Songs of Fellowship 2   234

I will sing about your love,
I will glorify your name,
I will be glad and rejoice in you,
I will praise you again:
  Praise the Lord,
    lift your voices high;
  praise the Lord, tell them he's alive;
  praise the Lord, praise the Lord!

Phil Potter
© Thankyou Music†

82 My God is so big
Jesus Praise 62

My God is so big/*great*, so strong,
  and so mighty,
there's nothing that he cannot do.
My God is so big/*great*, so strong,
  so mighty
there is nothing he cannot do!

The rivers are his,
  the mountains are his,
the stars are his handiwork too.

My God is so big/*great* . . .

Copyright controlled†

New Year (79–82)

83

CREED
All God's promises are 'yes' in Christ;
through him we give glory to God and
say, Amen:

**It is Christ
to whom we belong.
It is the Father
who assures us of our salvation
and anoints us for his service.
It is the Spirit
by whom we are sealed in love
for evermore.
We believe in one God:
Father, Son, and Holy Spirit. Amen.** †

after 2 Corinthians 1

84 Celeste
Hymns for Today's Church 450

1 How good is the God we adore,
our faithful, unchangeable friend
whose love is as great as his power
and knows neither measure
nor end!

2 For Christ is the first and the last;
his Spirit will guide us safe home:
we'll praise him for all that is past
and trust him for all that's to come.

J Hart (1712–1768)

85 Marching
Hymns for Today's Church 360(ii)

1 Father, hear the prayer we offer –
not for ease our prayer shall be,
but for strength that we may ever
live our lives courageously.

2 Not for ever in green pastures
do we ask our way to be;
but the steep and rugged pathway
may we tread rejoicingly.

3 Not for ever by still waters
would we idly rest and stay;
but would strike the living fountains
from the rocks along our way.

4 Be our strength
in hours of weakness,
in our wanderings be our guide;
through endeavour, failure, danger,
Father, be there at our side.

L M Willis (1824–1908)

86 Slane
Hymns for Today's Church 101

1 Lord of all hopefulness,
Lord of all joy,
whose trust, ever childlike,
no cares could destroy:
be there at our waking,
and give us, we pray,
your bliss in our hearts, Lord,
at the break of the day.

2 Lord of all eagerness,
Lord of all faith,
whose strong hands were skilled
at the plane and the lathe:
be there at our labours,
and give us, we pray,
your strength in our hearts, Lord,
at the noon of the day.

3 Lord of all kindliness,
Lord of all grace,
your hands swift to welcome,
your arms to embrace:
be there at our homing,
and give us, we pray,
your love in our hearts, Lord,
at the eve of the day.

(83–86) New Year

4 Lord of all gentleness,
    Lord of all calm,
  whose voice is contentment,
    whose presence is balm:
  be there at our sleeping,
    and give us, we pray,
  your peace in our hearts, Lord,
    at the end of the day.

J Struther (1901–1953)
© Oxford University Press

87

FOR GOD'S HELP IN THE NEW YEAR

O God our Father, at the beginning of
this new year, look upon our Christian
family. We come to you in prayer with
our hopes and resolutions. And we
come also with our doubts and fears,
knowing the power of the world, the
flesh and the devil. Yet we pray that
you will help us not to fall. At the
beginning of the new year,
Lord, hear our prayer.

Look upon us as we do our work, face
our exams, run our households, look
for jobs, earn our wages, maintain our
businesses, enjoy our leisure. At the
beginning of the new year,
Lord, hear our prayer.

Look upon our church as it loves and
cares and serves, as it learns and
worships and witnesses. At the beginning of the new year,
Lord, hear our prayer.

Look upon your world, with all its
waste and war and sorrow, yet all its
joys as well. At the beginning of the
new year,
Lord, hear our prayer.

**Father, grant us your presence
    and your peace;
keep us safe in the knowledge
of Jesus Christ our Lord. Amen.** †

88 Lord of the years
Hymns for Today's Church 328

1 Lord, for the years
    your love has kept and guided,
  urged and inspired us,
    cheered us on our way,
  sought us and saved us,
    pardoned and provided,
  Lord of the years,
    we bring our thanks today.

2 Lord, for that word,
    the word of life which fires us,
  speaks to our hearts
    and sets our souls ablaze;
  teaches and trains,
    rebukes us and inspires us;
  Lord of the word,
    receive your people's praise.

3 Lord, for our land,
    in this our generation,
  spirits oppressed
    by pleasure, wealth and care;
  for young and old,
    for commonwealth and nation,
  Lord of our land,
    be pleased to hear our prayer.

4 Lord, for our world;
    when we disown and doubt
    him,
  loveless in strength,
    and comfortless in pain;
  hungry and helpless,
    lost indeed without him;
  Lord of the world,
    we pray that Christ may reign.

5 Lord, for ourselves;
    in living power remake us –
  self on the cross
    and Christ upon the throne,
  past put behind us,
    for the future take us,
  Lord of our lives,
    to live for Christ alone.

© Timothy Dudley-Smith

New Year (87–88)

89

1 Praise to the Lord,
the almighty, the king of creation!
O my soul, praise him,
for he is your health and
salvation!
Come, all who hear:
brothers and sisters, draw near,
praise him in glad adoration!

2 Praise to the Lord,
above all things
so mightily reigning;
keeping us safe at his side,
and so gently sustaining.
Have you not seen
all you have needed has been
met by his gracious ordaining?

3 Praise to the Lord,
who shall prosper our work
and defend us;
surely his goodness and mercy
shall daily attend us.
Ponder anew
what the Almighty can do,
who with his love will befriend us.

4 Praise to the Lord –
O let all that is in me
adore him!
All that has life and breath
come now with praises before
him!
Let the 'Amen!'
sound from his people again –
gladly with praise we adore him!

from Psalm 103
after J Neander (1650–1680)
C Winkworth (1827–1878) and others

90

ASCRIPTION

Now to him who is able
to keep us from falling
and to present us
before his glorious presence
without fault and with great joy –
to the only God our Saviour
be glory, majesty,
power and authority,
through Jesus Christ our Lord,
before all ages,
now, and for evermore! **Amen.**

from Jude

NEW YEAR/THANKSGIVING FOR THE OLD YEAR

Other items appropriate to this theme

Hymns

Amazing Grace	158
Father, hear the prayer we offer	85
Great is your faithfulness	523
I love you, O Lord, you alone	248
Now thank we all our God	199
O God, our help in ages past	50

Psalm Versions (sung)

Lord, as I wake I turn to you (Psalm 5)	162
There is no moment of my life (Psalm 139)	164

Songs

Be bold, be strong	542
Fear not, rejoice	516
God is good	377
O give thanks to the Lord	493
The Lord has led forth	121
Through our God	540
We will praise	375

Prayers

Most merciful God (For forgiveness)	408
O God, we cannot measure your love (Thanksgiving)	187
Father Almighty, for your majesty and your mercy (Thanksgiving)	344

Readings

Be Strong and Courageous –
Joshua 1.1–9

Assurance for the Future –
Romans 8.28–39

The Lord is my Shepherd –
Psalm 23

David Praises God –
1 Chronicles 29.1–20

Running the Race –
Hebrews 12.1–3

(See also Minister's Section 710–713. The Lord's Prayer is printed inside the back cover.)

New Year (Other items)

10 The Wise Men/ The Escape to Egypt/ Epiphany

Arise, shine, for your light has come, and the glory of the Lord has risen upon you.   Isaiah 60.1

On coming to the house, the wise men saw the child with his mother Mary, and they bowed down and worshipped him.
Matthew 2.11

91

PRAISE

Sing a new song to the Lord;
sing to the Lord, all the earth!

Sing to the Lord, praise his name;
proclaim his triumph day by day!

Worship the Lord in the splendour of his holiness;
tremble before him all the earth!

For great is the Lord, and worthy to be praised. **Amen.**

from Psalm 96

 92 Was lebet
Hymns for Today's Church 344

1 O worship the Lord
    in the beauty of holiness,
bow down before him,
    his glory proclaim;
with gold of obedience
    and incense of lowliness,
kneel and adore him –
    the Lord is his name.

2 Low at his feet
    lay your burden of carefulness,
high on his heart
    he will bear it for you,
comfort your sorrows
    and answer your prayerfulness,
guiding your steps
    in the way that is true.

3 Fear not to enter his courts
    in the slenderness
of the poor wealth
    you would count as your own;
truth in its beauty
    and love in its tenderness –
these are the offerings
    to bring to his throne.

4 These, though we bring them
    in trembling and fearfulness,
he will accept
    for the name that is dear;
mornings of joy give
    for evenings of tearfulness,
trust for our trembling
    and hope for our fear.

5 O worship the Lord
    in the beauty of holiness,
bow down before him,
    his glory proclaim;
with gold of obedience
    and incense of lowliness,
kneel and adore him –
    the Lord is his name.

J S B Monsell (1811–1875)

(91–92) The Wise Men

1 Bethlehem, what greater city
   can in fame with you compare?
   For the gracious God of heaven
   chose to meet his people there.

2 Was there ever beauty brighter
   than the star which shone that night
   to proclaim the incarnation
   of our God, the world's true light?

3 From the East come men of learning
   rich the treasures that they hold –
   tributes to a greater wisdom,
   gifts of incense, myrrh and gold.

4 Sacrifice, redeemer, saviour!
   Incense shows that God has come,
   gold, our mighty king
         proclaims him,
   myrrh foretells his silent tomb.

5 Jesus Christ, to you be glory,
   Lord of lords whom we adore:
   Father, Son and Holy Spirit –
   God be praised for evermore!

after Prudentius
© Michael Perry/Jubilate Hymns

94

CONFESSION

Lord Jesus Christ, wise men from the East worshipped and adored you; they brought you gifts – gold, incense, and myrrh.

We too have seen your glory, but we have often turned away. Lord, in your mercy,
forgive us and help us.

We too have gifts, but we have not fully used them or offered them to you. Lord, in your mercy,
forgive us and help us.

We too have acclaimed you as King, but we have not served you with all our strength. Lord, in your mercy,
forgive us and help us.

We too have acknowledged you as God, but we have not desired holiness. Lord, in your mercy,
forgive us and help us.

We too have welcomed you as Saviour, but we have failed to tell others of your grace. Lord, in your mercy,
forgive us and help us.

**Make our trust more certain,
make our love more real,
make our worship more acceptable;
for your glory's sake. Amen.**   †

95

PSALM*

If the Lord had not been on our side – now let Israel say:

**If the Lord had not been on our side
^Awhen enemies attacked us,
^Bwhen their anger flared against us,
^Cthey would have swallowed us
     alive.**

^AThe flood would have engulfed us:
^Bthe torrent
     would have swept over us,
^Cthe waters would have drowned us.

Praise to the Lord:
who has not given us up to their teeth.

^AWe have escaped like a bird from the snare:
^Bthe snare is broken and we are free.

The Wise Men (93–95)

^C Our help is in the name of the Lord:
^{ALL} **who made heaven and earth.
Amen.**

from Psalm 124

(* The congregation/choir may divide at A,
B and C)

96 Come rejoice
Hymns for Today's Church 17

PSALM/CANTICLE

1 Come, rejoice before your maker
all you peoples of the earth;
serve the Lord your God
  with gladness,
come before him with a song!

2 Know for certain that Jehovah
is the true and only God:
we are his, for he has made us;
we are sheep within his fold.

3 Come with grateful hearts
  before him,
enter now his courts with praise;
show your thankfulness
  towards him,
give due honour to his name.

4 For the Lord our God is gracious –
everlasting in his love;
and to every generation
his great faithfulness endures.

from Psalm 100 (*Jubilate*)
© Michael Baughen/Jubilate Hymns

97 Llanfair
Hymns for Today's Church 345

PSALM

1 Every nation, praise the Lord,
  Alleluia,
praise his name with one accord;
  alleluia,
every land, your voices raise,
  alleluia,
praise the Lord, for ever praise
  alleluia!

2 For his steadfast love prevails,
  Alleluia,
his compassion never fails:
  alleluia,
of his faithfulness assured,
  alleluia,
evermore we'll praise the Lord
  alleluia!

from Psalm 117
J Montgomery (1771–1854)
© in this version David G Preston

98 Caswall
Hymns for Today's Church 364

CANTICLE

1 Lord, now let your servant
go his way in peace;
your great love has brought me
joy that will not cease:

2 For my eyes have seen him
promised from of old –
saviour of all people,
shepherd of one fold:

3 Light of revelation
to the gentiles shown,
light of Israel's glory
to the world made known.

from Luke 2 – The Song of Simeon (*Nunc dimittis*)
J E Seddon (1915–1983)
© Mrs M Seddon/Jubilate Hymns

(96–98) The Wise Men

ALL

1 We three kings of orient are,
bearing gifts we travel afar –
field and fountain,
    moor and mountain –
following yonder star.
    O star of wonder, star of night,
    star with royal beauty bright:
    westward leading,
    still proceeding,
    guide us to your perfect light!

FIRST

2 Born a king on Bethlehem's plain –
gold I bring to crown him again:
king for ever, ceasing never,
over us all to reign.
    ALL   O star of wonder . . .

SECOND

3 Frankincense to offer have I –
incense tells of deity nigh;
prayer and praising all are raising:
worship him – God most high!
    ALL   O star of wonder . . .

THIRD

4 Myrrh is mine – its bitter perfume
breathes a life of gathering gloom:
sorrowing, sighing, bleeding,
    dying,
sealed in the stone-cold tomb.
    ALL   O star of wonder . . .

ALL

5 Glorious now behold him arise –
king and God and sacrifice!
Heaven sings 'Alleluia!'
'Alleluia!' the earth replies.
    O star of wonder . . .

J H Hopkins (1820–1891)

1 When the Lord came to our land,
he was not a wealthy man;
he was born in poverty
and the stars looked down to see:
    and the brightest star of all
    was his.
Jesus was the Son of God,
and he came to earth for me.

2 When the Lord came to our land,
he was not a wealthy man;
he was born in poverty
and the angels came to see:
    and the angels
        sang their joyful news,
    and the brightest star of all
    was his.
Jesus was the Son of God . . .

3 When the Lord came to our land,
he was not a wealthy man;
he was born in poverty
and the shepherds came to see:
    and the shepherds
        knelt and worshipped him,
    and the angels
        sang their joyful news,
    and the brightest star of all
    was his.
Jesus was the Son of God . . .

4 When the Lord came to our land,
he was not a wealthy man;
he was born in poverty
and the wise men came to see:
    and the wise men
        brought rare gifts for him,
    and the shepherds
        knelt and worshipped him,
    and the angels
        sang their joyful news,
    and the brightest star of all
    was his.
Jesus was the Son of God . . .

The Wise Men (99–100)

5 When the Lord came to our land,
  he was not a wealthy man;
  he was born in poverty
  and the donkeys came to see:
    and the donkeys
      gave their stall for him,
    and the wise men
      brought rare gifts for him,
    and the shepherds
      knelt and worshipped him,
    and the angels
      sang their joyful news,
  and the brightest star of all
    was his.
Jesus was the Son of God,
and he came to earth for me.

101 Bergers
Hymns for Today's Church 63

1 Word of the Father everlasting,
  there at his side when time began;
  who but the Word reflects his glory,
  who but the Word
    may speak to man?
  Word of the Father everlasting,
  there at his side when time began.

2 Word once made flesh
    in Mary's keeping,
  source of all life and one true light;
  who of his own
    will dare receive him,
  or to their homes and hearts invite?
  Word once made flesh
    in Mary's keeping,
  source of all life
    and one true light.

3 Word full of grace,
    among us dwelling,
  Jesus our Lord, the Father's Son –
  give us the power,
    your name confessing,
  truly God's children to become:
  Word full of grace,
    among us dwelling,
  Jesus our Lord, the Father's Son.

102

CREED
We believe the grace of God has
dawned upon us with healing for all
the world, and so we rejoice to declare
our faith in him:

**We trust in God the Father,
who has revealed
  his love and kindness to us,
and in his mercy saved us,
not for any good deed of our own,
but because he is merciful.**

**We trust in Jesus Christ,
who gave himself up for us
to free us from our sin,
and set us apart for himself –
a people eager to do good.**

**We trust in the Holy Spirit,
whom God poured out on us
  generously
through Christ our saviour,
so that justified by grace
we might become heirs
with the hope of eternal life. Amen.** †

103

THEME PRAYER (COLLECT)

Eternal God,
who by the shining of a star
led the wise men
to the worship of your Son:
guide by his light
the nations of the earth,
that the whole world
may behold your glory;
through Jesus Christ our Lord. **Amen.**

Christmas 2 (year 2) collect – ASB

104
Dix
Carols for Today 146
Hymns for Today's Church 99

1 As with gladness men of old
did the guiding star behold,
as with joy they hailed its light,
leading onward, gleaming bright:
so, most gracious Lord, may we
evermore your splendour see.

2 As with joyful steps they sped
to that lowly manger bed,
there to bend the knee before
Christ whom heaven and earth
adore:
so with ever-quickening pace
may we seek your throne of grace.

3 As they offered gifts most rare
at your cradle plain and bare,
so may we with holy joy
pure and free from sin's alloy,
all our costliest treasures bring
Christ, to you, our heavenly king.

4 Holy Jesus, every day
keep us in the narrow way,
and when earthly things are past,
bring our ransomed souls at last:
where they need no star to guide,
where no clouds your glory hide.

5 In the heavenly country bright
none shall need created light –
Christ, its light, its joy, its crown,
Christ its sun which goes not down;
there for ever may we sing
alleluias to our king.

W C Dix (1837–1898)
© in this version Word & Music/Jubilate Hymns

105
Tyrolese
Songs of Worship 19

1 The wise may bring their learning,
the rich may bring their wealth,
and some may bring
their greatness,
and some their strength
and health:
we too would bring our treasures
to offer to the king:
how shall we greet our saviour,
what presents shall we bring?

2 We'll bring the many duties
we have to do each day,
we'll try our best to please him,
at home, at school, at play:
and better are these treasures
to offer to the king,
than richest gifts without them –
yet these we all may bring.

3 We'll bring him hearts that love him,
we'll bring him thankful praise,
and lives for ever striving
to follow in his ways:
and these shall be the treasures
we offer to the king,
the gifts that now and ever
our grateful hearts may bring!

Unknown

The Wise Men (103–105)

106

FOR CHILDREN EVERYWHERE

Heavenly Father,
whose children suffered
    at the hands of Herod
though they had done no wrong:
help us to defend all your children
from cruelty and oppression;
in the name of Jesus Christ
    who suffered for us,
but is alive and reigns
    with you and the Holy Spirit,
one God, now and for ever. **Amen.**

Holy Innocents collect – APB†

107

LITANY

Christ, born in a stable, give courage to
all who are homeless; in your mercy,
hear our prayer.

Christ, who fled into Egypt, give comfort to all refugees; in your mercy,
hear our prayer.

Christ, who fasted in the desert, give
relief to all who are hungry; in your
mercy,
hear our prayer.

Christ, who hung in torment on the
cross, give strength to all who suffer; in
your mercy,
hear our prayer.

Christ, who died to save us, give us the
assurance of your forgiveness; in your
mercy,
hear our prayer.

Save us today,
and use us in your loving purposes;
for your glory's sake. Amen.   †

108 Margaret
Hymns of Faith 141, Baptist Hymn Book 111

1 Lord, you left your throne
        and your kingly crown
    when you came to this earth for me,
    but in Bethlehem's home
        there was found no room
    for your holy nativity:
        O come to my heart, Lord Jesus;
        Emmanuel, come to me.

2 Heaven's arches rang
        when the angels sang
    proclaiming your royal degree,
    but to lowly birth
        you came here on earth,
    and in great humility:
        O come to my heart, Lord Jesus;
        Redeemer, be born in me.

3 You were sent, O Lord,
        with the living word
    that should set your people free;
    but with mocking scorn
        and with crown of thorn,
    they bore you to Calvary:
        O come to my heart, Lord Jesus,
        your cross is my only plea.

4 When the heavens shall ring,
        and the choirs shall sing
    at your coming to victory,
    let your voice call me home
        saying, 'Yes, there is room!' –
    there is room at your side for me.
    Then my heart shall rejoice,
        Lord Jesus,
    when you come
        and you call for me.

E Elliott (1836–1897)
© in this version Word & Music/Jubilate Hymns

1 The first nowell the angel did say
was to Bethlehem's shepherds
in fields as they lay;
in fields where they
lay keeping their sheep
on a cold winter's night
that was so deep:
Nowell, nowell, nowell, nowell,
born is the king of Israel!

2 Then wise men from a country far
looked up and saw a guiding star;
they travelled on by night and day
to reach the place where Jesus lay:
Nowell, nowell . . .

3 At Bethlehem they entered in,
on bended knee
they worshipped him,
and offered there in his presence
their gold and myrrh
and frankincense:
Nowell, nowell . . .

4 Then let us all with one accord
sing praises to our heavenly Lord;
for Christ has our salvation wrought
and with his blood
mankind has bought:
Nowell, nowell . . .

Unknown
© in this version Word & Music/Jubilate Hymns

THE WISE MEN/THE ESCAPE
TO EGYPT
Other items appropriate to this theme

Hymns and Carols
Angels from the realms of glory   661
Come and join the celebration   669
Jesus Christ the Lord is born   671
Joy to the world!   664
Shepherds came   670
There is singing in the desert   133

Psalm Version (sung)
O be glad in the Lord and rejoice
(Psalm 100)   443

Songs
God of glory   337
You are the King of glory   211
Worthy, O worthy   296

Prayers
We pray for those who will be
unhappy today (For Sad Families) 454
Lord Jesus Christ, born in a stable
(For The Homeless)   635

Readings
The Wise Men –
Matthew 2.1–12 or 2.7–18
The Servant Messiah –
Isaiah 42.1–9
Jesus Growing Up – Luke 2.41–52
Jesus' Wider Family –
Matthew 12.46–50; Mark 10.29–31

(See also Minister's Section 714–716.
The Lord's Prayer is printed inside the
back cover.)

The Wise Men (109)

11 The People of God/Covenant and Unity

You are a chosen people, a royal priesthood, a holy nation, a people belonging to God, that you may declare the praises of him who called you out of darkness into his marvellous light.

1 Peter 2.9

There is one body, and one Spirit, one hope to which God has called us: one Lord, one faith, one baptism, one God and Father of all, who is over all, and through all, and in all.

Ephesians 4.4–6

110

PRAISE

Praise the Lord, the God of Israel:
he alone does marvellous things.

Praise his glorious name for ever;
**let his glory fill the earth! Amen.
Amen.**

from Psalm 72

111 Mannheim
Hymns for Today's Church 525

1 *Lead us, heavenly Father, lead us
  through the world's
    tempestuous sea;
  guard us, guide us,
    keep us, feed us –
  now and to eternity,
  here possessing every blessing
  if our God our Father be.

2 Saviour, heal us and restore us:
  all our weakness you must know,
  for you trod this earth before us,
  felt its keenest pain and woe;
  through the dreary desert, weary
  and alone, you chose to go.

3 Spirit of our God, descending,
  fill our hearts with heavenly joy,
  love with every passion blending,
  pleasure that can never cloy:
  thus provided, pardoned, guided,
  nothing can our peace destroy.

J Edmeston (1791–1867)
© in this version Word & Music/Jubilate Hymns

(*See other version at number 365)

112

CONFESSION

O Lord our God, you brought your people out of slavery with a mighty hand, and made for yourself a name which endures to this day:

We have sinned, we have done wrong.
O Lord, hear:
O Lord, forgive!

(110–112) The People of God

In keeping with all your righteous acts, turn away your anger from your people. O Lord, hear:
O Lord, forgive!

Our sins have made us despised by those around us. O Lord, hear:
O Lord, forgive!

We do not come before you because we are righteous, but because of your great mercy. O Lord, hear:
O Lord, forgive!

**O Lord our God, do not delay but send your holy Spirit to revive your church, because your people
bear the name of Christ. Amen.** †

from Daniel 9

113

THEME PRAYER (COLLECT)

Almighty God,
without you
we are not able to please you.
Mercifully grant that your Holy Spirit
may in all things direct
and rule our hearts;
through Jesus Christ our Lord. **Amen.**

Pentecost 6 collect – ASB

114

PSALM*

Give thanks to the Lord, praise his name:
tell the nations what he has done.

Sing to him, sing praise to him:
tell of all his wonderful deeds.

Glory in his holy name:
let all who worship him rejoice.

Go to the Lord for help:
and worship him for ever.

Remember the wonders he does:
the miracles he performs.

^AHe is the Lord our God:
he judges the whole wide earth.

^BHe keeps his word and covenant:
for a thousand generations.

^AThe covenant he made with Abraham:
the oath he swore to Israel.

^BHe brought them out of Egypt:
and all of them were strong.

^AHe gave a cloud for covering:
a pillar of fire by night.

^BHe gave them bread from heaven:
and water from the rock.

^AHe brought his people out rejoicing:
his chosen ones with shouts of joy.

^{ALL}**Praise the Lord! Amen.**

from Psalm 105

(* The congregation may divide at A and B)

115 Calypso Carol
Hymns for Today's Church 91

PSALM/CANTICLE

1 Come, sing praises
        to the Lord above,
    rock of our salvation, God of love;
    with delight into his presence move,
    for the Lord our God is king!
        He's the king
        above the mountains high,
        the sea is his, the land and sky;
        mighty continents and islands lie
        within the hollow of his hand.

The People of God (113–115)

2 Come to worship him
  and bow the knee,
for the shepherd of the flock is he;
humble creatures in his hand
  are we –
sing the praise of God the king!
  He's the king
    above the mountains high,
the sea is his, the land and sky;
mighty continents and islands lie
within the hollow of his hand.

3 Hear the story of his people now,
  you with stubborn hearts
    who will not bow;
learn what happened long ago
  and how
God can show you he is king!
  He's the king above . . .

4 Forty years he kept the prize away,
  made them wander
    till they walked his way,
exiled all of them until the day
they should honour him as king:
  He's the king above . . .

from Psalm 95 (*Venite*)
© Michael Perry/Jubilee Hymns

116 Venice, Franconia
Hymns for Today's Church 34, 110

PSALM

1 How good a thing it is,
how pleasant to behold,
when all God's people live at one,
the law of love uphold!

2 As perfume, by its scent,
breathes fragrance all around,
so life itself will sweeter be
where unity is found.

3 And like refreshing dew
that falls upon the hills,
true union sheds its gentle grace,
and deeper love instils.

4 God grants his choicest gifts
to those who live in peace;
to them his blessings shall abound
and evermore increase.

from Psalm 133
J E Seddon (1915–1983)
© Mrs M Seddon/Jubilee Hymns

117 We have come into this house
Mission Praise 253

We have come into this house
and gathered in his name
  to worship him;
we have come into this house
and gathered in his name
  to worship him;
we have come into this house
and gathered in his name
  to worship Christ the Lord,
worship him, Christ the Lord.

Bruce Ballinger
© Sound III Incorporated†

118 You shall go out with joy
Mission Praise 281

You shall go out with joy
and be led forth in peace;
and the mountains and the hills
shall break forth before you,
singing songs of joy;
  and the trees of the field
    shall clap,
      shall clap their hands,
  and the trees of the field
    shall clap their hands,
  and the trees of the field
    shall clap their hands,
  and the trees of the field
    shall clap their hands,
as you go out with joy!

from Isaiah 55
Stuart Dauermann
© Lillenas Publishing Company/Thankyou Music

(116–118) The People of God

119
Bind us together
Mission Praise 21

Bind us together, Lord,
bind us together
with cords that cannot be broken;
bind us together, Lord,
bind us together,
O bind us together in love!

1 There is only one God,
there is only one King,
there is only one Body –
that is why we sing:
Bind us together . . .

2 We are the family of God,
joined by the Spirit above,
working together with Christ,
growing and building in love.
Bind us together . . .

Bob Gillman
© Thankyou Music†

120
We are one body
Jesus Praise 148

1 We are one body in the Lord,
we have one Spirit and one call;
there is
one hope,
one Lord,
one faith,
one life,
one Father of us all!

2 There are some
who can tend the flock,
there are some
who can preach the word,
so that
some lead,
some serve,
some teach,
some build
one body in the Lord.

from Ephesians 4 and 1 Corinthians 12
© Michael Perry/Jubilate Hymns

121
The Lord has led forth
Spirit of Praise 176

The Lord has led forth his people
with joy,
and his chosen ones with singing;
The Lord has led forth his people
with joy,
and his chosen ones with singing.

He has given to them
the lands of the nations,
to possess the fruit and keep his laws,
and praise, praise his name.
The Lord has led forth . . .

from Psalm 105
Chris Bowater
© Springtide/Word Music (UK)†

122

CREED

There is one God and Father:
from him all things come.

There is one Lord Jesus Christ:
through him we come to God.

There is one Holy Spirit:
**in him we are baptized
into one body. Amen.**

**We believe and trust in one God:
Father, Son, and Holy Spirit. Amen.** †

from 1 Corinthians 8 and 12

123

FOR CHRISTIAN UNITY (COLLECT)

Almighty and eternal God,
you have called us to be your people:
bring us to closer unity and fellowship
with you and one another,

The People of God (119–123)

so that every member of your Church
may serve you in holiness and truth;
through our Lord and Saviour
Jesus Christ. **Amen.**

Pentecost 2 collect – APB

124 Abridge
Hymns for Today's Church 374

1 O Lord our guardian and our guide,
be near us when we call;
uphold us when our footsteps slide,
and raise us when we fall.

2 The world, the flesh and Satan dwell
around the path we tread;
O save us from the snares of hell,
Deliverer from the dead!

3 And if we tempted are to sin,
and evil powers are strong;
be present, Lord, keep watch within
and save our souls from wrong.

4 Still let us always watch and pray,
and know that we are frail;
that if the tempter cross our way,
yet he may not prevail.

from Psalm 17
I Williams (1802–1865)
© in this version Jubilate Hymns

125 Binchester
Hymns for Today's Church 473

1 Happy are they, they who love God,
whose hearts have Christ confessed;
who by his cross
have found their life,
beneath his yoke, their rest.

2 Glad is the praise,
sweet are the songs,
when they together sing;

and strong the prayers
that bow the ear
of heaven's eternal king.

3 Christ gives their homes
pleasure and peace
and makes their loves his own;
but O what weeds the evil one
has in God's garden sown!

4 Sad were our life, evil this earth
did not its sorrows prove
the path by which the sheep
may find
the fold of Jesus' love.

5 Then they shall know,
they who love him,
how all their pain is good;
and death itself cannot unbind
their happy brotherhood.

after C Coffin (1676–1749)
R Bridges (1844–1930)

126

FOR GOD'S GRACE
O God, we are your people: in your Son
you have redeemed us; by your Spirit
you have sealed us as your own.

Make our hearts respond to your love.
Lord, receive our praise,
and hear our prayer.

Make our lives bear witness to your
mercy. Lord, receive our praise,
and hear our prayer.

Make our wills ready to obey. Lord,
receive our praise,
and hear our prayer.

**Show us your glory,
that we may delight in your presence,
and walk with you faithfully
all our days. Amen.**   †

127

THE TEN COMMANDMENTS

As we listen to God's Commandments,
we pray for strength to keep them:

'You shall have no other gods but me':
Lord, help us to love you
with all our heart, all our soul,
all our mind and all our strength.

'You shall not make for yourself any idol':
Lord, help us to worship you
in spirit and in truth.

'You shall not dishonour the name of the Lord your God':
Lord, help us to honour you
with reverence and awe.

'Remember the Lord's day and keep it holy':
Lord, help us to remember Christ
risen from the dead,
and to set our minds on things above,
not on things on the earth.

'Honour your father and your mother':
Lord, help us to live as your servants,
giving respect to all,
and love to our brothers and sisters
in Christ.

'You shall not murder':
Lord, help us to be reconciled
with each other,
and to overcome evil with good.

'You shall not commit adultery':
Lord, help us to realise
that our body is a temple
of the Holy Spirit.

'You shall not steal':
Lord, help us to be honest
in all we do,
and to care for those in need.

'You shall not be a false witness':
Lord, help us always to speak
the truth.

'You shall not covet anything which belongs to your neighbour':
Lord, help us to remember Jesus said,
'It is more blessed to give
than to receive',
and help us to love
our neighbours as ourselves;
for his sake. Amen.

from Exodus 20, Deuteronomy 5 etc†

128 Marching
Hymns for Today's Church 466

1 Through the night of doubt
 and sorrow
onward goes the pilgrim band,
singing songs of expectation,
marching to the promised land.

2 One the hymn a thousand voices
sing as from the heart of one;
one the conflict, one the danger,
one the march in God begun:

3 One the object of our journey,
one the faith that never tires,
one the urgent looking forward,
one the hope our God inspires:

4 Courage, therefore,
 Christian pilgrims;
with the cross before your eyes,
bear its shame, and fight its battle –
die with Christ, with Christ arise!

5 Soon shall come
 the great awakening,
soon the bursting of the tomb;
then the scattering of all shadows,
and the end of tears and gloom.

after B S Ingemann (1789–1862)
S Baring-Gould (1834–1924)
© in this version Jubilate Hymns

The People of God (127–128)

129 Cwm Rhondda
Hymns for Today's Church 528(i)

1 Guide me, O my great Redeemer,
   pilgrim through this barren land;
   I am weak, but you are mighty,
   hold me with your powerful hand:
      Bread of heaven, bread of heaven,
      feed me now and evermore!

2 Open now the crystal fountain
   where the healing waters flow;
   let the fiery, cloudy pillar
   lead me all my journey through:
      Strong Deliverer,
         strong Deliverer,
      ever be my strength and shield.

3 When I tread the verge of Jordan
   bid my anxious fears subside;
   Death of death,
         and hell's Destruction,
   land me safe on Canaan's side:
      songs of praises, songs of praises,
      I will ever sing to you.

                    after W Williams (1717–1791)
                    P Williams (1721–1796) and others

130* Thornbury
Hymns for Today's Church 536

1 Your hand, O God, has guided
   your flock, from age to age;
   your faithfulness is written
   on history's every page.
   Our fathers knew your goodness,
   and we their deeds record;
   and both to this bear witness:
      one church, one faith, one Lord.

2 Your heralds brought the gospel
   to greatest as to least;
   they summoned us to hasten
   and share the great king's feast!

(*Verse 3 may be omitted.)

(129–131) The People of God

And this was all their teaching
in every deed and word;
to all alike proclaiming:
   one church, one faith, one Lord.

3 Through many days of darkness,
   through many scenes of strife,
   the faithful few fought bravely
   to guard the nation's life.
   Their gospel of redemption –
   sin pardoned, peace restored –
   was all in this enfolded:
      one church, one faith, one Lord.

4 And we, shall we be faithless?
   shall hearts fail, hands hang down?
   shall we evade the conflict
   and throw away the crown?
   Not so! In God's deep counsels
   some better thing is stored;
   we will maintain, unflinching,
      one church, one faith, one Lord.

5 Your mercy will not fail us
   nor leave your work undone;
   with your right hand to help us,
   the victory shall be won.
   And then by earth and heaven
   your name shall be adored;
   and this shall be their anthem:
      one church, one faith, one Lord.

                    E H Plumptre (1821–1891)

131

ASCRIPTION

You are worthy, O Lord our God:
**to receive glory and honour
   and power.**

For you created all things:
**and by your will they existed
and were created.**

You are worthy, O Christ, for you were slain:
**and by your blood
you ransomed us for God.**

From every tribe and tongue and people and nation:
**you made us a kingdom of priests
to serve our God.**

To him who sits upon the throne, and to the Lamb:
**be blessing and honour
and glory and might
for ever and ever. Amen.** †

from Revelation 4

THE PEOPLE OF GOD/COVENANT
AND UNITY
Other items appropriate to this theme

Hymns

Children of the heavenly king	356
Christ, from whom all blessings flow (Unity)	463
Christ is made the sure foundation	483
Father, hear the prayer we offer	85
Glorious things of you are spoken	183
In Christ there is no east or west (Unity)	429
Let us praise God together	438
Spirit of God most high (Unity)	480
Through all the changing scenes of life	576

Songs

For I'm building a people of power	469
Here he comes, robed in majesty	57
In my life, Lord, be glorified	495

Let there be love shared among us (Unity)	58
Spirit of the living God, move among us	318

Psalm Version (spoken)

Praise the Lord: with my whole heart (Psalm 111)	604

Readings

One God, One People –
Exodus 3.7–15
The Shepherd and His Flock –
John 10.1–18
Chosen and Called –
Ephesians 1.1–14
One in Christ – Ephesians 2.11–22
The Unity of the Spirit –
Ephesians 4.1–5

(See also A Covenant Service, page 25, and Minister's Section 717–719. The Lord's Prayer is printed inside the back cover.)

The People of God (131)

12 Following Jesus/ Jesus' Teaching/ Transfiguration

Jesus said, 'I am the way and the truth and the life. No-one comes to the Father except through me.' John 14.6

Jesus said, 'I am the light of the world. Whoever follows me will never walk in darkness, but will have the light of life.' John 8.12

132

PRAISE

Praise the Lord,
  you servants of the Lord;
praise the name of the Lord.

Blessed be the name of the Lord;
both now and evermore. Amen.

from Psalm 113

133 Battle Hymn
Come and Praise 26

1 There is singing in the desert,
  there is laughter in the skies,
  there are wise men
    filled with wonder,
  there are shepherds with surprise:
  you can tell the world is dancing
  by the light that's in their eyes,
    for Jesus Christ is here:
    Come and sing aloud
      your praises,
    come and sing aloud
      your praises,
    come and sing aloud
      your praises,
    for Jesus Christ is here!

2 He hears deaf men by the lakeside,
  he sees blind men in the streets,
  he goes up to those
    who cannot walk,
  he talks to all he meets;
  touching silken robes or
    tattered clothes,
  it's everyone he greets –
    for Jesus Christ is here:
    Come and sing . . .

3 There is darkness on the hillside,
  there is sorrow in the town,
  there's a man upon a wooden cross,
  a man who's gazing down:
  you can see the marks of love
  and not the furrows of a frown,
    for Jesus Christ is here:
    Come and sing . . .

4 There is singing in the desert,
  there is laughter in the skies,
  there are wise men
    filled with wonder,
  there are shepherds with surprise:
  you can tell the world is dancing
  by the light that's in their eyes,
    for Jesus Christ is here:
    Come and sing . . .

© Geoffrey Marshall-Taylor/Jubilate Hymns

(132–133) Following Jesus

134

Ratisbon
Hymns for Today's Church 266

1 Christ whose glory fills the skies,
  Christ the true, the only light;
  Sun of righteousness, arise,
  triumph over shades of night:
    Dayspring from on high, be near,
    Daystar, in my heart appear!

2 Dark and cheerless is the dawn
  till your mercy's beams I see;
  joyless is the day's return
  till your glories shine on me:
    as they inward light impart,
    cheer my eyes
      and warm my heart.

3 Visit then this soul of mine,
  pierce the gloom of sin and grief;
  fill me, radiancy divine,
  scatter all my unbelief:
    more and more yourself display,
    shining to the perfect day!

C Wesley (1707–1788)

135

CONFESSION

Almighty God, our Father, we come to you with humble hearts, to confess our sins:

For turning away from you, and ignoring your will for our lives: Father, forgive us,
save us and help us.

For behaving just as we wish, without thinking of you: Father, forgive us,
save us and help us.

For failing you – not only by what we do, but also by our thoughts and words: Father, forgive us,
save us and help us.

For letting ourselves be drawn away from you by temptations in the world about us: Father, forgive us,
save us and help us.

For acting as if we were ashamed to belong to your dear Son Jesus: Father, forgive us,
save us and help us.

**Father, we have failed you often,
and humbly ask your forgiveness:
help us so to live
that others may see your glory;
through Jesus Christ our Lord. Amen.** †

136

PSALM

Happy are those who trust in God:
who do not worship idols.

Sacrifice and offering you do not desire:
but you want my ears to be open.

So I said, 'Lord I come:
obedient to your word.'

I long to do your will, O God:
and keep your teaching in my heart.

I'll tell the world your saving news:
you know my lips will not be sealed.

I have not kept you to myself:
but speak of all your faithfulness.

I do not hide your love away:
but share your mercy with them all.

May all who come to you be glad; may all who know your saving power for ever say:
'How great is the Lord!' Amen.

from Psalm 40

Following Jesus (134–136)

PSALM

1 The Lord my shepherd rules my life
and gives me all I need;
he leads me by refreshing streams,
in pastures green I feed.

2 The Lord revives
my failing strength,
he makes my joy complete;
and in right paths,
for his name's sake,
he guides my faltering feet.

3 Though in a valley dark as death,
no evil makes me fear;
your shepherd's staff
protects my way,
for you are with me there.

4 While all my enemies look on
you spread a royal feast;
you fill my cup, anoint my head,
and treat me as your guest.

5 Your goodness
and your gracious love
pursue me all my days;
your house, O Lord,
shall be my home –
your name, my endless praise.

6 To Father, Son and Spirit, praise!
to God, whom we adore,
be worship, glory, power and love,
both now and evermore!

from Psalm 23
© Christopher Idle/Jubilate Hymns

PSALM

1 Bless-ed is the man,
the man who does not walk
in the counsel of the ungodly –
bless-ed is that man;
he who rejects the way,
rejects the way of sin
and who turns away from scoffing –
bless-ed is that man:
but his delight
by day and night
is the law of God almighty.

2 He is like a tree –
a tree that flourishes
being planted by the water –
bless-ed is that man.
He will bring forth fruit –
his leaf will wither not,
for in all he does he prospers –
bless-ed is that man:
for his delight
by day and night
is the law of God almighty.

3 The ungodly are not so
for they are like the chaff
which the wind blows clean away –
the ungodly are not so;
the ungodly will not stand
upon the judgement day
nor belong to God's own people –
the ungodly will not stand:
but God knows the way
of righteous men
and ungodly ways will perish.

Bless-ed is the man,
the man who does not walk
in the counsel of the ungodly –
bless-ed is that man!

from Psalm 1
© Michael Baughen/Jubilate Hymns

(137–138) Following Jesus

139 From the rising of the sun
Mission Praise 54

PSALM

From the rising of the sun
to the going down of the same,
the Lord's name is to be praised;
from the rising of the sun
to the going down of the same
the Lord's name is to be praised.

Praise to the Lord:
praise him,
    all you servants of the Lord,
praise the name of the Lord;
blessed be the name of the Lord
from this time forth
    and for evermore!

from Psalm 113
© Paul Deming†

140 Christ in me
Jesus Praise 174

Christ in me is to live,
    to die is to gain;
Christ in me is to live,
    to die is to gain.

He's my king, he's my song,
    he's my life and he's my joy;
he's my strength, he's my sword,
he's my peace and he's my Lord!
    Christ in me . . .

from Philippians 1
Gary Garcia
© Maranatha! Music USA/Word Music (UK)†

141 I want to walk
Hymns for Today's Church S16

1 I want to walk with Jesus Christ
    all the days I live of this life on earth;
    to give to him complete control
    of body and of soul.
        Follow him, follow him,
        yield your life to him –
        he has conquered death,
        he is King of kings;
        accept the joy
            which he gives to those
        who yield their lives to him!

2 I want to learn to speak to him,
    to pray to him, confess my sin,
    to open my life and let him in,
    for joy will then be mine.

3 I want to learn to speak of him –
    my life must show
            that he lives in me;
    my deeds, my thoughts, my words
            must speak
    of his great love for me.

4 I want to learn to read his word,
    for this is how I know the way
    to live my life as pleases him,
    in holiness and joy.

5 O Holy Spirit of the Lord,
    now enter into this heart of mine;
    take full control of my selfish will
    and make me yours alone!
        Follow him, follow him,
        yield your life to him –
        he has conquered death,
        he is King of kings;
        accept the joy
            which he gives to those
        who yield their lives to him!

© C Simmonds and others†

Following Jesus (139–141)

142 If you want to be great
Church Family Worship Source Book

If you want to be great
   in God's kingdom,
learn to be the servant of all;
if you want to be great
   in God's kingdom,
learn to be the servant of all:
   Learn to be the servant of all,
   learn to be the servant of all.
If you want to be great
   in God's kingdom,
learn to be the servant of all.

from Mark 10 etc
Michael Ryan
© Maranatha! Music USA/Word Music (UK)†

143* I've made up my mind
Church Family Worship Source Book

So I've made up my mind
that I'm going to follow him –
wherever Jesus leads me I will go.
So I've . . .

1 I may be scared
   by the things I see
but Jesus won't
   let them destroy me.
So I've . . .; so I've . . .

2 I may be scared
   by the things I hear –
but Jesus won't
   let me live in fear.
So I've . . .; so I've . . .

3 I may be scared
   by the things I know –
but Jesus won't
   ever let me go.
So I've . . .; so I've . . .

Ian Smale
© Thankyou Music†

(*Written for children to sing)

144 Who does Jesus love
Jesus Praise 114

1 Who does Jesus love,
   Jesus love, Jesus love?
Who does Jesus love?
   He loves everyone!
Well, everybody should love Jesus,
   should love Jesus,
everybody should love Jesus too!

2 What did Jesus say,
   Jesus say, Jesus say?
What did Jesus say?
   He said: Love everyone!
Well, everybody
   should love each other,
   should love each other,
everybody
   should love each other, too!

3 Who did Jesus die for,
   Jesus die for, Jesus die for?
Who did Jesus die for?
   He died for everyone!
Well, everybody
   should live for Jesus,
   should live for Jesus,
everybody should live for Jesus, too!

Robert Stoodley
© Mustard Seed Music†

145 Shipston
Hymns for Today's Church 427

CREDAL HYMN

1 Firmly I believe and truly
   God is Three and God is One;
   and I next acknowledge duly
   manhood taken by the Son.

2 And I trust and hope most fully
   in that manhood crucified;
   and each thought and deed unruly
   do to death, for he has died.

3 Simply to his grace and wholly
  light and life and strength belong;
  and I love supremely, solely,
  Christ the holy, Christ the strong.

4 And I make this affirmation
  for the love of Christ alone:
  holy Church is his creation
  and his teachings are her own.

5 Honour, glory, power, and merit
  to the God of earth and heaven,
  Father, Son, and Holy Spirit –
  praise for evermore be given!

J H Newman (1801–1890)
© in this version Jubilate Hymns

3 Help me praise you every day,
  gladly serve you and obey;
  like your glorious ones above,
  happy in your precious love.

4 Loving Shepherd ever near,
  teach your lamb your voice to hear;
  let my footsteps never stray
  from the true and narrow way.

5 Where you lead me I will go,
  walking in your steps below;
  till, before my Father's throne,
  I shall know as I am known.

J Leeson (1809–1881)

146

THEME PRAYER (COLLECT)

Almighty God,
you have made us for yourself,
and our hearts are restless
till they find their rest in you.
Teach us to offer ourselves
    to your service,
that here we may have your peace,
and in the world to come
    may see you face to face;
through Jesus Christ our Lord. **Amen.**

Pentecost 18 collect – ASB

147 Buckland
Hymns for Today's Church 305

1 Loving Shepherd of your sheep,
  keep your lamb, in safety keep;
  nothing can your power withstand,
  none can tear me from your hand.

2 Loving Lord, you chose to give
  your own life that we might live;
  and your hands
      outstretched to bless
  bear the cruel nails' impress.

148 Ibstone, Quam dilecta
Hymns for Today's Church 250(ii), 558

1 Now let us learn of Christ:
  he speaks, and we shall find
  he lightens our dark mind;
  so let us learn of Christ.

2 Now let us love in Christ
  as he has first loved us;
  as he endured the cross,
  so let us love in Christ.

3 Now let us grow in Christ
  and look to things above,
  and speak the truth in love;
  so let us grow in Christ.

4 Now let us stand in Christ
  in every trial we meet,
  in all his strength complete;
  so let us stand in Christ.

© Christopher Idle/Jubilate Hymns

Following Jesus (146–148)

149

FOR STRENGTH
We pray for God's strength to keep Jesus' commandment:

'Love the Lord your God with all your heart, with all your mind, with all your soul, and with all your strength':
Lord, help us to obey. Amen.

'Love your neighbour as yourself':
Lord, help us to obey.

'Love one another as I have loved you':
Lord, help us to obey.

In your mercy strengthen us and move our hearts to do your will. Amen. †

from Matthew 22 and John 13

150

FOR STRENGTH TO FOLLOW JESUS

Jesus said: 'If one of you wants to be great, he must be the servant of the rest' – Master, we hear your call:
help us to follow.

Jesus said: 'Unless you change and become humble like little children, you can never enter the Kingdom of heaven' – Master, we hear your call:
help us to follow.

Jesus said: 'Happy are those who are humble; they will receive what God has promised' – Master, we hear your call:
help us to follow.

Jesus said: 'Be merciful just as your Father is merciful; love your enemies and do good to them' – Master, we hear your call:
help us to follow.

Jesus said: 'Love one another, just as I love you; the greatest love a person can have for his friends is to give his life for them' – Master, we hear your call:
help us to follow.

Jesus said: 'Go to all peoples everywhere and make them my disciples, and I will be with you always, to the end of the world' – Master, we hear your call:
help us to follow.

Lord, you have redeemed us and called us to your service: give us grace to hear your word and to obey your commandment; for your mercy's sake. Amen. †

151
Nottingham or Lübeck
Hymns for Today's Church 554

1 Take my life and let it be
all you purpose, Lord, for me;
consecrate my passing days,
let them flow in ceaseless praise.

2 Take my hands, and let them move
at the impulse of your love;
take my feet, and let them run
with the news of victory won.

3 Take my voice, and let me sing
always, only, for my King;
take my lips, let them proclaim
all the beauty of your name.

4 Take my wealth – all I possess,
make me rich in faithfulness;
take my mind that I may use
every power as you shall choose.

5 Take my motives and my will,
all your purpose to fulfil;
take my heart – it is your own,
it shall be your royal throne.

(149–151) Following Jesus

6 Take my love – my Lord, I pour
   at your feet its treasure-store;
   take myself, and I will be
   yours for all eternity.

F R Havergal (1836–1879)
© in this version Jubilate Hymns

152 Living Lord
Hymns for Today's Church 518

1 To him we come –
   Jesus Christ our Lord,
   God's own living Word,
   his dear Son:
   in him there is no east and west,
   in him all nations shall be blessed;
   to all he offers peace and rest –
       loving Lord!

2 In him we live –
   Christ our strength and stay,
   life and truth and way,
   friend divine:
   his power can break
       the chains of sin,
   still all life's storms without, within,
   help us the daily fight to win –
       living Lord!

3 For him we go –
   soldiers of the cross,
   counting all things loss
   him to know;
   going to every land and race,
   preaching to all redeeming grace,
   building his church in every place –
       conquering Lord!

4 With him we serve –
   his the work we share
   with saints everywhere,
   near and far;
   one in the task which faith requires,
   one in the zeal which never tires,
   one in the hope his love inspires –
       coming Lord!

5 Onward we go –
   faithful, bold, and true,
   called his will to do
   day by day
   till, at the last, with joy we'll see
   Jesus, in glorious majesty;
   live with him through eternity –
       reigning Lord!

J E Seddon (1915–1983)
© Mrs M Seddon/Jubilate Hymns

153

DEDICATION

Lord Jesus Christ,
redeemer, friend and brother:
may we know you more clearly,
love you more dearly,
and follow you more nearly,
day by day. **Amen.**   †

154 Quem pastores laudavere
Hymns for Today's Church 277

EVENING HYMN

1 Light of gladness, Lord of glory,
   Jesus Christ our king most holy,
   shine among us in your mercy:
       earth and heaven join their hymn.

2 Let us sing at sun's descending
   as we see the lights of evening,
   Father, Son, and Spirit praising
       with the holy seraphim.

3 Son of God, through all the ages
   worthy of our holiest praises,
   yours the life that never ceases,
       light which never shall grow dim.

from *Phos hilaron* (Eastern vesper hymn)
© Christopher Idle/Jubilate Hymns

Following Jesus (152–154)

FOLLOWING JESUS/JESUS' TEACHING/TRANSFIGURATION
Other items appropriate to this theme

Hymns

I am trusting you, Lord Jesus	406
Praise him, praise him, Jesus our mighty redeemer	379
When I survey the wondrous cross	238

Songs

From heaven you came	449
God's Spirit is in my heart	422
Seek ye first the kingdom of God	168
Send me out	425
The journey of life	210

Psalm

The Lord, my shepherd	137
My faithful shepherd	560

Prayer

Almighty God, we confess (Confession)	369

Readings

The Call of Samuel – 1 Samuel 3
Trust and Obey – Proverbs 3.1–8
The Alternatives – Matthew 7.13,14
The Call of the Disciples –
Mark 1.14–20; Mark 2.13–17;
John 1.35–51;
Jesus' Teaching – Luke 4.14–23
Transfiguration – Luke 9.28–36
The Cost of Discipleship –
Luke 9.57–62; Luke 9.18–27

(See also section Invitation to Faith 388–412 and Minister's Section 720. The Lord's Prayer is printed inside the back cover.)

13 The Life of Prayer/Forgiveness

Be alert and always keep on praying.   Ephesians 6.18

The Lord our God is merciful and forgiving, even though we have rebelled against him.
Daniel 9.9

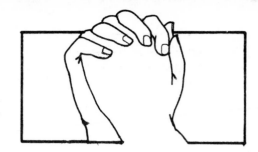

155

PRAISE

Turn to us, almighty God;
look down from heaven and see!

Renew us, O Lord God almighty;
show us your mercy
    that we may be saved! Amen.

from Psalm 80

156

INVITATION TO WORSHIP

Come close to God, and he will come close to you. The Lord our God is worthy to receive glory and honour and power, for he has created and redeemed us:
Heavenly Father,
in our worship
help us to sing your praise,
confess our sins,
hear your word
and bring our prayers to you,
through Jesus Christ our Lord. Amen.

†

from James 4 and Revelation 4

157
Gwalchmai
Hymns for Today's Church 272(ii)

1 King of glory, king of peace
    I will love you;
since your mercies never cease,
    faith shall prove you!
You have granted my request,
    you have heard me;
though my sinful soul transgressed,
    you have spared me.

2 Praises with my utmost art
    I will bring you;
songs of triumph from my heart
    I will sing you.
Though my sins against me cried,
    this shall cheer me:
God in Christ has justified
    and will clear me.

3 Seven whole days –
        not one in seven –
    I will praise you;
worship lifts the heart to heaven,
    love obeys you!
Once you died, when no-one sought
    to console you;
now eternity's too short
    to extol you!

G Herbert (1593–1633)
© in this version Word & Music/Jubilee Hymns

The Life of Prayer (155–157)

158

1 Amazing grace –
    how sweet the sound –
    that saved a wretch like me!
    I once was lost, but now am found;
    was blind, but now I see.

2 God's grace first taught my heart
        to fear,
    his grace my fears relieved;
    how precious did that grace appear
    the hour I first believed!

3 Through every danger,
        trial and snare
    I have already come;
    for grace has brought me safe
        thus far,
    and grace will lead me home.

4 The Lord has promised good to me,
    his word my hope secures;
    my shield and stronghold
        he shall be
    as long as life endures.

5 And when this earthly life is past,
    and mortal cares shall cease,
    I shall possess with Christ at last
    eternal joy and peace.

J Newton (1725–1807)
© in this version Jubilate Hymns

159

CONFESSION

**O God, our gracious Father,
we confess that we have sinned
        against you
and done many things to grieve you:
we have often been selfish,
we have sometimes forgotten
        to pray to you,**

**and we have not loved you
        as we should.
For these and all other sins
forgive us, we pray,
through him who died for us,
Jesus Christ our Lord. Amen.**   †

160

THEME PRAYER (COLLECT)

Almighty God,
you gave your Son Jesus Christ
to break the power of evil:
free us from all darkness
        and temptation,
and bring us to eternal light and joy;
through the power of him
who lives and reigns
with you and the Holy Spirit,
one God, now and ever. **Amen.**

Pentecost 22 collect – APB†

161

PSALM*

A Hear us, O Shepherd of Israel, leader of your flock. B Hear us from your throne above the cherubim. C Shine forth, awaken your strength, and come to save us:
**Bring us back, O God, and save us,
make your face to shine upon us.**

A O Lord God almighty, how long will you be angry with your people's prayers? B You have given us sorrow to eat and tears to drink. C You have made us a source of contention to our neighbours, and our enemies insult us:
**Bring us back, O God, and save us,
make your face to shine upon us.**

(158–161) The Life of Prayer

^AReturn to us, O God Almighty, look down from heaven and see. ^BLook on this vine that you planted with your own hand, this child you raised for yourself. ^CLet your hand rest upon the people you have chosen, then we will not turn away from you; revive us, and we shall praise your name:
Bring us back, O God, and save us, make your face to shine upon us. Amen.

from Psalm 80

(*This psalm may be led by three speakers. All say the refrain.)

162 Daniel
Hymns for Today's Church 267

PSALM

1 Lord, as I wake I turn to you,
  yourself the first thought of my day;
  my king, my God,
      whose help is sure,
  yourself the help for which I pray.

2 There is no blessing, Lord, from you
  for those who make their will
      their way,
  no praise for those
      who will not praise,
  no peace for those
      who will not pray.

3 Your loving gifts of grace to me,
  those favours I could never earn,
  call for my thanks
      in praise and prayer,
  call me to love you in return.

4 Lord, make my life a life of love,
  keep me from sin in all I do;
  Lord, make your law my only law,
  your will my will, for love of you.

from Psalm 5
Brian Foley
© Faber Music Limited†

163 Melling
Hymns for Today's Church 566(i)

CANTICLE*

1 Bless the Lord, creation sings;
  earth and sky his hand proclaim.
  Praise him, all created things;
  angel hosts, exalt his name.

2 Bless the Lord! To heaven's throne
  songs of endless glory rise;
  in the clouds his praise be shown,
  sun and moon and starry skies.

3 Bless the Lord with ice and snow,
  bitter cold and scorching blaze,
  floods and all the winds that blow,
  frosty nights and sunlit days.

4 Bless the Lord in mist and cloud,
  lightnings shine to mark his way;
  thunders speak his name aloud,
  wind and storm his word obey.

5 Bless the Lord who brings to birth
  life renewed by sun and rain;
  flowing rivers, fruitful earth,
  bird and beast on hill and plain.

6 Bless the Lord! From earth and sky,
  ocean depths and furthest shore,
  all things living bear on high
  songs of praise for evermore.

7 Bless the Lord! His name be blessed,
  worshipped, honoured,
      loved, adored;
  and with holy hearts confessed,
  saints and servants of the Lord.

8 Bless the Lord! The Father, Son,
  and the Holy Spirit, praise;
  high exalt the Three-in-One,
  God of everlasting days!

from *A Song of Creation/Benedicite*
© Timothy Dudley-Smith

(*For a shorter version of this canticle verses 1, 7 and 8 may be sung.)

The Life of Prayer (162–163)

PSALM

1 There is no moment of my life,
no place where I may go,
no action which God does not see,
no thought he does not know.

2 Before I speak,
my words are known,
and all that I decide.
To come or go:
God knows my choice,
and makes himself my guide.

3 If I should close my eyes to him,
he comes to give me sight;
if I should go where all is dark,
he makes my darkness light.

4 He knew my days before all days,
before I came to be;
he keeps me, loves me,
in my ways; –
no lover such as he.

from Psalm 139
Brian Foley
© Faber Music Limited†

1 Jesus is a friend of mine –
praise him;
Jesus is a friend of mine –
praise him,
praise him, praise him;
Jesus is a friend of mine –
praise him!

2 Jesus died to set us free –
praise him . . .

3 He gave us the victory –
praise him . . .

4 Jesus is the King of kings –
praise him . . .

Paul Mazak
© Celebration/Thankyou Music†

1 Jesus is the name we worship,
Jesus is the friend we love,
Jesus is our Lord and saviour,
king of heaven above.

2 Jesus knows when we are troubled,
Jesus hears our every prayer,
Jesus has our trials and sorrows
always in his care.

3 Jesus made the lame go walking,
Jesus made the blind to see,
Jesus healed the sick and wounded:
wondrous Lord is he!

4 Jesus is our great redeemer,
Jesus died for you and me,
Jesus took our sins and failings,
bore them on the Tree.

5 Jesus lives within us daily,
Jesus in our hearts will stay
till we meet with him in heaven
on that glorious day.

Diana Brand
© Scripture Union†

I'm going to say my prayers,
read my Bible every morning,
going to know God's fellowship,
witness every day:
I'm going to say . . .

I am going to pray every morning,
I am going to pray every day:
I am going to pray every morning,
I am going to pray every day.

Ian Smale
© Thankyou Music†

(*Written for children to sing)

168 Seek ye first
Mission Praise 201

1 Seek ye first the kingdom of God
    and his righteousness,
    and all these things
            shall be added unto you:
        Allelu-, alleluia!
        Alleluia, alleluia;
        alleluia, allelu-alleluia!

2 Ask, and it shall be given unto you;
    seek, and ye shall find;
    knock, and the door shall be opened
            unto you:
        Allelu-, alleluia!
        Alleluia . . .

3 Man does not live by bread alone,
    but by every word
    that proceeds
            from the mouth of the Lord:
        Allelu-, alleluia!
        Alleluia . . .

from Matthew 6 and 7
Karen Lafferty
© Maranatha! Music/Word (UK) Limited†

169 Jesus is king
Songs of Fellowship 2 236

1 Jesus is king,
        and we will extol him,
    give him the glory,
        and honour his name;
    he reigns on high,
        enthroned in the heavens –
    Word of the Father,
        exalted for us.

2 We have a hope
        that is steadfast and certain,
    gone through the curtain
        and touching the throne;
    we have a Priest
        who is there interceding,
    pouring his grace
        on our lives day by day.

3 We come to him
        our Priest and Apostle,
    clothed in his glory
        and bearing his name,
    laying our lives
        with gladness before him –
    filled with his Spirit
        we worship the King:

4 'O Holy One,
        our hearts do adore you;
    thrilled with your goodness
        we give you our praise!'
    Angels in light
        with worship surround him,
    Jesus, our Saviour,
        for ever the same.

Wendy Churchill
© Springtide/Word Music (UK)†

170

CREED
Let us affirm our faith in God:

**I believe and trust in God the Father,
who made the world.**

**I believe and trust
    in his Son Jesus Christ,
who redeemed mankind.**

**I believe and trust in his Holy Spirit,
who gives life to the people of God.**

**I believe and trust in one God:
Father, Son, and Holy Spirit. Amen.** †

171 Kum ba yah
Hymns for Today's Church 358

1 Father God in heaven,
        Lord most high:
    hear your children's prayer,
        Lord most high:
    hallowed be your name,
        Lord most high –
    O Lord, hear our prayer.

The Life of Prayer (168–171)

2 May your kingdom come
       here on earth;
  may your will be done
       here on earth,
  as it is in heaven
       so on earth –
       O Lord, hear our prayer.

3 Give us daily bread
       day by day,
  and forgive our sins
       day by day,
  as we too forgive
       day by day –
       O Lord, hear our prayer.

4 Lead us in your way,
       make us strong;
  when temptations come
       make us strong;
  save us from all sin,
       keep us strong –
       O Lord, hear our prayer.

5 All things come from you,
       all are yours –
  kingdom, glory, power,
       all are yours;
  take our lives and gifts,
       all are yours –
       O Lord, hear our prayer.

from *The Lord's Prayer*
J E Seddon (1915–1983)
© Mrs M Seddon/Jubilate Hymns

172

THEME PRAYER (COLLECT)

Almighty God,
the fountain of all wisdom,
you know our needs before we ask,
and our ignorance in asking:
have compassion on our weakness,
and give us those things

which for our unworthiness
       we dare not,
and for our blindness we cannot ask,
for the sake of your Son,
       Jesus Christ our Lord. **Amen.**

from Concluding Prayers – ASB

173 St Hugh
        Hymns for Today's Church 367

1 Lord, teach us how to pray aright
  with reverence and with fear:
  though dust and ashes in your sight,
  we may, we must draw near.

2 We perish if we cease from prayer:
  O grant us power to pray;
  and when to meet you we prepare,
  Lord, meet us by the way.

3 O God of love, before your face
  we come with contrite heart
  to ask from you these gifts of grace –
  truth in the inward part:

4 Faith in the only Sacrifice
  that can for sin atone;
  to found our hopes, to fix our eyes
  on Christ, and Christ alone:

5 Patience to watch and weep
       and wait,
  whatever you may send;
  courage that will not hesitate
  to trust you to the end.

6 Give these, and then
       your will be done;
  thus, strengthened with all might,
  we through your Spirit
       and your Son
  shall pray, and pray aright.

J Montgomery (1771–1854)

1 Speak, Lord, in the stillness,
all our longing see;
hush our hearts to listen
in expectancy.

2 Speak to us your servants –
let us hear you, Lord –
sinners, yet awaiting
your life-giving word.

3 Speak, O gracious Master,
in this quiet hour;
let us see your face, Lord,
feel your touch of power.

4 For the words you speak, Lord,
they are life indeed:
Living Bread from heaven,
all our spirits feed!

5 Fill us with the knowledge
of your perfect will;
then, your own good pleasure
in our lives fulfil.

E M Crawford (1868–1927)
© in this version Word & Music/Jubilate Hymns

176

FOR GOD'S BLESSING

O Lord,
open our eyes to see what is beautiful,
our minds to know what is true,
and our hearts to love what is good;
for Jesus' sake. **Amen.**   †

177

AN EVENING PRAYER

O God of all life,
thank you for looking after us today
and for all your goodness to us:
bless us tonight with your forgiveness,
send your peace into our hearts,
and take us and all we love
into your care;
for Jesus Christ our Saviour's sake.
Amen.   †

175

LITANY

By the prayers of Jesus,
Lord, teach us how to pray.

By the grace of Jesus,
Lord, teach us how to give.

By the labours of Jesus,
Lord, teach us how to work.

By the love of Jesus,
Lord, teach us how to love.

By the cross of Jesus,
Lord, teach us how to live. Amen.   †

178

THANKSGIVING

O God,
we cannot measure your love,
nor ever count your blessings:
we thank you for all your goodness;
for in our weakness
you make us strong,
in our darkness you give us light,
and in our sorrows
you bring comfort and peace.
And from everlasting to everlasting
you are our God,
Father, Son, and Holy Spirit. **Amen.** †

The Life of Prayer (174–178)

179 Converse
Hymns for Today's Church 373(ii)

1 What a friend we have in Jesus,
    all our sins and griefs to bear!
what a privilege to carry
    everything to God in prayer!
O what peace we often forfeit,
    O what needless pain we bear,
all because we do not carry
    everything to God in prayer.

2 Have we trials and temptations?
    is there trouble anywhere?
We should never be discouraged:
    take it to the Lord in prayer.
Can we find a friend so faithful
    who will all our sorrows share?
Jesus knows our every weakness –
    take it to the Lord in prayer.

3 Are we weak and heavy-laden,
    burdened with a load of care?
Jesus is our mighty saviour:
    he will listen to our prayer.
Do your friends despise,
        forsake you?
    take it to the Lord in prayer;
in his arms he will enfold you
    and his love will shield you there.

J M Scriven (1819–1886)

180 Crucifer
Hymns for Today's Church 508

Praise God today:
his glories never end;
our judge becomes in Christ
our greatest friend.

1 God brings us comfort
        where his anger burned,
so judgement and fear
        to peace and trust are turned:
    Praise God today:
    his mercies never end;
    our judge becomes in Christ
    our greatest friend.

2 Wells of salvation
        streams of life will bring;
with joy we shall draw
        from this refreshing spring.
    Praise God today:
    his blessings never end;
    our judge becomes in Christ
    our greatest friend.

3 Songs shall be his
        for this victorious day:
give thanks to his name
        and teach the earth to say,
    Praise God today:
    his triumphs never end;
    our judge becomes in Christ
    our greatest friend.

4 Love lives among us,
        Israel's holy One;
he comes to the rescue –
        see what God has done!
    Praise God today:
    his wonders never end;
    our judge becomes in Christ
    our greatest friend.

from Isaiah 12
© Christopher Idle/Jubilate Hymns

(179–180) The Life of Prayer

THE LIFE OF PRAYER/
FORGIVENESS
Other items appropriate to this theme

Hymns

And can it be that I should gain	389
Spirit Divine, inspire our prayers	309
When all your mercies, O my God	383

Songs

Caring, sharing	448
Jesus is the name we worship	166
Open our eyes, Lord, we want to see Jesus	612
Wonderful Counsellor, Jesus	641

Psalm Versions (sung)

I waited patiently for the Lord (Psalm 40)	392
Lord, all knowing, you have found me (Psalm 139)	394
My faithful Shepherd is the Lord (Psalm 23)	560
Safe in the shadow of the Lord (Psalm 91)	395
The Lord is king! lift up your voice (Psalm 97)	290

Psalm Version (spoken)

I love the Lord because he heard my voice (Psalm 116)	26

Prayer

We have not obeyed (Confession)	603
Lord Jesus, we give ourselves (Dedication)	32

Readings

Prayers for Wisdom and Power – Ephesians 1.15–23; 3.14–21
Prayer in a Crisis – Acts 4.23–31
Prayer, the Antidote to Worry – Matthew 6.5–15; Matthew 6.24–34
Parables of Forgiveness – Luke 15.11–24; Luke 18.9–14
Zacchaeus Accepted – Luke 19.1–10
Walking in the Light – 1 John 1.5–10; 2.1–2; John 3.16–21

(See also Minister's Section 721–722. The Lord's Prayer is printed inside the back cover.)

The Life of Prayer (Other items)

14 Mothering Sunday/The Family

Honour your father and your mother, so that you may live long in the land the Lord your God is giving you. Exodus 20.12

I bow my knees before the Father, from whom every family in heaven and on earth is named. Ephesians 3.14,15

181

PRAISE

Come, let us sing for joy to the Lord;
**let us shout
to the Rock of our salvation.**

Come before him with thanksgiving;
**sing him joyful songs of praise!
Amen.**

from Psalm 95

182 England's Lane
Hymns for Today's Church 298(i)

1 For the beauty of the earth,
for the beauty of the skies,
for the love which from our birth
over and around us lies,
Christ our God, to you we raise
this our sacrifice of praise.

2 For the beauty of each hour
of the day and of the night,
hill and vale, and tree and flower,
sun and moon and stars of light,
Christ our God . . .

3 For the joy of ear and eye,
for the heart and mind's delight,
for the mystic harmony
linking sense to sound and sight,
Christ our God . . .

4 For the joy of human love,
brother, sister, parent, child,
friends on earth and friends above,
pleasures pure and undefiled,
Christ our God . . .

5 For each perfect gift divine
to our race so freely given,
joys bestowed by love's design,
flowers of earth
and fruits of heaven,
Christ our God . . .

F S Pierpoint (1835–1917)

183 Austria
Hymns for Today's Church 494(i)

1 Glorious things of you are spoken,
Zion, city of our God;
he whose word cannot be broken
formed you for his own abode:
on the rock of ages founded,
what can shake your sure repose?
with salvation's walls surrounded
you may smile at all your foes.

(181–183) Mothering Sunday

2 See, the streams of living waters
  springing from eternal love!
  well supply your sons
      and daughters
  and all fear of want remove:
  who can faint while such a river
  ever flows their thirst to assuage?
  grace, which like the Lord the giver
  never fails from age to age.

3 Round each habitation hovering
  see the cloud and fire appear
  for a glory and a covering,
  showing that the Lord is near:
  thus they march, the pillar leading,
  light by night and shade by day;
  daily on the manna feeding
  which he gives them
      when they pray.

4 Saviour, since of Zion's city
  I through grace a member am,
  let the world deride or pity,
  I will glory in your name:
  fading are the world's
      best pleasures,
  all its boasted pomp and show;
  solid joys and lasting treasures
  none but Zion's children know.

J Newton (1725–1807)

(For a shorter version of this hymn, verse 3
  may be omitted.)

184

CONFESSION*

O God, the Father of us all, we come to
you in sorrow, for we have often failed
you.
ALL: **Lord, forgive us,
and help us to obey.**

You have taught us: 'Honour your

(*The leader may wish to omit the brack-
eted section)

father and mother, that it may go well
with you and that you may enjoy long
life on the earth.' We have often failed
you.
ALL: **Lord, forgive us,
and help us to obey.**

You have taught us as children: 'Obey
your parents in the Lord, for this is
right.' We have often failed you.
CHILDREN: **Lord, forgive us,
and help us to obey.**

You have taught us as fathers: 'Do not
exasperate your children; instead,
bring them up in the training and instruction of the Lord.' We have often
failed you.
FATHERS: **Lord, forgive us,
and help us to obey.**

You have taught us as mothers to live
with sincere faith and bring our children to Christ. We have often failed
you.
MOTHERS: **Lord, forgive us,
and help us to obey.**

[*You have taught us as husbands:
'Love your wives as you love
yourselves.' We have often failed you.
HUSBANDS: **Lord, forgive us,
and help us to obey.**

You have taught us as wives: 'Respect
your husbands.' We have often failed
you.
WIVES: **Lord, forgive us,
and help us to obey.**]

You have taught us as the Christian
family: 'Submit to one another out of
reverence for Christ.' We have often
failed you.
ALL: **Lord, forgive us,
and help us to obey.**

**Father, help us all to hear your word,
and to obey it;
for Jesus' sake. Amen.**

from Ephesians 5 and 6†

Mothering Sunday (184)

185

PSALM

A pilgrims' song:
**Blessed are those who fear the Lord,
who walk in his ways.**

You will eat the fruit of your work;
blessings and prosperity will be yours:
**Blessed are those who fear the Lord,
who walk in his ways.**

Your wife will be like a fruitful vine
within your house; your children will
be like young olive trees around your
table:
**Blessed are those who fear the Lord,
who walk in his ways.**

May the Lord bless you all the days of
your life; may you have prosperity;
may you live to see your children's
children. Peace be with you: **Amen.**

from Psalm 128

all the sea is the Lord's,
    for he made it –
by his hand the solid rock
    was formed.
Praise our maker . . .

3 Let us worship the Lord our maker,
    let us kneel to the Lord our God;
    for we all are the sheep
        of his pasture –
    he will guide us
        by his powerful hand.
    Praise our maker . . .

4 Let today be the time
        when you hear him!
    May our hearts not be hard or cold,
    lest we stray from the Lord
        in rebellion
    as his people did in time of old.
    Praise our maker . . .

from Psalm 95 (*Venite*)
© Richard Bewes/Jubilate Hymns

---

186 Give me joy
Mission Praise 58

PSALM

1 Let us sing to the God of salvation,
    let us sing to the Lord our rock;
    let us come to his house
        with thanksgiving,
    let us come before the Lord
        and sing!
    Praise our maker,
    praise our saviour,
    praise the Lord
    our everlasting king:
    every throne
    must bow before him –
    God is Lord of everything!

2 In his hand are the earth's
        deepest places,
    and the strength of the hills is his;

187 Woodlands
Hymns for Today's Church 42(i)

PSALM

1 Tell out, my soul,
        the greatness of the Lord!
    unnumbered blessings,
        give my spirit voice;
    tender to me
        the promise of his word;
    in God my saviour
        shall my heart rejoice.

2 Tell out, my soul,
        the greatness of his name!
    make known his might,
        the deeds his arm has done;
    his mercy sure,
        from age to age the same;
    his holy name –
        the Lord, the mighty one.

(185–187) Mothering Sunday

3 Tell out, my soul,
    the greatness of his might!
  powers and dominions
    lay their glory by.
  Proud hearts and stubborn wills
    are put to flight,
  the hungry fed,
    the humble lifted high.

4 Tell out, my soul,
    the glories of his word!
  firm is his promise,
    and his mercy sure.
  Tell out, my soul,
    the greatness of the Lord
  to children's children
    and for evermore!

from Luke 1 (*Magnificat*)
© Timothy Dudley-Smith

188 Michael, row the boat
       Jesus Praise 66

1 Come and praise the Lord our king,
    Alleluia,
  come and praise the Lord our king.
    alleluia!

2 Christ was born in Bethlehem,
    Alleluia,
  Son of God and Son of Man.
    alleluia!

3 He grew up an earthly child
    Alleluia,
  in the world, but undefiled.
    alleluia!

4 He who died at Calvary
    Alleluia,
  rose again triumphantly.
    alleluia!

5 He will cleanse us from our sin
    Alleluia,
  if we live by faith in him.
    alleluia!

6 Come and praise the Lord our king,
    Alleluia,
  come and praise the Lord our king.
    alleluia!

Copyright controlled†

189 He's got the whole world
       Sing to God 4

1 He's got the whole world
    in his hands,
  he's got the whole wide world
    in his hands,
  he's got the whole world
    in his hands,
  he's got the whole world
    in his hands!

2 He's got everybody here
    in his hands . . .

GIRLS AND LADIES
3 He's got the little tiny baby
    in his hands . . .

BOYS AND MEN
4 He's got you and me brother
    in his hands . . .

ALL
5 He's got the whole world . . .

© Marshall, Morgan & Scott/
Marshall Pickering Communications†

190 Turn the hearts of the children
       Songifts 58

Turn the hearts of the children
    to the parents;
turn the hearts of the parents
    to their young;
turn the hearts of us all to one another,
turn the hearts of the people
    to the Lord!

from Malachi 4 etc
Jimmy Owens
© Lexicon Music Inc (USA)/Word Music (UK)†

Mothering Sunday (188–190)

191 Father, we adore you
Mission Praise 44

1 Father, we adore you,
   lay our lives before you:
   how we love you!

2 Jesus, we adore you,
   lay our lives before you:
   how we love you!

3 Spirit, we adore you,
   lay our lives before you:
   how we love you!

Terrye Coelho
© Maranatha! Music/Word (UK) Limited†

192

CREED
Let us declare our faith in God:

We believe in God the Father,
from whom every family
in heaven and on earth is named.

We believe in God the Son,
who lives in our hearts through faith,
and fills us with his love.

We believe in God the Holy Spirit,
who strengthens us
   with power from on high.

We believe in one God;
Father, Son, and Holy Spirit. Amen. †

from Ephesians 3

193

FOR OUR FAMILIES (COLLECT)

God our Father,
your Son Jesus Christ
lived in a family at Nazareth:
grant that in our families on earth

(191–195) Mothering Sunday

we may so learn to love
   and to live together
that we may rejoice as one family
in your heavenly home;
through Jesus Christ our Lord. **Amen.**

Pentecost 14 collect – APB†

194 Albano, Amazing Grace
Hymns for Today's Church 135, 28

1 I love to think, though I am young,
   my saviour was a child;
   that Jesus walked this earth along
   with feet all undefiled.

2 I love to think that he who spoke
   and made the blind to see;
   that he for whom the dead awoke
   was once a child like me.

3 And though he wore a thorny crown
   and tasted death's despair,
   he had a mother like my own
   and knew her love and care.

4 I know it was for love of me
   that he became a child
   and left the heavens so fair to see
   and trod earth's pathway wild.

5 Lord Jesus, since to save this child,
   a child you had to be,
   then come in all your mercy mild,
   dear Saviour, come to me!

E P Hood (1820–1885)
© in this version Word & Music/Jubilee Hymns

195 Quem pastores laudavere
Hymns for Today's Church 96

1 Jesus, good above all other,
   gentle child of gentle mother;
   in a stable born our brother,
   whom the angel hosts adore:

2 Jesus, cradled in a manger,
    keep us free from sin and danger;
    and to all, both friend and stranger,
    give your blessing evermore.

3 Jesus, for your people dying,
    risen master, death defying;
    Lord of heaven,
        your grace supplying,
    come to us – be present here!

4 Lord, in all our doings guide us:
    pride and hate shall not divide us;
    we'll go on with you beside us,
    and with joy we'll persevere.

from the Latin (twelfth century)
J M Neale (1818–1866) verses 1 and 2
P Dearmer (1867–1936) verses 3 and 4
© Oxford University Press

196

FOR OUR FAMILIES

Lord God, our heavenly Father:
for our families and homes –
        thank you,
for your love and care – thank you,
for everything you give us –
        thank you:
make us thoughtful at home,
make us helpful to our parents,
and above all,
teach us to love you more day by day;
for Jesus' sake. **Amen.**   †

197

THANKSGIVING
We thank God for giving us other
people to be part of our lives:

For parents, and the love which
brought us to birth: we praise you, O
Lord,
and bring you thanks today.

For mothers who have cherished and
nurtured us: we praise you, O Lord,
and bring you thanks today.

For fathers who have loved and sup-
ported us: we praise you, O Lord,
and bring you thanks today.

For brothers and sisters with whom we
have shared our home: we praise you,
O Lord,
and bring you thanks today.

For children, entrusted to our care as
parents: we praise you, O Lord,
and bring you thanks today.

For other relatives and friends who
have been with us in our hopes and our
joys: we praise you, O Lord,
and bring you thanks today.

For all who first spoke to us of Jesus,
and have drawn us into the family of
our Father in heaven: we praise you, O
Lord,
and bring you thanks today.

**Help us to live
as those who belong to one another
and to you, now and always. Amen.**   †

198* Diademata
Hymns for Today's Church 174

1 Crown him with many crowns,
    the Lamb upon his throne,
    while heaven's
        eternal anthem drowns
    all music but its own!
    Awake, my soul, and sing
    of him who died to be
    your saviour
        and your matchless king
    through all eternity.   →

(*Verse 4, or verses 3 and 4 can be omitted
on Mothering Sunday; and verse 2, or
verses 2 and 5, at other times.)

Mothering Sunday (196–198)

2 Crown him as Mary's Son
   yet God incarnate born,
   whose mercy our redemption won
   through cross and cruel thorn;
   the shepherd of his fold,
   the branch of Jesse's stem,
   the eternal saviour long-foretold,
   the babe of Bethlehem.

3 Crown him the Lord of life
   triumphant from the grave,
   who rose victorious from the strife
   for those he came to save:
   his glories now we sing
   who died and reigns on high;
   he died eternal life to bring
   and lives that death may die.

4 Crown him the Lord of love,
   who shows his hands and side –
   those wounds yet visible above
   in beauty glorified.
   No angel in the sky
   can fully bear that sight,
   but downward bends
        his burning eye
   at mysteries so bright.

5 Crown him the Lord of peace –
   his kingdom is at hand;
   from pole to pole let warfare cease
   and Christ rule every land!
   His reign shall have no end,
   and round his nail-pierced feet
   the flowers of paradise shall blend
   in fragrance ever sweet.

6 Crown him the Lord of years,
   the potentate of time,
   creator of the rolling spheres
   in majesty sublime:

all hail Redeemer, hail,
for you have died for me;
your praise shall never, never fail
through all eternity!

M Bridges (1800–1894)
and G Thring (1823–1903)
© in this version Word & Music/Jubilate Hymns

199 Nun danket, Gracias
Hymns for Today's Church 33

1 Now thank we all our God,
   with hearts and hands and voices,
   who wondrous things has done,
   in whom this world rejoices;
   who from our mothers' arms
   has blessed us on our way
   with countless gifts of love,
   and still is ours today.

2 O may this bounteous God
   through all our life be near us,
   to fill our hearts with joy,
   and send us peace to cheer us;
   to keep us still in grace,
   and guide us when perplexed;
   to free us from all ills
   in this world and the next.

3 All praise and thanks to God
   who reigns in highest heaven;
   to Father and to Son
   and Spirit now be given;
   to the eternal God,
   whom heaven and earth adore:
   the one who was, is now,
   and shall be evermore.

after M Rinkart (1586–1649)
C Winkworth (1827–1878)

MOTHERING SUNDAY/THE FAMILY
Other items appropriate to this theme

Hymns
Father God in heaven, Lord most high	171
Father, in your presence kneeling	10
Help us to help each other, Lord	439

Psalm Version (spoken)
Praise the Lord: You servants of the Lord (Psalm 113)	4

Songs
Jesus put this song	423
One shall tell another	30

Readings
The Birth of Samuel –
   1 Samuel 1.1–20
Family Relationships –
   Ephesians 5.21–6.4; Colossians 3.15–4.1
Wives and Husbands –
   1 Peter 3.1–7
Jesus and Little Children –
   Mark 10.13–16
Care for a Mother – John 19.25–28

(See also Minister's Section 723–728. The Lord's Prayer is printed inside the back cover.)

15 Palm Sunday

Hosanna! Blessed is he who comes in the name of the Lord.

Mark 11.9

Shout for joy, you people of Jerusalem! Look, your king is coming to you – triumphant and victorious, but humble and riding on a donkey.

Zechariah 9.9

200

PRAISE

Shout for joy to the Lord, all the earth;
serve the Lord with gladness!

Come before him with joyful songs;
**give thanks to him
    and praise his name! Amen.**

from Psalm 100

4 Blessed be the Lord,
        who freely came
    to save our sinful race;
    he comes, in God his Father's name,
    with words of truth and grace.

5 Hosanna in the highest strains
    the church on earth can raise!
    the highest heaven
        in which he reigns
    shall give him nobler praise.

I Watts (1674–1748)

201   Bishopthorpe
        Hymns for Today's Church 379

1 This is the day the Lord has made,
    he calls the hours his own:
    let heaven rejoice, let earth be glad,
    and praise surround the throne.

2 Today he rose and left the dead,
    and Satan's empire fell;
    today the saints
        his triumphs spread,
    and all his wonders tell.

3 Hosanna to the anointed king,
    to David's holy Son!
    help us, O Lord; descend and bring
    salvation from your throne.

202   St Theodulph
        Hymns for Today's Church 120

    All glory, praise and honour,
    to you, redeemer, king,
    to whom the lips of children
    made sweet hosannas ring.

1 You are the king of Israel,
    great David's greater son;
    you ride in lowly triumph,
    the Lord's anointed one!
        All glory, praise . . .

2 The company of angels
    are praising you on high,

and mortal men, and all things
created, make reply:
　　All glory, praise . . .

3 The people of the Hebrews
with palms before you went;
our praise and prayer and anthems
before you we present.
　　All glory, praise . . .

4 To you before your passion
they sang their hymns of praise;
to you, now high exalted,
our melody we raise:
　　All glory, praise . . .

5 As you received their praises,
accept the prayers we bring,
for you delight in goodness
O good and gracious king!
　　All glory, praise . . .

after Theodulph (c 750–821)
J M Neale (1818–1866)
© in this version Jubilate Hymns

203

CONFESSION
On Palm Sunday, the crowds worshipped Jesus; on Good Friday they
shouted for him to die. Let us who
also worship him, confess that we
sometimes reject him, and ask his
forgiveness:

Lord Jesus Christ, you come to us in
peace, but we shut the door of our
mind against you. In your mercy:
forgive us and help us.

You come to us in humility, but we
prefer our own proud ways. In your
mercy:
forgive us and help us.

You come to us in judgement, but we
cling to our familiar sins. In your
mercy:

forgive us and help us.

You come to us in majesty, but we will
not have you to reign over us. In your
mercy:
forgive us and help us.

**Lord, forgive our empty praise,
fill our loveless hearts;
come to us and make our lives
your home for ever. Amen.**　　　　†

204

PSALM*

A The earth is the Lord's, and everything in it:
**the world and all who live in it
　　are his.**

A He founded it upon the seas:
and established it upon the waters.

B Who has the right to go up the Lord's
hill; who may enter his holy temple?
**Those who have clean hands
　　and a pure heart,
who do not worship idols
　　or swear by what is false.**

A The Lord will bless them and save
them:
God will declare them innocent.

A Such are the people who come to
God:
**who come into the presence
　　of the God of Jacob.**

C Fling wide the gates, open the ancient
doors:
that the king of glory may come in.

B Who is this king of glory?
**The Lord, strong and mighty,
the Lord mighty in battle.**

C Fling wide the gates, open the ancient
doors:
that the king of glory may come in.　→

^BWho is he, this king of glory?
The Lord almighty,
he is the king of glory. Amen.

Psalm 24

(*This psalm may be led by three speakers.
All say the refrain.)

205

Fulda
Hymns for Today's Church 16

PSALM/CANTICLE

1 Come with all joy to sing to God
   our saving rock, the living Lord:
   in glad thanksgiving seek his face
   with songs of victory and grace.

2 In holiness and light arrayed
   above all gods that we have made
   he is the one almighty king
   and his the glory that we sing.

3 The earth is his from east to west,
   from ocean-floor to mountain-crest:
   he made the seas
        and formed the lands,
   he shaped the islands by his hands.

4 Come near to worship!
        come with faith,
   bow down to him who
        gives us breath:
   God is our shepherd, he alone;
   we are his people, all his own.

5 But if you hear his voice today
   do not reject what he will say:
   when Israel wandered
        from God's path
   they suffered forty years of wrath.

6 That generation went astray;
   they did not want to know his way:
   they put their saviour to the test,
   and saw his power,
        but lost their rest.

7 So to the God of earth and heaven,
   the Father, Spirit, Son, be given
   praise now, as praise has ever been
   and ever shall be praise – Amen!

from Psalm 95 (Venite)
© Christopher Idle/Jubilate Hymns

206

Narenza
Baptist Hymn Book 313

CANTICLE

1 Before the heaven and earth
   were made by God's decree,
   the Son of God all-glorious dwelt
   in God's eternity.

2 Though in the form of God
   and rich beyond compare,
   he did not stay to grasp his prize;
   nor did he linger there.

3 From heights of heaven he came
   to this world full of sin,
   to meet with hunger, hatred, hell,
   our life, our love to win.

4 The Son became true Man
   and took a servant's role;
   with lowliness and selfless love
   he came, to make us whole.

5 Obedient to his death –
   that death upon a cross,
   no son had ever shown such love,
   nor father known such loss.

6 To him enthroned on high,
   by angel hosts adored,
   all knees shall bow,
        and tongues confess
   that Jesus Christ is Lord.

from Philippians 2
© Brian Black and Word & Music/Jubilate Hymns

(205–206) Palm Sunday

207
All the way
Jesus Praise 65

1 All the way, all the way,
he came all the way for me;
all the way, all the way,
he came all the way for me.

2 From heaven above to Bethlehem
he came all the way for me . . .

3 From Bethlehem to Jerusalem
he came all the way for me . . .

4 From Jerusalem to Calvary
he came all the way for me . . .

5 From Calvary to heaven above
he came all the way for me . . .

6 From heaven above into my heart
he came all the way for me . . .

7 Jesus came, Jesus came,
he came all the way for me . . .

Mo Wilkinson
© Thankyou Music†

208
Lift up your heads
Songs of Fellowship 2   248

Lift up your heads to the coming King;
bow before him and adore him,
    sing to his majesty:
let your praises be pure and holy,
giving glory to the King of kings.

Steven L Fry
© Birdwing Music/Cherry Lane Music Limited†

209
We cry hosanna Lord
Jesus Praise 50

    We cry hosanna, Lord;
    yes, hosanna, Lord;
    yes, hosanna, Lord, to you:
    we cry hosanna, Lord;
    yes, hosanna, Lord;
    yes, hosanna, Lord, to you!

1 Behold, our saviour comes!
behold the Son of our God!
He offers himself,
    and he comes among us,
a lowly servant to all.
    We cry hosanna . . .

2 Children wave their palms
as the King of all kings rides by;
should we forget to praise our God,
the very stones would sing.
    We cry hosanna . . .

3 He comes to set us free,
he gives us liberty;
his victory over death
    is the eternal sign
of God's love for us.
    We cry hosanna . . .

Mimi Farra
© Celebration/Thankyou Music†

210
Follow my leader
Praise God Together 113

1 The journey of life
may be easy, may be hard –
there'll be dangers on the way;
with Christ at my side
I'll do battle as I ride
with the foe
    that would lead me astray:
    Will you ride, ride, ride
    with the King of kings,
    will you follow my leader true;
    will you shout 'hosanna!'
    to the lowly Son of God,
    who died for me and you?

2 My burden is light,
and a song is in my heart
as I travel on life's way;
for Christ is my Lord
and he's given me his word
that by my side he'll stay:
    Will you ride . . .

Palm Sunday (207–210)

3 I'll follow my leader
   wherever he may go,
   for Jesus is my friend;
   he'll lead me on
   to the place where he has gone
   when I come
         to my journey's end.
   Will you ride, ride, ride
   with the King of kings,
   will you follow my leader true;
   will you shout 'hosanna!'
   to the lowly Son of God,
   who died for me and you?

as a man he humbled himself,
and was obedient to death –
even the death of the cross.
Therefore God has raised
      him on high,
and given him the name
      above every name:
that at the name of Jesus
every knee should bow,
and every voice proclaim
that Jesus Christ is Lord,
to the glory of God the Father. Amen.†

from Philippians 2

Valerie Collison
© High-Fye Music†

211 You are the king of glory
Mission Praise 279

You are the king of glory,
you are the prince of peace;
you are the Lord of heaven and earth,
you're the sun of righteousness!
Angels bow down before you,
      worship and adore
for you have the words of eternal life;
you are Jesus Christ the Lord!
   Hosanna to the Son of David;
   hosanna to the King of Kings!
   Glory in the highest heaven,
   for Jesus the messiah reigns!

Mavis Ford
© Springtide/Word Music (UK)†

212

CREED
Let us affirm our faith in Jesus Christ
the Son of God:

**Though he was divine,
he did not cling to equality with God,
but made himself nothing.
Taking the form of a slave,
he became as we are;**

213

THEME PRAYER (COLLECT)

Almighty and everlasting God,
who in your tender love
      towards mankind
sent your Son
      our Saviour Jesus Christ
to take upon him our flesh
and to suffer death upon the cross:
grant that we may follow the example
      of his patience and humility,
and also be made partakers
      of his resurrection;
through Jesus Christ our Lord. **Amen.**

Palm Sunday collect – ASB

214 Eudoxia
Hymns of Faith 564(ii)
Baptist Hymn Book 698

1 Jesus, high in glory,
   lend a listening ear;
   when we bow before you,
   thankful praises hear!

2 Though you are so holy,
   heaven's almighty king,
   you will stoop to listen
   while your people sing.

(211–214) Palm Sunday

3 Save us, Lord, from sinning –
  watch us day by day;
  help us love and serve you –
  take our sins away.

4 So when you shall call us
  to our heavenly home,
  we will gladly answer,
  'Saviour, Lord, we come!'

5 In your love eternal,
  from all sin set free,
  loud shall be our praises,
  when your face we see!

H B McKeever (1807–1886)
© in this version Word & Music/Jubilate Hymns

215* Love unknown
Hymns for Today's Church 136

1 My song is love unknown,
  my saviour's love for me;
  love to the loveless shown
  that they might lovely be:
  but who am I, that for my sake
  my Lord should take frail flesh
      and die?

2 He came from heaven's throne
  salvation to bestow;
  his own refused, and none
  the longed-for Christ would know:
  this is my friend, my friend indeed,
  who at my need his life did spend.

3 Sometimes they crowd his way
  and his sweet praises sing,
  resounding all the day
  hosannas to their king:
  then 'crucify' is all their breath,
  and for his death they thirst and cry.

4 Why, what has my Lord done
  to cause this rage and spite?
  he made the lame to run,
  and gave the blind their sight:
  what injuries! yet these are why
  the Lord most high so cruelly dies.

5 With angry shouts, they have
  my dear Lord done away;
  a murderer they save,
  the prince of life they slay!
  yet willingly he bears the shame
  that through his name
      all might be free.

6 Here might I stay and sing
  of him my soul adores;
  never was love, dear King,
  never was grief like yours! –
  this is my friend
      in whose sweet praise
  I all my days could gladly spend.

S Crossman (1624–1683)
© in this version Jubilate Hymns

(*Verses 4 and 5 may be omitted.)

216

FOR BLESSING
We pray that the Lord of Palm Sunday
will bless us today:

Come into our *city*, Lord; bring hope
and a cause for joy. Hosanna to the
King
who comes in the name of the Lord!

Come into our *fellowship*, Lord; cleanse
it of all that is not in accordance with
your will. Hosanna to the King
who comes in the name of the Lord!

Come into our hearts, Lord; teach us
your love and your truth. Hosanna to
the King
who comes in the name of the Lord!

Lord Jesus,
as you entered into Jerusalem
and its Temple, so come to us
that we may be a holy people,
worthy of your presence,
bringing glory to your name. Amen. †

Palm Sunday (215–216)

217 Bristol
Hymns for Today's Church 193

1 Hark the glad sound! –
    the Saviour comes,
  the Saviour promised long;
  let every heart prepare a throne
  and every voice a song.

2 He comes the prisoners to release
  in Satan's bondage held;
  the gates of brass before him burst,
  the iron fetters yield.

3 He comes the broken heart to bind,
  the wounded soul to cure;
  and with the treasures of his grace
  to enrich the humble poor.

4 Our glad hosannas, Prince of peace,
  your welcome shall proclaim;
  and heaven's eternal arches ring
  with your beloved name.

                          P Doddridge (1702–1751)

218 Winchester New, St Drostane
Hymns for Today's Church 119
Baptist Hymn Book 128

1 Ride on, ride on in majesty
  as all the crowds 'Hosanna!' cry:
  through waving branches
        slowly ride,
  O Saviour, to be crucified.

2 Ride on, ride on in majesty,
  in lowly pomp ride on to die:
  O Christ, your triumph now begin
  with captured death,
        and conquered sin!

3 Ride on, ride on in majesty –
  the angel armies of the sky
  look down
        with sad and wondering eyes
  to see the approaching sacrifice.

4 Ride on, ride on in majesty,
  the last and fiercest foe defy:
  the Father on his sapphire throne
  awaits his own anointed Son.

5 Ride on, ride on in majesty,
  in lowly pomp ride on to die:
  bow your meek head to mortal pain,
  then take, O God, your power
        and reign!

                          H Milman (1791–1868)
              © in this version Jubilate Hymns

PALM SUNDAY
Other items appropriate to this theme

Hymns
Name of all majesty   306
Praise him, praise him –
    Jesus, our mighty redeemer   304

Songs
Here he comes, robed in majesty   57
Make way, make way   587

Psalm Version (spoken)
Give thanks to the Lord
    (Psalm 118)   487

Psalm Versions (sung)
Fling wide the gates (Psalm 24)   291
This earth belongs to God
    (Psalm 24)   584

Readings
The Celebration – Psalm 118.15–29
The Prophecy of the King –
    Zechariah 9.9–12
Fulfilled on Palm Sunday –
    Matthew 21.1–11; Mark 11.1–10;
    Luke 19.28–40
Clearing the Temple –
    Mark 11.15–19

(See also Good Friday Section 219–238,
and Minister's Section 729–731. The
Lord's Prayer is printed inside the back
cover.)

16 Good Friday/ Easter Eve/ also Passiontide

Jesus died for all, that those who live should no longer live for themselves but for him who for their sake died and was raised again. 2 Corinthians 5.15

219 Horsley
Hymns for Today's Church 148

1 There is a green hill far away
   outside a city wall,
   where our dear Lord was crucified,
   who died to save us all.

2 We may not know, we cannot tell
   what pains he had to bear,
   but we believe it was for us
   he hung and suffered there.

3 He died that we might be forgiven,
   he died to make us good;
   that we might go at last to heaven,
   saved by his precious blood.

4 There was no other good enough
   to pay the price of sin;
   he, only, could unlock the gate
   of heaven – and let us in.

5 Lord Jesus, dearly you have loved;
   and we must love you too,
   and trust in your redeeming blood
   and learn to follow you.

C F Alexander (1818–1895)

220

CONFESSION

Lord Jesus Christ, we confess we have failed you as did your disciples, and we ask for your mercy and your help:

When we are tempted to betray you for the sake of selfish gain: Christ, have mercy;
Lord, forgive us and help us.

When we do not keep watch in prayer, and will not share the pain of your suffering: Christ, have mercy;
Lord, forgive us and help us.

When we allow the world to silence you, and run away from those who abuse you: Christ, have mercy;
Lord, forgive us and help us.

When we will not confess your name, and fear the consequences of being known to belong to you: Christ, have mercy;
Lord, forgive us and help us.

When we spurn your dying love, and will not offer you the sacrifice of our lives: Christ, have mercy;
Lord, forgive us and help us.

**Cleanse us from our sins
    by your precious blood,
and graciously restore us
    to your service;
for your praise and glory. Amen.** †

Good Friday (219–220)

221

SONG (CANTICLE)

The people reply:

Who has believed our message:
**to whom has the arm of the Lord
     been revealed.**

He grew up before him like a tender shoot:
and like a root out of dry ground.

He was despised and rejected:
**a man of sorrows
     and familiar with grief.**

Surely he took up our infirmities:
and carried our sorrows!

He was pierced for our transgressions;
he was crushed for our iniquities.

The punishment that brought us peace was upon him:
and by his wounds we are healed.

He was led like a lamb to the slaughter, and as a sheep before her shearers is silent:
so he did not open his mouth.

He was assigned a grave with the wicked:
and with the rich in his death.

We all, like sheep have gone astray; each of us has turned to our own way:
**and the Lord has laid on him
the iniquity of us all. Amen.**

from Isaiah 53

222 St Hugh
Hymns for Today's Church 367

PSALM

1 How long will you forget me, Lord?
   You hide your face away
   while sorrows trouble me by night
   and enemies by day.

2 Restore my strength,
      O Lord my God,
   and answer when I call!
   Protect me from my enemies,
   who love to see me fall.

3 My trust is in your constant love –
   to you, O Lord, I sing,
   for you have come to rescue me,
   my joy, my hope, my king!

from Psalm 13
© Christopher Idle/Jubilate Hymns

223 Passion Chorale, Ewing
Hymns for Today's Church 139, 573

CANTICLE

1 No weight of gold or silver
      can measure human worth;
   no soul secures its ransom
      with all the wealth of earth;
   no sinners find their freedom
      but by the gift unpriced,
   the Lamb of God unblemished,
      the precious blood of Christ.

2 Our sins, our griefs and troubles,
      he bore and made his own;
   we hid our faces from him,
      rejected and alone.
   His wounds are for our healing,
      our peace is by his pain:
   behold, the Man of sorrows,
      the Lamb for sinners slain!

3 In Christ the past is over,
      a new world now begins.
   With him we rise to freedom
      who saves us from our sins.
   We live by faith in Jesus
      to make his glory known:
   behold, the Man of sorrows,
      the Lamb upon his throne!

from 1 Peter 1, Isaiah 53, 2 Corinthians 5
© Timothy Dudley-Smith

(221–223) Palm Sunday

224 Alleluia my Father
Mission Praise 66

Alleluia, my Father,
    for giving us your Son;
sending him into the world
    to be given up for us,
knowing we would bruise him
    and smite him from the earth:
Alleluia, my Father,
in his death is my birth;
alleluia, my Father,
in his life is my life!

225 Cleanse me
Jesus Praise 175

Cleanse me from my sin Lord,
    put your power within Lord,
take me as I am Lord,
    and make me all your own;
keep me day by day Lord,
    underneath your sway Lord;
make my heart your palace
    and your royal throne.

226 Jesus name above all names
Jesus Praise 90

1 Jesus, name above all names,
    beautiful saviour, glorious Lord;
    Emmanuel – God is with us!
    bless-ed redeemer, living Word.

2 Jesus, bearer of my sins,
    beautiful saviour, glorious Lord:
    you suffered, giving me freedom:
    living redeemer, you are my Lord!

3 Jesus, name above all names,
    suffering servant, faithful friend;
    good shepherd, risen master,
    king of glory, Lord of all!

227 On Calvary's tree
Jesus Praise 100

On Calvary's tree,
    he died for me
that I his love might know;
to set me free
    he died for me –
that's why I love him so!

228 There is a Redeemer
Songs of Fellowship 3   499

1 There is a Redeemer,
    Jesus, God's own Son,
    precious Lamb of God, Messiah,
    holy One:
        Thank you, O my Father
        for giving us your Son,
        and leaving your Spirit
        till the work on earth is done.

2 Jesus, my Redeemer,
    Name above all names,
    precious Lamb of God, Messiah,
    O for sinners slain:
        Thank you . . .

3 When I stand in glory,
    I will see his face
    and there I'll serve my King for ever
    in that holy place:
        Thank you . . .

Palm Sunday (224–228)

229

CREED
Let us confess our faith in Christ:

Christ died for sins
once for all,
the just for the unjust,
to bring us to God:
he was put to death in the body,
but made alive by the Spirit;
he has gone up on high,
and is at God's right hand,
ruling over angels
and the powers of heaven. Amen.

†

from 1 Peter 3

230

THEME PRAYER (COLLECT)

Almighty Father,
look with mercy on this your family
for which our Lord Jesus Christ
was content to be betrayed
and given up
    into the hands of wicked men
and to suffer death upon the cross;
who is alive and glorified
    with you and the Holy Spirit,
one God, now and for ever. **Amen.**

Good Friday collect (i) – ASB

231 All for Jesus
Hymns for Today's Church 469

1 In the cross of Christ I glory
   towering over wrecks of time;
   all the light of sacred story
   gathers round his head sublime.

2 When earth's sorrows overtake me,
   hopes deceive and fears annoy,
   never shall the cross forsake me –
   Christ shall bring me peace and joy.

3 When the sun of bliss is beaming
   light and life upon my way,
   from the cross
        his radiance streaming
   adds more lustre to the day.

4 Joy and sorrow, pain and pleasure
   by the cross are sanctified;
   peace is there beyond all measure
   through the grace
        of Christ who died.

after J Bowring (1792–1872)
© in this version Word & Music/Jubilate Hymns

232 Herongate or Gideon
Hymns for Today's Church 131

1 It is a thing most wonderful –
   almost too wonderful to be –
   that God's own Son
        should come from heaven
   and die to save a child like me.

2 And yet I know that it is true:
   he came to this poor world below,
   and wept and toiled,
        and mourned and died,
   only because he loved us so.

3 I cannot tell how he could love
   a child so weak and full of sin;
   his love must be most wonderful
   if he could die my love to win.

4 I sometimes think about the cross,
   and shut my eyes, and try to see
   the cruel nails, and crown of thorns,
   and Jesus crucified for me.

5 But, even could I see him die,
   I could but see a little part
   of that great love which, like a fire,
   is always burning in his heart.

(229–232) Palm Sunday

6 How wonderful it is to know
   his love for me so free and sure;
   but yet more wonderful to see
   my love for him so faint and poor.

7 And yet I want to love you, Lord:
   O teach me how to grow in grace,
   that I may love you more and more
   until I see you face to face.

W W How (1823–1897)
© in this version Jubilate Hymns

233 The price is paid
Songs of Fellowship 3 497

1 The price is paid:
   come, let us enter in
to all that Jesus died
   to make our own.
For every sin
   more than enough he gave,
and bought our freedom
   from each guilty stain.
The price is paid, Alleluia –
amazing grace,
so strong and sure!
And so with all my heart,
my life in every part,
I live to thank you
for the price you paid.

2 The price is paid:
   see Satan flee away –
for Jesus, crucified,
   destroys his power.
No more to pay!
   Let accusation cease:
in Christ there is
   no condemnation now!
The price . . .

3 The price is paid:
   and by that scourging cruel,
he took our sicknesses
   as if his own.

And by his wounds,
   his body broken there,
his healing touch may now
   by faith be known.
The price . . .

4 The price is paid:
   'Worthy the Lamb!' we cry –
eternity shall never
   cease his praise.
The Church of Christ
   shall rule upon the earth:
in Jesus' name
   we have authority!
The price . . .

Graham Kendrick
© Thankyou Music†

234

FOR THOSE IN NEED

Lord Christ,
shine upon all who are in the darkness
   of suffering or grief,
that in your light
they may receive hope and courage,
in your mercy obtain
   relief and comfort,
and in your presence
find their rest and peace;
for your love's sake. **Amen.** †

235

FOR OURSELVES

O Saviour of the world,
by your cross and precious blood,
you have redeemed us:
**Save us and help us,
we humbly beseech you, O Lord.
Amen.**

Salvator mundi

Palm Sunday (233–235)

236

THANKSGIVING

O God our Father, you loved the world so much that you sent your only Son to die that we might live through him. *(For these, his words from the cross, we bring you thanks and praise:)

('Forgive . . .') For his willingness to forgive in the face of bitter hatred, Father, we thank you,
and praise your holy name.

('Today you shall be with me in paradise.') For his promise of heaven to the forgiven sinner, Father, we thank you,
and praise your holy name.

('Mother . . . behold your son.') For the example of his compassion to the last, Father, we thank you,
and praise your holy name.

('I thirst . . .') For his sharing in our physical suffering and longing, Father, we thank you,
and praise your holy name.

('Why have you forsaken me?') For his entering into our mental suffering and loneliness, Father, we thank you,
and praise your holy name.

('It is finished!') For the completion of his saving work, and for the covenant of love between God and his world, Father, we thank you,
and praise your holy name.

('Into your hands I commit my spirit.') For his triumph over death and the certainty of eternal life, Father, we thank you,
and praise your holy name.

(* The quotations in brackets are best used only when there has been specific reference in the service to Jesus' words from the cross.)

**Father, God, as you loved us,
so by your grace
help us to love one another,
through Jesus Christ our Lord. Amen.** †

237
Man of sorrows
Hymns for Today's Church 130

1 Man of sorrows! what a name
   for the Son of God, who came
   ruined sinners to reclaim:
     Alleluia! what a saviour!

2 Mocked by insults harsh and crude,
   in my place condemned he stood;
   sealed my pardon with his blood:
     Alleluia! what a saviour!

3 Guilty, helpless, lost were we:
   blameless Lamb of God was he,
   sacrificed to set us free:
     Alleluia! what a saviour!

4 He was lifted up to die:
   'It is finished!' was his cry;
   now in heaven exalted high:
     Alleluia! what a saviour!

5 When he comes, our glorious king,
   all his ransomed home to bring;
   then again this song we'll sing:
     'Alleluia! what a saviour!'

P Bliss (1838–1876)

238
Rockingham or O Waly Waly
Hymns for Today's Church 147

1 When I survey the wondrous cross
   on which the prince of glory died,
   my richest gain I count as loss,
   and pour contempt on all my pride.

2 Forbid it, Lord, that I should boast
   save in the cross of Christ my God;
   the very things
     that charm me most –
   I sacrifice them to his blood.

3 See from his head, his hands,
      his feet,
  sorrow and love
     flow mingled down:
  when did such love and sorrow
     meet,
  or thorns compose so rich a crown?

4 Were the whole realm of nature
      mine,
  that were an offering far too small;
  love so amazing, so divine,
  demands my soul, my life, my all!

I Watts (1674–1748)

GOOD FRIDAY/EASTER EVE/ also PASSIONTIDE Other items appropriate to this theme	

Prayers

| Almighty God, we confess (Confession) | 369 |
| Lord Jesus, we thank you | page 21 |

Hymns

He gave his life in perfect love	34
Loving shepherd of your sheep	147
My song is love unknown	215
The head that once was crowned with thorns	287

Readings

The Suffering Servant – Isaiah 53
The Humility of Christ – Philippians 2.1–11
Christ Died for our Sins – 1 Peter 2.21–25
The Criminal who Turned to Christ – Luke 23.32–47

Songs

From heaven you came	449
Salvation is found in no-one else	906
Worthy is the Lamb	45

(See also Minister's Section 729–731. The Lord's Prayer is printed inside the back cover.)

Palm Sunday (238)

17 Easter

'Why do you look for the living among the dead? He is not here; he has risen!' Luke 24.5,6

'God has raised this Jesus to life, and we are all witnesses of the fact.' Acts 2.32

239

PRAISE

O Lord our God,
we will praise you with all our heart.

O Lord our God,
**we will proclaim your greatness
for ever.**

Great is your constant love for us;
**you have saved us
from the grave itself! Amen.**

from Psalm 86

240

PRAISE

Praise be to the God and Father of our
Lord Jesus Christ!
**In his great mercy
he has given us new birth
into a living hope
through the resurrection
of Jesus Christ
from the dead. Amen.**

from 1 Peter 1

241

EASTER GREETING

We are risen with Christ –
the Lord is risen!

Eternal life is ours –
the Lord is risen!

Death has met its master –
the Lord is risen!

The way to heaven is open –
the Lord is risen!

He is risen indeed –
Alleluia! Amen.   †

242 Easter Hymn
     Hymns for Today's Church 155

1 Jesus Christ is risen today,
    Alleluia,
  our triumphant holy day;
    alleluia,
  who did once upon the cross
    alleluia,
  suffer to redeem our loss.
    alleluia!

2 Hymns of joy then let us sing
    Alleluia,
  praising Christ our heavenly king;
    alleluia,
  who endured the cross and grave
    alleluia,
  sinners to redeem and save!
    alleluia!

(239–242) Easter

3 But the pains which he endured
   Alleluia,
   our salvation have procured;
   alleluia,
   now above the sky he's king
   alleluia,
   where the angels ever sing.
   alleluia!

4 Sing we to our God above
   Alleluia,
   praise eternal as his love,
   alleluia,
   for the Lord from death is raised:
   alleluia,
   Father, Spirit, Son be praised.
   alleluia!

after a fourteenth-century author
Unknown (eighteenth century)

243 Victory or Vulpius
Hymns for Today's Church 163

1 The strife is past, the battle done;
   now is the victor's triumph won –
   O let the song of praise be sung,
   Alleluia!

2 Death's mightiest powers
      have done their worst;
   and Jesus has his foes dispersed –
   let shouts of praise and joy outburst,
   Alleluia!

3 On the third day he rose again,
   glorious in majesty to reign –
   sing out with joy the glad refrain,
   Alleluia!

4 Lord over death, our wounded king,
   save us from Satan's deadly sting
   that we may live for you and sing,
   Alleluia!

from the Latin
F Pott (1832–1909)
© in this version Jubilate Hymns

244

CONFESSION

O Jesus Christ, risen master and triumphant Lord, we come to you in sorrow
for our sins, and confess to you our
weakness and unbelief:

We have lived by our own strength,
and not by the power of your resurrection. In your mercy, forgive us:
Lord, hear us and help us.

We have lived by the light of our own
eyes, as faithless and not believing. In
your mercy, forgive us:
Lord, hear us and help us.

We have lived for this world alone, and
doubted our home in heaven. In your
mercy, forgive us:
Lord, hear us and help us.

**Lift our minds above earthly things,
set them on things above;
show us your glory and your power,
that we may serve you gladly
      all our days. Amen.**
                                    †

245

FOR JESUS' PRESENCE AND POWER

Lord Jesus, our risen Saviour,
we rejoice in your mighty victory
      over sin and death:
you are the Prince of Life;
you are alive for evermore.
Help us to know your presence
      in our worship,
and to receive your power in our lives;
until we rise to live with you for ever.
Amen.
                                    †

CANTICLE

1 Now lives the Lamb of God,
  our Passover, the Christ,
  who once with nails and wood
  for us was sacrificed:
      Come, keep the feast,
        the anthem sing
      that Christ indeed
        is Lord and king!

2 Now risen from the dead
  Christ never dies again;
  in us, with Christ as head,
  sin nevermore shall reign:
      Come, keep the feast . . .

3 In Adam all must die,
  forlorn and unforgiven;
  in Christ all come alive,
  the second Man from heaven.
      Come, keep the feast . . .

4 Give praise to God alone
  who life from death can bring;
  whose mighty power can turn
  the winter into spring:
      Come, keep the feast . . .

from the Easter Anthems
© David Mowbray/Jubilate Hymns

247

PSALM

When the Lord brought us back from
slavery:
we were like those who dream.

Our mouths were filled with laughter:
our tongues with songs of joy.

Then those around us said, 'The Lord
has done great things for them':
**The Lord has done great things for us,
and we are filled with joy.**

Those who sow in tears
shall reap with songs of joy. Amen.

from Psalm 126

PSALM

1 I love you, O Lord, you alone,
  my refuge on whom I depend;
  my maker, my saviour, my own,
  my hope and my trust without end:
  the Lord is my strength
      and my song,
  defender and guide of my ways;
  my master to whom I belong,
  my God who shall have
      all my praise.

2 The dangers of death
      gathered round,
  the waves of destruction came near;
  but in my despairing I found
  the Lord who released me from fear:
  I called for his help in my pain,
  to God my salvation I cried;
  he brought me his comfort again,
  I live by the strength he supplied.

3 My hope is the promise he gives,
  my life is secure in his hand;
  I shall not be lost, for he lives!
  he comes to my aid – I shall stand!
  Lord God, you are powerful to save,
  your Spirit will spur me to pray;
  your Son has defeated the grave:
  I trust and I praise you today!

from Psalm 18
© Christopher Idle/Jubilate Hymns

249

PSALM (CANTICLE)

1 Sing to God new songs of worship –
   all his deeds are marvellous;
   he has brought salvation to us
   with his hand and holy arm:
   he has shown to all the nations
   righteousness and saving power;
   he recalled his truth and mercy
   to his people Israel.

2 Sing to God new songs of worship –
   earth has seen his victory;
   let the lands of earth be joyful
   praising him with thankfulness:
   sound upon the harp his praises,
   play to him with melody;
   let the trumpets sound his triumph,
   show your joy to God the king!

3 Sing to God new songs of worship –
   let the sea now make a noise;
   all on earth and in the waters
   sound your praises to the Lord:
   let the hills rejoice together,
   let the rivers clap their hands,
   for with righteousness and justice
   he will come to judge the earth.

> from Psalm 98 (*Cantate Domino*)
> © Michael Baughen/Jubilate Hymns

250*

1 Come sing the praise of Jesus,
   sing his love with hearts aflame,
   sing his wondrous birth of Mary,
   when to save the world he came;
   tell the life he lived for others,
   and his mighty deeds proclaim, for
       Jesus Christ is king.

(* Verses 3 and 4 may be omitted.)

Praise and glory be to Jesus,
praise and glory be to Jesus,
praise and glory be to Jesus,
for Jesus Christ is king!

2 When foes arose and slew him,
   he was victor in the fight;
   over death and hell he triumphed
   in his resurrection-might;
   he has raised our fallen manhood
   and enthroned it in the height,
   for Jesus Christ is king.
       Praise and glory be to Jesus . . .

3 There's joy for all who serve him,
   more than human tongue can say;
   there is pardon for the sinner,
   and the night is turned to day;
   there is healing for our sorrows,
   there is music all the way,
   for Jesus Christ is king.
       Praise and glory be to Jesus . . .

4 We witness to his beauty,
   and we spread his love abroad;
   and we cleave the hosts of darkness,
   with the Spirit's piercing sword;
   we will lead the souls in prison
   to the freedom of the Lord,
   for Jesus Christ is king.
       Praise and glory be to Jesus . . .

5 To Jesus be the glory,
   the dominion, and the praise;
   he is Lord of all creation,
   he is guide of all our ways;
   and the world shall be his empire
   in the fulness of the days
   for Jesus Christ is king.
       Praise and glory be to Jesus . . .

> J C Winslow (1882–1974)
> © Mrs J Tyrrell

251 At your feet we fall
Songs of Fellowship 2   167

1 At your feet we fall,
        mighty risen Lord,
    as we come before your throne
        to worship you!
    By your Spirit's power
        you now draw our hearts,
    and we hear your voice
        in triumph ringing clear:
    'I am he that lives,
    that lives and was dead!
    Behold I am alive –
    alive evermore!'

2 There we see you stand,
        mighty risen Lord,
    clothed in garments pure and holy,
        shining bright;
    eyes of flashing fire,
        feet like burnished bronze,
    and the sound of many waters
        is your voice.
    'I am he that lives . . .'

3 Like the shining sun
        in its noon-day strength,
    we now see the glory
        of your wondrous face:
    once that face was marred,
        now you're glorified;
    and your words,
        like a two-edged sword,
        have mighty power.
    'I am he that lives . . .'

from Revelation 1
Dave Fellingham
© Thankyou Music†

252 Alleluia no. 1
Mission Praise 9

    Alleluia, alleluia,
    give thanks to the risen Lord!
    Alleluia, alleluia,
    give praise to his name!

1 Jesus is Lord of all the earth;
    he is the king of creation:
        Alleluia . . .

2 Spread the good news
        o'er all the earth –
    Jesus has died and has risen:
        Alleluia . . .

3 We have been crucified with Christ;
    now we shall live for ever:
        Alleluia . . .

4(5) Come let us praise the living God;
    joyfully sing to our saviour:
        Alleluia . . .

Don Fishel
© Word of God Music†

253 Led like a lamb
Mission Praise 282

1 Led like a lamb to the slaughter
    in silence and shame,
    there on your back
    you carried a world
    of violence and pain,
        bleeding, dying,
        bleeding, dying.
    You're alive – you're alive,
    you have risen –
        Alleluia . . .
    and the power
    and the glory is given –
        Alleluia . . .
    Jesus to you.

2 At the break of dawn – poor Mary,
    still weeping, she came:
    when through her grief
    she heard your voice
    now speaking her name,
        MEN 'Mary!' WOMEN 'Master!'
        MEN 'Mary!' WOMEN 'Master!'
    You're alive . . .

(251–253) Easter

3 At the right hand of the Father,
   now seated on high,
   you have begun your eternal reign
   of justice and joy:
      Glory, glory,
      glory, glory!
   You're alive . . .

Graham Kendrick
© Thankyou Music†

254 Sing glory glory
       Church Family Worship Source Book

Sing glory, glory,
   alleluia;
alleluia to the King!
Sing glory, glory,
   alleluia:
he is risen, so let us sing!
   (Everybody, sing!)

Traditional†

255 For this purpose
       Songs of Fellowship 3   364

1 For this purpose
      Christ was revealed,
   to destroy all the works
      of the evil one;
   Christ in us has overcome,
   so with gladness we sing
   and welcome his kingdom in.
      MEN
      Over sin he has conquered:
      WOMEN
      Alleluia! he has conquered.
      MEN
      Over death victorious:
      WOMEN
      Alleluia! victorious.
      MEN
      Over sickness he has triumphed:
      WOMEN
      Alleluia, he has triumphed.
      ALL
      Jesus reigns over all!

2 In the name of Jesus we stand;
   by the power of his blood
   we now claim this ground:
   Satan has no authority here,
   powers of darkness must flee,
   for Christ has the victory.
      MEN
      Over sin . . .

Graham Kendrick
© Thankyou Music†

256

CREED
Let us declare our faith in the resurrection of our Lord Jesus Christ:

**Christ died for our sins
in accordance with the scriptures;
he was buried;
he was raised to life on the third day
in accordance with the scriptures;
afterwards he appeared
      to his followers,
and to all the apostles:
this we have received,
      and this we believe.   Amen.**   †

from 1 Corinthians 15

257

THEME PRAYER (COLLECT)

Lord of all life and power,
who through the mighty resurrection
      of your Son
overcame the old order
      of sin and death
to make all things new in him:
grant that we, being dead to sin
and alive to you in Jesus Christ,
may reign with him in glory;
to whom with you and the Holy Spirit
be praise and honour,
      glory and might,
now and in all eternity. **Amen.**

Easter collect – ASB

1 Christ the Lord is risen again,
Christ has broken every chain;
hear the angel voices cry,
singing evermore on high:
Alleluia!

2 He who gave for us his life,
who for us endured the strife,
is our paschal lamb today;
we too sing for joy and say:
Alleluia!

3 He who bore all pain and loss
comfortless upon the cross
lives in glory now on high,
pleads for us and hears our cry:
Alleluia!

4 He who slumbered in the grave
is exalted now to save;
through the universe it rings
that the lamb is King of kings:
Alleluia!

5 Now he bids us tell abroad
how the lost may be restored,
how the penitent forgiven,
how we too may enter heaven:
Alleluia!

6 Christ, our paschal lamb indeed,
all your ransomed people feed!
take our sins and guilt away;
let us sing by night and day:
Alleluia!

after M Weisse (1480–1534)
C Winkworth (1827–1878)

(*For a shorter version of this hymn verses
5 and 6 may be omitted.)

1 Love's redeeming work is done;
fought the fight, the battle won:
see, our Sun's eclipse has passed;
see, the dawn has come at last!

2 Vain the stone, the watch, the seal:
Christ has burst the gates of hell;
death in vain forbids his rise –
Christ has opened paradise:

3 Now he lives, our glorious king;
now, O death, where is your sting?
Once he died, our souls to save –
where's your victory,
boasting grave?

4 So we rise where Christ has led,
following our exalted head;
made like him, like him we rise –
ours the cross, the grave, the skies:

5 Hail the Lord of earth and heaven!
praise to you by both be given;
every knee to you shall bow,
risen Christ, triumphant now!

C Wesley (1707–1788)
© in this version Jubilate Hymns

(*When this hymn is sung to the tune
'Württemberg', each verse ends, 'Alleluia!')

1 Shout for joy, loud and long,
God be praised with a song!
to the Lord we belong –
children of the Father,
God the great life-giver!
Shout for joy, joy, joy!
Shout for joy, joy, joy!
God is love, God is light,
God is everlasting!

(258–260) Easter

2 By God's word all was made,
heaven and earth, light and shade,
nature's wonders displayed,
man to rule creation
from its first foundation.
    Shout for joy . . .

3 Yet our pride makes us fall!
so Christ came for us all –
not the righteous to call –
by his cross and passion,
bringing us salvation!
    Shout for joy . . .

4 Now has Christ truly risen
and his Spirit is given
to all those under heaven
who will walk beside him,
though they once denied him!
    Shout for joy . . .

© David Mowbray/Jubilate Hymns

261

THANKSGIVING

Our Lord Jesus Christ, risen from
death, we praise you for changed lives
and new hopes at Easter:

You came to Mary in the garden, and
turned her tears into joy. For your love
and your mercy:
we give you thanks, O Lord.

You came to the disciples in the upper
room, and turned their fear into courage. For your love and your mercy:
we give you thanks, O Lord.

You came to the disciples by the lakeside, and turned their failure into faith.
For your love and your mercy:
we give you thanks, O Lord.

You came to the disciples on the
Emmaus road, and turned their despair
into hope. For your love and your
mercy:
we give you thanks, O Lord.

You come to us in our unworthiness
and shame, and turn our weakness
into triumph. For your love and your
mercy:
we give you thanks, O Lord.

Lord Jesus, wherever there are tears, or
fear, or failure, or despair, or weakness: come, reveal to us your love, your
mercy, and your risen power; for the
glory of your name. **Alleluia! Amen.** †

262 St Albinus
Hymns for Today's Church 156

1 Jesus lives! Your terrors now
can, O death, no more appal us:
Jesus lives! – by this we know
you, O grave, cannot enthral us:
    Alleluia!

2 Jesus lives! – henceforth is death
but the gate of life immortal;
this shall calm our trembling breath
when we pass its gloomy portal:
    Alleluia!

3 Jesus lives! – for us he died:
then, alone to Jesus living,
pure in heart may we abide,
glory to our saviour giving:
    Alleluia!

4 Jesus lives! – this bond of love
neither life nor death shall sever,
powers in hell or heaven above
tear us from his keeping never:
    Alleluia!

5 Jesus lives! – to him the throne
over all the world is given;
may we go where he is gone,
rest and reign with him in heaven:
Alleluia!

after C F Gellert (1715–1769)
F E Cox (1812–1897)
© in this version Jubilate Hymns

263 Maccabaeus
Hymns for Today's Church 167

1 Yours be the glory!
risen, conquering Son;
endless is the victory over death
you won;
angels robed in splendour
rolled the stone away,
kept the folded grave clothes
where your body lay:
Yours be the glory!
risen, conquering Son:
endless is the victory over death
you won.

2 See! Jesus meets us,
risen from the tomb,
lovingly he greets us,
scatters fear and gloom;
let the church with gladness
hymns of triumph sing!
for her Lord is living,
death has lost its sting:
Yours be the glory . . .

3 No more we doubt you,
glorious prince of life:
what is life without you?
aid us in our strife;
make us more than conquerors
through your deathless love,
bring us safe through Jordan
to your home above:
Yours be the glory . . .

after E L Budry (1854–1932)
R B Hoyle (1875–1939)
© World Student Christian Federation,
in this version Jubilate Hymns†

EASTER
Other items appropriate to this theme

Hymns

All creatures of our God and King	283
Crown him with many crowns	198
Lord Jesus Christ	390
Morning has broken	279
Rejoice, the Lord is King	301
This is the day the Lord has made	201

Songs

Because he died and is risen	568
Behold, I tell you a mystery	563
God of glory	337
He is Lord	295
How lovely on the mountains	421
I will sing about your love	81
This is the day	319
What a wonderful saviour is Jesus	567

Prayers

Come, Lord, in the fullness (For Christ's presence)	698
We praise you, O God and Father (Thanksgiving)	13

Readings

Song of Triumph – Isaiah 12
The Truth of the Resurrection –
1 Corinthians 15.1–11
The Lord of Glory –
Revelation 1.9–20
The Empty Tomb –
Matthew 28.1–10
On the Road to Emmaus –
Luke 24.13–35
Christ Appears to His Disciples –
Luke 24.36–49

(See also Minister's Section 733. The Lord's Prayer is printed inside the back cover.)

18 God's Creation

**God saw all that he had made,
and it was very good.** Genesis 1.31

264

PRAISE

O Lord, our Lord,
**how glorious is your name
in all the earth!**

High above the heavens
your majesty is praised. Amen.

from Psalm 8

265

INVITATION TO WORSHIP

Stand up and praise the Lord your God,
who is from everlasting.

Blessed be his glorious name, let it be exalted above all blessing and praise: Stand up and praise the Lord your God,
who is from everlasting.

He alone is the Lord, he made the highest heavens and all their starry host, the earth and all that is on it, the seas and all that is in them: Stand up and praise the Lord your God,
who is from everlasting.

He gives life to everything, and the multitudes of heaven worship him:

Stand up and praise the Lord your God,
who is from everlasting.

**We praise you O God
for you have created all things
and made us anew
in Jesus Christ our Lord. Amen.** †

from Nehemiah 9

266
All things bright or Royal Oak
Hymns for Today's Church 283

All things bright and beautiful,
all creatures great and small,
all things wise and wonderful –
the Lord God made them all.

1 Each little flower that opens,
each little bird that sings –
he made their glowing colours,
he made their tiny wings.
All things bright . . .

2 The purple-headed mountain,
the river running by,
the sunset, and the morning
that brightens up the sky:
All things bright . . .

3 The cold wind in the winter,
the pleasant summer sun,
the ripe fruits in the garden –
he made them every one.
All things bright . . .

God's Creation (264–266)

4 He gave us eyes to see them,
   and lips that we might tell
   how great is God almighty,
   who has made all things well!
      All things bright and beautiful,
      all creatures great and small,
      all things wise and wonderful –
      the Lord God made them all.

C F Alexander (1818–1895)

267 St Denio
Hymns for Today's Church 21

1 Immortal, invisible, God
         only wise,
   in light inaccessible
         hid from our eyes;
   most holy, most glorious,
         the ancient of days,
   almighty, victorious,
         your great name we praise.

2 Unresting, unhasting,
         and silent as light,
   nor wanting nor wasting,
         you rule us in might;
   your justice like mountains
         high soaring above,
   your clouds which are fountains
         of goodness and love.

3 To all life you give, Lord,
         to both great and small,
   in all life you live, Lord,
         the true life of all:
   we blossom and flourish,
         uncertain and frail;
   we wither and perish,
         but you never fail.

4 We worship before you,
         great Father of light,
   while angels adore you,
         all veiling their sight;

our praises we render,
      O Father, to you
whom only the splendour of light
      hides from view.

W C Smith (1824–1908)
© in this version Jubilate Hymns

268

CONFESSION

Almighty God, we confess that we
have often misused and ill-treated your
creation: hear us, and in your mercy
save us and help us.

For every act of carelessness that has
treated the world merely as a play-
ground: Father, forgive us –
save us and help us.

For every act of wastefulness that
forgets the crying of the needy: Father,
forgive us –
save us and help us.

For every act of selfishness that defies
your just rule over our lives: Father,
forgive us –
save us and help us.

Cleanse us from our sins
through the love of Christ,
and set us free for his service
through the power of the Spirit;
for the glory of your name. Amen.   †

269

PSALM*

Praise the Lord:

Praise the Lord from the heavens:
^A**praise him in the heights above.**

Praise him, all his angels:
^B**praise him, all his heavenly host.**   →

(* The congregation may divide at A and B)

(267–269) God's Creation

Praise him, sun and moon:
^A**praise him, all you shining stars.**

Let them praise the name of the Lord:
^{ALL}**praise the Lord!**

Praise the Lord from the earth:
^A**praise him, great sea creatures.**

Praise him, storms and clouds:
^B**praise him, mountains and hills.**

Praise him, fields and woods:
^A**praise him, animals and birds.**

Praise him, rulers and nations:
^B**praise him, old and young.**

Let them praise the name of the Lord:
^{ALL}**praise the Lord! Amen.**

from Psalm 148

270

PSALM/CANTICLE

May God be gracious to us and bless us:
and make his face to shine upon us.

Let your ways be known upon earth:
your saving grace to every nation.

Let the peoples praise you, O God:
let all the peoples praise you.

Let the nations be glad:
and sing aloud for joy.

Because you judge the peoples justly:
and guide the nations of the earth.

Let the peoples praise you, O God:
let all the peoples praise you.

Then the land will yield its harvest:
and God, our God, will bless us.

God will bless us:
and people will fear him.

To the ends of the earth. **Amen.**

Psalm 67 (Deus misereatur)

271

Es ist kein Tag, Almsgiving
Ancient and Modern NS 399(ii)
Hymns for Today's Church 287

PSALM

1 With wonder, Lord,
    we see your works,
we see the beauty you have made;
this earth, the skies,
    all things that are
    in beauty made.

2 With wonder, Lord,
    we see your works,
and child-like in our joy we sing
to praise you, bless you,
    maker, Lord
    of everything.

3 The stars that fill the skies above,
the sun and moon
    which give our light,
are your designing for our use
    and our delight.

4 We praise your works,
    yet we ourselves
are works of wonder made by you;
not far from you in all we are
    and all we do.

5 All you have made is ours to rule,
the birds and beasts at will to tame,
all things to order for the glory
    of your name.

from Psalm 8
Brian Foley
© Faber Music Limited†

God's Creation (270–271)

CANTICLE

1 Angels praise him,
   heavens praise him,
   waters praise him,
      Alleluia!
   powers of the Lord
   all praise him
      for evermore.

2 Sun praise him,
   moon praise him,
   stars praise him,
      Alleluia!
   showers praise him,
   dews praise him
      for evermore.

TREBLE VOICES:
3 Wind praise him,
   fire praise him,
   heat praise him,
      Alleluia!
   winter praise him,
   summer praise him
      for evermore.

MEN'S VOICES:
4 Nights praise him,
   days praise him,
   light praise him,
      Alleluia!
   lightnings praise him,
   clouds praise him
      for evermore.

TREBLE VOICES:
5 Earth praise him,
   mountains praise him,
   hills praise him,
      Alleluia!
   green things praise him,
   wells praise him
      for evermore.

MEN'S VOICES:
6 Seas praise him,
   floods praise him,
   creatures of the waters praise him,
   birds, beasts and cattle praise him
      for evermore.

7 Nations praise him,
   churches praise him,
   saints praise him,
      Alleluia!
   all his people
   join to praise him
      for evermore!

from *Benedicite*
© Michael Perry/Jubilate Hymns

273 The Butterfly Song
Sound of Living Waters 106

1 If I were a butterfly,
      I'd thank you, Lord,
         for giving me wings;
   and if I were a robin in a tree,
      I'd thank you, Lord,
         that I could sing;
   and if I were a fish in the sea,
      I'd wiggle my tail
         and I'd giggle with glee –
   but I just thank you, Father,
      for making me 'me'.
      For you gave me a heart
      and you gave me a smile,
      you gave me Jesus
      and you made me your child –
      and I just thank you, Father,
      for making me 'me'.

2 If I were an elephant,
      I'd thank you, Lord,
         by raising my trunk;
   and if I were a kangaroo,
      you know I'd hop right up to you;
   and if I were an octopus,
      I'd thank you, Lord,
         for my fine looks –

but I just thank you, Father,
for making me 'me'.
For you gave . . .

3 If I were a wiggly worm,
I'd thank you, Lord,
that I could squirm;
and if I were a billy goat
I'd thank you, Lord,
for my strong throat;
and if I were a fuzzy-wuzzy bear,
I'd thank you, Lord,
for my fuzzy-wuzzy hair –
but I just thank you, Father,
for making me 'me'.
For you gave . . .

Brian Howard
© Celebration/Thankyou Music†

274 Stand up clap hands
Jesus Praise 44

Stand up, clap hands,
shout: Thank you, Lord,
thank you for the world I'm in!
Stand up, clap hands,
shout: Thank you Lord
for happiness and peace within!

1 I look around and the sun's
in the sky;
I look around and then I think:
Oh my!
the world is such a wonderful place,
and all because of the good Lord's
grace:
Stand up, clap hands . . .

2 I look around –
and the creatures I see!
I look around and it amazes me
that every fox, and bird, and hare,
must fit in a special place
somewhere:
Stand up, clap hands . . .

3 I look around at all the joy I've had;
I look around, and then
it makes me glad
that I can offer thanks and praise
to him who guides me
through my days:
Stand up, clap hands . . .

Roger Dyer
© High-Fye Music Limited†

275 God knows me
Come and Praise 15

1 There are hundreds of sparrows,
thousands, millions;
they're two a penny, far too many
there must be:
there are hundreds and thousands,
millions of sparrows,
but God knows every one
and God knows me.

2 There are hundreds of flowers,
thousands, millions;
and flowers fair the meadows wear
for all to see:
there are hundreds and thousands,
millions of flowers,
but God knows every one . . .

3 There are hundreds of planets,
thousands, millions;
way out in space each has a place
by God's decree:
there are hundreds and thousands,
millions of planets,
but God knows every one . . .

4 There are hundreds of children,
thousands, millions;
and yet their names are written
on God's memory:
there are hundreds and thousands,
millions of children,
but God knows every one . . .

© John Gowans
Salvationist Publishing and Supplies Limited†

God's Creation (274–275)

276 Think of a world
Praise God Together 48

1 Think of a world
without any flowers,
think of a world without any trees,
think of a sky without any sunshine,
think of the air without any breeze:
we thank you, Lord,
for flowers and trees
and sunshine;
we thank you, Lord,
and praise your holy name.

2 Think of a world
without any animals,
think of a field without any herd,
think of a stream without any fishes,
think of a dawn without any bird:
we thank you, Lord,
for all your living creatures:
we thank you, Lord,
and praise your holy name.

3 Think of a world
without any people,
think of a street
with no one living there,
think of a town without any houses –
no one to love, and nobody to care:
we thank you, Lord,
for families and friendships:
we thank you, Lord,
and praise your holy name.

Doreen Newport
© Stainer & Bell Limited†

277 Shipston, Love divine
Hymns for Today's Church 427, 217(ii)

CREDAL HYMN

1 God the Father of Creation,
master of the realms sublime,
Lord of light and life's foundation:
we believe and trust in him.

(276–279) God's Creation

2 Christ who came from
highest heaven,
God from God before all time,
Son for our redemption given:
we believe and trust in him.

3 Spirit, God in us residing,
power of life and love supreme,
intercessor – pleading, guiding:
we believe and trust in him.

4 Trinity of adoration!
earth responds to heaven's theme;
one the church's acclamation:
we believe and trust in him!

© Michael Perry/Jubilate Hymns

278

THEME PRAYER (COLLECT)

Almighty God,
you have provided
the resources of the world
to maintain the life of your children,
and have so ordered our life
that we are dependent
upon each other.
Bless us all in our daily work
and, as you have given us
the knowledge to produce plenty
so give us the will
to bring it within reach of all;
through Jesus Christ our Lord. **Amen.**

Rogation Days collect – ASB

279 Bunessan
Hymns for Today's Church 265

1 Morning has broken
like the first morning;
blackbird has spoken
like the first bird:

praise for the singing,
  praise for the morning,
praise for them springing
  fresh from the word!

2 Sweet the rain's new fall,
    sunlit from heaven,
  like the first dew fall
    on the first grass:
  praise for the sweetness
    of the wet garden,
  sprung in completeness
    where his feet pass.

3 Mine is the sunlight,
    mine is the morning
  born of the one light
    Eden saw play:
  praise with elation,
    praise every morning,
  God's re-creation
    of the new day!

E Farjeon (1881–1965)
© David Higham Associates Limited†

280 Monkland
Hymns for Today's Church 23

1 Let us gladly with one mind
  praise the Lord, for he is kind:
    for his mercy shall endure,
    ever faithful, ever sure.

2 He has made the realms of space,
  all things have their ordered place:
    for his mercy . . .

3 He created sky and sea,
  field and mountain, flower and tree:
    for his mercy . . .

4 Every creature, great and small –
  God alone has made them all:
    for his mercy . . .

5 Then at last he fashioned man,
  crowning glory of his plan:
    for his mercy . . .

6 He has shaped our destiny –
  heaven for all eternity:
    for his mercy . . .

7 Glory then to God on high,
  'Glory!' let creation cry:
    for his mercy . . .

after J Milton (1608–1674)
© in this version Michael Saward/Jubilate Hymns

281

ABOUT OURSELVES AND GOD'S
CREATION

Lord of the universe,
we praise you for your creation;
for the wonder of space,
the beauty of the world
and the blessing of earth's resources:
keep us from spoiling these your gifts
    by our selfishness
and help us to use them
    for the good of all people
and the glory of your name. **Amen**   †

282

THANKSGIVING
Let us thank God for all his goodness to
us:

For creating the world and for preserving it until now: we give you thanks, O Lord,
and praise your holy name.

For the regular return of day and night, and of the seasons: we give you thanks, O Lord,
and praise your holy name.   →

God's Creation (280–282)

For the wonder of nature and the beauty of the earth: we give you thanks, O Lord,
and praise your holy name.

For our memory, which enables us to build on the experience of the past: we give you thanks, O Lord,
and praise your holy name.

For our imagination, which admits us to a wider world than we could otherwise know: we give you thanks, O Lord,
and praise your holy name.

For the grace by which you have revealed yourself to us: we give you thanks, O Lord,
and praise your holy name.

For your patience with our waywardness and your forgiveness for our sinfulness: we give you thanks, O Lord,
and praise your holy name.

Above all we thank you for the promise of all things made new, and for our re-creation in your dear Son, Jesus Christ our Lord. **Amen.**   †

283 Easter Song (Lasst uns erfreuen)
Hymns for Today's Church 13

1 All creatures of our God and king,
   lift up your voice and with us sing
      Alleluia, alleluia!
   Bright burning sun
         with golden beam,
   soft shining moon with silver gleam,
      O praise him, O praise him,
      Alleluia, alleluia, alleluia!

2 Swift rushing wind
         so wild and strong,
   white clouds that sail
         in heaven along,
      O praise him, alleluia!   →

(* Verses 3 and 6 may be omitted.)

(283) God's Creation

New rising dawn in praise rejoice,
you lights of evening find a voice;
   O praise him . . .

3 Cool flowing water, pure and clear,
   make music for your Lord to hear,
      Alleluia, alleluia!
   Fierce fire so masterful and bright
   giving to man
         both warmth and light,
      O praise him . . .

4 Earth ever fertile, day by day
   bring forth your blessings
         on our way,
      O praise him, alleluia!
   All fruit and crops that richly grow,
   all trees and flowers his glory show;
      O praise him . . .

5 People and nations take your part,
   love and forgive with all your heart;
      Alleluia, alleluia!
   All who long pain and sorrow bear,
   trust God and cast on him your care;
      O praise him . . .

6 Death, once the ancient enemy,
   hear now our Easter melody,
      O praise him, alleluia!
   You are the pathway home to God,
   our door to life
         through Christ our Lord;
      O praise him . . .

7 Let all things their creator bless
   and worship him in lowliness,
      Alleluia, alleluia!
   Praise, praise the Father,
         praise the Son,
   and praise the Spirit, Three-in-One,
      O praise him . . .

after Francis of Assisi (1182–1226)
W H Draper (1855–1933)
© in this version Jubilate Hymns

1 Praise the Lord, you heavens,
   adore him;
   praise him, angels in the height;
   sun and moon, rejoice before him;
   praise him, all you stars and light.
   Praise the Lord, for he has spoken,
   worlds his mighty voice obeyed;
   laws which never shall be broken
   for their guidance he has made.

2 Praise the Lord, for he is glorious,
   never shall his promise fail;
   God has made his saints victorious,
   sin and death shall not prevail.
   Praise the God of our salvation!
   hosts on high, his power proclaim;
   heaven and earth and all creation
   praise and glorify his name!

from Psalm 148
Anonymous
Foundling Hospital Collection (1796)

GOD'S CREATION
Other items appropriate to this theme

Hymns

For the beauty of the earth	182
Not the grandeur of the mountains	382
O worship the King	351

Songs

My God is so great, so strong and so mighty	82
Who put the colours in the rainbow?	518

Psalm Versions (sung)

O come, let us sing (Psalm 95)	76
O let his church rejoice (Psalm 147)	467
Praise the Lord (Psalm 148)	515
The earth is yours, O God (Psalm 65)	514

Canticle

Bless the Lord, creation sings	163

Prayers

We have come to worship (Call to Worship)	349
Lord God our Maker (Confession)	51
O Lord, open our eyes	176
Heavenly Father, we thank you (Thanksgiving)	385

Readings

The Story of Creation –
   Genesis 1 and 2
Praise to the God of Creation –
   Psalms 104, 139
God over all the World – Isaiah 40
The Word was God – John 1.1–14
New Heaven and New Earth –
   Revelation 21.1–7

(See also Harvest Section 508–527, and Minister's Section 734–737. The Lord's Prayer is printed inside the back cover.)

God's Creation (284)

19 Jesus is Lord

Be assured of this: God has made this Jesus . . . both Lord and Christ.

Acts 2.36

God has exalted him . . . and given him a name that is above every name.

Philippians 2.9

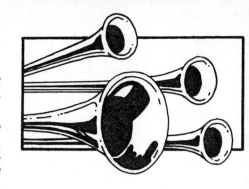

285

PRAISE

Sing to God, O kingdoms of the earth;
sing praises to the Lord!

Sing to God, O kingdoms of the earth;
proclaim his mighty power!

Praise the Lord! **Amen.**

from Psalm 68

286   Jesus is Lord
Mission Praise 119

1 Jesus is Lord!
 Creation's voice proclaims it,
 for by his power
 each tree and flower
  was planned and made.
 Jesus is Lord!
 The universe declares it –
 sun, moon and stars in heaven
  cry: 'Jesus is Lord!'
 Jesus is Lord, Jesus is Lord!
 Praise him with alleluias,
 for Jesus is Lord!

2 Jesus is Lord!
 Yet from his throne eternal
 in flesh he came
 to die in pain
  on Calvary's tree.
 Jesus is Lord!

From him all life proceeding –
 yet gave his life a ransom
  thus setting us free.
 Jesus is Lord . . .

3 Jesus is Lord!
 O'er sin the mighty conqueror;
 from death he rose
 and all his foes
  shall own his name.
 Jesus is Lord!
 God sent his Holy Spirit
 to show by works of power
  that Jesus is Lord.
 Jesus is Lord . . .

David Mansell
© Springtide/Word Music (UK)†

287   St Magnus
Hymns for Today's Church 182

1 The head that once was crowned
  with thorns
 is crowned with glory now;
 a royal diadem adorns
 the mighty victor's brow.

2 The highest place
  that heaven affords
 is his, is his by right;
 the King of kings and Lord of lords
 and heaven's eternal light.

(285–287) Jesus is Lord

3 The joy of all who dwell above,
   the joy of all below;
   to whom he demonstrates his love
   and grants his name to know.

4 To them the cross with all its shame,
   with all its grace is given;
   their name, an everlasting name,
   their joy, the joy of heaven.

5 They suffer with their Lord below,
   they reign with him above;
   their profit and their joy to know
   the mystery of his love.

6 The cross he bore is life and health,
   though shame and death to him;
   his people's hope,
       his people's wealth,
   their everlasting theme.

T Kelly (1769–1855)

289

PSALM

The Lord reigns:
let the nations tremble!

He sits enthroned on high:
let the earth shake!

Great is the Lord our God:
exalted over all the world.

Let the nations praise his awesome
name, and say:
'God is holy!'

Praise the Lord our God, and worship
at his feet:
God is holy!

Exalt the Lord our God, and worship
on his holy mountain:
the Lord our God is holy! Amen.

from Psalm 99

288

CONFESSION

**Lord Jesus Christ,
crucified, risen and ascended for us:
we have not loved you
       as our Redeemer,
nor obeyed you as our Lord;
we have not brought our prayers
       to you,
nor heeded your tears
       shed over the world.
Forgive us, we pray;
breathe into us a new spirit of service,
and make us joyfully obedient
       to your will:
for your glory's sake. Amen.**   †

290 Church triumphant
Hymns for Today's Church 183

PSALM

1 The Lord is king! Lift up your voice,
   O earth, and all you heavens,
       rejoice;
   from world to world
       the song shall ring:
   'The Lord omnipotent is king!'

2 The Lord is king!
       Who then shall dare
   resist his will, distrust his care
   or quarrel with his wise decrees,
   or doubt his royal promises?

3 The Lord is king! Child of the dust,
   the judge of all the earth is just;
   holy and true are all his ways –
   let every creature sing his praise!

Jesus is Lord (288–290)

4 God reigns! He reigns
    with glory crowned:
let Christians make a joyful sound!
And Christ is seated at his side,
the man of love, the crucified.

5 Come, make your needs,
    your burdens known:
he will present them at the throne;
and angel hosts are waiting there
his messages of love to bear.

6 One Lord one kingdom all secures:
he reigns, and life and death
    are yours;
through earth and heaven
    one song shall ring:
'The Lord omnipotent is king!'

from Psalm 97
J Conder (1789–1855)

291 Crucifer
Hymns for Today's Church 508

PSALM

Fling wide the gates,
unbar the ancient doors;
salute your king
in his triumphant cause!

1 Now all the world
    belongs to Christ our Lord:
let all creation
    greet the living Word!
Fling wide the gates . . .

2 Who has the right
    to worship him today?
All those who gladly
    serve him and obey.
Fling wide the gates . . .

3 He comes to save
    all those who trust his name,
and will declare them
    free from guilt and shame.
Fling wide the gates . . .

4 Who is the victor
    glorious from the fight?
He is our king, our life, our Lord,
    our right!
Fling wide the gates . . .

from Psalm 24
© Michael Perry/Jubilate Hymns

292 Alleluia alleluia
Jesus Praise 3

1 Alleluia, alleluia,
he is Lord, he is Lord;
alleluia, Jesus is Lord!
Alleluia, alleluia . . .
    Alleluia, Jesus is Lord!

2 Alleluia, alleluia,
he is King, he is King;
alleluia, Jesus is King!
Alleluia, alleluia . . .
    Alleluia, Jesus is King!

Frank Hernandez
© Sparrow Song/Cherry Lane Music Limited†

293 Freely freely
Mission Praise 60

1 God forgave my sin in Jesus' name;
I've been born again in Jesus' name,
and in Jesus' name I come to you
to share his love as he told me to.
    He said:
    Freely, freely you have received,
    freely, freely give;
    go in my name
    and because you believe,
    others will know that I live.

2 All power is given in Jesus' name,
in earth and heaven in Jesus' name;
and in Jesus' name I come to you
to share his power as he told me to.
    He said . . .

Jimmy and Carol Owens
© Lexicon Music Incorporated/Word (UK) Limited†

(291–293) Jesus is Lord

294 God has exalted him
Songs of Fellowship 3   371

God has exalted him
  to the highest place,
  given him the name
    that is above every name.
And every knee shall bow
  and every tongue confess
that Jesus Christ is Lord
  to the glory of God the Father.
  God has exalted him . . .

from Philippians 2
Austin Martin
© Thankyou Music†

295 He is Lord
Jesus Praise 70

1 He is Lord, he is Lord,
  he is risen from the dead,
    and he is Lord!
  Every knee shall bow,
    every tongue confess
  that Jesus Christ is Lord.

2 He's my Lord . . .

from Philippians 2
© Marvin V Frey†

296 Worthy, O worthy
Songs of Fellowship 3   520

Worthy, O worthy are you Lord,
worthy to be thanked and praised
and worshipped and adored;
worthy, O worthy are you Lord,
worthy to be thanked and praised
and worshipped and adored.

Singing alleluia,
  Lamb upon the throne,
we worship and adore you,
make your glory known.
Alleluia, glory to the King:
you're more than a conqueror,
you're Lord of everything!

Mark S Kinzer
© The Word of God†

297 We'll sing a new song
Mission Praise 260

We'll sing a new song
  of glorious triumph,
for we see the government of God
  in our lives;
we'll sing . . .
He is crowned –
  God of the whole world,
crowned king of creation,
crowned – ruling the nations now.
Yes, he is crowned . . .

Diane Fung
© Springtide/Word Music (UK)†

298

CREED
Let us confess our faith in Christ:

We believe in Christ
the King of glory,
the eternal Son of the Father:
he became man to set us free,
and did not despise
    the Virgin's womb;
he overcame death,
and opened the kingdom
    of heaven
to all believers;
he is seated at God's right hand
    in glory,
and will come to be our judge.
Amen.   †

from Te Deum

299

THEME PRAYER (COLLECT)

O God,
you are the light of the minds
    that know you,
the life of the souls that love you,

Jesus is Lord (294–299)

and the strength of the wills
    that serve you:
help us so to know you
    that we may truly love you,
and so to love you
    that we may truly serve you;
whom to serve is perfect freedom;
through Jesus Christ our Lord. **Amen.**

from The Gelasian Sacramentary

300
Christ triumphant, Guiting Power
Hymns for Today's Church 173

1 Christ triumphant, ever reigning,
  Saviour, Master, King!
  Lord of heaven, our lives sustaining,
  hear us as we sing:
    Yours the glory and the crown,
    the high renown,
      the eternal name.

2 Word incarnate, truth revealing,
  Son of Man on earth!
  power and majesty concealing
  by your humble birth:
    Yours the glory . . .

3 Suffering servant,
    scorned, ill-treated,
  victim crucified!
  death is through the cross defeated,
  sinners justified:
    Yours the glory . . .

4 Priestly king, enthroned for ever
  high in heaven above!
  sin and death and hell shall never
  stifle hymns of love:
    Yours the glory . . .

5 So, our hearts and voices raising
  through the ages long,
  ceaselessly upon you gazing,
  this shall be our song:
    Yours the glory . . .

© Michael Saward/Jubilate Hymns

301
Gopsal
Hymns for Today's Church 180

1 Rejoice, the Lord is king!
  your Lord and king adore:
  mortals, give thanks and sing,
  and triumph evermore:
    Lift up your heart,
      lift up your voice:
    rejoice! – again I say, rejoice!

2 Jesus, the saviour, reigns,
  the God of truth and love;
  when he had purged our stains
  he took his seat above:
    Lift up your heart . . .

3 His kingdom cannot fail,
  he rules both earth and heaven;
  the keys of death and hell
  to Jesus now are given:
    Lift up your heart . . .

4 He sits at God's right hand,
  till all his foes submit
  and bow to his command
  and fall beneath his feet:
    Lift up your heart . . .

5 Rejoice in glorious hope!
  Jesus the judge shall come
  and take his servants up
  to their eternal home:
    We soon shall hear
      the archangel's voice:
    the trumpet sounds –
      rejoice, rejoice!

C Wesley (1707–1788)

302

FOR STRENGTH

Lord Jesus Christ,
we thank you that you ascended
    as king of heaven and earth,

and that you are
in control of all things:
help us to trust you
in joy and in sorrow,
and to obey you always;
for the honour of your name. **Amen.** †

303

ACCLAMATION
We praise our ascended and exalted Lord:

Name above every name: Jesus, Lord,
we worship and adore you.

King of righteousness, king of peace,
enthroned at the right hand of Majesty
on high: Jesus, Lord,
we worship and adore you.

Great high priest, advocate with the
Father, living for ever to intercede for
us: Jesus, Lord,
we worship and adore you.

Pioneer of our salvation, bringing
many to glory through your death and
resurrection: Jesus, Lord,
we worship and adore you.

Let every knee bow to you,
and every tongue confess
that you are Lord,
to the glory of God the Father. Amen. †

304 Ludgrove
Mission Praise 186

1 Praise him, praise him –
Jesus, our mighty redeemer;
sing, O earth,
his wonderful love proclaim:
hail him, hail him,
highest archangels in glory;
strength and honour
give to his holy name!

Like a shepherd,
Jesus will guard his children,
in his arms
he'll carry them all day long.
Praise him, praise him,
tell of his excellent greatness;
praise him, praise him
ever in joyful song!

2 Praise him, praise him –
Jesus, our mighty redeemer;
for our sins he suffered,
and bled, and died:
he – our rock,
our hope of eternal salvation –
hail him, hail him,
Jesus, the crucified!
Sound his praises,
Jesus who bore our sorrows:
love unbounded,
wonderful, deep, and strong.
Praise him, praise him . . .

3 Praise him, praise him –
Jesus, our mighty redeemer;
heavenly arches,
loud with hosannas ring!
Jesus, Saviour,
reigning for ever and ever:
crown him, crown him,
prophet and priest, and king!
Christ is coming,
over the world victorious;
power and glory
now to the Lord belong:
Praise him, praise him . . .

F van Alstyne (1820–1915)
© in this version Word & Music/Jubilate Hymns

Jesus is Lord (303–304)

1 At the name of Jesus
    every knee shall bow,
every tongue confess him
    king of glory now;
this the Father's pleasure,
    that we call him Lord,
who from the beginning
    was the mighty word.

2 At his voice creation
    sprang at once to sight,
all the angel faces,
    all the hosts of light;
thrones and dominations,
    stars upon their way,
all the heavenly orders,
    in their great array.

3 Humbled for a season,
    to receive a name
from the lips of sinners
    unto whom he came;
faithfully he bore it
    spotless to the last,
brought it back victorious
    when from death he passed:

4 Bore it up triumphant
    with its human light,
through all ranks of creatures
    to the central height;
to the eternal Godhead,
    to the Father's throne,
filled it with the glory
    of his triumph won.

5 Name him, Christians, name him,
    with love strong as death,
but with awe and wonder,
    and with bated breath;
he is God the saviour,
    he is Christ the Lord,
ever to be worshipped,
    trusted and adored.

6 In your hearts enthrone him;
    there let him subdue
all that is not holy,
    all that is not true;
crown him as your captain
    in temptation's hour,
let his will enfold you
    in its light and power.

7 With his Father's glory
    Jesus comes again,
angel hosts attend him
    and announce his reign;
for all wreaths of empire
    meet upon his brow,
and our hearts confess him
    king of glory now.

C M Noel (1817–1877)
© in this version Jubilate Hymns

(* Verses 2 and 6 may be omitted.)

1 Name of all majesty,
    fathomless mystery,
king of the ages
    by angels adored;
    power and authority,
    splendour and dignity,
    bow to his mastery –
Jesus is Lord!

2 Child of our destiny,
    God from eternity,
love of the Father
    on sinners outpoured;
    see now what God has done
    sending his only Son,
    Christ the beloved One –
Jesus is Lord!

3 Saviour of Calvary,
  costliest victory,
  darkness defeated
  and Eden restored;
      born as a man to die,
      nailed to a cross on high,
      cold in the grave to lie –
  Jesus is Lord!

4 Source of all sovereignty,
  light, immortality,
  life everlasting
  and heaven assured;
      so with the ransomed, we
      praise him eternally,
      Christ in his majesty –
  Jesus is Lord!

© Timothy Dudley-Smith

JESUS IS LORD
Other items appropriate to this theme

Hymns

Before the heaven and earth	206
Come, let us join our cheerful songs	555
Crown him with many crowns	198
We have a gospel to proclaim	433

Songs

Holy, holy, holy is the Lord	338
Jesus is king, and we will extol him	169
Jesus, name above all names	226
Majesty – worship his majesty	339
Reign in me, sovereign Lord	403
Send me out from here, Lord	425

Psalm Version (spoken)

Clap your hands, all you nations (Psalm 47)	332

Prayer

O God, our Father in heaven	557
You are worthy, O Lord our God (Ascription)	131, 435

Creed

He was . . . taken up to glory	544
Though he was divine	212

Readings

Elijah and Elisha – 2 Kings 2.1–15
King Over All – Psalms 24, 47, 110
Lord Over All – Ephesians 1.15– end;
  Philippians 2.6–11
Worshipped and Adored –
  Revelation 5.6–end
The Ascension – Luke 24.46–end;
  Acts 1.1–11

(See also Minister's Section 738–739.
The Lord's Prayer is printed inside the
back cover.)

20 The Holy Spirit

'In the last days,' God says, 'I will pour out my Spirit on all people.'
Acts 2.17

God's love has been poured out into our hearts by the Holy Spirit whom he has given us.
Romans 5.5

307

PRAISE

Praise the Lord, O my soul;
all my being, praise his name!

Praise the Lord, O my soul;
and forget not all his blessings!

Praise the Lord, O my soul.
Praise the Lord! Amen.

from Psalm 103

308
Down Ampney
Hymns for Today's Church 231

1 Come down, O Love divine!
seek out this soul of mine
and visit it
with your own ardour glowing;
O Comforter, draw near,
within my heart appear,
and kindle it,
your holy flame bestowing.

2 O let it freely burn
till earthly passions turn
to dust and ashes
in its heat consuming;
and let your glorious light
shine ever on my sight,
and make my pathway clear,
by your illuming.

3 Let holy charity
my outward vesture be,
and lowliness
become my inner clothing;
true lowliness of heart
which takes the humbler part,
and for its own shortcomings
weeps with loathing.

4 And so the yearning strong
with which the soul will long
shall far surpass
the power of human telling;
for none can guess its grace
till we become the place
in which the Holy Spirit
makes his dwelling.

after Bianco da Siena (died 1434)
R F Littledale (1833–1890)
© in this version Jubilate Hymns

309
Beatitudo
Hymns for Today's Church 240

1 Spirit divine, inspire our prayers,
and make our hearts your home;
descend with all
your gracious powers –
O come, great Spirit, come!

(307–309) The Holy Spirit

2 Come as the light – reveal our need,
our hidden failings show,
and lead us in those paths of life
in which the righteous go.

3 Come as the fire,
and cleanse our hearts
with purifying flame;
let our whole life an offering be
to our redeemer's name.

4 Come as the dew and gently bless
this consecrated hour;
may barren souls rejoice to know
your life-creating power.

5 Come as the dove,
and spread your wings,
the wings of peaceful love,
and let your church on earth become
blessed as the church above.

6 Come as the wind,
with rushing sound
and pentecostal grace,
that all mankind with joy may see
the glory of your face.

A Reed (1787–1862)
© in this version Jubilate Hymns

310

CONFESSION

Almighty God,
we confess
that we have sinned against you:
for we have denied
your saving presence in our lives,
and we have grieved your Holy Spirit.
Come to us in the fire of your love,
and set our minds
on the things of the Spirit,
that we may bear his fruit
in love and joy and peace;
through Jesus Christ our Lord.
Amen.   †

311

PSALM

O Lord our God, you are very great;
you are clothed with splendour
and majesty.

You make winds your messengers;
and flashes of fire your servants.

How many are your works;
the earth is full of your creatures:

When you hide your face, they are
afraid;
when you take away their breath,
they die.

When you send your Spirit they are
created,
and you renew the face of the earth.
Amen.

from Psalm 104

312

PSALM

O Lord, I spread my hands out to you;
I thirst for you like dry ground:

Teach me to do your will, for you are
my God;
let your good Spirit lead me in safety.

You require sincerity and truth in me:
fill my mind with your wisdom.

Create in me a pure heart, O God;
and renew a faithful spirit in me.

Do not cast me from your presence,
or take your Holy Spirit from me.

Give me again the joy of your salvation,
and make me willing to obey. Amen.

from Psalms 143 and 51

The Holy Spirit (310–312)

PSALM

1 How great is God almighty
and how worthy to be praised,
for the city of our holy God
shall make the world amazed;
his mountain ever beautiful
before our vision raised –
the Joy of all the earth!
Glory be to God the Father,
glory be to God the Saviour,
glory to the Holy Spirit,
for ever, Three-in-One!

2 In Zion city God himself
will be our sure defence –
all the kings of earth
who ever reigned
are stripped of vain pretence;
they see his throne in glory
and in fear they scatter thence –
the Power of all the earth!
Glory be to God . . .

3 Like eastward wind
your mighty arm
will sweep your foes away;
we have seen fulfilled in Zion
all the truth of what you say:
we think of your eternal love
and worship every day
the Praise of all the earth!
Glory be to God . . .

4 The day shall come at last
when every wrong is turned to right;
we shall see in Zion's citadel
the ending of the night:
in every generation
we are passing on his light –
the God of all the earth!
Glory be to God . . .

from Psalm 48
© Richard Bewes/Jubilate Hymns

CANTICLE

1 The Spirit came, as promised,
in God's appointed hour;
and now to each believer
he comes in love and power:
and by his Holy Spirit,
God seals us as his own;
and through the Son and Spirit
makes access to his throne.

2 The Spirit makes our bodies
the temple of the Lord;
he binds us all together
in faith and true accord:
the Spirit in his greatness,
brings power from God above;
and with the Son and Father
dwells in our hearts in love.

3 He bids us live together
in unity and peace,
employ his gifts in blessing,
and let base passions cease:
we should not grieve the Spirit
by open sin or shame;
nor let our words and actions
deny his holy name.

4 The word, the Spirit's weapon,
will bring all sin to light;
and prayer, by his directing,
will add new joy and might:
be filled then with his Spirit,
live out God's will and word;
rejoice with hymns and singing,
make music to the Lord!

from Ephesians 1, 2, 5 and 6
J E Seddon (1915–1983)
© Mrs M Seddon/Jubilate Hymns

(313–314) The Holy Spirit

315 Rain Song
Cry Hosanna 106

Falling, falling, gently falling,
rain from heaven so gently falling:
on the earth,
　　so parched and thirsty,
God sends down his rain.

1 Even so, Lord, send your Spirit –
fall upon the poor and weary:
those who come to you sincerely
you'll not turn away.
　Falling, falling . . .

2 'In those latter days,' the Lord says,
'I'll pour out my Spirit on all flesh;
I shall come with power among you,
you shall know my name.'
　Falling, falling . . .

3 Even so, Lord, come among us;
lead and guide and purify us
in the fire of your refining,
in the Spirit's flame.
　Falling, falling . . .

4 Thank you, Jesus, Lord of heaven,
for the gift you've freely given,
gift of love and gift of living
in the Spirit's power.
　Falling, falling . . .

from Joel 2
Betty Pulkingham
© Celebration/Thankyou Music†

316 O Holy Spirit
Jesus Praise 125

1 O Holy Spirit breathe on me,
O Holy Spirit breathe on me
and cleanse away my sin;
fill me with love within:
O Holy Spirit breathe on me!

2 O Holy Spirit fill my life,
O Holy Spirit fill my life;

take all my pride from me,
give me humility:
O Holy Spirit breathe on me!

3 O Holy Spirit make me new,
O Holy Spirit make me new,
make Jesus real to me,
give me his purity:
O Holy Spirit breathe on me!

4 O Holy Spirit wind of God,
O Holy Spirit wind of God,
give me your power today,
to live for you always:
O Holy Spirit breathe on me!

© Norman Warren/Jubilate Hymns

317 Spirit of the living God
Mission Praise 209

Spirit of the living God,
　fall afresh on me;
Spirit of the living God,
　fall afresh on me:
break me, melt me,
mould me, fill me –
Spirit of the living God,
　fall afresh on me!

Daniel Iverson
© Moody Press†

318 Spirit of the living God
Mission Praise 209

Spirit of the living God,
　move among us all;
make us one in heart and mind,
　make us one in love:
humble, caring,
selfless, sharing –
Spirit of the living God,
　fill our lives with love!

© Michael Baughen/Jubilate Hymns

The Holy Spirit (315–318)

319
This is the day
Mission Praise 239

1 This is the day, this is the day,
that the Lord has made,
    that the Lord has made;
we will rejoice, we will rejoice,
and be glad in it, and be glad in it:
    This is the day
    that the Lord has made,
    we will rejoice and be glad in it;
    this is the day, this is the day
    that the Lord has made.

2 This is the day, this is the day
when he rose again . . .

3 This is the day, this is the day
when the Spirit came . . .

from Psalm 118

320
Capetown
Hymns for Today's Church 12

CREDAL HYMN

1 God the Father caused to be
all we can or cannot see,
life itself, creative, free:
    we believe in God.

2 Christ the everlasting Word,
who for us the cross endured,
is our true and living Lord:
    we believe in God.

3 God the Spirit, as a dove
sent in mercy from above,
brings us life and power and love:
    we believe in God.

4 One-in-Three and Three-in-One!
To the Father, Spirit, Son
be all praise and honour done:
    'We believe in God!'

© Michael Perry/Jubilate Hymns

321

THEME PRAYER (COLLECT)

Almighty God,
who sent your Holy Spirit
to be the life and light of your Church:
open our hearts
    to the riches of his grace,
that we may bring forth
    the fruit of the Spirit
in love and joy and peace;
through Jesus Christ our Lord. **Amen.**

Pentecost 8 collect – ASB

322
Lübeck
Hymns for Today's Church 554(ii)

1 Holy Spirit, truth divine,
dawn upon this soul of mine:
voice of God, and inward light,
wake my spirit, clear my sight.

2 Holy Spirit, love divine,
glow within this heart of mine:
kindle every high desire,
purify me with your fire.

3 Holy Spirit, power divine,
fill and nerve this will of mine:
boldly may I always live,
bravely serve and gladly give.

4 Holy Spirit, law divine,
reign within this soul of mine:
be my law, and I shall be
firmly bound, for ever free.

5 Holy Spirit, peace divine,
still this restless heart of mine:
speak to calm this tossing sea,
grant me your tranquillity.

6 Holy Spirit, joy divine,
gladden now this heart of mine:
in the desert ways I sing –
spring, O living water, spring!

S Longfellow (1819–1892)

Spirit of holiness,
wisdom and faithfulness,
Wind of the Lord,
blowing strongly and free:
strength of our serving
and joy of our worshipping –
Spirit of God,
bring your fulness to me!

1 You came to interpret
        and teach us effectively
all that the Saviour
        has spoken and done;
to glorify Jesus
        is all your activity –
Promise and Gift
        of the Father and Son:
Spirit of holiness . . .

2 You came with your gifts
        to supply all our poverty,
pouring your love
        on the church in her need;
you came with your fruit
        for our growth to maturity,
richly refreshing the souls
        that you feed:
Spirit of holiness . . .

© Christopher Idle/Jubilate Hymns

324

FOR GOD'S SPIRIT
We pray that God's Holy Spirit may
direct our lives.

'The fruit of the Spirit is love, joy and
peace' – Father, we know that our
world needs love and harmony: come
to bless us,
and fill us with your Spirit.

'The fruit of the Spirit is patience, kindness and goodness' – Father, we know

that our world is starved of compassion
and true fellowship: come to bless us,
and fill us with your Spirit.

'The fruit of the Spirit is faithfulness,
gentleness and self-control' – Father,
we know that our world is short of
truth and justice: come to bless us,
and fill us with your Spirit.

**Send us out in his power
to live and work
        to your praise and glory;
through him to whom we belong,
Jesus Christ our Lord. Amen.**   †

based on Galatians 5

325

THANKSGIVING

We thank you, God our Father,
for sending your Holy Spirit
to guide and strengthen us,
to help us understand the Bible,
and to love and serve the Lord Jesus;
for his sake. **Amen.**   †

1 Breathe on me, breath of God:
    fill me with life anew,
    that as you love, so I may love,
    and do what you would do.

2 Breathe on me, breath of God,
    until my heart is pure,
    until my will is one with yours
    to do and to endure.

3 Breathe on me, breath of God;
    fulfil my heart's desire,
    until this earthly part of me
    glows with your heavenly fire.

The Holy Spirit (323–326)

4 Breathe on me, breath of God;
  so shall I never die,
  but live with you the perfect life
  of your eternity.

E Hatch (1835–1889)
© in this version Jubilate Hymns

327 Veni Sancte Spiritus
Hymns for Today's Church 227

1 Come, most holy Spirit, come!
  and from your celestial home
  shed a ray of light divine;
  come, O Father of the poor,
  faithful advocate and sure,
  let your radiance in us shine.

2 Heal our wounds,
    our strength renew;
  on our dryness send your dew,
  wash the stains of guilt away;
  bend the stubborn heart and will,
  melt the frozen, warm the chill,
  guide the steps that go astray.

3 Send upon us from above
  fruits of joy and peace and love,
  gentleness, humility:
  faithfulness and self-control,
  goodness, kindness fill the soul –
  give us true nobility.

4 On the faithful, who adore
  and confess you, evermore
  in your grace and power descend;
  grant your kingdom's sure reward,
  grant us your salvation, Lord,
  grant us joys that never end.

after S Langton (c. 1160–1228)
and E Caswall (1814–1878)
© in this version Jubilate Hymns

THE HOLY SPIRIT
Other items appropriate to this theme

Hymns

Holy Spirit, gracious guest	476
Jesus is Lord	286
O Breath of Life, come sweeping through us	464
O Holy Spirit, come to bless	475
Spirit of God most high	480

Songs

Father, we adore you	191
Father, we love you	336
God's Spirit is in my heart	422
Put on the sword of the Spirit	541
Spirit of God, unseen as the wind	609
The King is among us	6
There is a redeemer	228

Prayer

Let us acclaim the Lord our God (Creed)	360

Readings

The Prophecy and its Fulfilment –
  Joel 2.28–32; Acts 2.1–21
Jesus Promises the Holy Spirit –
  John 14.15–27
Life through the Spirit –
  Romans 8.1–17
The Temple of the Holy Spirit –
  1 Corinthians 3.10–23
The Fruit of the Spirit –
  Galatians 5.16–26
Sealed by the Spirit –
  Ephesians 1.1–14

(See also the section God's Gifts to the Church/Renewal 462–480, and Minister's Section 740–741, 757–759. The Lord's Prayer is printed inside the back cover.)

21 The Holiness and Majesty of God

Holy, holy, holy is the Lord Almighty; the whole earth is full of his glory.   Isaiah 6.3

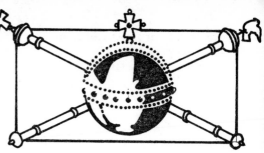

328

PRAISE

Praise the Lord, O my soul;
praise the Lord!

O Lord my God, how great you are;
robed in majesty and splendour.

Praise the Lord, O my soul;
praise the Lord! Amen.

from Psalm 104

329
Nicaea or Tersanctus
Hymns for Today's Church 7

1 Holy, holy, holy,
      Lord God almighty!
   Early in the morning
      our song of you shall be:
   holy, holy, holy,
      merciful and mighty,
   God in three persons,
      gracious Trinity!

2 'Holy, holy, holy!'
      cry the saints in glory,
   casting down their golden crowns
      before the glassy sea;
   cherubim and seraphim
      sing creation's story:
   God from of old
      to all eternity.

3 Holy, holy, holy,
      saviour of the lowly,
   here the sinner's darkened eye
      your glory may not see:
   God of earth and heaven,
      you alone are holy,
   perfect in power,
      in love and purity.

4 Holy, holy, holy,
      Lord God almighty!
   all your works shall praise your name,
      in earth and sky and sea:
   'Holy, holy, holy,
      merciful and mighty,
   God in three persons,
      glorious Trinity!'

R Heber (1783–1826)
© in this version Word & Music/Jubilate Hymns

330

CONFESSION

**O Lord our God,
enthroned on high,
filling the whole earth
   with your glory:
holy, holy, holy is your name.
Our eyes have seen the King,
the Lord almighty;
but our lips are unclean.**   →

The Holiness and Majesty of God (328–330)

**We cry to you in our sinfulness
to take our guilt away,
through Jesus Christ our Lord. Amen.** †

from Isaiah 6

The rulers of the nations come:
as subjects of our holy God.

The kings of earth belong to God:
he reigns supreme. Amen.

from Psalm 47

331

THEME PRAYER (COLLECT)

Almighty and eternal God,
you have revealed yourself
    as Father, Son, and Holy Spirit,
and live and reign
    in the perfect unity of love.
Hold us firm in this faith,
that we may know you
    in all your ways
and evermore rejoice
    in your eternal glory,
who are three Persons in one God,
now and for ever. **Amen**

Trinity Sunday collect – ASB

332

PSALM

Clap your hands, all you nations:
shout to God with cries of joy.

How awesome is the Lord most high:
**the king who rules
    the whole wide earth!**

God has ascended to his throne:
**with shouts of joy
    and sounds of trumpets.**

Sing praises to our God, sing praises:
sing praises to our king, sing praises.

For God is king of all the earth:
sing to him a psalm of praise.

God is seated on his throne:
he rules the nations of the world.

333

Savannah, Monkland
Hymns for Today's Church 150(ii), 23

PSALM

1 Sing we praise to God the king,
   Lord of splendoured majesty,
   robed with honour,
       armed with power,
   reigning through eternity:

2 Ruler from eternal years,
   founder of the land and sea,
   mightier than the roaring waves,
       God – from all eternity.

3 Firmly stands the law of God,
   honoured is his sanctuary;
   word and worship shall declare:
       'Lord for all eternity!'

from Psalm 93
© Michael Perry/Jubilate Hymns

334

In the presence of your people
Mission Praise 108

PSALM

In the presence of your people
   I will praise your name,
for you alone are holy,
   enthroned on the praises of Israel.
Let us celebrate your goodness
   and your steadfast love;
may your name be exalted
   here on earth and in heaven above!

from Psalm 22
Brent Chambers
© Scripture in Song/Thankyou Music†

(331–334) The Holiness and Majesty of God

335 Württemberg
Hymns for Today's Church 153

CANTICLE

1 Great and wonderful your deeds,
  God from whom all power proceeds:
  true and right are all your ways –
  who shall not give thanks
        and praise?
    To your name be glory!

2 King of nations, take your crown!
  every race shall soon bow down:
  holy God and Lord alone,
  justice in your deeds is shown;
    all have seen your glory.

3 To the one almighty God,
  to the Lamb who shed his blood,
  to the Spirit now be given
  by the hosts of earth and heaven;
    love and praise and glory!

from *Great and wonderful*
© Christopher Idle/Jubilate Hymns

336 Father we love you
Mission Praise 46

1 Father, we love you,
  we worship and adore you:
  glorify your name in all the earth,
    glorify your name,
    glorify your name,
  glorify your name in all the earth.

2 Jesus, we love you,
  we worship and adore you:
  glorify your name in all the earth,
    glorify your name . . .

3 Spirit, we love you,
  we worship and adore you:
  glorify your name in all the earth,
    glorify your name . . .

Donna Adkins
© Maranatha! Music (USA)/Word Music (UK)†

337 God of glory
Songs of Fellowship 2   197

God of glory, we exalt your name,
you who reign in majesty;
we lift our hearts to you
and we will worship,
      praise and magnify
your holy name.

In power resplendent
you reign in glory;
eternal King, you reign for ever:
your word is mighty,
releasing captives,
your love is gracious –
you are my God.

Dave Fellingham
© Thankyou Music†

338 Holy holy holy is the Lord
Mission Praise 74

1 Holy, holy, holy is the Lord;
  holy is the Lord God almighty!
  Holy, holy, holy is the Lord;
  holy is the Lord God almighty
    who was, and is, and is to come!
  Holy, holy, holy is the Lord!

2 Jesus, Jesus, Jesus is the Lord;
  Jesus is the Lord God almighty . . .

3 Worthy, worthy, worthy is the Lord;
  worthy is the Lord God almighty . . .

4 Glory, glory, glory to the Lord;
  glory to the Lord God almighty . . .

from Revelation 4
Copyright controlled†

The Holiness and Majesty of God (335–338)

339 Majesty
Mission Praise 151

Majesty – worship his majesty;
unto Jesus be glory,
　honour and praise!
Majesty, kingdom, authority,
flow from his throne unto his own:
　his anthem raise!
So exalt, lift upon high
　the name of Jesus;
magnify, come, glorify
　Christ Jesus the king.
Majesty – worship his majesty,
Jesus who died, now glorified,
　King of all kings!

Jack Hayford
© Rocksmith Music/Leosong Copyright Services Ltd†

340

CREED
Let us declare the universal Christian
Faith:

**We worship one God in trinity,
and trinity in unity;
neither confusing the persons
nor dividing the nature of God.
For there is one person of the Father,
another of the Son,
and another of the Holy Spirit;
but the Godhead of the Father,
of the Son, and of the Holy Spirit
　is all one –
the glory equal,
the majesty co-eternal:
what the Father is, so is the Son
and so is the Holy Spirit. Amen.**

The Athanasian Creed†

341 Westminster
Hymns for Today's Church 369

1 My God, how wonderful you are,
　your majesty how bright;
　how beautiful your mercy-seat
　in depths of burning light!

2 Creator from eternal years
　and everlasting Lord,
　by holy angels day and night
　unceasingly adored!

3 How wonderful, how beautiful
　the sight of you must be –
　your endless wisdom,
　　boundless power,
　and awesome purity!

4 O how I fear you, living God,
　with deepest, tenderest fears,
　and worship you
　　with trembling hope
　and penitential tears!

5 But I may love you too, O Lord,
　though you are all-divine,
　for you have stooped to ask of me
　this feeble love of mine.

6 Father of Jesus, love's reward,
　great king upon your throne,
　what joy to see you as you are
　and know as I am known!

F W Faber (1814–1863)
© in this version Jubilate Hymns

342 Barbara Allen
Hymns for Today's Church 4

1 My Lord of light
　　who made the worlds,
　in wisdom you have spoken;
　but those who heard
　　your wise commands
　your holy law have broken.

(339–342) The Holiness and Majesty of God

2 My Lord of love who knew no sin,
  a sinner's death enduring:
  for us you wore a crown of thorns,
  a crown of life securing.

3 My Lord of life who came in fire
  when Christ was high ascended:
  your burning love is now released,
  our days of fear are ended.

4 My Lord of lords, one Trinity,
  to your pure name be given
  all glory now and evermore,
  all praise in earth and heaven.

© Christopher Idle/Jubilate Hymns

Jesus, our Redeemer, for your humility
and your sacrifice – sharing our joys
and sorrows, dying and rising for our
salvation: we bring you our worship
and offer you thanksgiving.

Holy Spirit of God, for your guidance
and your encouragement – inspiring
and empowering the church, revealing
to us all truth: we bring you our
worship
and offer you thanksgiving.

**God of gods –
Father, Son and Holy Spirit,
eternal Lord, Three-in-One:
to you be glory, honour and praise,
for ever and ever. Amen.** †

343

FOR HOLINESS

Father, Son and Holy Spirit,
Lord of majesty,
Trinity of love and power:
accept and make holy
    all that we are,
    all that we have,
    and all that we offer you.
Keep us firm in our faith
and strong in your service;
create in us a new heart,
that we may respond
    to your great mercy:
one God, our saviour,
now and for ever. **Amen.** †

344

THANKSGIVING

Father Almighty, for your majesty and
your mercy – loving us still in our
waywardness, forgiving us in our unworthiness: we bring you our worship
and offer you thanksgiving.

345 Come Together or Tallis' Canon
Hymns for Today's Church 585/6

Praise God
    from whom all blessings flow,
in heaven above and earth below;
one God, three persons, we adore –
to him be praise for evermore!

after T Ken (1637–1710)
© in this version Jubilate Hymns

346 Capetown
Hymns for Today's Church 12

1 Three-in-One and One-in-Three,
  ruler of the earth and sea:
  hear, O mighty Trinity,
    songs of glad acclaim.

2 Light of lights, with morning shine,
  show to us your light divine;
  come, and all our love refine
    in your holy flame.

The Holiness and Majesty of God (343–346)

3 Light of lights, when falls the even,
  let it close on sins forgiven;
  keep us in the peace of heaven,
    free from guilt and blame.

4 Three-in-One and One-in-Three,
  feeble here our songs may be;
  with your saints hereafter we
    hope to praise your name.

G Rorison (1821–1869)
© in this version Word & Music/Jubilate Hymns

347

ASCRIPTION

Glory be to you, O God,
Father, Son, and Holy Spirit,
you have power, wisdom and majesty:
receive from us
honour, glory, worship and blessing.
Great and marvellous are your works,
just and true are your ways:
blessing and honour
    and glory and power
be to him who reigns upon the throne,
and to the Lamb,
through the one eternal Spirit,
now and for ever. **Amen.**

from Revelation 15

THE HOLINESS AND MAJESTY OF GOD
Other items appropriate to this theme

Hymns

Glory be to God in heaven	24
Glory in the highest	25
God the Father of creation (Credal hymn)	277
Immortal, invisible, God only wise	267
O worship the King	351

Songs

How lovely on the mountains	421
Jesus is King	169
The Lord is king, he is mighty	537
Worthy, O worthy	296
You are the king of glory	211

Prayer

Stand up and praise (Invitation to Worship)	265

Readings

Moses and the Burning Bush – Exodus 3.1–6
Holiness at Mount Sinai – Exodus 19
Psalms of Praise – Psalms 93, 96, 97
The Vision of Isaiah – Isaiah 6.1–8
The New Life and the Old – Ephesians 4.17–32
The Transfiguration of Jesus – Matthew 17.1–8; Luke 9.28–36

(See also Minister's Section 742. The Lord's Prayer is printed inside the back cover.)

22 Sea Theme/ Holidays

esus rebuked the wind and said o the waves: 'Be quiet!' The dis-:iples said: 'Who is this? Even he wind and the waves obey 1im!' Mark 4.39,41

348

PRAISE

Sing to the Lord a new song,
for he has done marvellous things!

Sing for joy to the Lord, all the earth;
**praise him with songs
and shouts of joy! Amen.**

from Psalm 98

349

APPROACH TO GOD
We have come to worship God our Father; to acknowledge his power and authority, to give thanks for his care and keeping, and to offer ourselves in the service of Christ:

He is Creator of the world:
he gives us life and breath.

He is Preserver of all life:
he sustains us day by day.

He is Redeemer of his people:
he shows us his love in Christ.

He is Lord of lords:
he controls all things.

O God our Father,
we bring you our love and praise
and give you thanks
for all your goodness,
through Jesus Christ our Lord. Amen. †

350   Melita
Hymns for Today's Church 285

1 Eternal Father, strong to save,
 whose arm restrains
  the restless wave,
 who told the mighty ocean deep
 its own appointed bounds to keep:
  we cry, O God of majesty,
  for those in peril on the sea.

2 O Christ,
  whose voice the waters heard
 and hushed their raging
  at your word,
 who walked across the surging deep
 and in the storm lay calm in sleep:
  we cry, O Lord of Galilee,
  for those in peril on the sea.

3 Creator Spirit, by whose breath
 were fashioned sea and sky
  and earth;
 who made the stormy chaos cease
 and gave us life and light and peace:
  we cry, O Spirit strong and free,
  for those in peril on the sea.

Sea Theme (348–350)

4 O Trinity of love and power,
  preserve their lives in danger's hour;
from rock and tempest,
    flood and flame,
protect them by your holy name,
  and to your glory let there be
  glad hymns of praise
    from land and sea.

W Whiting (1825–1878)
© in this version Jubilate Hymns

351 Hanover
Hymns for Today's Church 24

1 O worship the King
    all-glorious above,
and gratefully sing
    his power and his love,
our shield and defender,
    the Ancient of Days,
pavilioned in splendour
    and girded with praise.

2 O tell of his might
    and sing of his grace,
whose robe is the light,
    whose canopy space;
his chariots of wrath
    the deep thunder-clouds form,
and dark is his path
    on the wings of the storm.

3 The earth, with its store
    of wonders untold,
Almighty, your power
    has founded of old,
established it fast
    by a changeless decree,
and round it has cast
    like a mantle the sea.

4 Your bountiful care
    what tongue can recite?
it breathes in the air,
    it shines in the light;

it streams from the hills,
    it descends to the plain,
and sweetly distils
    in the dew and the rain.

5 We children of dust
    are feeble and frail –
in you we will trust,
    for you never fail;
your mercies how tender,
    how firm to the end,
our maker, defender,
    redeemer and friend!

6 O measureless Might,
    unchangeable Love,
whom angels delight
    to worship above:
your ransomed creation
    with glory ablaze,
in true adoration
    shall sing to your praise!

from Psalm 104
after W Kethe (died 1594)
R Grant (1779–1838)

352

CONFESSION

**Almighty God, our heavenly Father,
we have sinned against you,
through our own fault,
in thought and word and deed,
and in what we have left undone.
For your Son
    our Lord Jesus Christ's sake,
forgive us all that is past;
and grant that we may serve you
    in newness of life
to the glory of your name. Amen.**

Alternative Confession – ASB

(351–352) Sea Theme

353

PSALM

Give thanks to the Lord, for he is good:
his love endures for ever.

Repeat these words in praise to the Lord:
all those he has redeemed.

Some sailed the ocean in ships:
they earned their way on the seas.

They saw what the Lord can do:
his wonderful deeds in the deep.

For he spoke and stirred up a storm:
and lifted high the waves.

Their ships were thrown in the air:
and plunged into the depths.

Their courage melted away:
they reeled like drunken men.

They came to the end of themselves:
and cried to the Lord in their trouble.

He brought them out of distress:
and stilled the raging storm.

They were glad because of the calm:
he brought them safely to harbour.

Let them give thanks to the Lord:
for his unfailing love. Amen.

from Psalm 107

354 Golden Sheaves
Hymns for Today's Church 291

PSALM

1 Come, join to praise
   our God and king,
   his glories all-excelling:
   the heavenly hosts
   his wonders sing,
   his mercies we are telling!

His arm is stronger than the sea –
   he calms its fitful anger;
he comes to set his people free,
   and rescues us from danger.

2 For all who trust his saving name
   are happy in believing;
they know his presence every day,
   his kindnesses receiving.
His kingdom stands
   on righteousness,
   with justice as foundation:
so praise our God, our victory,
   our song, our celebration!

from Psalm 89
© Michael Perry/Jubilate Hymns

355 Kingly majesty
Psalm Praise 110

PSALM

1 Clothed in kingly majesty,
   robed in regal power,
      God is over all.

2 Lord of all, unshakeable,
   throned beyond all time,
      God is over all.

3 Greater than the river's roar
   and the surging sea,
      God is over all.

4 Changeless as his law's decrees,
   crowned our holy king,
      God is over all.

From Psalm 93
© Michael Saward/Jubilate Hymns

Sea Theme (353–355)

CANTICLE

1 Jesus, Saviour of the world,
    you have bought
        your people's freedom:
    by your cross, your life laid down,
    now bring in
        your glorious kingdom.
        Come to help us!

2 Christ, who once on Galilee
    came to your disciples' rescue:
    we, like them, cry out for help –
    free us from our sins, we ask you.
        Come to save us!

3 Lord, make known
        your promised power;
    show yourself our strong deliverer:
    so our prayer shall turn to praise –
    hear us, stay with us for ever.
        Come to rule us!

4 When you come, Lord Jesus Christ,
    filling earth and heaven
        with wonder,
    come to make us one with you –
    heirs of life, to reign in splendour.
        Alleluia!

from *Saviour of the world*
© Christopher Idle/Jubilate Hymns

Wide, wide as the ocean,
high as the heaven above;
deep, deep as the deepest sea
    is my Saviour's love:
I, though so unworthy,
still am a child of his care;
for his word teaches me
that his love reaches me
    everywhere.

©The Rodeheaver Company/Word Music (UK)†

(356–360) Sea Theme

The grace of the Lord,
    like a fathomless sea,
    sufficient for you, sufficient for me,
is tender and patient
    and boundless and free,
    sufficient for every need.

J S Holden
Copyright controlled†

I am a new creation,
no more in condemnation,
    here in the grace of God I stand;
my heart is overflowing,
my love just keeps on growing,
    here in the grace of God I stand:
and I will praise you, Lord,
yes I will praise you, Lord,
and I will sing
    of all that you have done.

A joy that knows no limit,
a lightness in my spirit –
    here in the grace of God I stand.

from 2 Corinthians 5
Dave Bilbrough
© Thankyou Music†

360

CREED
Let us acclaim the Lord our God:

**We believe in God
the eternal Father;
heaven and earth are full of his glory.**

**We believe in Jesus Christ,
his true and only Son;
he became man to set us free.**

We believe in the Holy Spirit;
he is our advocate and guide.

We believe in one God:
Father, Son, and Holy Spirit. Amen. †

from *Te Deum*

361

THEME PRAYER (COLLECT)

Almighty God,
you led your people through the sea,
and made a path for them
    in deep waters:
be near all those
who face the dangers of the seas;
protect them from disaster,
help them on their way,
and bring them safely
    to their desired haven
with hearts thankful for your mercy;
through Jesus Christ our Lord. **Amen.**

after the Scottish Prayer Book

362 St Aëlred
Baptist Hymn Book 117
Ancient and Modern R313 NS225

1 Fierce raged the tempest!
    On the deep
  watch did your anxious
      servants keep;
but you were wrapped
    in guileless sleep –
    calm and still.

2 'Save, Lord, we perish,'
    was their cry,
 'O save us in our agony!'
Your word
    above the storm rose high,
    'Peace, be still!'

3 The wild winds hushed,
    the angry deep
sank like a little child to sleep;
the sullen ocean ceased to leap,
    at your will.

4 So, when our life's fierce tempests
    roar
  and storm winds
      keep us from the shore,
say – lest we sink to rise no more –
    'Peace, be still!'

from Mark 4
J B Dykes (1823–1876)
© in this version Word & Music/Jubilate Hymns

363

FOR TRAVELLERS

O God, our Father,
we commend to your keeping
those who travel by land or sea or air:
give them your protection
    on their way,
and bring them safely to their
    journey's end;
through Jesus Christ our Lord. **Amen.** †

364

THANKSGIVING
We thank God for the wonderful world
he has given to us, and for all his love
and care:

For the warmth of the sun: O loving
Father,
we give you thanks and praise.

For the rain which makes things grow:
O loving Father,
we give you thanks and praise. →

For the woods and the fields: O loving Father,
we give you thanks and praise.

For the sea and the sky: O loving Father,
we give you thanks and praise.

For the flowers and the animals: O loving Father,
we give you thanks and praise.

For families and holidays: O loving Father,
we give you thanks and praise.

For all your gifts: O loving Father,
we give you thanks and praise.

**Everything around us rejoices,
therefore give us joyful hearts
to praise you in your glory;
through Jesus Christ our Lord. Amen.** †

365* Mannheim
Hymns for Today's Church 525

1 Lead us, heavenly Father, lead us
  through this world's
      tempestuous sea;
  guard us, guide us,
      keep us, feed us,
  now and to eternity:
  here possessing every blessing
  if our God our Father be.

2 Saviour, by your grace restore us –
  all our weaknesses are plain;
  you have lived on earth before us,
  you have felt our grief and pain:
  tempted, taunted, yet undaunted,
  from the depths you rose again.

3 Spirit of our God, descending,
  fill our hearts with holy peace;
  love with every passion blending,
  pleasure that can never cease:
  thus provided, pardoned, guided,
  ever shall our joys increase.

J Edmeston (1791–1867)
© in this version Jubilate Hymns

(*See other version at number 111)

SEA THEME/HOLIDAYS
Other items appropriate to this theme

Hymns
For the beauty of the earth   182
Not the grandeur of the mountains   382

Psalm Version (sung)
Let us sing to the God of salvation
    (Psalm 95)   186

Prayers
O Lord, open our eyes to see   176
Heavenly Father, we thank you
    (Thanksgiving)   385

Lord Jesus Christ, we give
    ourselves (Dedication)   32

Readings
Crossing the Red Sea –
    Exodus 13.17–14.31
Moses' Song of Praise – Exodus 15
The Soul that Longs for God – Psalm 42
Rest and Refreshment –
    Mark 6.30–34
Walking on the Water –
    Matthew 14.22–33; Mark 6.45–51

(See also Minister's Section 743–746. The
Lord's Prayer is printed inside the back
cover.)

(365) Sea Theme

23 God's Love to Us

God so loved the world that he gave his only Son, that whoever believes in him shall not perish but have eternal life. John 3.16

366

PRAISE

It is good to praise you, Lord,
and make music to your name:

To proclaim your constant love in the morning,
**and tell your faithfulness
in the evening:**

For you, O Lord, are exalted for ever.
Amen.

from Psalm 92

367
Old 100th
Hymns for Today's Church 14

1 All people that on earth do dwell
sing to the Lord with cheerful voice:
serve him with joy, his praises tell,
come now before him and rejoice!

2 Know that the Lord is God indeed,
he formed us all without our aid;
we are the flock he loves to feed,
the sheep who by his hand
are made.

3 O enter then his gates with praise,
and in his courts his love proclaim;
give thanks and bless him
all your days:
let every tongue confess his name.

4 The Lord our mighty God is good,
his mercy is for ever sure;
his truth at all times firmly stood,
and shall from age to age endure.

5 Praise God the Father, God the Son,
and God the Spirit evermore;
all praise to God the Three-in-One,
let heaven rejoice and earth adore!

from Psalm 100 (Jubilate)
W Kethe (died 1594)
© in this version Jubilate Hymns

368
Personent Hodie
Hymns for Today's Church 311

1 God is love – his the care,
tending each, everywhere;
God is love – all is there!
Jesus came to show him,
that mankind might know him:
Sing aloud, loud, loud;
sing aloud, loud, loud:
God is good,
God is truth, God is beauty –
praise him!

2 Jesus shared all our pain,
lived and died, rose again,
rules our hearts, now as then –
for he came to save us
by the truth he gave us:
Sing aloud . . .

God's Love to Us (366–368)

3 To our Lord praise we sing –
   light and life, friend and king,
   coming down love to bring,
   pattern for our duty,
   showing God in beauty:
       Sing aloud, loud, loud;
       sing aloud, loud, loud:
       God is good,
       God is truth, God is beauty –
           praise him!

P Dearmer (1867–1936)
omitting former verse 2
© Oxford University Press†

369

CONFESSION

Almighty God, we confess that too often we have taken the easy way of the world, rather than your way, and so have grieved your heart of love.

We have been slow to admit that we are not our own, but belong to you: in your mercy,
forgive us and help us.

We have been unwilling to see that we are bought with the price of Christ's blood: in your mercy,
forgive us and help us.

We have been unprepared to live out our lives as your servants: in your mercy,
forgive us and help us.

Raise us by the power of your love, and fill us with the joy of your Spirit; through Jesus Christ our Lord. Amen. †

370

PSALM

Your love, O Lord, reaches to the heavens,
your faithfulness to the skies.

Your righteousness is like the mighty mountains,
your justice like the great deep.

How precious is your love, O God;
we find shelter beneath your wings.

We feast on the food you provide,
**we drink
    from the river of your goodness:**

For with you is the fountain of life;
in your light we see light. Amen.

from Psalm 36

371

PSALM

Praise the Lord, all you nations:
praise him, all you people!

Great is his love towards us:
his faithfulness shall last for ever.

Praise the Lord: **Amen.**

Psalm 117

372   All Saints or Timeless Love
Hymns for Today's Church 215, 47(ii)

PSALM

1 Timeless love! We sing the story,
   praise his wonders, tell his worth;
   love more fair than heaven's glory,
   love more firm than ancient earth!
       Tell his faithfulness abroad:
       who is like him? Praise the Lord!

2 By his faithfulness surrounded,
   north and south his hand proclaim;

earth and heaven formed
and founded,
skies and seas, declare his name!
Wind and storm obey his word:
who is like him? Praise the Lord!

Truth and righteousness
enthrone him,
just and equal are his ways;
more than happy,
those who own him,
more than joy, their songs of praise!
Sun and shield and great reward:
who is like him? Praise the Lord!

from Psalm 89
© Timothy Dudley-Smith

73 The steadfast love of the Lord
Mission Praise 229

CANTICLE

The steadfast love of the Lord
never ceases,
his mercies never come to an end;
they are new every morning,
new every morning:
great is your faithfulness, O Lord,
great is your faithfulness!

The Lord is my portion,
says my soul,
therefore I will hope in him.
The steadfast love . . .

The Lord is good
to those who wait for him,
to the soul that seeks him:
it is good that we should
wait quietly
for the salvation of the Lord.
The steadfast love . . .

The Lord will not cast off for ever,
but will have compassion:
for he does not willingly afflict
or grieve the sons of men.
The steadfast love . . .

4 So let us examine all our ways,
and return to the Lord:
let us lift up our hearts and hands
to God in heaven.
The steadfast love . . .

from Psalm 37, Lamentations 3 etc
Edith McNeill
© Celebration/Thankyou Music†

374 Jesus' love is very wonderful
Jesus Praise 88

Jesus' love is very wonderful,
Jesus' love is very wonderful,
Jesus' love is very wonderful:
O wonderful love!

So high you can't get over it,
so low you can't get under it,
so wide you can't get round it:
O wonderful love!
Jesus' love . . .

H W Rattle
© Scripture Union†

375 * We will praise, we will praise
Church Family Worship Source Book

We will praise, we will praise,
we will praise the Lord,
we will praise the Lord
because he is good;
we will praise, we will praise,
we will praise the Lord,
because his love is everlasting.
We will praise . . .
Bring on the trumpets and harps,
let's hear the cymbals ring –
then in harmony,
lift our voices and sing, sing.
We will praise . . .

Ian Smale
© Thankyou Music†

(*Written for children to sing)

God's Love to Us (373–375)

376
O how good is the Lord
Jesus Praise 30

O how good is the Lord,
O how good is the Lord,
O how good is the Lord:
I never will forget
  what he has done for me!

1 He gives me salvation –
    how good is the Lord,
  he gives me salvation –
    how good is the Lord,
  he gives me salvation –
    how good is the Lord:
  I never will forget
    what he has done for me!
  O how good . . .

2 He gives me his blessings . . .
  O how good . . .

3 He gives me his Spirit . . .
  O how good . . .

4 He gives me his healing . . .
  O how good . . .

5 He gives me his glory . . .
  O how good . . .

377
God is good
Songs of Fellowship 3   372

God is good – we sing and shout it,
God is good – we celebrate;
God is good – no more we doubt it,
God is good – we know it's true!

And when I think of his love for me,
my heart fills with praise
and I feel like dancing;
for in his heart there is room for me,
and I run with arms open wide.
  God is good . . .

Graham Kendrick
© Thankyou Music†

378
Sing his praises
Jesus Praise 41

Sing his praises:
heaven raises
  songs of him who died for me;
his the glory,
mine the story
  of the love which sets me free;
love which never will deceive me,
love which never lets me go:
who can measure
half the treasure
  of his love, who loves me so!

M Cox

379
He is love
Hymns for Today's Church S21

1 Praise him, praise him,
  everybody praise him –
    he is love, he is love;
  praise him, praise him,
  everybody praise him –
    God is love, God is love!

2 Thank him, thank him,
  everybody thank him –
    he is love, he is love;
  thank him, thank him,
  everybody thank him –
    God is love, God is love!

3 Love him, love him,
  everybody love him –
    he is love, he is love;
  love him, love him,
  everybody love him –
    God is love, God is love!

4 Alleluia,
  glory, alleluia –
    he is love, he is love!
  Alleluia,
  glory, alleluia –
    God is love, God is love!

Unknown (c1890)
© in this version Jubilate Hymns

(376–379) God's Love to Us

380

CREED

**We believe in God the Father,
who reveals his love to us in Christ.**

**We believe in God the Son,
who pours out his Holy Spirit on us.**

**We believe in the Holy Spirit,
who teaches us God's truth.**

**We believe in one God:
Father, Son, and Holy Spirit. Amen.** †

after 1 John

381

THEME PRAYER ('COLLECT')

**Eternal God and Father,
you create us by your power
and redeem us by your love:
guide and strengthen us
by your Spirit,
that we may give ourselves
in love and service
to one another and to you;
through Jesus Christ our Lord. Amen.**

from Morning Prayer – ASB

382
Everton
Hymn's for Today's Church 511

1 Not the grandeur of the mountains,
nor the splendour of the sea,
can excel the ceaseless wonder
of my Saviour's love to me:
for his love to me is faithful,
and his mercy is divine;
and his truth is everlasting,
and his perfect peace is mine.

2 Not the streams that fill the valleys,
nor the clouds that drift along,
can delight me more than Jesus
or replace my grateful song:
for his love . . .

3 Yet these all convey his beauty
and proclaim his power and grace –
for they are among the tokens
of the love upon his face:
for his love . . .

© Michael Perry/Jubilate Hymns

383
Contemplation
Hymns for Today's Church 39

1 When all your mercies, O my God,
my thankful soul surveys,
uplifted by the view, I'm lost
in wonder, love and praise.

2 Unnumbered blessings to my soul
your tender care bestowed
before my infant heart perceived
from whom these blessings flowed.

3 Ten thousand thousand
precious gifts
my daily thanks employ;
nor is the least a thankful heart
that takes those gifts with joy.

4 In health and sickness, joy and pain,
your goodness I'll pursue;
and after death, in distant worlds,
the glorious theme renew.

5 Throughout eternity, O Lord,
a joyful song I'll raise;
but all eternity's too short
to utter all your praise!

J Addison (1672–1719)
© in this version Jubilate Hymns

God's Love to Us (380–383)

384

WE RESPOND TO GOD'S LOVE

O God,
we are your children and you love us:
so deep is your love
that nothing we have done,
   or thought to do,
can take away the peace you give;
so strong is your love
that no passing trouble
   shall tear us from your arms;
so precious is your love
that all our life
   shall be lived in your service –
and yours shall be the glory,
through Jesus Christ our Lord. **Amen.** †

385

THANKSGIVING

Heavenly Father, we thank you
for the beauty of the world around us;
for the love of parents and friends,
for work and play,
   for food and clothes,
for happiness, laughter and fun.
But most of all we thank you
   for your redeeming grace:
for the birth of Jesus Christ your Son,
for the example of his life,
and the love
   which made him die for us.
Help us to serve him faithfully
   all our days. **Amen.**   †

386 Blaenwern, Abbot's Leigh
Hymns for Today's Church 217(i), 494(ii)

1 God is love: let heaven adore him!
   God is love: let earth rejoice!
   Let creation sing before him
      and exalt him with one voice:
he who laid the earth's foundations,
   he who spread
      the heavens above,
he who breathes
      through all creation –
   he is love, eternal love!

2 God is love, and he enfolds us,
   all the world in one embrace;
with unfailing grasp he holds us,
   every child of every race:
and when human hearts
      are breaking
   under sorrow's iron rod,
then they find the self-same aching
   deep within the heart of God.

3 God is love;
      and though with blindness
   sin afflicts these human hearts,
God's eternal loving-kindness
   never from his world departs:
death and hell and Satan never
   shall their final triumph gain:
God is love, and love for ever
   through his universe shall reign.

T Rees (1874–1939)
© A R Mowbray & Co. Ltd.†,
in this version Word & Music/Jubilate Hymns

387 Blaenwern or Love Divine
Hymns for Today's Church 217

1 Love divine, all loves excelling,
   joy of heaven, to earth come down:
   fix in us your humble dwelling,
   all your faithful mercies crown.

2 Jesus, you are all compassion,
   pure, unbounded love impart;
   visit us with your salvation,
   enter every trembling heart.

3 Come, almighty to deliver,
   let us all your grace receive;
   suddenly return, and never,
   never more your temples leave.

(384–387) God's Love to Us

4 We would always give you blessing,
  serve you as your hosts above,
  pray, and praise you
        without ceasing,
  glory in your perfect love.

5 Finish then your new creation:
  pure and spotless let us be;
  let us see your great salvation,
  perfect in eternity:

6 Changed from glory into glory
  till in heaven we take our place,
  there to sing salvation's story
  lost in wonder, love and praise!

C Wesley (1707–1788)
© in this version Word & Music/Jubilate Hymns

God's Love to Us (387)

24 Invitation to Faith

The Lord says, 'I stand at the door and knock; if anyone hears my voice and opens the door, I will come in.' Revelation 3.20

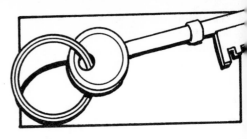

388

PRAISE

Give thanks to the Lord, for he is good;
his love endures for ever.

Tell of all his mighty acts;
and make his praises heard.

Praise be to the Lord, the God of Israel:
from everlasting to everlasting.

Let all the people say, 'Amen':
Amen, praise the Lord!

from Psalm 106

389* Sagina
Hymns for Today's Church 452

1 And can it be that I should gain
an interest in the Saviour's blood?
Died he for me,
who caused his pain;
for me, who him to death pursued?
Amazing love! – how can it be
that you, my God,
should die for me?

2 What mystery here!
– the Immortal dies;
who can explore his strange design?
In vain the first-born seraph tries
to sound the depths of love divine.
Such mercy this! – let earth adore;
let angel minds enquire no more.

3 He left his Father's throne above –
so free, so infinite his grace –
emptied himself of all but love,
and bled for Adam's helpless race.
What mercy this, immense and free,
for, O my God, it found out me!

4 Long my imprisoned spirit lay,
fast bound in sin and nature's night:
your sunrise
turned that night to day;
I woke –
the dungeon flamed with light.
My chains fell off,
my heart was free;
I rose, went out to liberty!

5 No condemnation now I dread;
Jesus, and all in him, is mine!
Alive in him, my living head,
and clothed in righteousness divine,
bold I approach the eternal throne
and claim the crown
through Christ my own.

C Wesley (1707–1788)

(*Verse 4 may be omitted.)

390 Living Lord
Hymns for Today's Church 417

1 Lord Jesus Christ,
you have come to us,
you are one with us, Mary's son;

cleansing our souls
    from all their sin,
pouring your love and goodness in:
Jesus, our love for you we sing –
    living Lord!

At communion, this may be sung:

2 Lord Jesus Christ,
    now and every day
teach us how to pray, Son of God;
you have commanded us to do
this in remembrance, Lord, of you:
into our lives
    your power breaks through –
    living Lord!

3 Lord Jesus Christ,
    you have come to us,
born as one of us, Mary's son;
led out to die on Calvary,
risen from death to set us free:
living Lord Jesus, help us see
    you are Lord!

4 Lord Jesus Christ,
    I would come to you,
live my life for you, Son of God;
all your commands I know are true,
your many gifts will make me new:
into my life your power breaks
    through – living Lord!

Patrick Appleford
© *Josef Weinberger Limited†*

391

CONFESSION

Let us confess our sins to God and ask
for his forgiveness:

For all the wrong things we have done:
in your mercy,
forgive us, O God.

For forgetting what we ought to have
remembered, for failing to do as we
promised, for turning away when we
should have listened, for being careless

when we should have been diligent: in
your mercy,
forgive us, O God.

For doing things we knew would
annoy, for acting in ways we knew
would hurt, for behaving in ways we
knew would disappoint: in your
mercy,
forgive us, O God.

O God, when we look back we can see
how foolish and wrong we have been.
Forgive us, and help us not to do the
same things again; through Jesus
Christ our Lord. **Amen.**
         †

392

PSALM

I waited patiently for the Lord:
he turned and heard my cry.

He pulled me out of the slimy pit:
out of the mud and mire.

He set my feet upon a rock:
and made my step secure.

He put a new song in my mouth:
a hymn of praise to God.

Many will see and fear:
and put their trust in the Lord. Amen.

from Psalm 40

393   Response Psalm
      Church Family Worship Source Book

PSALM/CANTICLE

Come let us sing to the Lord!
come let us . . .

Give a joyful shout in honour of the
Rock of our salvation:
give a joyful . . .   →

Invitation to Faith (391–393)

Come before him with thankful hearts:
come before him . . .

Let us sing to him psalms of praise:
let us sing . . .

For the Lord is a great God:
for the Lord . . .

And a great king above all gods:
and a great . . .

He controls the formation of the depths
of the earth and the mighty mountains:
he controls . . .

All are his!
all are his.

He made the sea and formed the land:
he made . . .

They too are his:
they too . . .

Come, kneel before the Lord our maker
for he is our God:
come, kneel . . .

We are his sheep and he is our
shepherd:
we are his . . .

O that you would hear him calling you
today:
O that you . . .

And come to him!
and come . . .

from Psalm 95 (*Venite*)
© Scott Willcox

394 Alton, Cross of Jesus
Hymns for Today's Church 52

PSALM

1 Lord all-knowing,
   you have found me;
every secret thought and word,
all my actions, all my longings
you have seen and you have heard.

2 Lord almighty, you have made me,
fashioned me to keep your laws;
your design and your creation –
every part of me is yours.

3 Lord all-holy, you have judged me
by a standard true and right;
all the best I have to offer
withers in your burning light.

4 Lord all-loving, you have saved me
in supreme and mighty grace;
by your Son's triumphant mercy,
suffering, dying in my place.

5 Lord all-glorious, you receive me
where your ransomed servants sing;
you have spoken,
   rescued, conquered,
Christ, our prophet, priest,
   and king!

from Psalm 139
Christopher Idle/Jubilate Hymns

395 Creator God
Hymns for Today's Church 445(i)

PSALM

1 Safe in the shadow of the Lord
beneath his hand and power,
   I trust in him,
   I trust in him,
my fortress and my tower.

2 My hope is set on God alone
though Satan spreads his snare,
   I trust in him,
   I trust in him,
to keep me in his care.

3 From fears and phantoms
      of the night,
from foes about my way,
   I trust in him,
   I trust in him,
by darkness as by day.

(394–395) Invitation to Faith

His holy angels keep my feet
secure from every stone;
   I trust in him,
   I trust in him,
and unafraid go on.

Strong in the everlasting name,
and in my Father's care,
   I trust in him,
   I trust in him,
who hears and answers prayer.

Safe in the shadow of the Lord,
possessed by love divine,
   I trust in him,
   I trust in him,
and meet his love with mine.

from Psalm 91
© Timothy Dudley-Smith

396 God is so good
Jesus Praise 56

God is so good,
God is so good,
God is so good:
   he's so good to me.

He took my sin,
he took my sin,
he took my sin:
   he's so good to me.

Now I am free,
now I am free,
now I am free:
   he's so good to me.

God is so good,
he took my sin,
now I am free:
   he's so good to me.

Copyright controlled†

397* Salvation is found
Church Family Worship Source Book

Salvation is found in no-one else,
for there is no other name under
   heaven given to us
by which we must be saved;
under heaven given to us
by which we must be saved.

Acts 4.12
Mick Gisbey
© Thankyou Music†

(*Written for children to sing)

398 Nothing but the love
Jesus Praise 96

1 Nothing but the love of Jesus –
   we have to sing about it;
nothing but the love of Jesus –
   we have to talk about it!
Nothing but the love of Jesus
   is changing the way we live;
nothing but the love of Jesus,
his good news of peace and joy –
   that's all we've got to give.
Do you know, do you know him;
do you love, do you love him?

Keith Routledge
© Kenwood Music/Word Music (UK)†

399 Abba Father
Mission Praise 1

Abba, Father, let me be
   yours and yours alone;
may my will for ever be,
   evermore your own.
Never let my heart grow cold,
   never let me go:
Abba, Father, let me be
   yours and yours alone!

Dave Bilborough
© Thankyou Music†

Invitation to Faith (396–399)

400

Jesus, I worship you
Jesus Praise 82

1 Jesus I worship you,
  Jesus I worship you,
  Jesus I worship you,
  Son of God:
    You came from heaven above
    to bring the Father's love:
    Jesus I worship you,
    Son of God!

2 Jesus I trust in you,
  Jesus I trust in you,
  Jesus I trust in you,
  Son of God:
    You died on Calvary
    to set my Spirit free:
    Jesus I trust in you,
    Son of God!

3 Jesus I feed on you,
  Jesus I feed on you,
  Jesus I feed on you,
  Son of God:
    You are the living bread,
    you meet my every need:
    Jesus I feed on you,
    Son of God!

4 Jesus I love you,
  Jesus I love you,
  Jesus I love you,
  Son of God:
    I give myself to you,
    lay down my life for you;
    Jesus I love you,
    Son of God!

© Norman Warren/Jubilate Hymns

401

Praise the name of Jesus
Mission Praise 189

Praise the name of Jesus,
praise the name of Jesus –
  he's my rock,
  he's my fortress,
he's my deliverer,
in him will I trust:
praise the name of Jesus!

Roy Hicks
© Latter Rain Music USA/Word Music (UK)†

402

Londonderry Air
Hymns for Today's Church 194

For God so loved the world
  he gave his only Son,
who came to die
  that we might ever live;
and on a cruel cross
  our full redemption won,
that we might know
  the peace he longs to give:
though he was rich,
  he came alone and poor for us;
though he was Lord,
  he served as if a slave;
though he was God,
  our human shape he bore for us;
to earth he came in love,
  his own to seek and save.

from John 3, 2 Corinthians 8 and Philippians 2
© Word & Music/Jubilate Hymns

403

Reign in me
Spirit of Praise 2   351

Reign in me, sovereign Lord,
  reign in me;
reign in me, sovereign Lord,
  reign in me –
captivate my heart,
let your kingdom come,
establish there your throne,
let your will be done.

Chris Bowater
© Word Music (UK)*

(400–403) Invitation to Faith

404

All for Jesus
Hymns for Today's Church 434

CREDAL HYMN

1 I believe in God the Father
who created heaven and earth,
source of wisdom and of power,
bringing light and life to birth.

2 I believe in God the Saviour,
Son of Man and Lord most high,
crucified to be redeemer,
raised to life that death may die.

3 I believe in God the Spirit,
wind of heaven and flame of fire,
pledge of all that we inherit,
sent to comfort and inspire.

4 Honour, glory, might and merit
be to God, and God alone!
Father, Son and Holy Spirit,
One-in-Three and Three-in-One.

© Michael Perry/Jubilate Hymns

405

THEME PRAYER (COLLECT)

Merciful Lord,
grant to your faithful people
pardon and peace:
that we may be cleansed
from all our sins
and serve you with a quiet mind;
through Jesus Christ our Lord. **Amen.**

Seventh Sunday before Easter collect – ASB

406

Bullinger
Hymns for Today's Church 433

1 I am trusting you, Lord Jesus,
you have died for me;
trusting you for full salvation
great and free.

2 I am trusting you for pardon –
at your feet I bow;
for your grace and tender mercy,
trusting now.

3 I am trusting you for cleansing,
Jesus, Son of God;
trusting you to make me holy
by your blood.

4 I am trusting you to guide me –
you alone shall lead;
every day and hour supplying
all my need.

5 I am trusting you for power –
yours can never fail;
words which you yourself
shall give me
must prevail.

6 I am trusting you, Lord Jesus –
never let me fall;
I am trusting you for ever,
and for all.

F R Havergal (1836–1879)

407

Old Yeavering or Quem pastores laudavere
Hymns for Today's Church 32

1 Like a mighty river flowing,
like a flower in beauty growing,
far beyond all human knowing
is the perfect peace of God.

2 Like the hills serene and even,
like the coursing clouds of heaven,
like the heart that's been forgiven
is the perfect peace of God.

3 Like the summer breezes playing,
like the tall trees softly swaying,
like the lips of silent praying
is the perfect peace of God.

Invitation to Faith (404–407)

4 Like the morning sun ascended,
   like the scents of evening blended,
   like a friendship never ended
       is the perfect peace of God.

5 Like the azure ocean swelling,
   like the jewel all-excelling,
   far beyond our human telling
       is the perfect peace of God.

© Michael Perry/Jubilate Hymns

408

WE ASK FOR GOD'S FORGIVENESS

**Most merciful God and Father,
give us true repentance for our sins.
Open our eyes
to recognise the truth
    about ourselves;
so that acknowledging our faults,
our weaknesses, and our failures,
we may receive your forgiveness,
and find in your love
the encouragement
    to make a new beginning;
for the sake of Jesus Christ our Lord.
Amen.**   †

409

A PRAYER OF INDIVIDUAL FAITH

Lord Jesus, my saviour,
my heart is cold,
    warm it by your selfless love,
my heart is sinful,
    cleanse it by your precious blood,
my heart is weak,

strengthen it by your joyful Spirit,
my heart is empty,
    fill it with your divine presence;
Lord Jesus,
my heart is yours,
possess it always and only
    for yourself. **Amen.**   †

410

THANKSGIVING
Heavenly Father, we come before you
with thanksgiving for all your mercy
and your grace:

For the beauty of the world around us,
we bring you our love,
and give you thanks and praise.

For our parents and our families,
we bring you our love,
and give you thanks and praise.

For work and play, for food and
clothes, we bring you our love,
and give you thanks and praise.

For the joy of friends, and for the
happiness we share, we bring you our
love,
and give you thanks and praise.

But most of all, for your Son Jesus
Christ, for his wonderful birth, for the
example of his life, for his death on the
cross to save us, for raising him from
the dead to be our living Lord, and for
sending upon us your Holy Spirit, we
bring you our love,
and give you thanks and praise.

**Help us to serve you
gladly and faithfully all our days,
until you call us
to worship you in heaven. Amen.**   †

Just as I am, without one plea
but that you died to set me free,
and at your bidding 'Come to me!'
O Lamb of God, I come.

Just as I am, without delay
your call of mercy I obey –
your blood can wash my sins away:
O Lamb of God, I come.

Just as I am, though tossed about
with many a conflict, many a doubt,
fightings within and fears without,
O Lamb of God, I come.

Just as I am, poor, wretched, blind!
Sight, riches, healing of the mind –
all that I need, in you to find:
O Lamb of God, I come.

Just as I am! You will receive,
will welcome, pardon,
cleanse, relieve:
because your promise I believe,
O Lamb of God, I come.

Just as I am! Your love unknown
has broken every barrier down:
now to be yours, yes, yours alone,
O Lamb of God, I come.

Just as I am! Of that free love
the breadth, length, depth and
height to prove,
here for a time and then above,
O Lamb of God, I come.

C Elliott (1789–1871)
© in this version Jubilate Hymns

1 To God be the glory!
    great things he has done;
so loved he the world
    that he gave us his Son
who yielded his life
    an atonement for sin,
and opened the life-gate
    that all may go in.
    Praise the Lord, praise the Lord!
    let the earth hear his voice;
    praise the Lord, praise the Lord!
    let the people rejoice:
    O come to the Father
    through Jesus the Son
    and give him the glory;
    great things he has done.

2 O perfect redemption,
    the purchase of blood!
To every believer
    the promise of God:
the vilest offender
    who truly believes,
that moment from Jesus
    a pardon receives.
    Praise the Lord . . .

3 Great things he has taught us,
    great things he has done,
and great our rejoicing
    through Jesus the Son:
but purer and higher and
    greater will be
our wonder, our gladness,
    when Jesus we see!
    Praise the Lord . . .

F J van Alstyne (1820–1915)

Invitation to Faith (411–412)

INVITATION TO FAITH
Other items appropriate to this theme

Hymns

Amazing grace	158
King of glory, king of peace	157
There is a green hill far away	219

Songs

All the way, all the way	207
One shall tell another	30
So I've made up my mind	143
The light of Christ has come	8
What a wonderful saviour is Jesus	567

Psalm and Canticle (spoken)

Happy are those who trust in God (Psalm 40)	136
The people reply (Isaiah 53)	221

Prayer

We praise you, O God and Father	13

Readings

Seek the Lord – Isaiah 55

Philip and the Ethiopian – Acts 8.26–40

Warning Against Being Lukewarm – Revelation 3.14–22

Come to Jesus – Matthew 11.25–30

One that was Lost – Luke 15

Zacchaeus Follows Jesus – Luke 19.1–10

(See also section, God's Love to Us 366–387, and Minister's Section 747–749. The Lord's Prayer is printed inside the back cover.)

25 The Missionary Church/The Worldwide Church

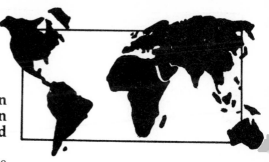

Jesus said, 'All authority in heaven and on earth has been given to me. Go therefore and make disciples of all nations.'

Matthew 28.18,19

413

PRAISE

Give thanks to the Lord, call on his name;
**make his deeds known
in the world around.**

Sing to him, sing praise to him;
**tell of the wonderful things
he has done.**

Glory in his holy name;
**let those who seek the Lord rejoice!
Amen.**

from Psalm 105

414

RESPONSE

Sing to the Lord, all the world,
for the Lord is a mighty God.

Sing a new song to the Lord,
for he has done marvellous things.

Proclaim his glory among the nations,
and shout for joy to the Lord our king!

415
Truro
Hymns for Today's Church 516

1 Jesus shall reign where'er the sun
does his successive journeys run;
his kingdom stretch
from shore to shore
till moons shall rise and set no more.

2 People and realms of every tongue
declare his love in sweetest song,
and children's voices shall proclaim
their early blessings on his name.

3 Blessings abound
where Jesus reigns –
the prisoner leaps to lose his chains,
the weary find eternal rest,
the hungry and the poor
are blessed.

4 To him shall endless prayer
be made,
and princes throng
to crown his head;
his name like incense shall arise
with every morning sacrifice.

5 Let all creation rise and bring
the highest honours to our king;
angels descend with songs again
and earth repeat the loud 'Amen!'

from Psalm 72
I Watts (1674–1748)
© in this version Jubilate Hymns

The Missionary Church (413–415)

1 God, whose almighty word
chaos and darkness heard,
and took their flight:
hear us, we humbly pray,
and where the gospel-day
sheds not its glorious ray,
let there be light!

2 Saviour, who came to bring
on your redeeming wing
healing and sight,
health to the sick in mind,
sight to the inly blind:
O now to all mankind
let there be light!

3 Spirit of truth and love,
life-giving, holy dove,
speed on your flight;
move on the water's face
bearing the lamp of grace
and, in earth's darkest place,
let there be light!

4 Gracious and holy Three,
glorious Trinity,
wisdom, love, might:
boundless as ocean's tide
rolling in fullest pride
through the world far and wide,
let there be light!

J Marriott (1780–1825)

417

CONFESSION

**Father eternal,
giver of light and grace,
we have sinned against you
    and against our fellow men,
in what we have thought,
in what we have said and done,**

through ignorance,
    through weakness,
through our own deliberate fault.
We have wounded your love,
and marred your image in us.
We are sorry and ashamed,
and repent of all our sins.
For the sake of your Son Jesus Christ,
    who died for us,
forgive us all that is past;
and lead us out from darkness
to walk as children of light. Amen.

Alternative Confession – ASB

418

PSALM*

Sing to the Lord a new song:
A **sing to the Lord, all the earth.**

Sing to the Lord, praise his name:
B **proclaim his salvation each day.**

Declare his glory among the nations:
A **his marvellous deeds
    among the peoples.**

Great is the Lord, and most worthy of
praise:
B **honour him above all gods.**

Splendour and majesty surround him:
A **power and beauty fill his temple.**

Praise the Lord all people on earth:
B **praise his glory and might.**

Give him the glory due to his name:
A **bring an offering into his temple.**

Worship the Lord in his beauty and
holiness:
B **tremble before him all the earth.**

Say to the nations:
ALL **'The Lord is king!'**

Let the heavens rejoice and the earth be
glad:
A **let all creation sing for joy.**

For God shall come to judge the world:
B and rule the people with his truth.
Amen.

from Psalm 96

(*The congregation may divide at A and B)

419
Deus tuorum militum
Hymns for Today's Church 580

PSALM

1 From all who live beneath the skies
let the Creator's praise arise!
let the Redeemer's name be sung
through every land,
by every tongue!

2 Eternal are your mercies, Lord,
eternal truth attends your word;
your praise shall sound
from shore to shore
till suns shall rise and set no more.

from Psalm 117
I Watts (1674–1748)

420
Onslow Square or Littlebourne
Hymns for Today's Church 349

PSALM/CANTICLE

1 Sing a new song to the Lord,
he to whom wonders belong!
Rejoice in his triumph
and tell of his power –
O sing to the Lord a new song!

2 Now to the ends of the earth
see his salvation is shown;
and still he remembers
his mercy and truth,
unchanging in love to his own.

3 Sing a new song and rejoice,
publish his praises abroad!
Let voices in chorus,
with trumpet and horn,
resound for the joy of the Lord!

4 Join with the hills and the sea
thunders of praise to prolong!
In judgment and justice
he comes to the earth –
O sing to the Lord a new song!

from Psalm 98 (*Cantate Domino*)
© Timothy Dudley-Smith

421
How lovely on the mountains
Mission Praise 79

1 How lovely on the mountains
are the feet of him
who brings good news, good news,
proclaiming peace, announcing
news of happiness:
our God reigns, our God reigns!
Our God reigns, our God reigns,
our God reigns, our God reigns!

2 You watchmen, lift your voices
joyfully as one,
shout for your king, your king;
see eye to eye the Lord
restoring Zion:
your God reigns, your God reigns!
Your God reigns . . .

3 Waste places of Jerusalem,
break forth with joy –
we are redeemed, redeemed;
the Lord has saved and comforted
his people:
your God reigns, your God reigns!
Your God reigns . . .

4 Ends of the earth, see the salvation
of your God –
Jesus is Lord, is Lord!
Before the nations he has bared
his holy arm:
your God reigns, your God reigns!
Your God reigns . . .

from Isaiah 52
Leonard E Smith
© Thankyou Music†

The Missionary Church (419–421)

422 Go tell everyone
Sound of Living Waters 93

1 'God's Spirit is in my heart,
  he has called me and set me apart;
  this is what I have to do,
  what I have to do:
    He sent me
    to give the good news to the poor,
    tell prisoners
    that they are prisoners no more;
    tell blind people that they can see,
    and set the down-trodden free.
    And go tell everyone the news
    that the kingdom of God
      has come,
    and go tell everyone the news
    that God's kingdom has come!'

2 'Just as the Father sent me,
  so I'm sending you out to be
  my witness throughout the world,
  the whole of the world.'
    He sent . . .

3 'Don't carry a load in your pack –
  you don't need two shirts
    on your back,
  a workman can earn his own keep,
  can earn his own keep.'
    He sent . . .

4 'Don't worry what you have to say,
  don't worry because on that day
  God's spirit will speak in your heart,
  will speak in your heart.'
    He sent . . .

from Luke 4 and Matthew 10
Alan Dale
© Oxford University Press†

423 Jesus put this song . . .
This Is Your God 42

1 Jesus put this song into our hearts,
  Jesus put this song into our hearts;
  it's a song of joy
    no-one can take away.
  Jesus put this song into our hearts.

2 Jesus taught us
    how to live in harmony,
  Jesus taught us
    how to live in harmony;
  different faces, different races,
    he made us one –
  Jesus taught us
    how to live in harmony.

3 Jesus taught us how to be a family,
  Jesus taught us how to be a family;
  loving one another
    with the love that he gives –
  Jesus taught us how to be a family.

4 Jesus turned our sorrow
    into dancing,
  Jesus turned our sorrow
    into dancing,
  changed our tears of sadness
    into rivers of joy –
  Jesus turned our sorrow into dance.

Graham Kendrick
© Thankyou Music†

424 Go tell it on the mountain
Jesus Praise 181

  Go, tell it on the mountain,
  over the hills and everywhere;
  go, tell it on the mountain
  that Jesus Christ is Lord!

1 O when I was a seeker,
  I sought both night and day;
  I asked the Lord to guide me –
  and he showed me the way.
    Go, tell it on the mountain . . .

2 Then he made me a watchman
  upon a city wall,
  to tell of his salvation –
  that Jesus died for all.
    Go, tell it on the mountain . . .

3 Go tell it to your neighbour
   in darkness here below;
   go with the words of Jesus –
   that all the world may know.
     Go, tell it on the mountain . . .

425
Send me out from here
Songifts 54

Send me out from here Lord,
to serve a world in need;
may I know no-one
    by the coat they wear,
but the heart that Jesus sees.
And may the light of your face
shine upon me Lord –
You have filled my heart
    with the greatest joy
and my cup is overflowing.

1 'Go now, and carry the news
    to all creation –
every race and every tongue;
take no purse with you,
    take nothing to eat
for he will supply your every need.
    Send me out . . .

2 'Go now, bearing the light,
    living for others,
fearlessly walking into the night;
take no thought for your lives –
like lambs among wolves –
full of the Spirit, ready to die.'
    Send me out . . .

John Pantry
© Ears and Eyes Music†

426

CREED

There is one God and Father:
from him all things come.

There is one Lord Jesus Christ:
through him we come to God.

There is one Holy Spirit:
**in him we are baptized
    into one body.**

**We believe in one God:
Father, Son, and Holy Spirit. Amen.** †

from 1 Corinthians 8 and 12

427

THEME PRAYER (COLLECT)

Almighty Father,
whose Son Jesus Christ has taught us
that what we do
    for the least of our brethren
we do also for him;
give us the will
    to be the servant of others
as he was the servant of all,
who gave up his life and died for us,
but is alive and reigns
    with you and the Holy Spirit,
one God, now and for ever. **Amen.**

Pentecost 11 collect – ASB

428
Eisenach
Hymns for Today's Church 510

1 Lord, speak to me that I may speak
   in living echoes of your tone;
   as you have sought, so let me seek
   your wandering children,
       lost, alone.

2 O lead me, Lord, that I may lead
   the stumbling and the straying feet;
   and feed me, Lord, that I may feed
   your hungry ones
       with manna sweet.

The Missionary Church (425–428)

3 O teach me, Lord, that I may teach
the precious truths
which you impart;
and wing my words
that they may reach
the hidden depths of many a heart.

4 O fill me with your fulness, Lord,
until my heart shall overflow
in kindling thought
and glowing word,
your love to tell;
your praise to show.

5 O use me Lord, use even me,
just as you will,
and when, and where;
until at last your face I see,
your rest, your joy,
your glory share.

F R Havergal (1836–1879)

429 Kilmarnock
Hymns for Today's Church 448

1 In Christ there is no east or west,
in him no pride of birth;
the chosen family God has blessed
now spans the whole wide earth.

2 For God in Christ has made us one
from every land and race;
he reconciled us through his Son
and met us with his grace.

3 It is by grace we are assured
that we belong to him:
the love we share in Christ our Lord,
the Spirit's work within.

4 So brothers, sisters, praise his name
who died to set us free
from sin, division, hate and shame,
from spite and enmity!

(429–432) The Missionary Church

5 In Christ there is no east or west –
he breaks all barriers down;
by Christ redeemed,
by Christ possessed,
in Christ we live as one.

after W A Dunkerley (1852–1941)
© Michael Perry/Jubilate Hymns

430

FOR THE WORLDWIDE CHURCH

Heavenly Father,
we thank you for making us
in our baptism
members of your worldwide family
the Church,
and for our brothers and sisters
in every land
who love the Lord Jesus:
keep us loyal to one another,
faithful to our promises,
and active in your service,
for Jesus Christ's sake. **Amen.**   †

431

ABOUT OUR WITNESS

O Lord God,
we are all called to be your witnesses:
help us to make Jesus our saviour
known to others –
through our words and our lives,
through our prayers and our gifts;
for his sake. **Amen.**   †

432

FOR MISSIONARIES

Heavenly Father,
we pray for those
who have gone to other countries
with the good news of Jesus:

when their work is difficult and tiring,
make them strong;
when they are lonely and homesick,
remind them that you are with them;
when they are uncertain what to do,
guide them.
Keep them at all times loving you;
for Jesus' sake. **Amen.**

†

433
Fulda
Hymns for Today's Church 519

1 We have a gospel to proclaim,
   good news for all
      throughout the earth;
   the gospel of a saviour's name:
   we sing his glory, tell his worth.

2 Tell of his birth at Bethlehem,
   not in a royal house or hall
   but in a stable dark and dim:
   the Word made flesh, a light for all.

3 Tell of his death at Calvary,
   hated by those he came to save;
   in lonely suffering on the cross
   for all he loved, his life he gave.

4 Tell of that glorious Easter morn:
   empty the tomb, for he was free;
   he broke the power of death and hell
   that we might share his victory.

5 Tell of his reign at God's right hand,
   by all creation glorified;
   he sends his Spirit on his church
   to live for him, the lamb who died.

6 Now we rejoice to name him king:
   Jesus is Lord of all the earth;
   this gospel-message we proclaim:
   we sing his glory, tell his worth.

© Edward J Burns

434
Thornbury
Hymns for Today's Church 521

1 Tell all the world of Jesus,
   our saviour, Lord and king;
   and let the whole creation
   of his salvation sing:
   proclaim his glorious greatness
   in nature and in grace;
   creator and redeemer,
   the Lord of time and space.

2 Tell all the world of Jesus,
   that everyone may find
   the joy of his forgiveness –
   true peace of heart and mind:
   proclaim his perfect goodness,
   his deep, unfailing care;
   his love so rich in mercy,
   a love beyond compare.

3 Tell all the world of Jesus,
   that everyone may know
   of his almighty triumph
   defeating every foe:
   proclaim his coming glory,
   when sin is overthrown,
   and he shall reign in splendour –
   the King upon his throne!

J E Seddon (1915–1983)
© Mrs M Seddon/Jubilate Hymns

435

ASCRIPTION

You are worthy, O Lord our God:
**to receive glory
and honour and power.**

For you created all things:
**and by your will they existed
and were created.**

You are worthy, O Christ, for you were
slain:
**and by your blood
you ransomed us for God.**

→

The Missionary Church (433–435)

From every tribe and tongue and people and nation:
**you made us a kingdom of priests
to serve our God.**

To him who sits upon the throne, and to the Lamb:
**be blessing and honour
and glory and might
for ever and ever. Amen.**   †

from Revelation 4

436 St Clement
        Hymns for Today's Church 280

EVENING HYMN

1 The day you gave us, Lord,
        is ended,
    the sun is sinking in the west;
    to you our morning hymns
        ascended,
    your praise shall sanctify our rest.

2 We thank you that your church,
        unsleeping

while earth rolls onward into light,
through all the world
        her watch is keeping
and rests not now by day or night.

3 As to each continent and island
    the dawn proclaims another day,
    the voice of prayer is never silent,
    nor dies the sound of praise away.

4 The sun that bids us rest is waking
    your church
        beneath the western sky;
    fresh voices hour by hour
        are making
    your mighty deeds resound on high.

5 So be it, Lord:
        your throne shall never,
    like earth's proud empires,
        pass away;
    your kingdom stands,
        and grows for ever,
    until there dawns that glorious day.

J Ellerton (1826–1893)
© in this version Jubilate Hymns

THE MISSIONARY CHURCH/
THE WORLDWIDE CHURCH
Other items appropriate to this theme

Hymns

Go forth and tell	506
God is love: let heaven adore	368
Let all the world in every corner sing	49
This is the truth which we proclaim	2

Songs

Alleluia, alleluia, give thanks	252
Because he has died	568
God forgave my sin in Jesus' name	293
The earth was dark	447
To God's loving-kindness we commit you	5

Psalm Versions (spoken)

Happy are those who trust in God (Psalm 40)	136
Praise the Lord, all you nations (Psalm 117)	437

Prayer

O Lord our God, enthroned on high
(based on Isaiah 6) 330

Readings

Proclaim the Good News –
Isaiah 52.7–10; 61.1–3
Paul's Missionary Journeys –
Acts 16.6–10
Sent to Preach – Romans 10.8–18
Christ's Ambassadors –
2 Corinthians 5.11–6.2;
Luke 10.1–9
Light for the World –
Matthew 5.13–16
Jesus Prays for the Church –
John 17.20–26

(See also section The Caring Church
437–461, and Minister's Section 750–
753, 756–757. The Lord's Prayer is
printed inside the back cover.)

26 The Caring Church/Healing

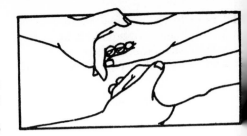

God is love; those who live in love live in God, and God lives in them.

1 John 4.16

The Lord heals the broken-hearted and binds up their wounds.

Psalm 147.3

437

PRAISE

Praise the Lord, all you nations;
extol him all you peoples.

For his love protecting us is strong;
**his faithfulness endures for ever.
Amen.**

from Psalm 117

3 Let us serve God together,
   him obey;
let our lives show his goodness
   through each day:
Christ the Lord
   is the world's true light –
let us serve him with all our might,
   his name be exalted on high!

J E Seddon (1915–1983)
© Mrs M Seddon/Jubilate Hymn

---

438 Calhoun Melody
Hymns for Today's Church S18

1 Let us praise God together,
   let us praise;
let us praise God together
   all our days:
he is faithful in all his ways,
he is worthy of all our praise,
   his name be exalted on high!

2 Let us seek God together,
   let us pray;
let us seek his forgiveness
   as we pray:
he will cleanse us from all our sin,
he will help us the fight to win,
   his name be exalted on high!

---

439 St Hugh
Hymns for Today's Church 367

1 Help us to help each other, Lord,
   each other's load to bear;
that all may live in true accord,
   our joys and pains to share.

2 Help us to build each other up,
   your strength within us prove;
increase our faith, confirm our hope
   and fill us with your love.

3 Together make us free indeed –
   your life within us show;
and into you, our living head,
   let us in all things grow.

(437–439) The Caring Church

4 Drawn by the magnet of your love
we find our hearts made new:
nearer each other let us move,
and nearer still to you.

after C Wesley (1707–1788)
© in this version Jubilate Hymns

440

FOR FORGIVENESS (CONFESSION)

O God our Father, we ask your forgiveness for the times when we have failed
you:

When we have not cared enough for
your world: in your great mercy,
forgive us, O God.

When we have not cared enough for
you: in your great mercy,
forgive us, O God.

When we have been content with
ourselves as we are: in your great
mercy,
forgive us, O God.

**Give us the will and the power
to live in the spirit of Jesus,
now and always. Amen.**

†

441

THEME PRAYER (COLLECT)

Almighty God,
you have taught us through your Son
that love is the fulfilling of the law.
Grant that we may love you
with our whole heart
and our neighbours as ourselves;
through Jesus Christ our Lord. **Amen.**

Pentecost 16 collect – ASB

442

PSALM*

Praise the Lord, my soul:
all my being, praise his holy name!

Praise the Lord, my soul:
and do not forget how kind he is.

[A]He forgives all my sins:
[B]**and heals all my diseases.**

[A]He keeps me from the grave:
[B]**and blesses me with love and mercy.**

The Lord is merciful and kind:
[ALL]**slow to become angry
and full of constant love.**

[A]He does not keep on rebuking:
[B]**he is not angry for ever.**

[A]He does not punish us as we deserve:
[B]**or repay us for our sins and wrongs.**

[A]As far as the east is from the west:
[B]**so far does he remove our sins
from us.**

As kind as a Father to his children:
[ALL]**so kind is the Lord
to those who honour him.**

Praise the Lord, all his creation:
praise the Lord, my soul. Amen.

from Psalm 103

(*The congregation may divide at A and B)

443
Jane (adapted)
Hymns for Today's Church 475

PSALM/CANTICLE

1 O be glad in the Lord, and rejoice;
all you lands of the earth,
come and sing;
with his praises
now lift up your voice,
to his presence
your thanksgiving bring!

The Caring Church (440–443)

Our creator is God, be assured;
it is not by ourselves we were made:
God himself is our Shepherd
and Lord
in his hand we shall not be afraid!

2 Through his gates
let us gratefully move;
to his courts let us come
with our praise!
O give thanks to the Lord
for his love;
O rejoice in his works and his ways!
For our God is abounding in grace,
and his mercy is faithful and sure:
generations to come, seek his face,
praise and worship the Lord
evermore!

from Psalm 100 (*Jubilate*)
© Stephen Wilcockson

444 Lux Eoi
Hymns for Today's Church 504

CANTICLE

1 Church of God, elect and glorious,
holy nation, chosen race;
called as God's own special people,
royal priests and heirs of grace:
know the purpose of your calling,
show to all his mighty deeds;
tell of love which knows no limits,
grace which meets
all human needs.

2 God has called you out of darkness
into his most marvellous light;
brought his truth to life within you,
turned your blindness into sight.
Let your light so shine around you
that God's name is glorified;
and all find fresh hope and purpose
in Christ Jesus crucified.

3 Once you were an alien people,
strangers to God's heart of love;

but he brought you home in mercy,
citizens of heaven above.
Let his love flow out to others,
let them feel a Father's care;
that they too may know his welcome
and his countless blessings share.

4 Church of God, elect and holy,
be the people he intends;
strong in faith and swift to answer
each command
your master sends:
royal priests, fulfil your calling
through your sacrifice and prayer;
give your lives in joyful service –
sing his praise, his love declare.

from 1 Peter 2
J E Seddon (1915–1983)
© Mrs M Seddon/Jubilate Hymns

445 New Commandment
Jesus Praise 132

The new commandment
that I give to you
is to love one another
as I have loved you;
is to love one another
as I have loved you.
By this shall people know
you are my disciples:
if you have love one for another;
by this shall people know
you are my disciples:
if you have love one for another.

from John 1

446 Give me joy
Mission Praise 58

1 Give me joy in my heart,
keep me praising;
give me joy in my heart, I pray:
give me joy in my heart,
keep me praising –
keep me praising
till the break of day.

Sing hosanna, sing hosanna,
   sing hosanna to the King of kings;
sing hosanna, sing hosanna,
   sing hosanna to the King.

2 Give me peace in my heart,
      keep me resting;
   give me peace in my heart, I pray:
   give me peace in my heart,
      keep me resting –
   keep me resting
      till the break of day.
      Sing hosanna . . .

3 Give me love in my heart,
      keep me serving;
   give me love in my heart, I pray:
   give me love in my heart,
      keep me serving –
   keep me serving
      till the break of day.
      Sing hosanna . . .

Unknown

447 Lights to the World
Songifts 45

1 The earth was dark
      until you spoke –
   then all was light and all was peace;
   yet still, O God, so many wait
   to see the flame of love released.
      Lights to the world!
      O Light divine,
      kindle in us a mighty flame,
      till every heart, consumed by love
      shall rise to praise
      your holy name!

2 In Christ you gave your gift of life
   to save us
      from the depths of night:
   O come and set our spirits free
   and draw us to your perfect light!
      Lights to the world . . .

3 Where there is fear may we bring joy
   and healing to a world of pain:
   Lord, build your kingdom
      through our lives
   till Jesus walks this earth again.
      Lights to the world . . .

4 O burn in us, that we may burn
   with love that triumphs
      in despair;
   and touch our lives with such a fire
   that souls may search
      and find you there.
      Lights to the world . . .

John Daniels and Phil Thomson
© Ears and Eyes Music†

448* Living the Jesus way
Songifts 153

1 Caring (caring), sharing (sharing),
   loving (loving), giving (giving);
      living the Jesus way.

2 Seeing (seeing), helping (helping),
   loving (loving), trusting (trusting);
      living the Jesus way.

3 Praying (praying),
      obeying (obeying),
   loving (loving),
      forgiving (forgiving),
      living the Jesus way.

(*Written for children to sing)

© Linda Caroe†

449 From heaven you came
Songs of Fellowship 3   368

1 From heaven you came,
      helpless Babe –
   entered our world your glory veiled,
   not to be served but to serve,
   and give your life that we might live.

The Caring Church (447–449)

This is our God – the servant king,
he calls us now to follow him,
to bring our lives
as a daily offering
of worship to the servant king.

2 There in the garden of tears
my heavy load he chose to bear,
his heart with sorrow was torn:
'Yet not my will but yours,' he said.
This is our God . . .

3 Come, see his hands and his feet,
the scars that speak of sacrifice,
hands that flung stars into space
to cruel nails surrendered.
This is our God . . .

4 So let us learn how to serve
and in our lives enthrone him,
each other's needs to prefer –
for it is Christ we're serving.
This is our God . . .

Graham Kendrick
© Thankyou Music†

450

CREED
Let us declare our faith and trust in
God:

Do you believe and trust in God the
Father, who made the world and loves
it and sustains it?
We believe and trust in him.

Do you believe and trust in God the
Son, who came into the world not to be
served but to serve, and to give his life
as a ransom for many?
We believe and trust in him.

Do you believe and trust in God the
Holy Spirit, who fills all creation and

who pours out his love in the hearts of
those who seek him?
We believe and trust in him.

Will you then constantly ask for the
grace of the Holy Spirit, that you may
love and serve God, your neighbours
and each other, after the example of
Christ and in accordance with the
Father's will?
By God's help we will. Amen.

after an Induction Creed
used in the Diocese of London

451

FOR SICK PEOPLE (COLLECT)

Creator and Father of all,
we pray for those who are ill.
Bless them,
    and those who serve their needs,
that they may put their whole trust
    in you
and be filled with your peace;
through Jesus Christ our Lord. **Amen.**

Collect for the Sick – ASB

452
St Leonard's
Hymns for Today's Church 550

1 May the mind of Christ my saviour
live in me from day to day,
by his love and power controlling
all I do and say.

2 May the word of God enrich me
with his truth, from hour to hour;
so that all may see I triumph
only through his power.

3 May the peace of God my Father
in my life for ever reign,
that I may be calm to comfort
those in grief and pain.

4 May the love of Jesus fill me
  as the waters fill the sea,
  him exalting, self abasing –
  this is victory!

5 May his beauty rest upon me
  as I seek to make him known;
  so that all may look to Jesus,
  seeing him alone.

K B Wilkinson (1859–1928)
© in this version Jubilate Hymns

453 Melcombe
      Hymns for Today's Church 318

1 We give God thanks
    for those who knew
  the touch of Jesus' healing love;
  they trusted him
    to make them whole,
  to give them peace,
    their guilt remove.

2 We offer prayer for all who go
  relying on his grace and power,
  to help the anxious and the ill,
  to heal their wounds,
    their lives restore.

3 We dedicate our skills and time
  to those who suffer where we live,
  to bring such comfort as we can
  to meet their need,
    their pain relieve.

4 So Jesus' touch of healing grace
  lives on within our willing care;
  by thought and prayer and gifts
    we prove
  his mercy still, his love we share.

© Michael Perry/Jubilate Hymns

454

FOR SAD FAMILIES
We pray for those who will be unhappy
today:

For mothers who cannot provide for
their children – Lord, in your mercy,
hear our prayer.

For fathers who cannot earn enough
money for their families – Lord, in your
mercy,
hear our prayer.

For children who are ill or frightened –
Lord, in your mercy,
hear our prayer.

For all who are alone, and without people to love them – Lord, in your mercy,
hear our prayer.

**Bless those who give their lives
in service to the poor and hungry,
and strengthen us to help
in meeting their needs;
through Jesus Christ our Lord. Amen.** †

455

FOR A SPIRIT OF CARING

O God our Father,
we praise you
that through Jesus Christ
    your only Son,
you have adopted us
    into your family the Church
and made us your children:
help us to show
    our love and thanks to you
by care and concern for one another;
use us to spread your love
    in all the world
by the power of your Holy Spirit,
and to the honour of your name.
Amen.
        †

The Caring Church (453–455)

456

FOR HEALING

O Lord, heal us,
and we shall be healed,
save us,
and we shall be saved:
and the praise shall be yours alone.
Amen.

from Jeremiah 17

457

THANKSGIVING

Almighty God,
we thank you for your mercy
  and your grace:
you are our light in darkness,
our strength in weakness,
and our comfort in sorrow.
You heal our bodies and our minds;
you ease our pain,
you lift our anxieties
and give us hope.
So fill us with your Spirit's power
that we may take your healing love
to a world in need,
and bring glory to your name;
through Jesus Christ our Lord. **Amen.** †

458 Regent Square
Hymns for Today's Church 128

1 Christians, join in celebration,
  lift your voices, rise and sing!
  Praise to him
      who brought redemption
  Jesus – prophet, priest and king:
  in resounding songs of worship
  let your Alleluias ring!

2 Let the Church fulfil its calling,
  preaching Christ to every race,
  guided by his word and Spirit,
  strengthened
      by his power and grace:
  we are told to share that mission,
  each in our appointed place.

3 Let the Church be strong and active,
  as it cares for human needs;
  open to the Spirit's promptings,
  quick to follow where he leads;
  true in worship, life and witness,
  sharing Christ in loving deeds.

4 Glory, honour, power and blessing
  be to him whose name we bear,
  Jesus, living Lord and saviour –
  in his risen life we share:
  lift your voices, all his people,
  let your songs his praise declare!

J E Seddon (1915–1983)
© Mrs M Seddon/Jubilate Hymns

459 Praise, my soul
Hymns for Today's Church 38

1 Praise, my soul, the king of heaven!
  to his feet your tribute bring:
  ransomed, healed,
      restored, forgiven,
  who like me his praise should sing?
      Alleluia, alleluia!
  praise the everlasting king!

2 Praise him for his grace and favour
  to our fathers in distress;
  praise him still the same as ever,
  slow to blame and swift to bless:
      Alleluia, alleluia!
  glorious in his faithfulness!

3 Father-like, he tends and spares us;
  all our hopes and fears he knows,
  in his hands he gently bears us,
  rescues us from all our foes,
      Alleluia, alleluia!
  widely as his mercy flows.

4 Angels, help us to adore him –
  you behold him face to face;
  sun and moon,
      bow down before him –
  praise him, all in time and space:
      Alleluia, alleluia!
  praise with us the God of grace!

from Psalm 103
H F Lyte (1793–1847)

460

OFFERTORY PRAYER

Heavenly Father,
let these gifts go where we cannot go,
and help those
      whom we cannot reach;
through them
let the unlearned be taught,
the hungry fed,
the sick healed,
and the lost found;
for Jesus' sake. **Amen.**   †

461 Stracathro or Charnwood
Hymns for Today's Church 144(i)
Church Family Worship Source Book

EVENING HYMN

1 Now evening comes
      to close the day,
  and soon the silent hours
  shall banish all our fears away,
  and sleep renew our powers.

2 Into your hands, eternal Friend,
  we give ourselves again,
  and to your watchful care commend
  all those in grief or pain.

3 In waking, lift our thoughts above,
  in sleeping guard us still,
  that we may rise to know your love
  and prove your perfect will.

4 To Father, Son and Spirit – praise,
  all mortal praise be given,
  till sleep at last shall end our days
  and we shall wake in heaven!

© Michael Perry/Jubilate Hymns

THE CARING CHURCH/HEALING
Other items appropriate to this theme

Hymns

Come, most holy Spirit	327
God of mercy, God of grace	527
God, whose almighty word	416
Praise to the Lord, the almighty	89

Songs

If you want to be great	142
Jesus is the name we worship	166
Jesus put this song	423
Let there be love shared among us	58
Make me a channel of your peace	470
Send me out	425
Who does Jesus love	144

Prayers

O God our Father, who in Jesus came (For Vision and Strength)	65
We pray for God's strength (Commandment)	149

Almighty Father, whose Son (Collect)	427
Lord Jesus Christ, born in a stable (For the Homeless)	635
Lord, make us instruments of your peace	page 21

Readings

Learning to Care –
Leviticus 19.9–18
No Favouritism: Faith and Deeds –
James 2.1–13; 2.14–26
Christ the Healer – James 5.13–16;
Matthew 8.5–17; Mark 2.1–12
The Sheep and Goats –
Matthew 25.31–46
The Greatest Commandment –
Mark 12.28–34
The Good Samaritan –
Luke 10.25–37

(See also section God's Gifts to the Church 462–480, and Minister's Section 754–756. The Lord's Prayer is printed inside the back cover.)

27 God's Gifts to the Church/Renewal

In Christ we who are many form one body, and each member belongs to all the others. We have different gifts, according to the grace given us.   Romans 12.5,6

462

PRAISE

Shout with joy to God, all the earth;
sing to the glory of his name!

Come and see what God has done:
how awesome are his works!

Praise our God, all you people;
sound aloud his praise: Amen.

from Psalm 66

4 Gladly may we all agree,
bound in one community;
kindly for each other care –
all our joys and sorrows share.

5 Love has all our strife destroyed,
rendered all divisions void;
sects and names and parties fall:
you, O Christ, are all in all.

C Wesley (1707–1788)
© in this version Jubilate Hymns

463   Culbach
Hymns for Today's Church 491

1 Christ,
from whom all blessings flow,
by whose grace your people grow;
Christ whose nature now we share,
work in us, your body here.

2 Send your Spirit from above
and unite us in your love;
still for more to you we call –
with your fulness fill us all.

3 Move and motivate and guide,
varying gifts for each provide;
placed according to your will,
let us all our work fulfil.

464   Spiritus Vitae
Hymns for Today's Church 237

1 O Breath of life,
come sweeping through us,
revive your church
with life and power;
O Breath of life,
come, cleanse, renew us
and fit your church
to meet this hour.

2 O Breath of love,
come breathe within us,
renewing thought
and will and heart;
come, love of Christ, afresh
to win us,
revive your church in every part!

God's Gifts to the Church (462–464)

3 O Wind of God,
        come bend us, break us
    till humbly
        we confess our need;
    then, in your tenderness
        remake us,
    revive, restore –
        for this we plead.

E A P Head (1850–1936)
© Mrs F M Charlton

465

CONFESSION

O God, we come to you in repentance, conscious of our sins:

When we are self-satisfied, you expose our failure. Lord, forgive us:
save us and help us.

When we are self-assertive, you challenge our pride. Lord, forgive us:
save us and help us.

When we are self-opinionated, you show us we do not know everything. Lord, forgive us:
save us and help us.

When we are self-indulgent, you condemn our greed. Lord, forgive us:
save us and help us.

When we are self-centred, you take our peace away. Lord, forgive us:
save us and help us.

Give us a new vision of your holiness, make us worthy to be your people, and help us to live up to our calling in Jesus Christ our Lord. Amen. †

466

PSALM

Praise the Lord:

Praise God in his sanctuary:
praise him in his mighty heavens.

Praise him for his acts of power:
**praise him
        for his surpassing greatness.**

Praise him with the sounding of the trumpet:
praise him with the harp and lyre.

Praise him with tambourine and dancing:
praise him with the strings and flute.

Praise him with the clash of cymbals:
praise him with resounding cymbals.

Let everything that has breath praise the Lord:
Praise the Lord! Amen.

Psalm 150

467
Christchurch
Hymns for Today's Church 565

PSALM

1 O let the Church rejoice
    in God our saviour's grace,
    for it is good to voice
    his all deserving praise:
        Sing alleluia, praise the Lord –
        he builds his church
        and spreads his word!

2 Our God commands the storm
    and sends the warming breeze;
    he can within us form
    a life of joy and peace.
        Sing alleluia . . .

3 He makes the meadow flower,
   the clouds, the wind and rain;
   the humble, by his power
   he'll lovingly sustain.
      Sing alleluia . . .

4 The broken-hearted sigh –
   he bears their guilt and shame;
   like numbered stars on high
   he knows them all by name.
      Sing alleluia . . .

5 Hope in the Lord above –
   he will provide our needs;
   trust his unfailing love,
   praise all his gracious deeds!
      Sing alleluia . . .

from Psalm 147
© Barbara Woollett/Jubilate Hymns

468 Praise him on the trumpet
Songs of Fellowship 2   280

PSALM

Praise him on the trumpet,
the psaltery and harp;
praise him on the timbrel
      and the dance;
praise him with stringed instruments
      too;
praise him on the loud cymbals,
praise him on the loud cymbals:
let everything that has breath
   praise the Lord!

Alleluia – praise the Lord;
alleluia – praise the Lord:
let everything that has breath
   praise the Lord!

Alleluia . . .

from Psalm 150
John Kennett
© Thankyou Music†

469 For I'm building a people of power
Mission Praise 50

For I'm building a people of power –
and I'm making a people of praise,
that will move through this land
      by my Spirit,
and will glorify my holy name.

Build your Church, Lord;
      make us strong, Lord,
join our hearts, Lord,
      through your Son;
make us one, Lord, in your Body,
in the kingdom of your Son!

Dave Richards
© Thankyou Music†

470 St Francis
Jesus Praise 161

1 Make me a channel of your peace:
   where there is hatred
         let me bring your love,
   where there is injury,
         your pardon, Lord,
   and where there's doubt,
         true faith in you:
      O Master, grant
      that I may never seek
      so much to be consoled
      as to console;
      to be understood
      as to understand,
      to be loved,
      as to love with all my soul!

2 Make me a channel of your peace:
   where there's despair in life
         let me bring hope,
   where there is darkness, only light,
   and where there's sadness, ever joy:
      O Master, grant . . .

God's Gifts to the Church (468–470)

3 Make me a channel of your peace:
   it is in pardoning
      that we are pardoned,
   in giving of ourselves
      that we receive,
   and in dying that we're born
      to eternal life.

471
The Seed Song
Cry Hosanna 103

One must water, one must weed,
one must sow the precious seed:
we'll all work in unity –
to tend the garden of love.

1 You take a little seed
      and put it in the ground,
   spread a little love
      and cheer around:
   plant a little kindness from above –
   and you'll have a garden of love.
      One must water . . .

2 Tend it patiently in prayer,
   root out the weeds of doubt
      and care;
   trust God's Spirit from above –
   to nourish the seed of love.
      One must water . . .

3 Till the garden
      through and through –
   as Jesus Christ directs you to;
   pour forgiveness all around –
   and you'll have a fruitful ground.
      One must water . . .

472
When the Spirit of the Lord
Songs of Fellowship 2   316

1 When the Spirit of the Lord
      is within my heart,
   I will sing as David sang;
   when the Spirit of the Lord
      is within my heart,
   I will sing as David sang:
      I will sing, I will sing,
      I will sing as David sang;
      I will sing, I will sing,
      I will sing as David sang.

2 When the Spirit of the Lord
      is within my heart,
   I will clap . . .

3 When the Spirit of the Lord
      is within my heart,
   I will dance . . .

4 When the Spirit of the Lord
      is within my heart,
   I will praise . . .

473

CREED
Let us declare our faith in God:

**We believe in God the Father;
the almighty,
who is, and was, and is to come.**

**We believe in Jesus Christ;
the faithful witness,
the firstborn from the dead,
the King of kings,
who loves us,
and has freed us from our sins
      by his blood.**

**We believe in the Spirit;
giver of many gifts,
proceeding from the throne on high.**

We believe in one God:
Father, Son, and Holy Spirit. Amen. †

from Revelation 1

474

THEME PRAYER (COLLECT)

Almighty God,
without you
    we are not able to please you.
Mercifully grant that your Holy Spirit
may in all things direct and rule
    our hearts;
through Jesus Christ our Lord. **Amen.**

Pentecost 6 collect – ASB

475
St Timothy, St Stephen
Hymns for Today's Church 269, 483(ii)

1 O Holy Spirit, come to bless
  your waiting church, we pray:
  we long to grow in holiness
  as children of the day.

2 Great Gift of our ascended king,
  his saving truth reveal,
  our tongues inspire
     his praise to sing,
  our hearts his love to feel.

3 O come, creator Spirit, move
  as on the formless deep;
  give life and order, light and love,
  where now is death or sleep.

4 We offer up to you, O Lord,
  ourselves to be your throne,
  our every thought and deed
     and word
  to make your glory known.

5 O Holy Spirit, Lord of might,
  through you all grace is given:
  grant us to know and serve aright
  one God in earth and heaven.

H W Baker (1821–1877)
© in this version Jubilate Hymns

476
Charity
Hymns for Today's Church 474(i)

1 Holy Spirit, gracious guest,
  hear and grant our heart's request
  for that gift supreme and best:
    holy heavenly love.

2 Faith that mountains could remove,
  tongues of earth or heaven above,
  knowledge, all things, empty prove
    if I have no love.

3 Though I as a martyr bleed,
  give my goods the poor to feed,
  all is vain if love I need:
    therefore give me love.

4 Love is kind and suffers long,
  love is pure and thinks no wrong,
  love than death itself more strong:
    therefore give us love.

5 Prophecy will fade away,
  melting in the light of day;
  love will ever with us stay:
    therefore give us love.

6 Faith and hope and love we see
  joining hand in hand agree –
  but the greatest of the three,
    and the best, is love.

from 1 Corinthians 13
C Wordsworth (1807–1885)
© in this version Jubilate Hymns

God's Gifts to the Church (474–476)

477

FOR THE BODY OF CHRIST

O God our Father, you grant your people gifts, that we may work together in the service of your Son:

Bless those who lead, that they may be strong and true, yet be humble before you: Lord, through your Spirit,
answer our prayer.

Bless those who teach, that they may enlighten our understanding, yet be taught by your wisdom: Lord, through your Spirit,
answer our prayer.

Bless those who offer healing, that they may extend your touch of grace, yet always know your healing presence: Lord, through your Spirit,
answer our prayer.

Bless those through whom you speak, that they may proclaim your word in power, yet have their ears open to your gentle whisper: Lord, through your Spirit,
answer our prayer.

Bless those who administer, help, and organise, that they may be diligent in their duty, yet seek your kingdom first: Lord, through your Spirit,
answer our prayer.

Grant that as one Body
we may grow up into him
who is the head of the Church,
even Jesus Christ our Lord. Amen.   †

478

THANKSGIVING
We give thanks to God for all his gifts to us:

For birth and life and strength of body, for safety and shelter and food: we give you thanks, O God,
and praise your holy name.

For sight and hearing and the beauty of nature, for words and music and the power of thought: we give you thanks, O God,
and praise your holy name.

For work and leisure and the joy of achieving, for conscience and will and depth of feeling: we give you thanks, O God,
and praise your holy name.

For grace and truth in Jesus Christ, for the gifts of the Spirit and the hope of heaven: we give you thanks, O God,
and praise your holy name.

We shall not forget
that you are our God,
and we are your people,
in Jesus Christ our Lord. Amen.   †

479
Carlisle or Venice
Hymns for Today's Church 515

1 Revive your church, O Lord,
  in grace and power draw near;
  speak with the voice
     that wakes the dead,
  and make your people hear!

2 Revive your church, O Lord,
  disturb the sleep of death;
  give life to smouldering embers now
  by your almighty breath.

3 Revive your church, O Lord,
  exalt your precious name;
  and by your Holy Spirit come
  and set our love aflame.

(477–479) God's Gifts to the Church

4 Revive your church, O Lord,
  give us a thirst for you,
  a hunger for the bread of life
  our spirits to renew.

5 Revive your church, O Lord,
  and let your power be shown;
  the gifts and graces shall be ours,
  the glory yours alone!

A Midlane (1825–1909)
© in this version Jubilate Hymns

480 Little Cornard
Hymns for Today's Church 242

1 Spirit of God most high,
  Lord of all power and might;
  source of our Easter joy,
  well-spring of life and light:
      strip from the Church
        its cloak of pride,
      a stumbling-block
        to those outside.

2 Wind of God's Spirit, blow!
  into the valley sweep,
  bringing dry bones to life,
  wakening each from sleep:
      speak to the Church
        your firm command
      and bid a scattered army stand.

3 Fire of God's Spirit, melt
  every unbending heart;
  your people's love renew
  as at their journey's start:
      your reconciling grace release
      to bring the Christian family
        peace.

4 Spirit of Christ our Lord,
  send us to do your will;
  nothing need hold us back
  for you are with us still:
      forgetful of ourselves, may we
      receive your gift of unity!

© David Mowbray/Jubilate Hymns

GOD'S GIFTS TO THE CHURCH/
RENEWAL
Other items appropriate to this theme

Hymns

Breathe on me, breath of God	326
Come down, O love divine	308
Jesus is Lord! Creation's voice proclaims it	286
Spirit of holiness	323
We have a gospel to proclaim	433

Songs

Spirit of the living God, move among us	318
We are being built into a temple	491
We are one body in the Lord	120

Prayers
Almighty God, who sent your
  Holy Spirit (For the Fruits of the
  Spirit)   321
Almighty God, whose Holy
  Spirit   page 21

Readings
Differing Gifts – Romans 12.1–13;
  1 Corinthians 12.4–13
A Healthy Body –
  Ephesians 4.7–16
Unity in Diversity – John 17.13–23;
  1 Corinthians 3; Ephesians 4.1–6

(See also section The Holy Spirit 307–
327, and Minister's Section 757–762. The
Lord's Prayer is printed inside the back
cover.)

28 The Church Anniversary/Giving

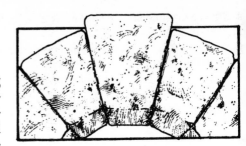

Come to the Lord, the living stone, rejected by man as worthless but chosen by God as valuable. Come as living stones, and let yourselves be used in building the spiritual temple.

1 Peter 2.4,5

Each one should give as he has decided, not with regret or out of a sense of duty; for God loves the one who gives gladly.

2 Corinthians 9.6

481

PRAISE

Praise God in his sanctuary;
praise him in his mighty heavens.

Praise him for his acts of power;
**praise him
for his surpassing greatness.**

Let everything that has breath praise the Lord:
praise the Lord! Amen.

from Psalm 150

482
Darwall's 148th, Harewood
Hymns for Today's Church 171, 564

1 Christ is our corner-stone,
on him alone we build;
with his true saints alone
the courts of heaven are filled;
on his great love
our hopes we place
of present grace
and joys above.

2 With psalms and hymns of praise
this holy place shall ring;
our voices we will raise,
the Three-in-One to sing;
and thus proclaim
in joyful song
both loud and long,
that glorious name.

3 Here, gracious God, draw near
as in your name we bow;
each true petition hear,
accept each faithful vow;
and more and more
on all who pray
each holy day
your blessings pour.

4 Here may we gain from heaven
the grace which we implore;
and may that grace, once given,
be with us evermore,
until that day
when all the blessed
to endless rest
are called away.

from the Latin (c seventh century)
J Chandler (1806–1876)

(481–482) The Church Anniversary

1 Christ is made the sure foundation,
Christ the head and corner-stone
chosen of the Lord and precious,
binding all the Church in one;
holy Zion's help for ever,
and her confidence alone.

2 All within that holy city
dearly loved of God on high,
in exultant jubilation
sing, in perfect harmony;
God the One-in-Three adoring
in glad hymns eternally.

3 We as living stones invoke you:
Come among us, Lord, today!
with your gracious loving-kindness
hear your children as we pray;
and the fulness of your blessing
in our fellowship display.

4 Here entrust to all your servants
what we long from you to gain –
that on earth and in the heavens
we one people shall remain,
till united in your glory
evermore with you we reign.

5 Praise and honour to the Father,
praise and honour to the Son,
praise and honour to the Spirit,
ever Three and ever One:
one in power and one in glory
while eternal ages run.

from the Latin (c seventh century)
J M Neale (1818–1866)
© in this version Jubilate Hymns

When we lose patience,
when we are unkind,
when we are envious,
when we are rude or proud,
when we are selfish or irritable,
and when we will not forgive:
have mercy on us, O God.

Help us not to delight in evil,
but to rejoice in the truth;
help us always to protect, to trust,
to hope and to persevere:
then shall we see you face to face,
and learn to love as you love us
in Jesus Christ our Lord. Amen.   †

from 1 Corinthians 13

485

THEME PRAYER (COLLECT)

Almighty God,
to whose glory we celebrate
the *dedication/consecration*
      of this house of prayer:
we praise you for the many blessings
you have given to those
      who worship here;
and we pray
that all who seek you in this place
may find you,
and being filled with the Holy Spirit
may become a living temple
acceptable to you;
through Jesus Christ our Lord. **Amen.**

Dedication or Consecration collect – ASB

484

CONFESSION
'Be kind and compassionate to one
another, forgiving each other, just as in
Christ God forgave you.' Let us confess
our lack of love, and our need of grace:

486 St Clement
Hymns for Today's Church 280

CANTICLE

1 Come, praise the Lord,
      all you his servants,
who stand within his house
      by night!

The Church Anniversary (483–486)

Come, lift your hands and hearts
   in worship;
make him your praise
   and your delight:

2 Come, bless the Lord,
   all those who love him,
who serve within his holy place:
may God who made
   both earth and heaven
grant us the blessings of his grace.

from Psalm 134 (*Come praise the Lord*)
© Christopher Idle/Jubilate Hymns

487

PSALM*

^MGive thanks to the Lord, for he is good:
His love endures for ever.

^MLet those who fear the Lord say:
His love endures for ever.

^WOpen for me the gates of the temple; I will go in and give thanks to the Lord.

^MThis is the gate of the Lord, only the righteous can come in.

^WI will give thanks because you heard me; you have become my salvation.

^CThe stone which the builders rejected as worthless turned out to be the most important of all:
**The Lord has done this –
what a wonderful sight it is!**

^CThis is the day of the Lord's victory – let us be happy, let us celebrate:
**O Lord save us;
O Lord, grant us success.**

^MMay God bless the one who comes in the name of the Lord:
**The Lord is God –
he has been good to us!**

^CFrom the temple of the Lord, we bless you.

(^MWith branches in your hands, start the procession and march round the altar:)

**You are my God,
   and I will give you thanks.
You are my God, and I will exalt you.**

^MGive thanks to the Lord, for he is good:
His love endures for ever! Amen.

from Psalm 118†

(*Parts as follows: M-minister, W-worshipper, C-choir, **bold print**-all. The worshipper stands towards the back of the congregation.)

488 Truro
Hymns for Today's Church 516

PSALM

1 Great is the Lord; his praise is great
on Zion's mount, his holy place:
the royal city crowns the earth,
and shines on all with radiant grace.

2 God is the tower
      whose strength was shown
when Satan's armies
      threatened harm:
they gathered round,
      and looked, and ran
like boats before the driving storm.

3 Our ears have heard,
      our eyes have seen
what God the Lord of hosts
      has done:
within these walls we celebrate
his steadfast love,
      his ageless throne.

(487–488) The Church Anniversary

4 God is the Judge
whose mighty name
across the world
with praise shall ring:
for his resplendent victories
let Zion shout and Judah sing!

5 God is the King,
whose kingdom's power
we see built up on every side:
we tell our children of our God
who will for ever be our guide.

from Psalm 48
© Christopher Idle/Jubilate Hymns

489

DOXOLOGY

Oh, the depth of the riches of the wisdom and knowledge of God!
**How unsearchable his judgements,
and his paths beyond tracing out!**

Who has known the mind of the Lord?
Or who has been his counsellor?
**Who has ever given to God,
that God should repay?**

For from him and through him and to
him are all things.
To God be the glory for ever! Amen.

from Romans 11

490 Laudate Dominum
Hymns for Today's Church 354

PSALM

1 Sing praise to the Lord!
praise him in the height;
rejoice in his word
you angels of light:
you heavens adore him
by whom you were made,
and worship before him
in brightness arrayed.

2 Sing praise to the Lord!
praise him upon earth
in tuneful accord,
you saints of new birth:
praise him who has brought you
his grace from above;
praise him who has taught you
to sing of his love.

3 Sing praise to the Lord!
all things that give sound,
each jubilant chord
re-echo around:
loud organs, his glory
proclaim in deep tone,
and sweet harp, the story
of what he has done.

4 Sing praise to the Lord!
thanksgiving and song
to him be outpoured
all ages along:
for love in creation,
for heaven restored,
for grace of salvation,
sing praise to the Lord!

(Amen, amen.)

from Psalms 148, 150
H W Baker (1821–1877)
© in this version Jubilate Hymns

491 We are being built into a temple
Songs of Fellowship 1   139

We are being built into a temple
fit for God's own dwelling place;
into the house of God
which is the Church
the pillar and the ground of truth;
a precious stone that Jesus owns,
fashioned by his wondrous grace.
And as we love and trust each other,
so the building grows and grows.

Ian Traynar
© Thankyou Music†

The Church Anniversary (489–491)

492 There's a city to build
Songs of Fellowship 2   301

There's a city to build,
　　there are walls to repair,
where the people of God
　　are to dwell;
let us strengthen our hands
　　for the work of the Lord,
let us rise up, rise up and build.

Rise up and fight with the weapons
　　our God has supplied;
take up your tools
　　he has taught you to use:
rise up and serve in your place:
so we'll move as one man,
that our God may be glorified!

from Nehemiah 2 and 4
Rita Pratt
© Springtide/Word Music (UK)†

493 O give thanks
Songs of Fellowship 1   97

O give thanks to the Lord,
all you his people.
　　O give thanks to the Lord,
　　　　for he is good;
let us praise, let us thank,
let us celebrate and dance:
　　O give thanks to the Lord,
　　　　for he is good.

Joanne Pond
© Thankyou Music†

494 We really want to thank you
Mission Praise 256

　　We really want to thank you, Lord,
　　we really want to bless your name:
　　Alleluia – Jesus is our king!

1 We thank you, Lord,
　　for your gift to us,
　　your life so rich beyond compare,

the gift of your body here on earth
of which we sing and share.
　　We really . . .

2 We thank you, Lord,
　　for our life together –
to live and move
　　in the love of Christ,
your tenderness which sets us free
to serve you with our lives.
　　We really . . .

3 Praise God
　　from whom all blessings flow,
in heaven above and earth below;
one God, three persons, we adore –
to him be praise for evermore!

Ed Baggett
© Celebration/Thankyou Music†
v 3 after T Ken (1637–1710)
© in this version Jubilate Hymns

495 In my life Lord
Mission Praise 105

1 In my life, Lord, be glorified,
　　be glorified;
in my life, Lord, be glorified today!

2 In my song, Lord, be glorified,
　　be glorified;
in my song, Lord, be glorified today!

3 In your church, Lord, be glorified,
　　be glorified;
in your church, Lord, be glorified
　　today!

4 In my speech, Lord, be glorified,
　　be glorified;
in my speech, Lord, be glorified
　　today!

Bob Kilpatrick
© Prism Tree Music†

(492–495) The Church Anniversary

496

CREED

Let us confess our faith in the Son of God:

Christ is the image
　　of the invisible God,
the firstborn over all creation.
By him all things were created:
things in heaven and on earth,
visible and invisible,
thrones, powers,
　　rulers, and authorities;
all things were created by him
　　and for him.
He is before all things
and in him all things hold together.
He is the head of the body,
　　the Church;
he is the beginning
and the firstborn from the dead. Amen.

†

from Colossians 1

497　Quam dilecta
Hymns for Today's Church 558

1 We love the place, O God,
　in which your honour dwells:
　the joy of your abode,
　all earthly joy excels.

2 We love the house of prayer:
　for where Christ's people meet,
　our risen Lord is there
　to make our joy complete.

3 We love the word of life,
　the word that tells of peace,
　of comfort in the strife
　and joys that never cease.

4 We love the cleansing sign
　of life through Christ our Lord,
　where with the name divine
　we seal the child of God.

5 We love the holy feast
　where, nourished with this food,
　by faith we feed on Christ,
　his body and his blood.

6 We love to sing below
　of mercies freely given,
　but O, we long to know
　the triumph-song of heaven.

7 Lord Jesus, give us grace
　on earth to love you more,
　in heaven to see your face
　and with your saints adore.

W Bullock (1798–1874) and
H W Baker (1821–1877)
© in this version Jubilate Hymns

498　Almsgiving
Hymns for Today's Church 287

1 O Lord of heaven and earth and sea,
　to you all praise and glory be,
　who loved us from eternity
　　and gave us all.

2 The golden sunshine, gentle air,
　sweet flowers and fruit,
　　your love declare;
　when harvests ripen you are there –
　　you give us all.

3 For peaceful homes
　　and healthful days,
　for all the blessings earth displays,
　we owe you thankfulness
　　and praise –
　　you give us all.

4 Freely you gave your only Son,
　who on the cross salvation won;
　and in the life through him begun
　　you give us all.

The Church Anniversary (496–498)

5 You sent your Spirit from above
   as wind and fire and gentle dove;
   and in his gifts of power and love
      you gave us all.

6 For souls redeemed,
      for sins forgiven,
   for means of grace
      and hopes of heaven,
   to you, O Lord, what can be given?
      you give us all.

7 We lose what on ourselves
      we spend;
   we have as treasure without end
   whatever, Lord, to you we lend –
      you give us all.

8 Father, from whom we all derive
   our life, our gifts, our power to give:
   O may we ever with you live;
      you give us all.

C Wordsworth (1807–1885)
© in this version Jubilate Hymns

499

FOR LEADERS (COLLECT)

Almighty God,
you have given your Holy Spirit
      to the church
that he may lead us into all truth.
Bless with his grace and presence
the leaders of this church;
keep them steadfast in faith
      and united in love,
that they may reveal your glory
and prepare the way of your kingdom;
through Jesus Christ our Lord. **Amen.**

after collect for a Synod – ASB

500

ABOUT OUR POSSESSIONS

Lord Jesus Christ,
you have taught us
that we cannot love both God
      and money
and that all our possessions
are a trust from you:
teach us to be faithful stewards
of our time, our talents,
      and our money,
that we may help others
      extend your kingdom;
for your name's sake. **Amen.**   †

501

FOR PATIENCE

Grant, our Father,
that in this church
the younger may respect the traditions
      of the older,
and the older may understand
      the impatience of the younger;
so that young and old
may share together in your service,
and gladly recognise
that all are one in Jesus Christ. **Amen.** †

502

ACT OF DEDICATION
The Act of Dedication at number 784 may be
adapted here for local use. The appropriate
responses are as follows:

. . . this is our resolve.
May God be with you.

To God be glory in the Church and in
Christ Jesus:
**Yours, Lord, is the greatness,
the power, the glory,**

the splendour, and the majesty;
or everything in heaven and on earth
is yours.
**All things come from you,
and of your own do we give you.**

from 1 Chronicles 29.11
page 129 – ASB

503

PRAYER OF DEDICATION
We offer to God our skills and our
service, our lives and our worship:

O God, you have given us life and
health and strength, and in Jesus Christ
you have given us a saviour and a
friend.

For the love that made you enter our
world in Jesus to share our joys and
sorrows and to die for our sin: Father,
receive the gift of our love.

For the forgiveness you promise to all
who confess their sins and trust in his
sacrifice on the cross: Father,
receive the gift of our penitence.

For the hope of eternal life we have in
Christ because you raised him from the
dead: Father,
receive the gift of our lives.

For the blessing of friendship and the
satisfaction of working together, for the
stretching of mind and the exercise of
body: Father,
receive the gift of our service.

Because you are the Lord of all, yet
your ears are open to our cry; and because we delight to praise you: Father,
receive the gift of our worship.

**Holy, holy, holy Lord,
God of power and might,
heaven and earth
are full of your glory.
Hosanna in the highest. Amen.** †

504 Halton Holgate (Sharon)
Hymns for Today's Church 370

1 May the grace of Christ our saviour
and the Father's boundless love,
with the Holy Spirit's favour,
rest upon us from above.

2 So may we remain in union
with each other and the Lord,
and possess, in sweet communion,
joys which earth cannot afford.

from 2 Corinthians 13
J Newton (1725–1807)

505 All Saints
Hymns for Today's Church 215

1 God of light and life's creation,
reigning over all supreme,
daunting our imagination,
prospect glorious yet unseen:
Lord, whom earth and heaven obey,
turn towards this house today!

2 God of alien, God of stranger,
named by nations of the earth;
poor and exile in a manger,
God of harsh and humble birth:
let us all with love sincere
learn to welcome strangers here.

3 God of justice in our nation,
fearing neither rich nor strong,
granting truth its vindication,
passing sentence on all wrong:
Lord, by whom we die or live,
hear, and as you hear, forgive.

4 God the Father, Son, and Spirit,
Trinity of love and grace,
through our fathers we inherit
word and worship in this place:
let our children all their days
to this house return with praise!

from 1 Kings 8
© Michael Perry/Jubilate Hymns

The Church Anniversary (503–505)

1 Go forth and tell!
O church of God, awake!
God's saving news
to all the nations take:
proclaim Christ Jesus,
saviour, Lord, and king,
that all the world
his worthy praise may sing.

2 Go forth and tell!
God's love embraces all;
he will in grace
respond to all who call:
how shall they call
if they have never heard
the gracious invitation of his word?

3 Go forth and tell!
where still the darkness lies;
in wealth or want,
the sinner surely dies:
give us, O Lord,
concern of heart and mind,
a love like yours
which cares for all mankind.

4 Go forth and tell!
The doors are open wide:
share God's good gifts –
let no one be denied;
live out your life

as Christ your Lord
shall choose,
your ransomed powers
for his sole glory use.

5 Go forth and tell!
O church of God, arise!
go in the strength
which Christ your Lord
supplies;
go till all nations
his great name adore
and serve him, Lord and king
for evermore.

J E Seddon (1915–1983)
© Mrs M Seddon/Jubilate Hymns

507

ASCRIPTION

Now to him who is able to do
immeasurably more
than all we ask or imagine,
according to his power
that is at work within us;
to him be glory in the church
and in Christ Jesus
throughout all generations,
for ever and ever! **Amen.**   †

from Ephesians 3

THE CHURCH
ANNIVERSARY/GIVING
Other items appropriate to this theme

Sentence

Give, and it will be given   Section **29**

Hymns

Church of God, elect and glorious   444
Lord, speak to me that I may speak   428
May the mind of Christ my saviour   452
O God beyond all praising   47
Praise God from whom all blessings   70

Songs

Jesus put this song   423
So we're marching along   543
The Lord has led forth   121

Psalm Version (sung)

I was glad when they said
    (Psalm 122)   559

Psalm Versions (spoken)

I was glad when they said
    (Psalm 122)   53
Praise the Lord, praise God in his
    sanctuary (Psalm 150)   466

Prayers

All God's promises are 'yes' (Creed)   83
O God our Father, you grant (For
    the Body of Christ)   477
O God, we cannot measure your
    love (Thanksgiving)   178
Heavenly Father, let these gifts
    (Offertory Prayer)   460
Lord God of our fathers
    (Acclamation)   69

Readings

Dedication of the Temple –
    1 Kings 8.22–30
David's Prayer –
    1 Chronicles 29.10–20
Giving Generously –
    1 Chronicles 29.1–9;
    2 Corinthians 8; 9.1–15
Exhortation to God's People –
    Hebrews 10.19–25
The People of God – 1 Peter 2.1–10
The Light of the World –
    Matthew 5.11–16

(See also Minister's Section 757–762. The
Lord's Prayer is printed inside the back
cover.)

29 Harvest

The land has yielded its harvest: God, our own God, has blessed us. Psalm 67.6

Give, and it will be given to you – a good measure, pressed down, shaken together and running over. Luke 6.38

508

PRAISE

Shout for joy to the Lord, all the earth;
serve the Lord with gladness!

Come before him with joyful songs;
**give thanks to him
and praise his name! Amen.**

from Psalm 100

509
Wir pflügen
Hymns for Today's Church 292

1 We plough the fields, and scatter
the good seed on the land;
but it is fed and watered
by God's almighty hand:
he sends the snow in winter,
the warmth to swell the grain;
the breezes and the sunshine,
and soft refreshing rain.
     All good gifts around us
     are sent from heaven above:
     then thank the Lord,
     O thank the Lord
     for all his love.

2 He only is the maker
of all things near and far;
he paints the wayside flower,
he lights the evening star:
the winds and waves obey him,

by him the birds are fed;
much more, to us his children
he gives our daily bread.
     All good gifts . . .

3 We thank you, then, our Father,
for all things bright and good;
the seed-time and the harvest,
our life, our health, our food:
accept the gifts we offer
for all your love imparts;
and that which you most welcome
our humble, thankful hearts!
     All good gifts . . .

after M Claudius (1740–1815)
J M Campbell (1817–1878)

510
Golden Sheaves
Hymns for Today's Church 291

1 To you, O Lord, our hearts we raise
     in hymns of adoration:
accept our sacrifice of praise,
     our shouts of exultation;
for by your hand our souls are fed –
     what joys our love has given!
You give to us our daily bread,
     so give us bread from heaven!

2 And now on this our festal day,
     your love to us expressing
our gifts before you, Lord, we lay,
     the firstfruits of your blessing:

bright robes of gold the fields adorn,
   the hills with joy are ringing;
the valleys stand so thick with corn
   that even they are singing.

3 Yet in your presence we confess,
   O Lord of earth and heaven,
our pride, our greed
      and selfishness –
   we ask to be forgiven:
and where the hungry suffer still
   because of our ambition,
there let our riches serve your will
   your love be our commission.

4 There is a country bright as day
   beyond the crystal river,
where hunger will be done away
   and thirst be gone for ever;
where praises ring out
      loud and strong
   that now with ours are blending;
where we shall sing
      the harvest-song
   that never has an ending.

after W C Dix (1837–1898)
© in this version Word & Music/Jubilee Hymns

511

CONFESSION

O God our Father, we confess that we
have often used your gifts carelessly,
and acted as though we were not grateful. Hear our prayer, and in your mercy
forgive us and help us:

When we enjoy the fruits of the harvest, but forget they come from you –
then, Father, in your mercy,
forgive us and help us.

When we are full and satisfied, but
ignore the cry of the hungry and those
in need – then, Father, in your mercy,
forgive us and help us.

When we are thoughtless, and do not
treat with respect or care the wonderful
world you have made – then, Father, in
your mercy,
forgive us and help us.

When we store up goods for ourselves
alone, as if there were no God and no
heaven – then, Father, in your mercy,
forgive us and help us.

**Grant us thankful hearts
and a loving concern for all people;
through Jesus Christ our Lord. Amen.** †

512

PSALM*

O God, it is right for us to praise you,
and keep our promises to you, because
you answer our prayers:

You care for the land and water it:
you make it rich and fertile.

^AYou fill the running streams with
water:
and irrigate the land.

^BYou soften the ground with showers:
and make young crops grow.

^AYou crown the year with goodness:
and give us a plentiful harvest.

^BThe pastures are filled with flocks:
^A**the hillsides are full of joy.**

The fields are covered with grain:
^{ALL}**they shout for joy and sing. Amen.**

from Psalm 65

(*The congregation may divide into two at
A and B)

513 Regent Square
Hymns for Today's Church 30

PSALM

1 Fill your hearts with joy
        and gladness,
    sing and praise your God and mine!
    Great the Lord in love and wisdom,
    might and majesty divine!
    He who framed the starry heavens
    knows and names them
        as they shine.

2 Praise the Lord, his people,
        praise him!
    wounded souls his comfort know.
    Those who fear him find his
        mercies,
    peace for pain and joy for woe;
    humble hearts are high exalted,
    human pride and power laid low.

3 Praise the Lord
        for times and seasons,
    cloud and sunshine, wind and rain;
    spring to melt the snows of winter
    till the waters flow again;
    grass upon the mountain pastures,
    golden valleys thick with grain.

4 Fill your hearts with joy
        and gladness,
    peace and plenty crown your days;
    love his laws,
        declare his judgements,
    walk in all his words and ways,
    he the Lord and we his children;
    praise the Lord, all people, praise!

from Psalm 147
© Timothy Dudley-Smith

514 Venice, Franconia, Rossleigh
Hymns for Today's Church 34, 110, 290

PSALM

1 The earth is yours, O God –
    you nourish it with rain;

(513–515) Harvest

the streams and rivers overflow,
the land bears seed again.

2 The soil is yours, O God –
    the shoots are moist with dew;
    and ripened by the burning sun
    the corn grows straight and true.

3 The hills are yours, O God –
    their grass is lush and green,
    providing pastures for the flocks
    which everywhere are seen.

4 The whole rich land is yours
    for fodder or for plough;
    and so, for rain, sun, soil and seed,
    O God, we thank you now.

from Psalm 65
© Michael Saward/Jubilate Hymns

515 Kum ba yah
Hymns for Today's Church 358

PSALM

1 Praise the Lord our God,
        praise the Lord;
    praise him from the heights,
        praise the Lord;
    praise him, angel throngs,
        praise the Lord –
    praise God, all his host!

2 Praise him, sun and moon,
        and the stars;
    praise him, sky and clouds,
        and the rain;
    let them praise his name,
        works of God –
    all creatures, praise the Lord!

3 Praise him, wind and storm,
        mountains steep;
    praise him, fruitful trees,
        cedars tall;
    beasts and cattle herds,
        birds that fly –
    all creatures, praise the Lord!

4 Kings of earth, give praise,
    rulers all;
all young men and girls,
    praise the Lord;
old men, children small,
    praise the Lord –
all people, praise the Lord!

from Psalm 148
© Richard Bewes/Jubilate Hymns

4 'My children shall dwell
    in a body of love,
a light to the world they will be;
life shall come forth
    from the Father above –
my body will set mankind free.'
    Fear not . . .

from Joel 2
Priscilla Wright Porter
© Celebration/Thankyou Music†

516 Fear not
Mission Praise 47

Fear not, rejoice and be glad:
the Lord has done a great thing –
has poured out his Spirit on all
    mankind,
on those who confess his name.

1 The fig-tree is budding,
    the vine bears us fruit,
the wheat fields
    are golden with grain:
thrust in the sickle,
    the harvest is ripe –
the Lord has given us rain.
    Fear not . . .

2 You shall eat in plenty
    and be satisfied,
the mountains
    will drip with sweet wine:
'My children shall drink
    of the fountain of life,
my children will know
    they are mine.'
    Fear not . . .

3 'My people shall know
    that I am the Lord,
their shame I have taken away;
my Spirit
    will lead them together again,
my Spirit will show them the way.'
    Fear not . . .

517 I will sing, I will sing
Jesus Praise 21

1 I will sing, I will sing
    a song unto the Lord,
I will sing, I will sing
    a song unto the Lord,
I will sing, I will sing
    a song unto the Lord:
Alleluia, glory to the Lord!
    Allelu, alleluia, glory to the Lord,
    allelu, alleluia, glory to the Lord,
    allelu, alleluia, glory to the Lord,
    alleluia, glory to the Lord!

2 We will come, we will come
    as one before the Lord . . .
Alleluia, glory to the Lord!
    Allelu, alleluia . . .

3 If the Son, if the Son
    shall make you free . . .
you shall be free indeed:
    Allelu, alleluia . . .

4 They that sow in tears
    shall reap in joy . . .
Alleluia, glory to the Lord!
    Allelu, alleluia . . .

Max Dyer
© Celebration/Thankyou Music†

Harvest (516–517)

1 Who put the colours in the rainbow?
Who put the salt into the sea?
Who put the cold
into the snowflake?
Who made you and me?
Who put the hump upon the camel?
Who put the neck on the giraffe?
Who put the tail upon the monkey?
Who made hyenas laugh?
Who made whales and snails
and quails?
Who made hogs and dogs
and frogs?
Who made bats and rats and cats?
Who made everything?

2 Who put the gold into the sunshine?
Who put the sparkle in the stars?
Who put the silver in the moonlight?
Who made Earth and Mars?
Who put the scent into the roses?
Who taught the honey bee to dance?
Who put the tree inside the acorn?
It surely can't be chance!
Who made seas and leaves
and trees?
Who made snow and winds
that blow?
Who made streams and rivers
flow?
God made all of these!

© Paul Booth

They say he's wonderful,
they say he's wonderful;
the sun, the moon,
the stars that shine –
the sun, the moon,
the stars that shine,
say God is wonderful.

(518–521) Harvest

1 He makes the rain to fall,
he sees the wheat grow tall;
the harvest of the land and sea,
the harvest of the land and sea
in love he gives it all.
They say . . .

2 When I see babies small,
and I hear children call,
and think of family life and fun –
and think of family life and fun,
I know he's behind it all.
They say . . .

© Hugh Pollock

CREED

**We believe and trust
in God the Father
who made the world.**

**We believe and trust
in his Son Jesus Christ,
who redeemed mankind.**

**We believe and trust
in his Holy Spirit,
who gives life to the people of God.**

**We believe and trust in one God:
Father, Son, and Holy Spirit. Amen.** †

THEME PRAYER (COLLECT)

Almighty and everlasting God,
we offer you our hearty thanks
for your fatherly goodness and care
in giving us the fruits of the earth
in their seasons.

give us grace to use them rightly,
   to your glory,
   for our own well-being,
   and for the relief of those in need;
through Jesus Christ our Lord. **Amen.**

Harvest collect – ASB

522 East Acklan, All through the night
Hymns for Today's Church 286, 81

For the fruits of his creation,
   thanks be to God;
for his gifts to every nation,
   thanks be to God;
for the ploughing, sowing, reaping,
silent growth while we are sleeping,
future needs in earth's safe-keeping,
   thanks be to God.

In the just reward of labour,
   God's will is done;
in the help we give our neighbour,
   God's will is done;
in our worldwide task of caring
for the hungry and despairing,
in the harvests we are sharing,
   God's will is done.

For the harvests of his Spirit,
   thanks be to God;
for the good we all inherit,
   thanks be to God;
for the wonders that astound us,
for the truths that still confound us,
most of all that love has found us,
   thanks be to God.

F Pratt Green
© Stainer & Bell Limited†

523 Great is thy faithfulness
Hymns for Today's Church 260

1 Great is your faithfulness,
      O God my Father,
   you have fulfilled
      all your promise to me;
   you never fail
      and your love is unchanging –
   all you have been
      you for ever will be.
   Great is your faithfulness,
   great is your faithfulness,
   morning by morning
   new mercies I see;
   all I have needed
   your hand has provided –
   great is your faithfulness,
      Father, to me.

2 Summer and winter,
      and springtime and harvest,
   sun, moon and stars
      in their courses above
   join with all nature
      in eloquent witness
   to your great faithfulness,
      mercy and love.
   Great is your faithfulness . . .

3 Pardon for sin,
      and a peace everlasting,
   your living presence
      to cheer and to guide;
   strength for today,
      and bright hope for
         tomorrow –
   these are the blessings
      your love will provide.
   Great is your faithfulness . . .

T O Chisholm (1866–1960)
in this version Jubilate Hymns
© Hope Publishing Company†

524

ABOUT OUR POSSESSIONS

Lord Jesus Christ,
you have taught us
that we cannot love both God
and money,
and that all our possessions
are a trust from you:
teach us to be faithful stewards
of our time, our talents,
and our money,
that we may help others extend
your kingdom;
for your name's sake. **Amen**. †

525

THANKSGIVING

For the rich soil of the countryside, for good seed, and for the green corn springing out of the earth, we thank you O God,
and praise your holy name.

For the warm sweetness of the fertile rain, for the hot days of ripening sun, and for the harvest, we thank you O God,
and praise your holy name.

For the yield of the forests, the earth and the sea, we thank you O God,
and praise your holy name.

For all who work on the land, in the mines, or on the waters, and for their courage in days of difficulty and disappointment, we thank you O God,
and praise your holy name.

For those who work in office, shop, factory and in transport, to meet our needs, we thank you O God,
and praise your holy name.

For these and all your blessings we make our harvest thanksgiving and give you all the glory: →

Glory be to the Father, and to the Son, and to the Holy Spirit,
as it was in the beginning, is now, and shall be for ever. Amen. †

526 St George's Windsor
Hymns for Today's Church 284

1 Come, you thankful people, come,
   raise the song of harvest home!
 fruit and crops are gathered in
   safe before the storms begin:
 God our maker will provide
   for our needs to be supplied;
 come, with all his people, come,
   raise the song of harvest home!

2 All the world is God's own field,
   harvests for his praise to yield;
 wheat and weeds together sown
   here for joy or sorrow grown:
 first the blade and then the ear,
   then the full corn shall appear –
 Lord of harvest, grant that we
   wholesome grain and pure
     may be.

3 For the Lord our God shall come
   and shall bring his harvest home;
 he himself on that great day,
   worthless things shall take away,
 give his angels charge at last
   in the fire the weeds to cast,
 but the fruitful ears to store
   in his care for evermore.

4 Even so, Lord, quickly come –
   bring your final harvest home!
 gather all your people in
   free from sorrow, free from sin,
 there together purified,
   ever thankful at your side –
 come, with all your angels, come,
   bring that glorious harvest home!

H Alford (1810–1871)
© in this version Jubilate Hymns

1 God of mercy, God of grace,
   show the brightness of your face:
shine upon us, Saviour, shine,
   fill your church with light divine,
and your saving health extend
   to the earth's remotest end.

2 Let the people praise you, Lord!
   be by all who live adored:
let the nations shout and sing

glory to their saviour king,
at your feet their tribute pay,
   and your holy will obey.

3 Let the people crown you king!
   then shall earth her harvest bring,
God to man his blessing give,
   man to God devoted live;
all below and all above,
   one in joy and light and love.

from Psalm 67 (*Deus misereatur*)
H F Lyte (1793–1847)

HARVEST
Other items appropriate to this theme

Hymns

All creatures of our God and king	283
All things bright and beautiful	266
O Lord of Heaven	498

Songs

One must water, one must weed	471
Stand up, clap hands, shout: Thank you, Lord	274

Psalm Version (spoken)

May God be gracious (Psalm 67)	270

Canticles

Angels, praise him	272
Bless the Lord, creation sings	163

Prayer

Lord of the universe (About Ourselves and God's Creation)	281

Readings

The Harvest of God's Creation –
   Genesis 1.1–3, 24–31;
   Deuteronomy 8.1–10
Psalms of Praise – Psalm 104, 148
Honour God Who Provides –
   Luke 12.16–31
Jesus, the Living Bread –
   John 6.27–35

(See also sections God's Creation 264–284, Christ's Coming 579–599, and Minister's Section 735–737, 762–763. The Lord's Prayer is printed inside the back cover.)

30 Christian Conflict and Character/Our Work, Schools

Stand firm, let nothing move you. Always give yourselves fully to the work of the Lord, because you know that your labour in the Lord is not in vain.

1 Corinthians 15.58

528

PRAISE

Praise the Lord, all you nations;
extol him, all you peoples.

For his love protecting us is strong;
**his faithfulness endures for ever.
Amen.**

from Psalm 117

529
St Ethelwald or From strength to strength
Hymns for Today's Church 533

1 Soldiers of Christ, arise
    and put your armour on;
strong in the strength
        which God supplies
        through his eternal Son:

2 Strong in the Lord of hosts,
    and in his mighty power –
who in the strength of Jesus trusts
    is more than conqueror.

3 Stand then in his great might,
    with all his strength endued;
and take, to arm you for the fight,
    the weapons of our God:

4 To keep your armour bright
    attend with constant care,
still walking in your captain's sight
    and keeping watch with prayer.

5 From strength to strength go on –
    wrestle and fight and pray,
tread all the powers
        of darkness down
    and win the well-fought day:

6 Till, having all things done
    and all your conflicts past,
you overcome through Christ alone
    and stand complete at last.

C Wesley (1707–1788)

530
University College
Hymns for Today's Church 524

1 Christian soldiers, onward go!
Jesus' triumph you shall know;
fight the fight, maintain the strife,
strengthened with the bread of life.

2 Join the war and face the foe!
Christian soldiers, onward go;
boldly stand in danger's hour,
trust your captain, prove his power.

(528–530) Christian Conflict and Character

3 Let your drooping hearts be glad,
  march in heavenly armour clad;
  fight, nor think the battle long –
  soon shall victory be your song.

4 Sorrow must not dim your eye,
  soon shall every tear be dry;
  banish fear, you shall succeed –
  great your strength
        if great your need.

5 Onward, then, in battle move!
  more than conquerors
        you shall prove;
  though opposed by many a foe
  Christian soldiers, onward go!

H K White (1785–1806)
© in this version Jubilate Hymns

531

CONFESSION

Heavenly Father,
we are here to worship you,
but first we ask you
to forgive us all our sins:
so many wrong things
      we ought not to have done,
we have done;
so many right things
      we ought to have done
we have not done.
In your mercy forgive us –
help us to do right,
and to reject what is wrong;
through Jesus Christ our Lord. Amen. †

532

THEME PRAYER (COLLECT)

Almighty God,
you call us to your service:
give us strength to put on
      the armour you provide
that we may resist
      the assaults of the devil,
and ever trust in the salvation
which you have promised us
in Jesus Christ our Lord. **Amen.**

Pentecost 9 collect – APB†

533

PSALM*

God is our refuge and strength:
ALL **an ever-present help in trouble.**

Therefore we will not fear:
A **though the earth should shake,**
B **though the mountains**
      fall into the sea,
A **though the waters surge and foam,**
B **though the mountains**
      shake and roar.

There is a river whose streams make glad the city of God: the holy place where the Most High dwells.
A **God is within her, she shall not fall:**
B **God will help her at break of day.**

Nations are in uproar, and kingdoms fall: God lifts his voice – the earth melts away.
A **The Lord almighty is with us:**
B **the God of Jacob is our refuge.**

Come and see what God has done:
ALL **his wonders wrought upon the**
      earth.

He stops the wars throughout the earth:
A **he breaks the bow**
      and shatters the spear,
B **he sets the shield on fire.**

'Be still and know that I am God:
A **I will be exalted over the nations,**
B **I will be exalted over the earth.'** →

(*The congregation may divide at A and B)

Christian Conflict and Character (531–533)

The Lord almighty is with us:
ALLthe God of Jacob is our refuge.
Amen.

from Psalm 46

534 Let God arise
Song of Fellowship 3 428

PSALM

Let God arise,
and let his enemies be scattered,
and let those who hate him
flee before him;
let God arise,
and let his enemies be scattered
and let those who hate him
flee away.

MEN
But let the righteous be glad;
let them exult before God,
let them rejoice with gladness,
building up a highway for the king:
we go in the name of the Lord –
let the shout go up
in the name of the Lord!

WOMEN
The righteous be glad,
let them exult before God;
O let them rejoice
for the king
in the name of the Lord!

from Psalm 68
Graham Kendrick
© Thankyou Music†

535 Sing a new song
Songs of Worship 139

PSALM

Sing a new song – Alleluia!
sing aloud to God the king;
let the saints of God adore him,
let their joyful praises ring!

1 Let instruments and voices
make music to the Lord;
be glad, O ransomed people,
rejoice with one accord!
The Lord accepts the service
of those who love his name;
he leads them on in triumph
his greatness to proclaim.
Sing a new song . . .

2 They wield the sword of justice,
for God their hands are strong;
they challenge kings and nations,
and fight all forms of wrong:
they work for truth and goodness,
the noble and the right;
and this will be their glory –
to triumph in the fight.
Sing a new song . . .

from Psalm 14
J E Seddon (1915–1983)
© Mrs M Seddon/Jubilate Hymn

536 Lux Eoi
Hymns for Today's Church 151

CANTICLE

1 God, we praise you!
God, we bless you!
God, we name you sovereign Lord!
Mighty King whom angels worship,
Father, by your church adored:
all creation shows your glory,
heaven and earth
draw near your throne
singing 'Holy, holy, holy,'
Lord of hosts, and God alone!

2 True apostles, faithful prophets,
saints who set their world ablaze,
martyrs, once unknown, unheeded
join one growing song of praise,
while your church on earth
confesses
one majestic Trinity:
Father, Son, and Holy Spirit,
God, our hope eternally.

(534–536) Christian Conflict and Character

Jesus Christ, the king of glory,
everlasting Son of God,
humble was your virgin mother,
hard the lonely path you trod:
by your cross is sin defeated,
hell confronted face to face,
heaven opened to believers,
sinners justified by grace.

Christ,
    at God's right hand victorious,
you will judge the world you made;
Lord, in mercy help your servants
for whose freedom you have paid:
raise us up from dust to glory,
guard us from all sin today;
King enthroned above all praises,
save your people, God, we pray.

from *Te Deum*
© Christopher Idle/Jubilate Hymns

537[*] The Lord is king
Songs of Fellowship 3   493

1 The Lord is king,
    he is mighty in battle,
working wonders,
    glorious in majesty.

2 The Lord is king –
    so majestic in power!
His right hand has
    shattered the enemy.

3 ᴬThis is my God
    and I will praise him;
ᴮthis is my God
    and I will praise him:

4 ᴬMy strength and song
    and my salvation,
ᴮmy strength and song
    ᴬᴸᴸand my salvation.

Graham Kendrick
© Thankyou Music†

(*The singers may divide at A and B)

538 Rejoice rejoice
Songs of Fellowship 3   478

Rejoice, rejoice! Christ is in you –
the hope of glory in our hearts.
He lives, he lives!
his breath is in you.
Arise! A mighty army we arise!

1 Now is the time for us
    to march upon the land –
into our hands
    he will give the ground
    we claim;
he rides in majesty
    to lead us into victory,
the world shall see
    that Christ is Lord.
Rejoice . . .

2 God is at work in us
    his purpose to perform –
building a kingdom
    of power not of words;
where things impossible
    by faith shall be made possible:
let's give the glory
    to him now.
Rejoice . . .

3 Though we are weak,
    his grace is everything
    we need –
we're made of clay,
    but this treasure is within;
he turns our weaknesses
    into his opportunities,
so that the glory
    goes to him.
Rejoice . . .

Graham Kendrick
© Thankyou Music†

Christian Conflict and Character (537–538)

539 Thanks be to God
Jesus Praise 209

Thanks be to God
who gives us the victory,
gives us the victory
through our Lord Jesus Christ;
thanks be to God
who gives us the victory,
gives us the victory
through our Lord Jesus Christ!

1 He is able to keep us from falling,
and to set us free from sin:
so let us each live up to our calling,
and commit our way to him.
Thanks be to God . . .

2 Jesus knows all about
our temptations –
he has had to bear them too;
he will show us how to escape them,
if we trust him he will lead us
through.
Thanks be to God . . .

3 He has led us
from the power of darkness
to the kingdom of his bless-ed Son:
so let us join in praise together,
and rejoice
in what the Lord has done.
Thanks be to God . . .

4 Praise the Lord for sending Jesus
to the Cross of Calvary:
now he's risen, reigns in power,
and death is swallowed up
in victory.
Thanks be to God . . .

> from 1 Corinthians 15 etc.
> Robert Stoodley
> © Mustard Seed Music†

540 Victory Song
Songs of Fellowship 2   307

1 Through our God
we shall do valiantly –
it is he who will tread down
our enemies;
we'll sing and shout his victory:
Christ is king!

2 For God has won the victory
and set his people free,
his word has slain the enemy,
the earth shall stand and see
that through our God . . .
Christ is king;
Christ is king; Christ is king!

> from Psalm 108
> Dale Garratt
> © Scripture in Song/Thankyou Music†

541* Put on the sword of the Spirit
Church Family Worship Source Book

Put on the sword of the Spirit,
(Trumpet, or equivalent vocal sounds)
the helmet of salvation,
(Trumpet, or equivalent vocal sounds)
the belt of truth and the shield of faith,
(Trumpet, or equivalent vocal sounds)
the breastplate of righteousness
and the shoes of the gospel,
the shoes of the gospel,
the shoes of the gospel of peace.

> from Ephesians 6
> Ian Smale
> © Thankyou Music†

(*Written for children to sing)

542 Be bold, be strong
Spirit of Praise 2   215

Be bold, be strong,
for the Lord your God is with you;
be bold, be strong,
for the Lord your God is with you!
I am not afraid,

(539–542) Christian Conflict and Character

I am not dismayed,
because I'm walking in faith
    and victory:
come on and walk in faith and victory,
for the Lord your God is with you!

Morris Chapman
© Word Music (UK)†

543* Lord's Army
Church Family Worship Source Book

So we're marching along,
    singing a song,
    we're in the Lord's army,
we're fighting for right as we're
    learning what's wrong,
    for we're in the Lord's army.
He's got the victory,
    so let's really shout,
    we're in the Lord's army,
we're in the Lord's, (yes!)
    we're in the Lord's (right!)
    we're in the Lord's army.

Ian Smale
© Thankyou Music†

(*Written for children to sing)

544

CREED

Let us proclaim the mystery of our
faith:

We believe in one Lord Jesus Christ:
he was revealed in the flesh,
attested by the Spirit,
seen by angels,
proclaimed to the nations,
believed in throughout the world,
and taken up to glory. Amen.

If we died with him,
we shall live with him.

If we endure,
we shall reign with him. Amen.   †

from 1 Timothy 3 and 2 Timothy 2

545

THEME PRAYER (COLLECT)

Lord God almighty,
grant your people grace
to withstand the temptations
of the world, the flesh,
    and the devil,
and with pure hearts and minds
to follow you, the only God;
through Jesus Christ, our Lord. **Amen.**

Lent 2 collect – ASB

546 Duke Street
Hymns for Today's Church 526(i)

1 Fight the good fight
    with all your might,
Christ is your strength,
    and Christ your right;
lay hold on life, and it shall be
your joy and crown eternally.

2 Run the straight race
    through God's good grace,
lift up your eyes, and seek his face:
life with its way before you lies,
Christ is the path
    and Christ the prize.

3 Cast care aside, lean on your guide,
his boundless mercy will provide;
trust, and your trusting soul
    shall prove
Christ is its life, and Christ its love.

4 Faint not, nor fear,
    his arms are near;
he does not change,
    and you are dear;
only believe, and Christ shall be
your all-in-all eternally.

J S B Monsell (1811–1875)

Christian Conflict and Character (543–546)

1 Strong in Christ, our great salvation,
   called to be his new creation,
   Christians, sing in celebration,
        living by our faith.
   Saints of old were led and guarded,
   famous names or unrecorded,
   all alike in God rewarded,
        living by their faith.
      All who love and fear him
      learn by faith to hear him,
      in distress his name confess,
      believing it an honour
      to be near him.
   He who chooses this world's bruises
   knows that in Christ
   he never loses
   gaining far more than he refuses,
        living by his faith.

2 Abraham inspired a nation
   searching for a sure foundation
   made his God his destination,
        living by his faith.
   Moses left his power and pleasure,
   Egypt's wealth
        that none could measure,
   finding God a greater treasure,
        living by his faith.
      Many more were hated,
      driven out, ill-treated;
      facing death they kept the faith
      and sang about the glory
      that awaited.
   No derision, pain, or prison
   ever destroyed
   their heavenly vision;
   we with them say 'Christ is risen!'
        living by our faith.

from Hebrews 11
Christopher Idle/Jubilate Hymns

FOR CHRISTIAN MATURITY

Strengthen us, O God,
that we may add to our faith,
        goodness;
to goodness, knowledge;
to knowledge, self-control;
to self-control, endurance;
to endurance, godliness;
to godliness, care for one another;
and to care for one another, love:
that we may be effective
        and productive
in the knowledge
of Jesus Christ our Lord. **Amen.**   †

from 2 Peter 1

549

FOR THOSE IN SCHOOLS

Heavenly Father,
we pray for every boy and girl
        among us
who goes to school,
and for every adult who is a teacher:
let our schools teach what is true,
and make each one of us
willing to learn;
for Jesus sake. **Amen.**

550[*]   Sine Nomine
Hymns for Today's Church 567

1 For all the saints,
        who from their labours rest;
   who to the world
        by faith their Lord confessed,
   your name, O Jesus,
        be for ever blessed:
      Alleluia, alleluia!

(*Verses 4–7, or 4 and 6, may be omitted)

2 You were their rock,
        their fortress and their might;
you, Lord, their captain
        in the well-fought fight,
and in the darkness
        their unfailing light.
    Alleluia, alleluia!

3 So may your soldiers,
        faithful, true and bold,
fight as the saints
        who nobly fought of old
and win with them
        the victor's crown of gold.
    Alleluia, alleluia!

4 One holy people,
        fellowship divine!
we feebly struggle,
        they in glory shine –
in earth and heaven
        the saints in praise combine:
    Alleluia, alleluia!

5 And when the fight is fierce,
        the warfare long,
far off we hear
        the distant triumph-song;
and hearts are brave again,
        and arms are strong.
    Alleluia, alleluia!

6 The golden evening brightens
        in the west:
soon, soon to faithful warriors
        comes their rest,
the peaceful calm
        of paradise the blessed.
    Alleluia, alleluia!

7 But look! – there breaks
        a yet more glorious day;
saints all-triumphant
        rise in bright array –
the king of glory
        passes on his way!
    Alleluia, alleluia!

8 From earth's wide bounds,
        from dawn to setting sun,
through heaven's gates
        to God the Three-in-One
they come, to sing
        the song on earth begun:
    Alleluia, alleluia!

W W How (1823–1897)
© in this version Jubilee Hymns

551 St Gertrude
Hymns for Today's Church 532

1 Onward, Christian soldiers!
        marching as to war,
with the cross of Jesus
        going on before.
Christ, the royal master,
        leads his armies on:
forward into battle
        till the fight is won!
    Onward, Christian soldiers,
    marching as to war
    with the cross of Jesus
    going on before.

2 At the name of Jesus,
        Satan's armies flee:
on then, Christian soldiers,
        on to victory!
Hell's foundations tremble
        at the shout of praise –
sing the song of triumph!
        loud your voices raise!
    Onward, Christian soldiers . . .

3 Like a mighty army
        moves the church of God:
we are humbly treading
        where the saints have trod;
Christ is not divided –
        all one body we,
one in hope and calling,
        one in charity,
    Onward, Christian soldiers . . .

Christian Conflict and Character (551)

4 Crowns and thrones may perish,
    kingdoms rise and wane,
but the church of Jesus
    ever shall remain;
death and hell and Satan
    never shall prevail –
we have Christ's own promise
    and that cannot fail.
    Onward, Christian soldiers,
    marching as to war
    with the cross of Jesus
    going on before.

5 Onward then, you people!
    march in faith, be strong!
blend with ours your voices
    in the triumph song:
Glory, praise and honour
    be to Christ the king!
this through countless ages
    we with angels sing.
    Onward, Christian soldiers . . .

S Baring-Gould (1834–1924)
© in this version Jubilate Hymns

552

ASCRIPTION
Let us give glory to God:

Our Lord and God! You are worthy to receive glory, honour, and power. For you created all things, and by your will they were given existence and life:
Glory to God in the highest!

O Lamb of God! You are worthy to receive wisdom, strength, and praise. For by your death you bought for God people from every tribe, language, nation, and race. You have made them a kingdom of priests to serve our God, and they shall rule on earth:
Glory to God in the highest!

**To him who sits upon the throne
and to the Lamb,**

**be praise and honour,
    glory and power,
for ever and ever! Amen.** †

from Revelation 4 and 5

553   Ellers
Hymns for Today's Church 281

EVENING HYMN

1 Saviour, again to your dear name
    we raise
with one accord
    our parting hymn of praise;
we give you thanks
    before our worship cease –
then, in the silence,
    hear your word of peace.

2 Give us your peace, Lord,
    on our homeward way:
with you began,
    with you shall end the day;
guard now the lips from sin,
    the hearts from shame,
that in this house have called upon
    your name.

3 Give us your peace, Lord,
    through the coming night,
turn all our darkness
    to your perfect light;
then, through our sleep,
    our hope and strength renew,
for dark and light
    are both alike to you.

4 Give us your peace
    throughout our earthly life:
comfort in sorrow,
    courage in the strife;
then, when your voice
    shall make our conflict cease,
call us, O Lord,
    to your eternal peace.

J Ellerton (1826–1893)

(552–553) Christian Conflict and Character

CHRISTIAN CONFLICT AND CHARACTER/OUR WORK, SCHOOLS

Other items appropriate to this theme

Hymns

Here from all nations	577
Lord of all hopefulness	86
Praise the Lord, you heavens adore him	284
Through all the changing scenes of life	576
To him we come	152

Psalm Version (spoken)

If the Lord had not been on our side (Psalm 124)	95

Songs

For this purpose	255
The Lord has led forth	121

Prayers

Lord God almighty, grant your people (Collect)	545
Almighty God, you have provided (Collect)	278

Now to him who is able (Ascription)	90
When we are tempted (For strength)	617

Readings

The Triumph of Joshua –
   Joshua 1.1–9
David's strength –
   1 Samuel 17.31–50
Daniel's Courage – Daniel 6.10–23
God's Law in the Heart –
   Jeremiah 31.31–34
Manifesto of God's Kingdom –
   Matthew 5.1–12
Call to Discipline –
   1 Corinthians 9.19–27
Suffering for Christ –
   2 Corinthians 6.3–10
The Fight – Ephesians 6.10–20
Running for the Prize –
   Philippians 3.12–21

(See also section Following Jesus 132–154, and Minister's Section 720–722, 764–766. The Lord's Prayer is printed inside the back cover.)

Christian Conflict and Character (Other items)

31 Heaven/God's Peace

Our homeland is in heaven, and from heaven comes the Saviour we are waiting for, the Lord Jesus Christ. Philippians 3.20

Since we have been justified by faith, we have peace with God through our Lord Jesus Christ. Romans 5.1

554

PRAISE

O Lord our God,
we will praise you with all our heart.

O Lord our God,
**we will proclaim your greatness
    for ever.**

Great is your constant love for us;
**you have saved us
    from the grave itself! Amen.**

from Psalm 86

3 Jesus is worthy to receive
   all praise and power divine;
   and all the blessings we can give
   with songs of heaven combine.

4 Let all who live beyond the sky,
   the air and earth and seas
   unite to lift his glory high
   and sing his endless praise!

5 Let all creation join in one
   to bless the sacred name
   of him who reigns upon the throne,
   and to adore the Lamb!

from Revelation 5
I Watts (1674–1748

555 Nativity
Hymns for Today's Church 206

1 Come let us join our cheerful songs
   with angels round the throne;
   ten thousand thousand
       are their tongues,
   but all their joys are one.

2 Worthy the Lamb who died,
       they cry,
   to be exalted thus!
   Worthy the Lamb, our lips reply,
   for he was slain for us!

556 Innocents
Hymns for Today's Church 566(ii)

1 Children of the heavenly king,
   as you journey, sweetly sing;
   sing your saviour's worthy praise,
   glorious in his works and ways.

2 We are travelling home to God
   in the way the saints have trod;
   they are happy now, and we
   soon their happiness shall see.

(554–556) Heaven

3 Lift your eyes to seek the light –
God's own city is in sight;
there our endless home shall be,
there our Lord we soon shall see.

4 Never fear, but boldly stand
on the borders of your land;
Christ, the everlasting Son
gives you strength to journey on.

5 Lord, obediently we go,
gladly leaving all below:
Master, be our guide indeed –
we shall follow where you lead.

J Cennick (1718–1755)

557

CONFESSION

O God, our Father in heaven, we
confess to you our failure to live as
children of your grace and heirs of your
promises:

When we make this world's goods our
treasure, and are mindless of your
kingdom and your reward: in your
mercy,
Father, forgive us and help us.

When we forget that here we have no
enduring city, and fail to look for the
city which is to come: in your mercy,
Father, forgive us and help us.

When we measure worth by the stan-
dards of this passing age and reject
your eternal truth: in your mercy,
Father, forgive us and help us.

When we lose the vision of Christ and
no longer run to win the prize of your
call to heaven: in your mercy,
Father, forgive us and help us.

**Father,
you have raised us
together with Christ:**

set our hearts and minds
on things above,
where he is seated in glory
at your right hand for evermore.
Amen.

†

558

PSALM*

Sing joyfully to the Lord, you righteous:
ALLit is right that his people
should praise him.

Praise the Lord with the harp:
Amake music to him on the strings.

Sing to the Lord a new song:
Bplay skilfully, and shout for joy.

For the word of the Lord is right and
true:
ALLhe is faithful in all he does.

The Lord loves justice and truth:
Band his faithful love fills the earth.

By the word of the Lord the heavens
were formed:
ALLthe moon and stars
by his right hand.

Let all the earth fear the Lord:
Athe people of the world revere him.

For he spoke, and it came to be:
Bhe commanded, and all was made.

The Lord holds back the nations:
ALLhe thwarts their evil intent.

God's purposes are sure:
Ahis plans endure for ever.

Happy is the nation whose God is the
Lord:
Bhappy the people he makes his own.

→

(*The congregation may divide at A and B)

Heaven (557–558)

The eyes of the Lord are on those who fear him:
ALL**who trust in his unfailing love.**

We wait in hope for the Lord:
A**he is our help and shield.**

In him our hearts rejoice:
B**we trust his holy name.**

May your constant love be with us, Lord:
ALL**as we put our hope in you. Amen.**

from Psalm 33

3 'You bring to those who hate me,
    shame;
you spread a feast and fill my cup.
It overflows! You raise me up
to live with you
    and bless your name.'

4 To God the Father, Spirit, Son,
be glory now, until the song
of mercy through the ages long
in heaven shall greet
    the Three-in-One!

from Psalm 23
© Michael Perry/Jubilate Hymns

559 I was glad
Church Family Worship Source Book

PSALM

I was glad when they said to me
let us go to the house of the Lord:
here we are in the presence of God,
giving thanks to our mighty Lord.

DURING REPEAT VERSE
Pray for peace,
pray for peace for the city of God:
Peace be with you, peace be with you;
peace be with you, peace be with you!

from Psalm 122
© Norman Warren/Jubilate Hymns

560 Herongate
Hymns for Today's Church 131(i)

PSALM

1 My faithful shepherd is the Lord,
he leads me
        through the pastures green
to pools of water sweet and clean,
and makes me stronger by his word.

2 His promise is my certain guide,
his way is true, his path is right:
'I shall not fear the darkest night
for you, O Lord, are at my side!'

561 God of gods
Hymns for Today's Church 340

CANTICLE

1 God of gods, we sound his praises,
highest heaven its homage brings;
earth and all creation raises
glory to the King of kings.
Holy, holy, holy, name him,
Lord of all his hosts proclaim him,
to the everlasting Father
every tongue in triumph sings.

2 Christians in their hearts
        enthrone him,
tell his praises wide abroad;
prophets, priests, apostles own him
martyrs' crown and saints' reward.
Three-in-One his glory sharing,
earth and heaven
        his praise declaring,
praise the high majestic Father,
praise the everlasting Lord!

3 Hail the Christ, the King of glory,
he whose praise the angels cry,
born to share our human story,
love and labour, grieve and die.
By his cross his work completed,
sinners ransomed, death defeated,
in the glory of the Father
Christ ascended reigns on high.

(559–561) Heaven

4 Lord, we look for your returning,
  teach us so to walk your ways,
  hearts and minds
      your will discerning,
  lives alight with joy and praise.
  In your love and care enfold us,
  by your constancy uphold us;
  may your mercy, Lord and Father,
  keep us now and all our days!

from *Te Deum*
© Timothy Dudley-Smith

562 Faithful vigil
Hymns for Today's Church 55(i)

CANTICLE

1 Faithful vigil ended,
  watching, waiting cease:
  Master, grant your servant
  his discharge in peace.

2 All the Spirit promised,
  all the Father willed,
  now these eyes behold it
  perfectly fulfilled.

3 This your great deliverance
  sets your people free;
  Christ their light uplifted
  all the nations see.

4 Christ, your people's glory!
  watching, doubting cease;
  grant to us your servants
  our discharge in peace.

from Luke 2 (*The Song of Simeon/Nunc dimittis*)
© Timothy Dudley-Smith

563 Behold I tell you a mystery
Songs of Fellowship 3   339

1 Behold, I tell you a mystery;
  behold, I tell you a mystery!
  We shall not all sleep,
  but we shall all be changed –

in a moment,
in a twinkling of an eye;
in a moment,
in a twinkling of an eye.
    For the last trumpet shall sound,
    and the dead shall be raised
        incorruptible
    and we shall be changed,
    we shall be changed.

2 Death is swallowed up in victory;
  death is swallowed up in victory!
  O death, where is your sting?
  The sting of death is sin –
  but thanks be to God
  who gives us the victory
  through Jesus Christ our Lord!
      For the . . .

from 1 Corinthians 15
Phil Rogers
© Thankyou Music†

564 Come and go with me
Jesus Praise 136

1 Come and go with me
      to my Father's house,
  to my Father's house,
      to my Father's house;
  come and go with me
      to my Father's house
    where there's joy, joy, joy!

2 It's not very far to my Father's
  house . . .

3 There is room for all in my Father's
  house . . .

4 Everything is free in my Father's
  house . . .

5 Jesus is the way to my Father's
  house . . .

6 Jesus is the light in my Father's
  house . . .

Copyright controlled†

Heaven (562–564)

565 Sing alleluia
Mission Praise 204

1 Sing alleluia to the Lord,
   sing alleluia to the Lord,
   sing alleluia, sing alleluia,
   sing alleluia to the Lord!

2 Jesus is risen from the dead,
   Jesus is risen from the dead,
   Jesus is risen, Jesus is risen,
   Jesus is risen from the dead!

3 Jesus is Lord of heaven and earth,
   Jesus is Lord of heaven and earth,
   Jesus is Lord, Jesus is Lord,
   Jesus is Lord of heaven and earth!

4 Jesus is coming for his own,
   Jesus is coming for his own,
   Jesus is coming, Jesus is coming,
   Jesus is coming for his own.

verse 1 © Linda Stassen/New Song Ministries†
verses 2–4 anonymous

566 Soon and very soon
Mission Praise 208

1 Soon – and very soon –
   we are going to see the King*
   Alleluia, alleluia,
   we're going to see the King!

2 No more crying there . . .*
   Alleluia . . .

3 No more dying there . . .*
   Alleluia . . .

   Alleluia, alleluia, alleluia, alleluia!

4 Soon and very soon . . .*
   Alleluia . . .

   Alleluia, alleluia, alleluia, alleluia!

Andrae Crouch
© Lexicon Music Incorporated/
Crouch Music (USA)/Word Music (UK)†

(*These sentences are twice repeated)

567* Give me joy
Mission Praise 58

1 What a wonderful saviour is Jesus,
   what a wonderful friend is he:
   for he left all the glory of heaven,
   came to earth to die on Calvary.
      Sing hosanna, sing hosanna,
      sing hosanna to the King of kings;
      sing hosanna, sing hosanna,
      sing hosanna to the king!

2 He arose from the grave – alleluia!
   and he lives never more to die;
   at the Father's right hand
         interceding
   he will hear and heed
         our faintest cry.
      Sing hosanna . . .

3 He is coming some day
         to receive us,
   we'll be caught up to heaven above:
   what a joy it will be to behold him –
   sing for ever of his gracious love.
      Sing hosanna . . .

Copyright controlled†

(*Written for children to sing)

568 Because he died
Junior Praise 81

1 Because he died and is risen,
   because he died and is risen,
   because he died and is risen,
   we now have peace with God
         through Jesus Christ our Lord.
      Hévénu shalóm aléchem,
      hévénu shalóm aléchem,
      hévénu shalóm aléchem,
      hévénu shalóm, shalóm, shalóm
         aléchem!

2 His peace destroys walls between us,
   his peace destroys walls between us,
   his peace destroys walls between us,

for only he
   can reconcile us both to God.
   Hévénu shalóm . . .

3 'My peace I give you,' said Jesus;
   'My peace I give you,' said Jesus;
   'My peace I give you,' said Jesus,
   'Don't let your heart be troubled,
      do not be afraid.'
   Hévénu shalóm . . .

4 The peace beyond understanding,
   the peace beyond understanding,
   the peace beyond understanding,
   will guard the hearts and minds
      of those who pray to him.
   Hévénu shalóm . . .

from Romans 5 etc.
© Michael Baughen/Jubilate Hymns

569

CREED
Let us proclaim our faith:

**We believe in God the Father,
by whose great mercy
we have been born again
to a living hope,
through the resurrection
   of Jesus Christ
from the dead.**

**We believe in God the Son,
who died for our sin,
and rose again for our justification.**

**We believe in God the Holy Spirit,
who bears witness with our spirit
that we are the children of God.**

**We believe in one God:
Father, Son, and Holy Spirit. Amen.** †

from 1 Peter 1, Romans 4 and 8

570

THEME PRAYER (COLLECT)

Merciful God,
you have prepared
   for those who love you
such good things
   as pass our understanding.
Pour into our hearts
   such love towards you
that we, loving you above all things,
may obtain your promises,
which exceed all that we can desire;
through Jesus Christ our Lord. **Amen.**

Last Sunday after Pentecost collect – ASB

571 Pastor pastorum
Hymns for Today's Church 29

1 Faithful Shepherd, feed me
   in the pastures green;
   faithful Shepherd, lead me
   where your steps are seen:

2 Hold me fast, and guide me
   in the narrow way;
   so, with you beside me,
   I need never stray:

3 Daily bring me nearer
   to the heavenly shore;
   make my faith grow clearer,
   help me love you more:

4 Consecrate each pleasure,
   every joy and pain;
   you are all my treasure,
   all I hope to gain:

5 Day by day prepare me
   as you purpose best,
   mercy shall pursue me
   to your promised rest.

T B Pollock (1836–1896)
© in this version Jubilate Hymns

Heaven (569–571)

572

1 There's a song for all the children
    that makes the heavens ring,
  a song that even angels
    can never, never sing;
  they praise the Lord as maker
    and see him glorified,
  but we can call him Saviour
    because for us he died.

2 There's a place for all the children
    where Jesus reigns in love,
  a place of joy and freedom
    that nothing can remove;
  a home that is more friendly
    than any home we know,
  where Jesus makes us welcome
    because he loves us so.

3 There's a friend for all the children
    to guide us every day,
  whose care is always faithful
    and never fades away;
  there's no-one else so loyal –
    his friendship stays the same;
  he knows us and he loves us,
    and Jesus is his name.

                    after A Midlane (1825–1909)
                    © in this version Jubilate Hymns

573

FOR INWARD PEACE

O Lord, your way is perfect:
help us, we pray,
always to trust in your goodness;
that walking with you in faith,
and following you in all simplicity,
we may possess
        quiet and contented minds,
and leave all our worries with you,
because you care for us;
for the sake of Jesus Christ our Lord.
Amen.   †

574

FOR STRENGTH

Heavenly Father,
in your Son Jesus Christ
you have given us a true faith
        and a sure hope.
Strengthen this faith and hope
        in us all our days,
that we may live
        as those who believe
in the communion of saints,
the forgiveness of sins,
and the resurrection
to eternal life;
through your Son Jesus Christ
        our Lord. **Amen.**

                    from the Funeral Service – ASB

575

DEDICATION

And now, O Father in heaven,
we entrust ourselves to you;
that joyful or sorrowing,
living or dying,
we may ever be with our Lord Jesus,
safe in your eternal care. **Amen.**   †

576

1 Through all the changing scenes
        of life,
    in trouble and in joy,
    the praises of my God shall still
    my heart and tongue employ.

2 O glorify the Lord with me,
    with me exalt his name!
    when in distress, to him I called –
    he to my rescue came.

(572–576) Heaven

3 The hosts of God encamp around
    the dwellings of the just;
his saving help he gives to all
who in his mercy trust.

4 O taste his goodness, prove his love!
experience will decide
how blessed they are,
    and only they,
who in his truth confide.

5 Fear him, you saints,
    and you will then
have nothing else to fear;
his service shall be your delight,
your needs shall be his care.

6 To Father, Son and Spirit, praise!
to God, whom we adore,
be worship, glory, power and love,
both now and evermore!

from Psalm 34
N Tate (1652–1715) and
N Brady (1659–1726)
© in this version Jubilate Hymns

577   O quanta qualia, Epiphany Hymn
        Hymns for Today's Church 571, 338(i)

1 Here from all nations,
    all tongues, and all peoples,
countless the crowd
    but their voices are one;
vast is the sight
    and majestic their singing –
'God has the victory:
    he reigns from the throne!'

2 These have come out of
    the hardest oppression,
now they may stand
    in the presence of God,
serving their Lord
    day and night in his temple,
ransomed and cleansed
    by the Lamb's precious blood.

3 Gone is their thirst
    and no more shall they hunger,
God is their shelter,
    his power at their side;
sun shall not pain them,
    no burning will torture,
Jesus the Lamb
    is their shepherd and guide.

4 He will go with them
    to clear living water
flowing from springs
    which his mercy supplies;
gone is their grief
    and their trials are over –
God wipes away
    every tear from their eyes.

5 Blessing and glory
    and wisdom and power
be to the Saviour
    again and again;
might and thanksgiving
    and honour for ever
be to our God:
    Alleluia! Amen.

from Revelation 7
© Christopher Idle/Jubilate Hymns

578   Marching through Georgia
        Hymns for Today's Church 188

1 Come and see the shining hope
    that Christ's apostle saw;
on the earth, confusion,
    but in heaven an open door,
where the living creatures
    praise the Lamb for evermore:
Love has the victory for ever!
    Amen, he comes!
to bring his own reward!
    Amen, praise God!
for justice now restored;
kingdoms of the world become
the kingdoms of the Lord:
    Love has the victory for ever!

Heaven (577–578)

2 All the gifts you send us, Lord,
      are faithful, good, and true;
holiness and righteousness
      are shown in all you do:
who can see your greatest Gift
      and fail to worship you?
Love has the victory for ever!
    Amen, he comes!
to bring his own reward!
Amen, praise God!
for justice now restored;
kingdoms of the world become
the kingdoms of the Lord:
Love has the victory for ever!

3 Power and salvation
      all belong to God on high!
So the mighty multitudes of heaven
      make their cry,
singing Alleluia!
      where the echoes never die:
Love has the victory for ever!
    Amen, he comes! . . .

from Revelation 4–5 etc
© Christopher Idle/Jubilate Hymns

HEAVEN/GOD'S PEACE
Other items appropriate to this theme

Hymns

Psalm Version (sung)

Canticle

Songs

Prayers

Readings

The New Jerusalem –
    Isaiah 33.17–22; Revelation 21
The Resurrection Body –
    1 Corinthians 15.12–58
Pressing On – Philippians 3.7–21
Worship in Heaven –
    Revelation 7.9–17
Treasure in Heaven –
    Matthew 6.19–21
Jesus, the Way to Heaven –
    John 14.1–14
True Peace – John 14.27–31

(See also the Easter section 239–263, and
Minister's Section 767–769. The Lord's
Prayer is printed inside the back cover.)

32 Christ's Coming

Look, he is coming with the clouds, and every eye will see him.
Revelation 1.7

You also must be ready, because the Son of Man will come at an hour when you do not expect him.
Matthew 24.44

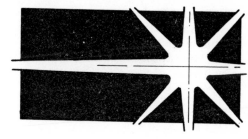

579

PRAISE

Come, O God, and rule the earth:
all the nations are yours!

Let them know that you are king,
sovereign over all the world! Amen.

from Psalms 82, 83

580
Bristol
Hymns for Today's Church 193

1 Hark the glad sound! –
    the Saviour comes,
the Saviour promised long;
let every heart prepare a throne
and every voice a song.

2 He comes the prisoners to release
in Satan's bondage held;
the gates of brass before him burst,
the iron fetters yield.

3 He comes the broken heart to bind,
the wounded soul to cure;
and with the treasures of his grace
to enrich the humble poor.

4 Our glad hosannas, Prince of peace,
your welcome shall proclaim;
and heaven's eternal arches ring
with your beloved name.

from Isaiah 61
P Doddridge (1702–1751)

581
Winchester New
Hymns for Today's Church 112

1 On Jordan's bank the Baptist's cry
announces that the Lord is nigh:
awake and listen for he brings
glad tidings of the King of kings.

2 Let every heart be cleansed from sin,
make straight
    the way for God within,
and so prepare to be the home
where such a mighty guest
    may come.

3 For you are our salvation, Lord,
our refuge and our great reward;
without your grace we waste away
like flowers that wither and decay.

4 To heal the sick,
    stretch out your hand,
and make the fallen sinner stand;
shine out, and let your light restore
earth's own true loveliness
    once more!

Christ's Coming (579–581)

5 To you, O Christ, all praises be,
  whose advent sets your people free;
  whom with the Father we adore
  and Holy Spirit evermore!

after C Coffin (1676–1749)
J Chandler (1806–1876)
© in this version, Word & Music/Jubilate Hymns

582

CONFESSION
We must give account of our stewardship: let us ask forgiveness for our sin
and failure.

Lord, we have not used your gifts
wisely: forgive us for being unprofit-
able; in your mercy,
hear us and help us.

Lord, we have not kept brightly
burning the light you entrusted to us:
forgive us for being unprepared; in
your mercy,
hear us and help us.

Lord, we have sometimes ended the
day in anger or bitterness: forgive us for
being unrepentant; in your mercy,
hear us and help us.

Renew our vision,
restore our watchfulness,
make us faithful as you are faithful,
that when you come in glory
we may hear you say:
'Enter into the joy of your Lord.'
Amen.

                                       †

583

PSALM*

Sing to the Lord a new song:
for he has done marvellous things.

(*The congregation may divide at A and B)

His right hand and his holy arm:
have brought his salvation to us.

ᴬHe makes his great victory known:
ᴮ**his triumph he shows to the world.**

ᴬTo us he remembers his love:
ᴮ**his glory is witnessed by all.**

Shout for joy to the Lord, all the earth:
and burst into jubilant song.

ᴬMake music to God with the harp:
ᴮ**with a song**
    and the sound of your praise.

ᴬWith trumpets and blast of the horn:
ᴮ**sing praises to God as your king.**

Let rivers and streams clap their hands:
and the mountains together
    sing praise.

For God comes to judge the whole
world:
to rule all the people in truth. Amen.

from Psalm 98

584   Trumpet Voluntary
         Songs of Worship 126

PSALM*

1 This earth belongs to God,
  the world, its wealth,
    and all its people;
  he formed the waters wide
  and fashioned every sea and shore.
    ᴬWho may go up
    the hill of the Lord
    and stand in the place of holiness?
    ᴮOnly the one whose heart is pure,
    whose hands and lips are clean.

2 Lift high your heads, you gates,
  rise up, you everlasting doors, as
  here now the king of glory
  enters into full command.

(*The congregation may divide at A and B)

^AWho is the king,
this king of glory,
where is the throne
he comes to claim?
^BChrist is the king,
the Lord of glory,
fresh from his victory.

Lift high your heads, you gates,
and fling wide open
the ancient doors, for
here comes the king of glory
taking universal power.
^AWho is the king,
this king of glory,
what is the power
by which he reigns?
^BChrist is the king,
his cross his glory,
and by love he rules.

All glory be to God
the Father, Son, and Holy Spirit;
from ages past it was,
is now, and evermore shall be.

from Psalm 24
© Christopher Idle/Jubilate Hymns

585 Morning Light
Hymns for Today's Church 535

CANTICLE

O bless the God of Israel
who comes to set us free;
who visits and redeems us,
with love for all to see.
The prophets spoke of mercy,
of rescue and release:
God shall fulfil his promise
and bring our people peace.

He comes! the Child of David,
the Son whom God has given;
he comes to live among us
and raise us up to heaven:

before him goes his herald –
forerunner in the way,
the prophet of salvation,
the harbinger of Day.

3 Where once were fear and darkness,
the sun begins to rise –
the dawning of forgiveness
upon the sinner's eyes.
He guides the feet of pilgrims
along the paths of peace:
O bless our God and Saviour,
with songs that never cease!

from Luke 1 (*Benedictus*)
© Michael Perry/Jubilate Hymns

586 He is Lord
Jesus Praise 70

1 He is Lord, he is Lord,
he is risen from the dead
and he is Lord!
Every knee shall bow,
every tongue confess
that Jesus Christ is Lord.

2 He will come, he will come,
he has promised in his word
that he will come;
some glad day or night,
with great power and might,
the risen Lord will come.

verse 1: from Philippians 2, © Marvin V Frey†
verse 2: © Michael Baughen/Jubilate Hymns

587 Make Way
This is Your God 57

1 Make way, make way,
for Christ the king
in splendour arrives;
fling wide the gates
and welcome him into your lives.
Make way, make way
for the King of kings;
make way, make way
and let his kingdom in!

Christ's Coming (585–587)

2 He comes the broken hearts to heal
   the prisoners to free;
   the deaf shall hear,
       the lame shall dance,
   the blind shall see.
       Make way, make way
       for the King of kings;
       make way, make way
       and let his kingdom in!

3 And those who mourn
       with heavy hearts,
   who weep and sigh,
   with laughter, joy and royal crown
   he'll beautify.
       Make way . . .

4 We call you now to worship
   the Lord of all,
   to have no gods before him –
   their thrones must fall!
       Make way . . .

from Isaiah 61
Graph Kendrick
© Thankyou Music†

588 My Lord he is a-coming
Jesus Praise 94

   My Lord, he is a-coming soon –
   prepare the way of the Lord!
   get everything ready
   for that day –
   prepare the way of the Lord!

1 If you're asleep,
       it's time to wake up –
   awake, O sleeper, arise!
   If you're in the dark,
       it's time to be lit –
   awake, O sleeper, arise!
   My Lord . . .

2 Come, Lord Jesus,
       come into my heart –
   prepare the way of the king!
   He is coming, he's coming soon:
   prepare the way of the king!
       My Lord . . .

Laura Winnei
© Celebration/Thankyou Music

589 Restore O Lord
Mission Praise 196

1 Restore, O Lord,
   the honour of your name
   in works of sovereign power;
   come shake the earth again
   that all may see,
   and come with reverent fears
   to the living God
   whose Kingdom shall outlast
       the years.

2 Restore, O Lord,
   in all the earth your fame,
   and in our time revive
   the Church that bears your name;
   and in your anger,
   Lord, remember mercy –
   O living God,
   whose mercy shall outlast the years.

3 Bend us, O Lord,
   where we are hard and cold,
   in your refiner's fire;
   come purify the gold:
   though suffering comes,
   and evil crouches near,
   still our living God
   is reigning – he is reigning here!

Graham Kendrick and Chris Rowlinsor
© Thankyou Music†

Tell me, why do you weep;
tell me, why do you mourn;
tell me, why do you look so sad?
Tell me, why don't you dance;
tell me, why don't you sing;
tell me, why don't you look
    to the sky?

Don't you know
    that your king is coming;
don't you know
    that your king is nigh?
He is even at the gates of Jerusalem,
he is coming on the morning sky.
    Tell me . . .

Don't you know
    that the feast is ready –
ready for the bride to come?
Christians,
    keep your lamps a-burning –
the ending of the age is come.
    Tell me . . .

Don't you know
    you are the Lord's invited;
don't you know
    you are the chosen ones?
You in whom he has delighted
shall rise with Jesus when he comes.
    Tell me . . .

Come arise, my love,
    my fairest daughter:
the winter and the rain are gone,
the flowers of summer
    are appearing,
the time of singing songs has come.
    Tell me . . .

Don't you know
    that your king is coming;
don't you know
    that your king is nigh?

He is even at the gates of Jerusalem,
he is coming on the morning sky.

from Matthew 25
Graham Kendrick
© Thankyou Music†

591

CREED
We say together in faith:

**Holy, holy, holy
is the Lord God Almighty,
who was, and is, and is to come.**

We believe in God the Father, who created all things:
**for by his will they were created
and have their being.**

We believe in God the Son, who was slain:
**for with his blood,
he purchased us for God,
from every tribe and language
and people and nation.**

We believe in God the Holy Spirit –
**the Spirit and the Bride say, 'Come!'
Even so, come, Lord Jesus! Amen.**   †

from Revelation 4 and 5

592

THEME PRAYER (COLLECT)

Almighty God,
give us grace
to cast away the works of darkness
and to put on the armour of light,
now in the time of this mortal life,
in which your Son Jesus Christ
    came to us in great humility:
so that on the last day,
when he shall come again
    in his glorious majesty   →

Christ's Coming (590–592)

to judge the living and the dead,
we may rise to the life immortal;
through him who is alive and reigns
   with you and the Holy Spirit,
one God, now and for ever. **Amen.**

Advent collect – ASB

593 Cloisters
Hymns for Today's Church 529

EVENING HYMN

1 Lighten our darkness
    now the day is ended –
Father in mercy, guard your
    children sleeping;
from every evil,
    every harm defended,
safe in your keeping:

2 To that last hour,
    when heaven's day is dawning,
far spent the night
    that knows no earthly waking;
keep us as watchmen,
    longing for the morning,
till that day's breaking.

© Timothy Dudley-Smith

594 Tempus adest floridum
Hymns for Today's Church 160

1 When the King shall come again
    all his power revealing,
splendour shall announce his reign,
    life and joy and healing:
earth no longer in decay,
    hope no more frustrated;
this is God's redemption day
    longingly awaited.

2 In the desert trees take root
    fresh from his creation;
plants and flowers
    and sweetest fruit
    join the celebration:

rivers spring up from the earth,
    barren lands adorning;
valleys, this is your new birth,
    mountains, greet the morning!

3 Strengthen feeble hands and knees,
    fainting hearts, be cheerful!
God who comes for such as these
    seeks and saves the fearful:
now the deaf can hear the dumb
    sing away their weeping;
blind eyes see the injured come
    walking, running, leaping.

4 There God's highway shall be seen
    where no roaring lion,
nothing evil or unclean
    walks the road to Zion:
ransomed people homeward bound
    all your praises voicing,
see your Lord with glory crowned,
    share in his rejoicing!

from Isaiah 3
© Christopher Idle/Jubilate Hymn

595 Benson
Hymns for Today's Church 187

1 City of God, Jerusalem,
    where he has set his love;
church of Christ that is one on earth
    with Jerusalem above:
here as we walk this changing world
    our joys are mixed with tears,
but the day will be soon
    when the Saviour returns
and his voice will banish our fears.

2 Sing and be glad, Jerusalem,
    for God does not forget;
he who said he would come to save
    never failed his people yet.
Though we are tempted by despair
    and daunted by defeat,
our invincible Lord
    will be seen in his strength,
and his triumph will be complete.

(593–595) Christ's Coming

3 Sorrow no more, Jerusalem,
    discard your rags of shame!
take your crown as a gift from God
    who has called you by his name.
Put off your sin, and wear the robe
    of glory in its place;
you will shine in his light,
    you will share in his joy,
you will praise his wonderful grace.

4 Look all around, Jerusalem,
    survey from west to east;
sons and daughters of God the king
    are invited to his feast.
Out of their exile far away
    his scattered family come,
and the streets will resound
    with the songs of the saints
when the Saviour
    welcomes us home.

from Baruch 4–5
© Christopher Idle/Jubilate Hymns

596

ABOUT BEING READY

Lord Jesus Christ,
whose advent all shall see:
let your coming be with triumph,
but not to our shame;
let your coming be with glory,
but not to our surprise;
let your coming be with justice,
but not to our judgement.
Make our love burn bright for you,
our loyalty endure,
and our faith increase;
that with you we may rejoice
    on that day,
and so enter into
    your eternal kingdom. **Amen.** †

597

ACT OF PRAISE

Jesus, you came to live among us, born
of the virgin Mary. We give you thanks:
and praise your holy name.

Jesus, you come to us as we read your
story in the Bible. We give you thanks:
and praise your holy name.

Jesus, you come to us as we take in faith
the bread and wine. We give you
thanks:
and praise your holy name.

Jesus, you will come to reign in glory.
We give you thanks:
and praise your holy name.
Amen. Come, Lord Jesus! †

598   Land of hope
      Church Family Worship Source Book

1 Christ is surely coming
    bringing his reward,
omega and alpha,
    first and last and Lord;
root and stem of David,
    brilliant morning star –
Meet your judge and saviour,
    nations near and far;
meet your judge and saviour,
    nations near and far!

2 See the holy city!
    There they enter in,
all by Christ made holy,
    washed from every sin;
thirsty ones, desiring
    all he loves to give:
Come for living water,
    freely drink, and live;
come for living water,
    freely drink, and live!

3 Grace be with God's people!
    Praise his holy name –
Father, Son, and Spirit,
    evermore the same!
Hear the certain promise
    from the eternal home:
    'Surely I come quickly!' –
      Come, Lord Jesus, come;
    'Surely I come quickly!' –
      Come, Lord Jesus, come!

from Revelation 22
© Christopher Idle/Jubilate Hymns

599 Helmsley
Hymns for Today's Church 196

1 Jesus comes
    with clouds descending –
see the Lamb for sinners slain!
thousand thousand saints attending
join to sing the glad refrain:
    Alleluia, alleluia, alleluia!
God appears on earth to reign.

2 Every eye shall then behold him
robed in awesome majesty;
those who jeered at him
    and sold him,
pierced and nailed him to the tree,
    shamed and grieving . . .
shall their true Messiah see.

3 All the wounds of cross and passion
still his glorious body bears;
cause of endless exultation
to his ransomed worshippers.
    With what gladness . . .
we shall see the Saviour's scars!

4 Yes, Amen! let all adore you
high on your eternal throne;
crowns and empires
    fall before you –
claim the kingdom for your own.
    Come, Lord Jesus . . .
everlasting God, come down!

after J Cennick (1718–175?
C Wesley (1707–1788) an?
M Madan (1726–179?
© in this version Jubilate Hymr?

(599) Christ's Coming

CHRIST'S COMING
Other items appropriate to this theme

Hymns

At the name of Jesus, every knee shall bow	305
Come and see the shining hope	578
Joy to the world! The Lord has come	664
Praise God today	180
Praise him, praise him, Jesus our mighty redeemer	304
Rejoice, the Lord is king	301

Songs

At your feet we fall	251
God has exalted him	294
How lovely on the mountains	421
Lift up your heads to the coming king	208
What a wonderful saviour is Jesus	567

Psalm Versions (sung)

Fling wide the gates (Psalm 24)	291
How great is God almighty (Psalm 48)	313
Sing to God new songs of worship (Psalm 98)	249

Prayer

We praise you, O God and Father (Thanksgiving)	13

Readings

Prophecy – Isaiah 52.7–11; Malachi 3.1–18

The Coming of the Lord – 1 Thessalonians 4.13–5.11; 2 Peter 3

Signs of the End of the Age – Matthew 24

Parables – Matthew 25.1–13, 31–46; Luke 12.35–48

(See also Minister's Section 770–772. The Lord's Prayer is printed inside the back cover.)

33 God's Word to Us

All Scripture is inspired by God, and is useful for teaching the truth, rebuking error, correcting faults, and giving instruction for right living.

2 Timothy 3.16

Your word is a lamp to my feet and a light for my path.

Psalm 119.105

600

PRAISE

Let the people praise you, O God;
let all the people praise you!

Let your ways be known on earth;
your saving power in all the world!
Amen.

from Psalm 67

601

Southwell (Irons)
Hymns for Today's Church 247

1 Father of mercies, in your word
 what endless glory shines!
 For ever be your name adored
 for this celestial lines.

2 Here may the blind and hungry
 come
 and light and food receive;
 here shall the humble guest
 find room
 and taste and see and live.

3 Here the redeemer's welcome voice
 spreads heavenly peace around,
 and life and everlasting joys
 attend the glorious sound.

4 Here springs of consolation rise
 to cheer the fainting mind,
 and thirsty souls receive supplies
 and sweet refreshment find.

5 Divine instructor, gracious Lord,
 be now and always near:
 teach us to love your sacred word
 and view our saviour here.

A Steele (1717–1778)

602

North Coates
Hymns for Today's Church 384

1 Holy Spirit, hear us,
 help us while we sing;
 breathe into the music
 of the praise we bring.

2 Holy Spirit, lead us
 when we kneel to pray;
 nearer come and teach us
 what we ought to say.

3 Holy Spirit, teach us
 when your word we read;
 shine upon the pages
 with the light we need.

Holy Spirit, give us
each a humble mind;
make us more like Jesus,
strong and good and kind.

Holy Spirit, help us
walking in your light
what is wrong to conquer
and to choose the right.

W H Parker (1845–1929)
© in this version Word & Music/Jubilate Hymns

03

ONFESSION

we confess our sins, God is faithful
ad just, and will forgive our sins and
urify us from all unrighteousness:

ord, we have not obeyed your word,
or heeded
hat is written in the scriptures.
Ve repent with all our heart,
ad humble ourselves before you:
your mercy forgive us,
rant us your peace
ad the strength to keep your laws;
trough Jesus Christ our Lord. Amen. †

from 2 Kings 22

04

HEME PRAYER (COLLECT)

Almighty God,
ve thank you for the gift
of your holy word.
Iay it be a lantern to our feet,
light to our paths,
nd a strength to our lives.
ake us and use us
 love and serve all people

in the power of the Holy Spirit
and in the name of your Son,
Jesus Christ our Lord. **Amen.**

A Prayer of Dedication – ASB

605

PSALM

Praise the Lord:

With my whole heart I will thank the Lord:
in the company of his people.

Great are the works of the Lord:
all who see them wonder.

Glorious and majestic are his deeds:
his goodness lasts for ever.

He reminds us of his works of grace:
he is merciful and kind.

He sustains those who fear him:
he keeps his covenant always.

All he does is right and just:
all his words are faithful.

They will last for ever and ever:
for they were given in truth.

He provided redemption for his people, and made an eternal covenant with them:
holy and awesome is his name!

The fear of the Lord is the beginning of wisdom; he gives understanding to those who obey:
to God belongs eternal praise. Amen.

from Psalm 111

God's Word to Us (603–605)

PSALM/CANTICLE

1 Come, worship God
  who is worthy of honour,
enter his presence
  with thanks and a song!
he is the rock
  of his people's salvation,
to whom
  our jubilant praises belong.

2 Ruled by his might
  are the heights
    of the mountains,
held in his hands
  are the depths of the earth;
his is the sea,
  his the land, for he made them,
king of creation,
  who gave us our birth.

3 We are his people,
  the sheep of his pasture,
he is our maker
  and to him we pray;
gladly we kneel
  in obedience before him –
great is the God
  whom we worship this day!

4 Now let us listen,
  for God speaks among us,
open our hearts
  and receive what he says:
peace be to all
  who remember his goodness,
trust in his promises,
  walk in his ways!

from Psalm 95 (*Venite*)
© Michael Perry/Jubilate Hymns

PSALM

1 The will of God to mark my way,
  the word of God for light;
eternal justice to obey
  in everlasting right.

2 Your eyes of mercy keep me still,
  your gracious love be mine;
so work in me your perfect will
  and cause your face to shine.

3 With ordered step
  secure and strong,
from sin's oppression freed,
redeemed from every kind of wrong
  in thought and word and deed –

4 So set my heart to love your word
  and every promise prove,
to walk with truth before the Lord
  in righteousness and love.

from Psalm 11
© Timothy Dudley-Smith

1 All Scriptures are given
    by the breath of God,
  are inspired of God,
  are the word of the Lord;
all Scriptures are given
    by the breath of God,
and glorify his name!
  They can make you wise
    to a saving faith
    in Jesus Christ the Lord;
  they can make the child of God
      complete,
    and are made to be his sword!

2 So study to show yourself
    approved to God,
  fit to use his word,

(606–608) God's Word to Us

fit to speak in his name;
so study to show yourself
    approved to God,
a workman not ashamed:
  They'll reprove, correct,
    and a training in
all righteous living afford;
they will yield up all
    that we need to know
of the teaching of the Lord!

All Scriptures are given
    by the breath of God,
are inspired of God,
  are the word of the Lord;
all Scriptures are given
    by the breath of God,
and glorify his name!

from 2 Timothy 3
© Michael Baughen/Jubilate Hymns

609 Skye Boat Song
Songs of Worship 36

Spirit of God, unseen as the wind,
gentle as is the dove:
teach us the truth
and help us believe,
show us the Saviour's love!

You spoke to us – long, long ago –
gave us the written word;
we read it still, needing its truth,
through it God's voice is heard.
Spirit of God . . .

Without your help we fail our Lord,
we cannot live his way;
we need your power,
  we need your strength,
following Christ each day.
Spirit of God . . .

Margaret Old
© Scripture Union†

610* The Word of God
Church Family Worship Source Book

The word of God is living and active,
sharper than any double-edged sword;
the word of God is living and active,
sharper than any double-edged sword.

Hebrews 4.12
Mick Gisbey
© Thankyou Music†

(*Written for children to sing)

611 God has spoken
Jesus Praise 183

God has spoken to his people,
    Alleluia,
and his words are words of
    wisdom. Alleluia!

1 Open your ears, O Christian people,
open your ears and hear good news;
open your hearts,
    O royal priesthood,
God has come to you,
    God has come to you.
God has spoken . . .

2 They who have ears
    to hear his message,
they who have ears,
    then let them hear;
they who would learn
    the way of wisdom,
let them hear God's word,
    let them hear God's word!
God has spoken . . .

3 Israel comes to greet the saviour,
Judah is glad to see his day;
from east and west
    the peoples travel,
he will show the way,
    he will show the way.
God has spoken . . .

© Willard F Jabusch†

God's Word to Us (609–611)

612 Open our eyes, Lord
Mission Praise 181

Open our eyes, Lord,
   we want to see Jesus –
to reach out and touch him
   and say that we love him;
open our ears, Lord,
   and help us to listen:
O open our eyes, Lord,
   we want to see Jesus!

Robert Cull
© Maranatha! Music (USA)/Word Music (UK)†

613 Unser Herrscher
Hymns for Today's Church 324

1 We believe in God Almighty,
   maker of the earth and sky;
   all we see and all that's hidden
   is his work unceasingly:
   God our Father's loving kindness
   with us till the day we die.

2 We believe in Christ the Saviour,
   Son of God and Son of Man;
   born of Mary, preaching, healing,
   crucified, yet risen again:
   he ascended to the Father,
   there for evermore to reign.

3 We believe in God the Spirit,
   present in our lives today;
   speaking through
         the prophets' writings,
   guiding travellers on their way:
   to our hearts he brings forgiveness
   and the hope of endless joy.

© David Mowbray/Jubilate Hymns

614 Lathbury
Hymns of Faith 260

1 Break now the bread of life,
      dear Lord, to me
   as you once broke the bread
      beside the sea:

beyond the sacred page
   I seek you, Lord;
my spirit longs for you,
   the living Word.

2 You are the bread of life,
      O Lord, to me;
   your holy word, your truth,
      is food for me:
   grant I may eat and live
      with you above;
   teach me to love your truth,
      for you are love.

3 Now send your Spirit, Lord,
      to strengthen me,
   so let him touch my eyes
      that I may see:
   show me the truth concealed
      within your word;
   and in your love revealed
      I'll see you, Lord.

4 Bless now the bread of life
      to me, to me,
   as you once blessed the loaves
      by Galilee:
   then shall all bondage cease,
      all fetters fall,
   and I shall find my peace,
      my all in all.

M A Lathbury (1841–1913)
and A Groves (1843–1929)
© in this version Word & Music/Jubilate Hymns

615 St Michael
Hymns of Faith 342, Baptist Hymn Book 49

1 Help us, O Lord, to learn
      the truths your word imparts,
   to study that your laws may be
      inscribed upon our hearts.

2 Help us, O Lord, to live
      the faith which we proclaim,
   that all our thoughts
         and words and deeds
      may glorify your name.

(612–615) God's Word to Us

Help us, O Lord, to teach
the beauty of your ways,
that yearning souls
may find the Christ
and sing aloud his praise.

William W Reid, Junior
© The Hymn Society of America/
Hope Publishing Company†

16

)R UNDERSTANDING

eavenly Father,
u have shown
e wonder of your love for us
in Jesus Christ
rough the Bible:
lp us to understand it
with our minds,
d apply it in our lives;
r his name's sake. **Amen.** †

17

)R STRENGTH

e pray for God's help as we read his
mmands in the Bible, or as we listen
his word:

hen we are tempted to do or say
ong things, Lord, speak to us in our
lfishness:
lp us to be strong.

hen we are anxious or afraid, Lord,
eak to us in our fearfulness:
lp us to be strong.

hen we are ill or in pain, Lord, speak
us in our helplessness:
lp us to be strong.

hen things we have to do seem too
rd for us, Lord, speak to us in our
eakness:
lp us to be strong.

O God,
we will listen to your word;
and by your strength
we will do what you command,
and bring glory to your name. Amen. †

618

THANKSGIVING FOR THE BIBLE
Let us give thanks to God:

For the majesty of the Law, for the
power of the Prophets, for the wisdom
of the Proverbs and the beauty of the
Psalms, and above all for the grace of
the Gospel, we lift up our hearts in
praise:
thanks be to God!

For the Bible in our own language, for
those who long ago gave us trans-
lations, for those who down the years
improved them, enabling the Scriptures to penetrate deeply into our
national life, we lift up our hearts in
praise:
thanks be to God!

For the continuing work of revision to
match our changing language, for all
that the Bible means to Christians
throughout the world, we lift up our
hearts in praise:
thanks be to God!

For those who interpret, publish and
distribute the Scriptures in every
tongue, so that all peoples may come to
the knowledge of salvation, we lift up
our hearts in praise:
thanks be to God!

To you, O gracious Father,
with the living Word,
through the one eternal Spirit,
be glory now and for ever. Amen. †

God's Word to Us (616–618)

Or **619**

THANKSGIVING FOR GOD'S WORD
Let us thank God for all his blessings:

For your creative word, by which the earth and sky were made: we thank you, Father,
and praise your holy name.

For making us in your own image, able to hear and answer your call: we thank you, Father,
and praise your holy name.

For revealing yourself to people through the ages, and changing their lives: we thank you, Father,
and praise your holy name.

For your word to us in these days, calling us to repentance and assuring us of forgiveness: we thank you, Father,
and praise your holy name.

For promising to hear our prayers, and faithfully meeting our every need: we thank you, Father,
and praise your holy name.

**Grant that we may worship you,
not only with our voices,
but in true and willing service,
through Jesus Christ our Lord. Amen.** †

---

620 Ravenshaw or Chesterton
Hymns for Today's Church 251

1 Lord your word shall guide us
and with truth provide us:
teach us to receive it
and with joy believe it.

2 When our foes are near us,
then your word shall cheer us –
word of consolation,
message of salvation.

3 When the storms distress us
and dark clouds oppress us,
then your word protects us
and its light directs us.

4 Who can tell the pleasure,
who recount the treasure
by your word imparted
to the simple-hearted?

5 Word of mercy, giving
courage to the living;
word of life, supplying
comfort to the dying.

6 O that we discerning
its most holy learning,
Lord, may love and fear you –
evermore be near you!

H W Baker (1821–18
© in this version Jubilate Hym

---

621 St Helen
Hymns for Today's Church 416

1 Thanks to God
whose word was spoken
in the deed that made the earth;
his the voice that called a nation,
his the fires that tried her worth.
God has spoken:
praise him for his open word!

2 Thanks to God
whose Word incarnate
glorified the flesh of man;
deeds and words and death
and rising
tell the grace in heaven's plan.
God has spoken:
praise him for his open word!

3 Thanks to God
whose word was written
in the Bible's sacred page,
record of the revelation

(619–621) God's Word to Us

showing God to every age.
God has spoken:
praise him for his open word!

4 Thanks to God
whose word is published
in the tongues of every race;
see its glory undiminished
by the change of time or place.
God has spoken:
praise him for his open word!

5 Thanks to God
whose word is answered
by the Spirit's voice within;
here we drink of joy unmeasured,
life redeemed from death and sin.
God is speaking:
praise him for his open word!

Reginald Brooks
© Hope Publishing Company†

GOD'S WORD TO US
Other items appropriate to this theme

Hymns

Songs

Psalm Version (sung)

Prayers

Readings

Josiah and the Book of the Law –
2 Kings 22; 23.1–3
Listen and Enquire –
Isaiah 55.1–13
The Psalmist's Testimony –
Psalm 1; 19.7–14; 119.129–144
The Power of God's Word –
Hebrews 4.12–13
Using God's Word –
Luke 4.1–13; 4.14–21;
2 Timothy 3.14–4.8
The Scriptures Point to Jesus –
John 5.36–47

(See also Minister's Section 773–775. The
Lord's Prayer is printed inside the back
cover.)

34 Christmas Prayers and Readings

Let the heavens rejoice, and let the earth be glad before the Lord: for he comes!

1 Chronicles 16.31,33

I bring you good news of great joy that will be for all the people. Today in the town of David a Saviour has been born to you; he is Christ the Lord.

Luke 2.10,11

(Other suitable sentences may be found at 776–777)

622

WELCOME, EVERYBODY!

At Christmas time we delight again to hear the story of the journey to Bethlehem, the song of the angels, the surprise of the shepherds, and their joy as they found Jesus in the manger. But lest we forget he was born to poverty, we remember at this season all who are hungry or cold. And lest we forget he became a refugee, we remember the stranger and the lonely among us. And lest we forget he felt the pain of life and death, we remember now those who are ill, or anxious, or bereaved. And because we know he came for our salvation, let us in heart and mind go once again to Bethlehem, to hear the message of the angels and worship afresh the Son of God.   †

(Opening carols 638–639, 672)

623

CONFESSION

We confess that amid all the joys and festivities of this season we have sometimes forgotten what Christmas really means, and have left the Lord Jesus out of our thinking and living:
Father, forgive us.

Help us to remember that you loved the world so much that you gave your only Son, who was born to be our Saviour:
Lord, help us.

We confess that we have allowed the most important event in history to become dulled by familiarity:
Father, forgive us.

Help us in this act of worship to recapture a sense of wonder, and to discover again the stupendous fact that the Creator of the universe has come to us as a newborn baby:
Lord, help us.

We confess to a selfish enjoyment of Christmas while we do little to help the homeless families of your world:
Father, forgive us.

Fill our hearts with the love that cares, that understands and gives; show us how we can best serve those in need;

for the sake of him
   who was born in a stable,
Jesus Christ our Lord. Amen.   †

(Other suitable prayers may be found between 778 and 783; The Lord's Prayer is
printed inside the back cover)

624 Christmas Readings Set A (see also section 39: 34–35)

THE PROPHETS PROMISE THE SAVIOUR
(Numbers 24.16,17; Isaiah 7.14; Jeremiah 23.5,6; Micah 5.2,4; Isaiah 9.6: corresponding carols 640–642, 647)

Numbers
The oracle of one who hears the words of God, who has knowledge from the Most High: I see him, but not now; I behold him, but not near. A star will come out of Jacob; a sceptre will rise out of Israel.

Isaiah
The Lord himself will give you a sign: The virgin will be with child and will give birth to a son, and will call him Immanuel.

Jeremiah
The days are coming,' declares the Lord, 'when I will raise up to David a righteous Branch, a King who will reign wisely and do what is just and right in the land. This is the name by which he will be called: The Lord Our Righteousness.'

Micah
Bethlehem Ephrathah, though you are small among the clans of Judah, out of you will come for me one who will be ruler over Israel, whose origins are from of old, from ancient times. He will stand and shepherd his flock in the strength of the Lord, in the majesty of the name of the Lord his God.

Isaiah
To us a child is born, to us a son is given, and the government will be on his shoulders. And he will be called Wonderful Counsellor, Mighty God, Everlasting Father, Prince of Peace.

Reader: This is the word of the Lord.
All: Thanks be to God.

625

MARY HEARS THE NEWS
(from Luke 1.26–38: corresponding carols 187, 585, 642–643)

Narrator
In the sixth month, God sent the angel Gabriel to Nazareth, a town in Galilee, to a virgin pledged to be married to a man named Joseph, a descendant of David. The virgin's name was Mary. The angel went to her and said:

Angel
Greetings, you who are highly favoured! The Lord is with you.

Narrator
Mary was greatly troubled at his words and wondered what kind of greeting this might be. But the angel said to her:

Angel
Do not be afraid, Mary, you have found favour with God. You will be with child and give birth to a son, and you are to give him the name Jesus. He will be great and will be called the Son of the Most High. The Lord God will give him the throne of his father David, and he will reign over the house of Jacob for ever; his kingdom will never end.

Narrator
Mary asked the angel:

Mary
How will this be, since I am a virgin?

Christmas Prayers and Readings (624–625)

Angel
The Holy Spirit will come upon you, and the power of the Most High will overshadow you. So the holy one to be born will be called the Son of God.

Narrator
Mary answered:

Mary
I am the Lord's servant. May it be to me as you have said.

Narrator
Then the angel left her.

Reader: This is the word of the Lord.
All: Thanks be to God.

Narrator
All this took place to fulfil what the Lord had said through the prophet:

Prophet
The virgin will be with child and will give birth to a son, and they will call him Immanuel – God with us.

Narrator
When Joseph woke up, he did what the angel of the Lord had commanded him and took Mary home as his wife. But he had no union with her until she gave birth to a son. And he gave him the name Jesus.

Reader: This is the word of the Lord.
All: Thanks be to God.

626

JOSEPH LEARNS THE TRUTH
(from Matthew 1.18–25: corresponding carols 642, 649–652, 659, 665)

Narrator
This is how the birth of Jesus Christ came about. His mother Mary was pledged to be married to Joseph, but before they came together, she was found to be with child through the Holy Spirit. Because Joseph her husband was a righteous man and did not want to expose her to public disgrace, he had in mind to divorce her quietly. But after he had considered this, an angel of the Lord appeared to him in a dream and said:

Angel
Joseph son of David, do not be afraid to take Mary home as your wife, because what is conceived in her is from the Holy Spirit. She will give birth to a son, and you are to give him the name Jesus, because he will save his people from their sins.

627

THE ANGELS ANNOUNCE THE BIRTH
(from Luke 2.8–14: corresponding carols 648, 657–661)

Narrator
There were shepherds living out in the fields near Bethlehem, keeping watch over their flocks at night. An angel of the Lord appeared to them, and the glory of the Lord shone around them and they were terrified. But the angel said to them:

Angel
Do not be afraid. I bring you good news of great joy that will be for all the people. Today in the town of David a Saviour has been born to you; he is Christ the Lord. This will be a sign to you: You will find a baby wrapped in strips of cloth and lying in a manger.

Narrator
Suddenly a great company of the heavenly host appeared with the angel praising God and saying:

Chorus
Glory to God in the highest, and on earth peace to those on whom his favour rests.

Reader: This is the word of the Lord.
All: Thanks be to God.

628

THE SHEPHERDS FIND THE BABY
(from Luke 2.15–20: corresponding carols 195, 656, 662–668)

Narrator
When the angels had left them and gone into heaven, the shepherds said to one another:

Shepherds
Let's go to Bethlehem and see this thing that has happened, which the Lord has told us about.

Narrator
So they hurried off and found Mary and Joseph, and the baby, who was lying in the manger. When they had seen him, they spread the word concerning what had been told them about this child, and all who heard it were amazed at what the shepherds said to them. But Mary treasured up all these things and pondered them in her heart. The shepherds returned, glorifying and praising God for all the things they had heard and seen, which were just as they had been told.

Reader: This is the word of the Lord.
All: Thanks be to God.

629

THE WISE MEN FOLLOW THE STAR
(from Matthew 2.1–11: corresponding carols 661, 669–671, and see 91–109)

Narrator
After Jesus was born in the town of Bethlehem in Judea, during the time of King Herod, Magi from the east came to Jerusalem and asked:

Magi
Where is the one who has been born king of the Jews? We saw his star in the east and have come to worship him.

Narrator
When King Herod heard this, he was disturbed, and all Jerusalem with him. When he had called together all the chief priests and teachers of the law, he asked them:

Herod
Where will the Christ be born?

Narrator
They replied:

Teachers
In Bethlehem in Judea, for this is what the prophet has written: 'Bethlehem in the land of Judah, out of you will come a ruler who will be the shepherd of my people Israel.'

Narrator
Then Herod called the Magi secretly and found out from them the exact time the star had appeared. He sent them to Bethlehem and said:

Herod
Go and make a careful search for the child. As soon as you find him, report to me, so that I too may go and worship him.

Narrator
After they had heard the king, they went on their way, and the star they

Christmas Prayers and Readings (628–629)

had seen in the east went ahead of them until it stopped over the place where the child was. When they saw the star, they were overjoyed. On coming to the house, they saw the child with his mother Mary, and they bowed down and worshipped him. Then they opened their treasures and presented him with gifts of gold and of incense and of myrrh.

Reader: This is the word of the Lord.
All: Thanks be to God.

630

THE CHILD ESCAPES THE SWORD
(from Matthew 2.13–18: corresponding carols 93, 100. This reading may be omitted at Christmas, if desired.)

Narrator
When the Magi had gone, an angel of the Lord appeared to Joseph in a dream. He said:

Angel
Get up, take the child and his mother and escape to Egypt. Stay there until I tell you, for Herod is going to search for the child to kill him.

Narrator
So Joseph got up, took the child and his mother during the night and left for Egypt, where he stayed until the death of Herod. And so was fulfilled what the Lord had said through the prophet:

Prophet
Out of Egypt I called my son.

Narrator
When Herod realised that he had been outwitted by the Magi, he was furious, and he gave orders to kill all the boys in Bethlehem and its vicinity who were two years old and under, in accordance

with the time he had learned from the Magi. Then what was said through the prophet Jeremiah was fulfilled:

Prophet
A voice is heard in Ramah, weeping and great mourning, Rachel weeping for her children and refusing to be comforted, because they are no more.

Reader: This is the word of the Lord.
All: Thanks be to God.

631

SIMEON RECOGNISES THE MESSIAH
(from Luke 2.25–32: corresponding carols 98, 562, 664. This reading may be omitted at Christmas, if desired.)

Narrator
Now there was a man in Jerusalem called Simeon, who was righteous and devout. He was waiting for the consolation of Israel, and the Holy Spirit was upon him. It had been revealed to him by the Holy Spirit that he would not die before he had seen the Lord's Christ. Moved by the Spirit, he went into the temple courts. When the parents brought in the child Jesus to do for him what the custom of the Law required, Simeon took him in his arms and praised God saying:

Simeon
Sovereign Lord, as you have promised, you now dismiss your servant in peace. For my eyes have seen your salvation, which you have prepared in the sight of all people, a light for revelation to the Gentiles and for glory to your people Israel.

Narrator
The child's father and mother marvelled at what was said about him.

en Simeon blessed them and said to
ary, his mother:

meon

his child is destined to cause the fall-
g and rising of many in Israel, and to
a sign that will be spoken against, so
at the thoughts of many hearts will be
vealed. And a sword will pierce your
wn soul too.

eader: This is the word of the Lord.
ll: Thanks be to God.

32

HE APOSTLES EXPLAIN THE
EANING
ohn 1.1,3,14; Colossians 1.15,17;
ebrews 1.1–3; 2 Corinthians 4.6; 8.9;
ilippians 2.6,7; John 1.11, 12: cor-
sponding carols 101, 108, 206, 639,
3, 656, 673)

hn

the beginning was the Word, and the
ord was with God, and the Word was
od. Through him all things were
ade. The Word became flesh and
ved for a while among us. We have
en his glory, the glory of the one and
lly Son, who came from the Father,
ll of grace and truth.

olossians

hrist is the image of the invisible God,
e firstborn over all creation. He is
fore all things, and in him all things
ld together.

ebrews

the past God spoke to our forefathers
rough the prophets, but in these last
ays he has spoken to us by his Son,
ho is the radiance of his glory and the
xact representation of his being.

Corinthians

od, who said, 'Let light shine out of

darkness,' made his light shine in our
hearts to give us the light of the knowledge of the glory of God in the face of
Christ. You know the grace of our Lord
Jesus Christ, that though he was rich,
yet for your sakes he became poor, so
that you through his poverty might
become rich.

Philippians
Christ Jesus, being in very nature God,
did not consider equality with God
something to be grasped, but made
himself nothing, taking the very nature
of a servant, being made in human
likeness.

John
He came to that which was his own, but
his own did not receive him. Yet to all
who received him, to those who believed in his name, he gave the right to
become children of God.

Reader: This is the word of the Lord.
All: Thanks be to God.

633

CREED
Let us confess our faith in the Son of
God:

In the beginning was the Word,
and the Word was with God,
and the Word was God.
Through him all things were made;
without him nothing was made
     that has been made.
In him was life,
and that life was the light of us all.

The Word became flesh
and lived for a while among us;
we have seen his glory,
the glory of the one and only Son
who came from the Father,
full of grace and truth. Amen.

from John 1

Christmas Prayers and Readings (632–633)

634

THANKSGIVING

God our Father, we listen again to the story of Christmas, and we are glad that Jesus has come to be our saviour and our friend.

We hear how Mary laid her baby in a manger. Jesus has come:
thank you, Father.

We hear how the angels sang over the Bethlehem hills: 'Glory to God; peace for the world.' Jesus has come:
thank you, Father.

We hear how the shepherds hurried to see that what the angel said was true. Jesus has come:
thank you, Father.

We hear how the wise men came to bring their worship and their precious gifts. Jesus has come:
thank you, Father.

O God,
we thank you
that Jesus has come to be our saviour
and our friend:
we welcome him with love,
and worship him with gladness,
for your glory's sake. Amen.   †

635

FOR THE HOMELESS

Lord Jesus Christ, born in a stable:
hear the cry
    of the homeless and refugee,
and so move our wills
    by your Holy Spirit

that we may not rest content
until all have found home
    and livelihood;
for your name's sake. **Amen.**

636

ACT OF PRAISE
Let us worship the Saviour:

Heavenly king, yet born of Mary; Jesus Son of God,
we praise and adore you.

Eternal Word, yet child without speech; Jesus, Son of God,
we praise and adore you.

Robed in glory, yet wrapped in infant clothes; Jesus, Son of God,
we praise and adore you.

Lord of heaven and earth, yet laid in a manger; Jesus, Son of God,
we praise and adore you.

To you, O Jesus,
strong in your weakness,
glorious in your humility,
mighty to save,
be all praise and glory,
with the Father and the Holy Spirit,
now and for ever. Amen.

637

BLESSING

The joy of the angels, the wonder of the shepherds, and the peace of the Christ child, fill your hearts this Christmas time; and the blessing of God the Father, God the Son, and God the Holy Spirit, be with you now and always
Amen.

CHRISTMAS
Other items appropriate to this theme

Carols
See sections The Wise Men etc. 91–109,
and Christmas Carols 639–673.

Prayers
Lord Jesus Christ, wise men
  (Confession)   94
Eternal God, who by the shining of
  a star (Collect)   103
Christ, born in a stable (For the
  Homeless, Hungry etc.)   107

Readings
Prophecies – Isaiah 40.1–5; 11.1–9;
  Micah 5.2–4; Zechariah 2.10–13

Jesus' Birth Foretold –
  Luke 1.26–38
The Magnificat – Luke 1.46–55
Jesus' Birth – Luke 2.1–7;
  Matthew 1.18–25
The Shepherds – Luke 2.8–20
The Eternal Word – John 1.1–14
The Final Revelation –
  Hebrews 1.1–5

(Further sets of Christmas readings may
be found at section 39: 34–35. They are
set out in full in the New International
Version in *Carols for Today* published by
Hodder and Stoughton. See also Minister's Section 714–716 and 776–783. The
Lord's Prayer is printed inside the back
cover.)

35 Christmas Carols

We have seen his glory, the glory of the one and only Son, who came from the Father, full of grace and truth.

John 1.14

(Note: The recommended source of the tune is the one supplied at the head of each carol. For instance, a carol exclusively referenced to 'Carols for Today' may also appear in 'Hymns for Today's Church'.)

638 All through the night
Hymns for Today's Church 81

1 Come and sing the Christmas story
   this holy night!
Christ is born: the hope of glory
   dawns on our sight.
Alleluia! earth is ringing
with a thousand angels singing –
hear the message they are bringing
   this holy night.

2 Jesus, Saviour, child of Mary
   this holy night,
in a world confused and weary
   you are our light.
God is in a manger lying,
manhood taking, self denying,
life embracing, death defying
   this holy night.

3 Lord of all! Let us acclaim him
   this holy night;
king of our salvation name him,
   throned in the height.
Son of Man – let us adore him,
all the earth is waiting for him;
Son of God – we bow before him
   this holy night.

© Michael Perry/Jubilate Hymns

639 Jubilate everybody
Praise God Together 56

1 Happy Christmas, everybody!
all the world is singing;
come to worship, everybody,
praise and glory bringing:
   Come to greet the Lord
   with joy;
   come to worship
   and adore him . . .

2 Happy Christmas, everybody!
join the people praying;
God is speaking, everybody –
hear what love is saying:
   Come to greet . . .

3 Happy Christmas, everybody!
God's new day is dawning;
meet the Saviour, everybody –
Christ is born this morning:
   Come to greet . . .

Happy Christmas, everybody!
Christ is born this morning.

© Michael Perry/Jubilate Hymns

40 His name is higher
Jesus Praise 74

is name is higher than any other,
s name is Jesus, his name is Lord;
his name is higher than any other,
his name is Jesus, his name is Lord.
is name is Wonderful,
    his name is Counsellor,
s name is Prince of peace,
    the mighty God;
his name is higher than any other,
his name is Jesus, his name is Lord.

from Isaiah 9
Copyright controlled†

41 Wonderful Counsellor
Spirit of Praise 196

Wonderful Counsellor, Jesus:
search me, know me, Jesus;
lead me, guide me, Jesus –
Wonderful Counsellor, Jesus.

Mighty God, Son of God, Jesus;
name above all other names, Jesus:
glorify, magnify, Jesus –
Mighty God, Son of God, Jesus.

Everlasting Father, Jesus;
holy and unchangeable, Jesus:
fill me with your presence, Jesus –
Everlasting Father, Jesus.

Prince of peace,
    rule my heart, Jesus;
know my every anxious thought,
    Jesus;
calm my fears, dry my tears, Jesus –
Prince of peace,
    rule my heart, Jesus.

Wonderful Counsellor, Jesus;
Mighty God, Son of God, Jesus;
Everlasting Father, Jesus –
Prince of Peace,
    rule my heart, Jesus!

from Isaiah 9
Bill Yarger
© Maranatha! Music (USA)/Word Music (UK)†

642 Emmanuel Emmanuel
Jesus Praise 68

Emmanuel, Emmanuel,
his name is called Emmanuel –
    God with us,
    revealed in us –
his name is called Emmanuel.

from Isaiah 7
Bob McGee
© Christian Arts Music (USA)/Word Music (UK)†

643 Mary sang a song; Pavenham
Jesus Praise 28; Carol Praise

CANTICLE

1 Mary sang a song, a song of love,
    magnified the mighty Lord above;
    melodies of praise his name extol
    from the very depths of Mary's soul:

2 'God the Lord
        has done great things for me,
    looked upon my life's humility;
    happy they shall call me
        from this day –
    merciful is he whom we obey.

3 'To the humble soul our God is kind,
    to the proud
        he brings unease of mind:
    who uplifts the poor,
        pulls down the strong?
    God alone
        has power to right the wrong!

4 'He who has been Israel's
        strength and stay
    fills the hungry,
        sends the rich away;
    he has shown his promise
        firm and sure,
    faithful to his people evermore.'

Christmas Carols (640–643)

5 This was Mary's song as we recall,
mother to the saviour of us all:
magnify his name
and sing his praise,
worship and adore him,
all your days!

from Luke 1 (*Magnificat*)
© Michael Perry/Jubilate Hymns

644 Little donkey
Carol, Gaily Carol 3; Carol Praise

1 Little donkey, little donkey,
on a dusty road,
got to keep on plodding onward
with your precious load:

2 Been a long time, little donkey,
through the winter's night –
don't give up now, little donkey,
Bethlehem's in sight.
Ring out those bells tonight,
Bethlehem, Bethlehem;
follow that star tonight,
Bethlehem, Bethlehem!

3 Little donkey, little donkey,
had a heavy day –
little donkey, carry Mary
safely on her way.
Little donkey, carry Mary
safely on her way.

Eric Boswell
© Chappell and Company Limited/
International Music Publications†

645 Mary's Boy Child
Carol Praise

1 Long time ago in Bethlehem,
so the Holy Bible say,
Mary's boy-child, Jesus Christ,
was born on Christmas Day.
Hark now, hear the angels sing –
a new king born today!
And we may live for evermore
because of Christmas Day.

Trumpets sound
and angels sing –
listen to what they say,
that we may live for evermore
because of Christmas Day.

2 While shepherds watch their flocks
by night,
them see a bright new shining star;
them hear a choir sing –
the music seems to come from afar.

3 Now Joseph and his wife Mary
come to Bethlehem that night;
she have no place
to bear her child –
not a single room was in sight.

4 By and by they find a little nook
in a stable all forlorn,
and in a manger cold and dark,
Mary's little boy-child was born.

5 Long time ago in Bethlehem
so the Holy Bible say,
Mary's boy-child, Jesus Christ,
was born on Christmas Day.
Hark now, hear . . .

Jester Hairston
© Bourne Music Ltd

646 Irby
Carols for Today 41

1 Once in royal David's city
stood a lowly cattle shed,
where a mother laid her baby
in a manger for his bed:
Mary was that mother mild,
Jesus Christ, her little child.

2 He came down to earth from heaven
who is God and Lord of all;
and his shelter was a stable
and his cradle was a stall:
with the poor and meek and lowly
lived on earth our saviour holy.

And through all his wondrous
        childhood
he would honour and obey,
love and watch the gentle mother
in whose tender arms he lay:
Christian children all should be
kind, obedient, good as he.

For he is our childhood's pattern:
day by day like us he grew;
he was little, weak and helpless;
tears and smiles like us he knew:
and he feels for all our sadness,
and he shares in all our gladness.

And our eyes at last shall see him,
through his own redeeming love;
for that child, so dear and gentle,
is our Lord in heaven above:
and he leads his children on
to the place where he has gone.

Not in that poor lowly stable
with the oxen standing by,
we shall see him, but in heaven,
set at God's right hand on high:
there his children gather round
bright like stars,
        with glory crowned.

C F Alexander (1818–1895)

647 Forest Green or Christmas Carol
Hymns for Today's Church 88

O little town of Bethlehem,
how still we see you lie!
Above your deep and dreamless
        sleep
the silent stars go by:
yet in your dark streets shining
is everlasting light;
the hopes and fears of all the years
are met in you tonight.

2 For Christ is born of Mary
and, gathered all above
while mortals sleep, the angels keep
their watch of wondering love:
O morning stars, together
proclaim the holy birth,
and praises sing to God the king,
and peace to all the earth.

3 How silently, how silently
the wondrous gift is given!
So God imparts to human hearts
the blessings of his heaven:
no ear may hear his coming,
but in this world of sin,
where meek souls will receive him –
        still
the dear Christ enters in.

4 O holy child of Bethlehem,
descend to us, we pray;
cast out our sin and enter in,
be born in us today!
We hear the Christmas angels
the great glad tidings tell –
O come to us, abide with us,
our Lord Emmanuel.

P Brooks (1835–1893)

648 Stille nacht
Hymns for Today's Church 95

1 Silent night! holy night!
all is calm, all is bright
round the virgin and her child:
holy infant, so gentle and mild,
        sleep in heavenly peace;
        sleep in heavenly peace!

2 Silent night! holy night!
shepherds quail at the sight,
glory streams from heaven afar:
heavenly hosts sing, 'Alleluia,
        Christ the saviour is born,
        Christ the saviour is born.'

Christmas Carols (647–648)

3 Silent night! holy night!
　　Son of God, love's pure light:
　　radiant beams your holy face
　　with the dawn of saving grace,
　　　Jesus, Lord, at your birth,
　　　Jesus, Lord, at your birth.

after J Möhr (1792–1848)
J F Young (1820–1885)

649　Christmas Lullaby
Cry Hosanna 140; Carol Praise

1 Cradle rocking, cattle lowing,
　　bright star guiding men to see
　little Christ-child in the manger,
　　light of all the world to be:
　　　Alleluia, holy Child,
　　　hosanna in the highest;
　　　gloria, Emmanuel,
　　　hosanna in the highest!

2 Mother Mary, watching carefully
　　by the light of one bright star;
　bread of heaven, softly sleeping,
　　gentle gift of God to man:
　　　Alleluia . . .

3 Who could guess,
　　　to see you lie there,
　　that you came to bring a sword?
　Prince of peace, born in a manger,
　　with a price upon your soul.
　　　Alleluia . . .

4 Do you know –
　　　so weak and helpless –
　of the grace you bear to us;
　do you dream yet of the kingdom
　　you will some day bring to pass?
　　　Alleluia . . .

Jodi Page Clark
© Celebration/Thankyou Music†

650　Mary had a baby
Carols for Today 49

1 Mary had a baby, yes Lord;
　　Mary had a baby, yes my Lord;
　　Mary had a baby, yes Lord!
　　　The people keep a-coming
　　　for to see her child!

QUESTION:
2 What did she name him?
　　yes, Lord . . .

ANSWER:
3 Mary named him Jesus!
　　yes, Lord . . .

QUESTION:
4 Where was he born?
　　yes, Lord . . .

ANSWER:
5 Born in a stable!
　　yes, Lord . . .

QUESTION:
6 Where did she lay him?
　　yes, Lord . . .

ANSWER:
7 Laid him in a manger!
　　yes, Lord . . .

West Indian Spiritual
© in this version Word & Music/Jubilate Hymns

651　Cradle Song
Carols for Today 57

1 Away in a manger,
　　no crib for a bed,
　the little Lord Jesus
　　laid down his sweet head;
　the stars in the bright sky
　　looked down where he lay;
　the little Lord Jesus
　　asleep on the hay.

The cattle are lowing,
   the baby awakes,
but little Lord Jesus
   no crying he makes:
I love you, Lord Jesus –
   look down from on high
and stay by my side
   until morning is nigh.

Be near me, Lord Jesus;
   I ask you to stay
close by me for ever
   and love me, I pray;
bless all the dear children
   in your tender care,
and fit us for heaven
   to live with you there.

verses 1, 2 unknown (nineteenth century)
verse 3 J T McFarland (c 1906)

652 Bunessan
Hymns for Today's Church 51

1 Child in the manger, infant of Mary,
outcast and stranger, Lord of all!
child who inherits
   all our transgressions,
all our demerits on him fall.

2 Once the most holy
   child of salvation
gentle and lowly lived below:
now as our glorious
   mighty redeemer,
see him victorious over each foe.

3 Prophets foretold him,
   infant of wonder;
angels behold him on his throne:
worthy our saviour
   of all their praises;
happy for ever are his own.

after M MacDonald (1789–1872)
L Macbean (1853–1931)

653 Holy Child
Carols for Today 56

1 Holy child, how still you lie!
safe the manger, soft the hay;
faint upon the eastern sky
breaks the dawn of Christmas Day.

2 Holy child, whose birthday brings
shepherds from their field and fold,
angel choirs and eastern kings,
myrrh and frankincense and gold:

3 Holy child, what gift of grace
from the Father freely willed!
In your infant form we trace
all God's promises fulfilled.

4 Holy child, whose human years
span like ours delight and pain;
one in human joys and tears,
one in all but sin and stain:

5 Holy child, so far from home,
all the lost to seek and save,
to what dreadful death you come,
to what dark and silent grave!

6 Holy child, before whose name
powers of darkness faint and fall;
conquered,
   death and sin and shame –
Jesus Christ is Lord of all!

7 Holy child, how still you lie!
safe the manger, soft the hay;
clear upon the eastern sky
breaks the dawn of Christmas Day.

© Timothy Dudley-Smith

654 A joyful song
Cry Hosanna 139; Carol Praise

1 Sing a song, a joyful song,
   sing unto the Lord;
Sing a song, a joyful song,
   sing unto the Lord.

Christmas Carols (652–654)

Clap your hands,
all you people,
clap your hands unto the Lord;
dance your feet, all you people,
dance unto the Lord!

2 See the baby in a manger,
    see the baby softly sleeping;
see the baby in a manger –
    come with me and see.
        Clap your hands . . .

3 See the mother rock the baby,
    rock the baby, rock the baby;
see the mother rock the baby –
    come with me and see.
        Clap your hands . . .

4 Hear the donkey hee and hawing,
    hee and hawing, hee and hawing;
hear the donkey hee and hawing –
    come with me and see.
        Clap your hands . . .

5 Shepherds on the hills a-watching,
    hills a-watching, hills a-watching;
shepherds on the hills a-watching:
    come with me and see.
        Clap your hands . . .

Colleen O'Meara
© Celebration/Thankyou Music†

655 The Virgin Mary
Carols for Today 121

1 The virgin Mary had a baby boy,
the virgin Mary had a baby boy,
the virgin Mary had a baby boy
and they say that his name is Jesus.
    He come from the glory,
    he come from
        the glorious kingdom;
    he come from the glory,
    he come from
        the glorious kingdom:
    O yes, believer!

O yes, believer!
He come from the glory,
he come from
    the glorious kingdom.

2 The angels sang
    when the baby was born,
the angels sang
    when the baby was born,
the angels sang
    when the baby was born
and they sang that his name is Jesus.
    He come from the glory . . .

3 The shepherds came
    where the baby was born,
the shepherds came
    where the baby was born,
the shepherds came
    where the baby was born
and they say that his name is Jesus.
    He come from the glory . . .

West Indian carol
© Collected Boosey & Hawkes Incorporated†

656 Calypso Carol
Carols for Today 110, 111

1 See him lying on a bed of straw:
a draughty stable
    with an open door;
Mary cradling the babe she bore –
the prince of glory is his name.
    O now carry me to Bethlehem
    to see the Lord appear to men –
    just as poor as was the stable then,
    the prince of glory when he came.

2 Star of silver,
    sweep across the skies,
show where Jesus
    in the manger lies;
shepherds,
    swiftly from your stupor rise
to see the saviour of the world!
    O now carry . . .

(655–656) Christmas Carols

3 Angels,
      sing again the song you sang,
   bring God's glory
      to the heart of man;
   sing that Bethl'em's little baby can
   be salvation to the soul.
      O now carry . . .

4 Mine are riches, from your poverty,
   from your innocence, eternity;
   mine forgiveness
      by your death for me,
   child of sorrow for my joy.
      O now carry . . .

© Michael Perry/Jubilate Hymns

657 Look to the skies
Graham Kendrick Song Book 18;
Carol Praise

1 Look to the skies,
      there's a celebration,
   lift up your heads,
      join the angel song,
   for our creator
      becomes our saviour,
   as a baby born!
   Angels amazed bow in adoration:
   'Glory to God
      in the highest heaven' –
   send the good news out
      to every nation,
   for our hope has come.
      Worship the king –
      come, see his brightness;
      worship the king,
      his wonders tell:
      Jesus our king is born today –
      we welcome you, Emmanuel!

2 Wonderful Counsellor, Mighty God,
   Father for ever, the Prince of Peace:
   there'll be no end
      to your rule of justice,
   for it shall increase.
   Light of your face,
      come to pierce our darkness;

joy of your heart
      come to chase our gloom;
   star of the morning,
      a new day dawning,
   make our hearts your home.
      Worship the king . . .

3 Quietly he came as a helpless baby,
   one day in power
      he will come again;
   swift through the skies
      he will burst with splendour
   on the earth to reign.
   Jesus I bow at your manger lowly:
   now in my life let your will be done;
   live in my flesh by your Spirit holy
   till your kingdom come.
      Worship the king . . .

Graham Kendrick
© Thankyou Music†

658 Winchester Old
Carols for Today 77

1 While shepherds
      watched their flocks by night,
   all seated on the ground,
   the angel of the Lord came down
   and glory shone around.

2 'Fear not,' said he –
      for mighty dread
   had seized their troubled mind –
   'Glad tidings of great joy I bring
   to you and all mankind:

3 'To you in David's town this day
   is born of David's line
   a saviour, who is Christ the Lord.
   And this shall be the sign:

4 'The heavenly babe
      you there shall find
   to human view displayed,
   all tightly wrapped
      in swathing bands
   and in a manger laid.'

Christmas Carols (657–658)

5 Thus spoke the seraph,
    and forthwith
  appeared a shining throng
  of angels praising God, who thus
  addressed their joyful song:

6 'All glory be to God on high,
  and to the earth be peace;
  goodwill henceforth
      from highest heaven
  begin and never cease!'

N Tate (1652–1715)

Christ was born to be our Lord
  on Christmas Day,
      on Christmas Day;
  Christ was born to be our Lord
  on Christmas Day in the morning.

4 Where God no longer calls in vain
  and human hearts are love's domain,
  there Christ is born in us again
  on Christmas Day in the morning:
      Christ is born in us again
      on Christmas Day,
          on Christmas Day;
      Christ is born in us again
      on Christmas Day in the morning.

© Michael Perry/Jubilate Hymns

659
Greensleeves
Hymns for Today's Church 145

1 When shepherds watched
    and angels sang
  and Judah's hills with glory rang,
  then Christ was born the Son of Man
  on Christmas Day in the morning:
      Christ was born the Son of Man
      on Christmas Day,
          on Christmas Day;
      Christ was born the Son of Man
      on Christmas Day in the morning.

2 Where Joseph knelt and Mary
      bowed
  and beasts of burden brayed aloud,
  there Christ was born
      for all our good
  on Christmas Day in the morning:
      Christ was born for all our good
      on Christmas Day,
          on Christmas Day;
      Christ was born for all our good
      on Christmas Day in the morning.

3 When wise men sought
    and Herod feared
  and when a royal star appeared,
  then Christ was born to be our Lord
  on Christmas Day in the morning:

660
Mendelssohn
Carols for Today 84

1 Hark! the herald angels sing
  glory to the new-born King;
  peace on earth and mercy mild,
  God and sinners reconciled!
  Joyful all you nations rise,
  join the triumph of the skies;
  with the angelic host proclaim,
  'Christ is born in Bethlehem':
      Hark! the herald angels sing
      glory to the new-born King.

2 Christ, by highest heaven adored,
  Christ, the everlasting Lord;
  late in time behold him come,
  offspring of a virgin's womb:
  veiled in flesh the Godhead see,
  hail the incarnate Deity!
  pleased as man with us to dwell,
  Jesus our Emmanuel:
      Hark! the herald . . .

3 Hail the heaven-born
      Prince of peace,
  hail the Sun of righteousness;

(659–660) Christmas Carols

light and life to all he brings,
risen with healing in his wings:
mild, he lays his glory by,
born that we no more may die;
born to raise us from the earth,
born to give us second birth:
    Hark! the herald . . .

C Wesley (1707–1788) and others

661 Iris
Carols for Today 86

1 Angels from the realms of glory,
wing your flight
    through all the earth;
heralds of creation's story
now proclaim Messiah's birth!
    Come and worship
    Christ, the new-born king:
    come and worship,
    worship Christ
    the new-born king.

2 Shepherds in the fields abiding,
watching by your flocks at night,
God with us is now residing:
see, there shines the infant light!
    Come and worship . . .

3 Wise men,
    leave your contemplations!
brighter visions shine afar;
seek in him the hope of nations,
you have seen his rising star:
    Come and worship . . .

4 Though an infant now we view him,
he will share his Father's throne,
gather all the nations to him;
every knee shall then bow down:
    Come and worship . . .

J Montgomery (1771–1854)
© in this version Jubilate Hymns

662 Nos Galan
Carols for Today 106

1 Come and hear the joyful singing,
    Alleluia, gloria,
set the bells of heaven ringing:
    alleluia, gloria,
God the Lord has shown us favour –
    alleluia, gloria,
Christ is born to be our saviour.
    Alleluia, gloria!

2 Angels of his birth are telling,
    Alleluia, gloria,
prince of peace all powers excelling;
    alleluia, gloria,
death and hell can not defeat him –
    alleluia, gloria,
go to Bethlehem and greet him.
    Alleluia, gloria!

3 Choir and people, shout in wonder,
    Alleluia, gloria,
let the merry organ thunder;
    alleluia, gloria,
thank our God for love amazing,
    alleluia, gloria,
Father, Son and Spirit praising.
    Alleluia, gloria!

© Michael Perry/Jubilate Hymns

663 I saw three ships
Carols for Today 100

1 When God from heaven
    to earth came down
on Christmas Day,
    on Christmas Day,
the songs rang out
    in Bethlehem town
on Christmas Day in the morning.

WOMEN AND GIRLS
2 For Christ was born to save us all,
    on Christmas Day,
    on Christmas Day,
and laid within a manger stall
    on Christmas Day in the morning.

Christmas Carols (661–663)

MEN AND BOYS

3 The shepherds
          heard the angels sing
    on Christmas Day,
        on Christmas Day,
  to tell them of the saviour-king
    on Christmas Day in the morning.

ALL

4 Now joy is ours and all is well,
    on Christmas Day,
        on Christmas Day,
  so sound the organ, chime the bell
    on Christmas Day in the morning!

after the traditional carol
© in this version Word & Music†/Jubilate Hymns

664 Antioch
Carols for Today 18

1 Joy to the world! The Lord has come:
  let earth receive her king,
  let every heart prepare him room
      and heaven and nature sing,
      and heaven and nature sing,
      and heaven, and heaven
        and nature sing!

2 Joy to the earth! The saviour reigns:
  your sweetest songs employ,
  while fields and streams and hills
      and plains
      repeat the sounding joy,
      repeat the sounding joy,
      repeat, repeat the sounding joy.

3 He rules the world
      with truth and grace,
  and makes the nations prove
  the glories of his righteousness,
      the wonders of his love,
      the wonders of his love,
      the wonders, wonders of his love.

I Watts (1674–1748)

665 Past three a clock
Carols for Today 129

  Ring out the bells –
  the joyful news is breaking;
  ring out the bells
  for Jesus Christ is born!

1 Angels in wonder
      sing of his glory;
  shepherds returning
      tell us the story.
  Ring out . . .

2 Let all creation
      worship before him:
  earth bring him homage,
      heaven adore him!
  Ring out . . .

3 Prophets have spoken –
      hark to their warning:
  shadows are passing,
      soon comes the morning!
  Ring out . . .

© Michael Perry/Jubilate Hymns

666 Russian Air
Carols for Today 114

1 Christ is born within a stable:
      greet the day
          when heaven smiled!
  Shepherds, fast as they are able,
      run to see the holy Child.
          Alleluia, alleluia,
          alleluia! Amen.

2 Eastern skies are brightly shining,
          hope has come upon the earth;
  angel songs with ours combining
      tell the world of Jesus' birth.
          Alleluia, alleluia,
          alleluia! Amen.

(664–666) Christmas Carols

Peal the bells and set them ringing,
  spread the joyful news abroad;
come with faith and join our singing
  to acclaim the incarnate Lord!
    Alleluia, alleluia,
    alleluia! Amen.

67 Branle de l'Official
Carols for Today 99

Ding-dong! Merrily on high
  in heaven the bells are ringing.
Ding-dong! Verily the sky
  is riven with angels singing:
    Gloria, hosanna in excelsis;
    gloria, hosanna in excelsis!

E'en so here below, below,
  let steeple bells be swungen;
and i-o, i-o, i-o,
  by Christian people sungen!
    Gloria . . .

Pray you, dutifully prime
  your matin chime, you ringers;
may you, beautifully rhyme
  your evetime song, you singers:
    Gloria . . .

G R Woodward (1848–1934)

68 Zither Carol
Carol Gaily Carol 12; Carols for Today 115

Girls and boys, leave your toys,
  make no noise,
kneel at his crib and worship him.
For this shrine, Child divine,
  is the sign
our Saviour's here.
  Alleluia, the church bells ring,
  'Alleluia!' the angels sing,
  alleluia from everything –
all must draw near!

2 On that day, far away, Jesus lay –
  angels were watching
    round his head.
Holy Child, mother mild, undefiled,
we sing your praise.
  Alleluia . . .
our hearts we raise.

3 Shepherds came at the fame
    of your name,
  angels their guide to Bethlehem;
in that place, saw your face
    filled with grace,
stood at your door.
  Alleluia . . .
love evermore.

669 Celebrations
Songs of Worship 12; Carol Praise

  Come and join the celebration –
    it's a very special day;
  come and share our jubilation –
    there's a new king born today!

1 See the shepherds
    hurry down to Bethlehem,
  gaze in wonder at the Son of God
    who lies before them:
  come and join . . .

2 Wise men journey,
    led to worship by a star,
  kneel in homage, bringing precious
    gifts from lands afar, so
  come and join . . .

3 'God is with us!' – round the world
    the message bring;
  he is with us – 'Welcome!'
    all the bells on earth are pealing:
  come and join . . .

Christmas Carols (667–669)

670 Quem pastores laudavere
Hymns for Today's Church 74

1 Shepherds came,
      their praises bringing,
   who had heard the angels singing:
   'Far from you be fear unruly,
   Christ is king of glory born.'

2 Wise men whom a star had guided
   incense, gold, and myrrh provided,
   made their sacrifices truly
   to the king of glory born.

3 Jesus born the king of heaven,
   Christ to us through Mary given,
   to your praise and honour duly
   be resounding glory done.

from *Quem pastores laudavere* (fifteenth century)
G B Caird (1917–1984)
© Mrs V Caird

671 Puer nobis
Carols for Today 130

1 Jesus Christ the Lord is born,
   all the bells are ringing!
   angels greet the holy One
      and shepherds hear them singing,
      and shepherds hear them singing:

2 'Go to Bethlehem today,
   find your king and saviour:
   glory be to God on high,
      to earth his peace and favour,
      to earth his peace and favour!'

3 Held within a cattle stall,
   loved by love maternal,
   see the master of us all,
      our Lord of lords eternal,
      our Lord of lords eternal!

4 Soon shall come the wise men three,
   rousing Herod's anger;
   mothers' hearts shall broken be
      and Mary's son in danger,
      and Mary's son in danger.

5 Death from life and life from death,
   our salvation's story:
   let all living things give breath
      to Christmas songs of glory,
      to Christmas songs of glory!

after German authors (from the fifteenth century)
© Michael Perry/Jubilate Hymns

672 Adeste fideles
Carols for Today 102

1 O come, all ye faithful,
   joyful and triumphant!
   O come ye,
      O come ye to Bethlehem!
   Come and behold him,
      born the king of angels:
      O come, let us adore him,
      O come, let us adore him,
   O come let us adore him,
      Christ the Lord!

2 God from God,
   Light from light –
   lo, he abhors not the virgin's womb
   Very God, begotten, not created:
      O come . . .

3 Sing, choirs of angels,
   sing in exultation!
   Sing, all ye citizens of heaven above
   'Glory to God in the highest!'
      O come . . .

4 Yea, Lord, we greet thee,
   born for our salvation;
   Jesus, to thee be glory given!
   Word of the Father
      now in flesh appearing:
      O come . . .

(670–672) Christmas Carols

r, on Christmas Day:

Yea, Lord, we greet thee,
born this happy morning;
Jesus, to thee be glory given!
Word of the Father
    now in flesh appearing:
O come . . .

after J F Wade (1711–1786)
F Oakeley (1802–1880) and others

3 Lord, you are love
        beyond all telling,
    Saviour and King, we worship you;
    Emmanuel, within us dwelling,
    make us and keep us pure and true:
    Lord, you are love
        beyond all telling,
    Saviour and King, we worship you.

F Houghton (1894–1972)
© Mrs D Houghton/Overseas Missionary Fellowship†
and in this version Jubilee Hymns

73 Bergers
Hymns for Today's Church 63

Lord, you were rich
    beyond all splendour,
yet, for love's sake, became so poor;
leaving your throne
    in glad surrender,
sapphire-paved courts
    for stable floor:
Lord, you were rich
    beyond all splendour,
yet, for love's sake, became so poor.

You are our God
    beyond all praising,
yet, for love's sake, became a man;
stooping so low, but sinners raising
heavenwards, by your eternal plan:
you are our God,
    beyond all praising,
yet, for love's sake, became a man.

CHRISTMAS CAROLS

Other Christmas Hymns and Songs

All the way, all the way	207
As with gladness, men of old	104
Before the heaven and earth	206
Bethlehem, what greater city	93
Faithful vigil ended	562
From heaven you came	449
Jesus, good above all other	195
Jesus, name above all names	226
Lord, now let your servant	98
Lord, you left your throne	108
O bless the God of Israel	585
Tell out, my soul	187
The first nowell the angel did say	109
The light of Christ has come	8
We three kings of Orient are	99
When the Lord came to our land	100

(See also sections The Wise Men/The Escape to Egypt/Epiphany 91–109, and Christ's Coming 579–599.)

36 Prayers Through The Year

and bring you to everlasting life through Jesus Christ our Lord. **Amen.**

674–677

ASSURANCE OF FORGIVENESS

674

If we say that we have no sin, we deceive ourselves, and there is no truth in us. But if we confess our sins to God, he will keep his promise and do what is right: he will forgive us our sins and purify us from all our wrongdoing.

from 1 John 1

675

May the Almighty and all-loving Father, forgive us for the sins we have now confessed to him, and help us to serve him better in the days to come. **Amen.**

676

May God, our heavenly Father, who has promised to forgive all those who sincerely turn to him, have mercy on each one of you, deliver you from your sins, and strengthen you for his service: through Jesus Christ our Lord. **Amen.**

677

Almighty God, our heavenly Father, who in his great mercy has promised to forgive the sins of all who turn to him with heartfelt repentance and sincere faith; have mercy on you, pardon and set you free from all your sins, establish and strengthen you in all goodness,

678–681

BLESSINGS

678

God the Father keep you in his care,
the Lord Jesus Christ
    be your constant friend,
and the Holy Spirit
    guide you in all you do,
now and always. **Amen.**

679

May the Lord bless you
    and take care of you;
may the Lord be kind
    and gracious to you;
may the Lord look on you with favour
    and give you peace. **Amen.**

from Numbers

680

The Lord bless and watch over you, the Lord make his face shine upon you and be gracious to you, the Lord look kindly on you and give you peace; and the blessing of God almighty, the Father, the Son, and the Holy Spirit, be among you and remain with you always. **Amen.**

from Numbers

681

The love of the Lord Jesus draw you to himself, the power of the Lord Jesus strengthen you in his service, the joy of the Lord Jesus fill your hearts; and the blessing of God almighty, the Father, the Son, and the Holy Spirit, be among you and remain with you always. **Amen.**

Prayers for Various Occasions – ASB

(674–681) Prayers Through The Year

PRAYERS THROUGH THE YEAR
(Other items for the minister)

Dedications
Almighty God, we thank you
(after Communion) — p. 16
Almighty God, whose Holy Spirit
(Renewal of Vows) — p. 21
And now, O father — 575
('Ever with the Lord')
Father of all, we give you thanks
(after Communion) — p. 16
Father, we dedicate ourselves
(from A Covenant Service) — p. 26; 720
Lord Jesus Christ, redeemer, friend
(after Richard of Chichester) — 153
Lord Jesus Christ, we give ourselves
(Morning dedication) — 32
Lord Jesus, my saviour, my heart
is cold
(Individual faith) — 409
O God of all life, thank you
(Evening dedication) — 177
O God, we are your children
(We respond to God's love) — 384

Thanksgivings
Almighty God, we thank you
(For healing) — 457
Heavenly father, we thank you
(General) — 385
O God our father, we thank you
(At Holy Communion) — 700
O God, we cannot measure
(after St Boniface) — 178
O heavenly father, we thank you
(For all God's gifts) — 762
We praise you, O God
(For making Jesus Lord) — 739
We praise you, O God
(For the hope of heaven) — 13
We thank you, God our Father
(For the Holy Spirit) — 325

Offertory Prayers
Heavenly Father, let these gifts
(For their use to God's glory) — 460
Yours, Lord is the greatness
(1 Chronicles 29)
— p. 9; 502, 784; back cover

Ascriptions
And now to him who is able
(After Martin Luther King) — 769
Blessing and honour, thanksgiving
(after Lancelot Andrewes) — 742
Glory be to you, O God
(from Revelation 15) — 66, 347
Lord God, may you be praised
(from 1 Chronicles 29) — 36
Now to him who is able to do
(from Ephesians) — 507
Now to him who is able to keep
(from Jude) — 90
Oh, the depth of the riches . . .
(from Romans 11) — 489
Our Lord and God! You are worthy
(from Revelation 4 and 5) — 552
You are worthy, O Lord
(Revelation 4) — 131, 435

Additional Blessings
Go in peace, be very courageous
(from 1 Thessalonians 5) — 701
May the spirit of the Lord
(from Isaiah 11) — 12
N . . . the Lord bless you
(Thanksgiving for a child) — 690
The joy of the angels
(Christmas Blessing) — 637, 783
The Lord bless you and watch
over you
(At a Baptism) — p. 23
The love of the Lord Jesus
(At a Baptism) — p. 23
The peace of God
(At Holy Communion) — p. 16
Upon all people of this nation
(At Local Festivals) — 709

Prayers Through The Year (Other items)

37 Prayers to Match the Themes

6 At a Baptism/Thanksgiving for a Child

(See also prayers in 'Renewal of Baptismal Vows', page 21.)

682

SENTENCES

Children are a gift from the Lord. They are his blessing. *Psalm 127.3*

Hannah said, 'I prayed for this child, and the Lord has granted me what I asked of him. So now I give him to the Lord.' *1 Samuel 1.27,28*

Jesus said, 'Let the little children come to me, and do not hinder them, for the kingdom of God belongs to such as these.' *Mark 10.14*

683–686

READING(S)
Let us hear the word of the Lord:

683 *Mark 10.13–16*
People were bringing little children to Jesus to have him touch them, but the disciples rebuked them. When Jesus saw this, he was indignant. He said to them, 'Let the little children come to me, and do not hinder them, for the kingdom of God belongs to such as these. I tell you the truth, anyone who will not receive the kingdom of God like a little child will never enter it.' And he took the children in his arms, put his hands on them and blessed them.

684 *Matthew 18.1–5, 10*
At that time the disciples came to Jesus and asked, 'Who is the greatest in the kingdom of heaven?' He called a little child and had him stand among them. And he said: 'I tell you the truth, unless you change and become like little children, you will never enter the kingdom of heaven. Therefore, whoever humbles himself like this child is the greatest in the kingdom of heaven. And whoever welcomes a little child like this in my name welcomes me. See that you do not look down on one of these little ones. For I tell you that their angels in heaven always see the face of my Father in heaven.'

685 *Deuteronomy 6.4–7*
Hear, O Israel: The Lord is our God, the Lord alone. Love the Lord your God with all your heart and with all your soul and with all your strength. These commandments that I give you today are to be upon your hearts. Impress them on your children. Talk about them when you sit at home and when you walk along the road, when you lie down and when you get up.

686 *Ephesians 6.1–*
Children, obey your parents in the Lord, for this is right. 'Honour your father and mother' – which is the first commandment with a promise – 'that it may go well with you and that you may enjoy long life on the earth.' Parents do not exasperate your children; instead, bring them up in the training and instruction of the Lord.

FOR THE PARENTS

God our heavenly Father, we thank you for your creative power and love, through which these parents have been granted the gift of a child; and for the skill and care of all who have guarded the health of mother and baby. Grant that N and N may always remember your love for them, and serve you faithfully in all their responsibilities as parents. So may they give to *this child* a sure knowledge of that love, through Jesus Christ our Lord. **Amen.**

Patrick Goodland

PARENTS' PRAYERS

(Mother)
God, my heavenly Father,
you have shown me your love
in giving me this child:
  thank you with all my heart.
Help me to fulfil my responsibilities
    as a mother,
so that our child
may know and feel your love;
for Jesus' sake. **Amen.**

(Father)
God our Father,
  thank you for the child
    you have given us.
Help me to fulfil my responsibilities
    as a father,
that together
we may love and serve you faithfully,
through Jesus Christ our Lord. **Amen.**

689

FOR THE HOME

We remember that Jesus shared an earthly home at Nazareth:

Bless, Lord, the home of this child we dedicate today; give all needed wisdom to these parents, and to all who will have care and oversight of *him*, so that *he* may grow up to know you, to love and to honour you. Grant with growth in stature, growth also in wisdom and understanding, safety through childhood, and your help to overcome the temptations of youth. Above all, grant that *he* may respond to your grace in Jesus Christ, gladly identifying with your church, and confessing Jesus as saviour and Lord. **Amen.**

Patrick Goodland

690

BLESSING

N . . . the Lord bless you and keep you; the Lord make his face to shine upon you and be gracious to you; the Lord turn his face towards you and give you peace. **Amen.**

from Numbers 6

7 At Holy Communion

(See also Family Communion Prayer, 785)

691

AN INTRODUCTION

We have gathered in the name of Jesus our saviour and living Lord. We recall

Prayers to Match the Themes (687–691)

how Jesus made himself known to his friends in the breaking of bread, and how their hearts were set ablaze as they talked and communed with him. May our hearts rejoice and our tongues be filled with praise as we come to meet him here.

Patrick Goodland

692

CONFESSION

Our loving and forgiving Father, we now confess that our lives do not measure up to the pure ideals and teaching of our Lord Jesus Christ. We are conscious that no part of our life is worthy of your holy presence. We confess that often we have been forgetful of you, careless of others and have followed our own selfish ways. We are aware that we have not reflected the love and concern of the Lord Jesus in the world. Our Father in heaven, we know we are sinners: but help us here and now to accept your forgiveness and the freedom from guilt which you offer. We ask this in the name of your Son, our saviour, Jesus Christ. **Amen.**

Patrick Goodland

693

WORDS OF COMFORT

Hear the words of comfort our Saviour Christ says to all who truly turn to him:

Come to me, all who labour and are heavy laden, and I will give you rest.

Matthew 11.28

God so loved the world that he gave his only Son, that whoever believes in him should not perish but have eternal life.

John 3.16

Hear what Saint Paul says: This saying is true and worthy of full acceptance, that Christ Jesus came into the world to save sinners.

1 Timothy 1.15

Hear what Saint John says: If anyone sins, we have an advocate with the Father, Jesus Christ the righteous; and he is the propitiation for our sins.

1 John 2.1

694

INTERCESSION

Let us pray for the whole Church of God in Christ Jesus, and for all people according to their needs:

O God, the creator and preserver of all mankind, we pray for people of every race, and in every kind of need: make your ways known on earth, your saving power among all nations. (Especially we pray for . . .) Lord, in your mercy
hear our prayer.

We pray for your Church throughout the world: guide and govern us by your Holy Spirit, that all who profess and call themselves Christians may be led into the way of truth, and hold the faith in unity of spirit, in the bond of peace, and in righteousness of life. (Especially we pray for . . .) Lord, in your mercy
hear our prayer.

We commend to your fatherly goodness all who are anxious or distressed in mind or body; comfort and relieve them in their need; give them patience in their sufferings, and bring good out

their troubles. (Especially we pray
r . . .) Merciful Father,
:cept these prayers
or the sake of your Son,
or Saviour Jesus Christ. Amen.

Alternative Form of Intercession – ASB

95

[M]EDITATION

n memory now we travel back two
ousand years; in faith Christ comes to
s across the ages. We break bread, as
e did, and remember his body broken
r us; we pour out wine, as he did, and
member his blood poured for us to
e ground. We hold out our hands to
ceive his grace; we eat to feed on his
ve, and drink to pledge our loyalty;
e rise to take up our cross; we go out
o serve him in his world.

Michael Perry

96

[IN]VOCATION

ome to us, Lord Jesus, in your risen
ower, when we receive the bread of
fe and the cup of salvation; cleanse
ur hearts from sin, that they may be
orthy of so great a guest; and keep us
oiding in your love, for your great
ame's sake. Amen.

F W Street

97

[C]OMMUNION PRAYER

ord Jesus Christ, we are your disciples
ith whom you desire to eat; and we

come to your table. Our hearts were
burning within us as you talked with us
on the way and opened the Scriptures
to us. Now in your name we break
bread, and give thanks and receive it:
open our eyes, confirm our faith and fill
us with your grace, that we may believe
and declare to all: 'It is true! The Lord
has risen'. Amen.

from Luke 24

698

FOR CHRIST'S PRESENCE

Come, Lord, in the fullness of your
risen presence, and make yourself
known to your people again through
the breaking of the bread, and the sharing of the cup. Amen.

+ Robert Runcie
WCC World Conference, Vancouver

699

FOR A SPIRIT OF WORSHIP

Lord Christ, who said 'Do this in remembrance of me': help us at every
communion service to look back, and
remember your death for us on the
cross; to look up, and know that you
are the risen saviour in our midst; to
look around, and rejoice in our
fellowship with one another; and to
look forward in hope to the coming of
your kingdom and the heavenly banquet. For your name's sake. Amen.

Llewellyn Cumings

700

THANKSGIVING

O God, our Father, we thank you for this sacrament. For all who down the centuries at your table have found the light that never fades, the joy that no man takes from them, the forgiveness of their sins, the love which is your love, the presence of their Lord; we thank you in his name. **Amen.**

from Worship Now†

They shall grow not old, as we who are left grow old: age shall not weary them, nor the years condemn. At the going down of the sun and in the morning, we will remember them:
we will remember them.

Laurence Binyon (1869–1943)
from 'With proud thanksgiving'

The Silence is observed. Then may be sounded the Last Post and Reveille.

from A Service for Remembrance Sunday 1968

701

A BLESSING

Go in peace, be very courageous, hold on to what is good, do not return evil for evil, strengthen the faint-hearted, support the weak, help the afflicted, honour all people, love and serve the Lord, rejoicing in the power of the Holy Spirit; and the grace of the Lord Jesus be with you. **Amen.**

from 1 Thessalonians 5

8 At Local Festivals (Civic Occasions, Parades, Remembrance, Pentecost 15)/ For the Peace of the World

702

ACT OF REMEMBRANCE
(Remembrance Sunday)
Let us remember before God those we have commended to his sure keeping:

Those to be remembered may be named.

The following may be said by all, or as a response.

(700–704) Prayers to Match the Themes

703

FOR PEACE IN THE WORLD

Almighty Father, whose will is to restore all things in your beloved Son, the king of all: govern the hearts and minds of those in authority, and bring the families of the nations, divided and torn apart by the ravages of sin, to be subject to his just and gentle rule; who is alive and reigns with you and the Holy Spirit, one God, now and for ever. **Amen.**

Pentecost 15 collect – ASB

704

FOR COMMUNITY LEADERS

Almighty and eternal God, to whom we must all give account: guide with your Spirit the . . . of *this city*, that *they* may be faithful to the mind of Christ and seek in all *their* purposes to enrich our common life; through Jesus Christ our Lord. **Amen.**

Collect for Civic Occasions – ASB

705

FOR WORLD LEADERS

O Lord God, guide the leaders of many different countries at the meetings where they try, by working together, to make the world a better and safer place. Help them to want peace rather than power, and show them how they can share the food in the world so that no one need be hungry. For Jesus' sake. **Amen.**

†

706

REMEMBRANCE

Almighty Father, we remember before you those who sacrificed their lives in the struggle for freedom, and we pray that the justice and peace for which they fought may become established today among the families of the nations: we ask this in him who taught us to pray for the coming of your kingdom on earth as it is in heaven, through Jesus Christ our Lord. **Amen.**

†

707

FOR SECURITY

Heavenly Father, we thank you for the safety and peace we have in this land, and for those who preserve it for us at the risk of their lives. Bless the leaders of the nations of the world: lest they think of war, put your peace in their minds; lest they are tempted to be cruel, let your love fill their hearts; for Jesus Christ's sake. **Amen.**

Michael Perry

708

FOR THE OPPRESSED

We plead with you today, O God, for those nations in East and West where totalitarian governments give little freedom: for their leaders, we ask that they may learn to govern in justice, mercy and truth; for their people, we ask that they may be able to hear your gospel and heed your word; and for all your servants in these lands, we pray for great faithfulness, great courage, and great love; through Jesus Christ our Lord. **Amen.**

Christopher Idle

709

BLESSING

Upon all people of this nation whose lives are dedicated to the service of others, may God bestow his blessings of faithfulness and peace. **Amen.**

St George's Windsor

9 New Year/Thanksgiving for the Old Year

710

FOR FORGIVENESS

O God, our loving Father, we are very sorry for all the things we have done which make you sad: we have sometimes been selfish or bad-tempered or disobedient. And we are sorry for the things we have failed to do: for the work we did not finish, the thank-you we forgot to say, the friends we did not

Prayers to Match the Themes (705–710)

help, the quarrel we never made up. For these and all our failings, forgive us, through Jesus Christ our Lord. **Amen.**

St Bartholomew's, Oxford

whether for ourselves, for our family for our church, for our employer, or fo a friend; help us to do all that we do, a Jesus did, to bring honour and glory to your name. **Amen.**

Paul Simmond

711

FOR PEACE IN OUR WORLD

O God of love, in whose will is our peace: so set your peace in human hearts that the nations of the world may learn to live as members of one family and children of one God and Father, to the glory of your name; through Jesus Christ our Lord. **Amen.**

from Contemporary Parish Prayers

712

FOR GOD'S PROTECTION

'I said to the man who stood at the Gate of the Year, "Give me a light that I may tread safely into the unknown." And he replied, "Go out into the darkness and put your hand into the hand of God. That shall be to you better than light and safer than a known way."' May that Almighty hand guide and uphold us all; through Jesus Christ our Lord. **Amen.**

after Minnie Haskins (1875–1957)†

713

FOR OUR WORK

O God, we thank you for the gifts you have given to each of us, and for the satisfaction of a task well done –

(711–714) Prayers to Match the Themes

10 The Wise Men/The Escape to Egypt (Christmas 2ii, Epiphany 1)

714

EPIPHANY SENTENCES

1
Arise, shine, Jerusalem, for your ligh has come, and the glory of the Lord ha risen upon you.   Isaiah 60

2
From the rising of the sun to its setting my name is great among the nations says the Lord.   Malachi 1.

3
We have seen his star in the east an have come with gifts to worship th Lord.   Matthew 2

4
There came a voice from heaven: this my Son, the Beloved, in whom I a well pleased.   Matthew 3.

5
We have beheld his glory, glory as the only Son from the Father.
John 1

selected by the Alternative Service Bo

715

FOR THOSE IN NEED

Remember, O merciful God, all those in need: people with no good food or proper clothes, no home of their own or no work to do, no family or friends, or no knowledge of your love. Move us to respond to their plight, and strengthen us to help them; through Jesus Christ, our Lord. **Amen.**

Christopher Idle

716

FOR REFUGEES

Loving Father, we pray for millions of spent people today: the homeless, the refugees – forced to live in tents or shacks, often in camps, herded together. We pray for people whose harvest has failed for years, who must listen to the sobs of children with daily hunger pains. Strengthen every missionary, every church organisation, every national fund seeking to help the forgotten millions; and show us how we can best love these our neighbours in need. Hear our prayer and enliven our response; for Jesus' sake. **Amen.**

Patrick Goodland

1 **The People of God** (6 before Christmas, Lent 3)/**Covenant and Unity** (Pentecost 2, 12, The Unity of the Church)

717

Lord God our redeemer, who heard the cry of your people and sent your servant Moses to lead them out of slavery: free us from the tyranny of sin and death and, by the leading of your Spirit, bring us to our promised land; through Jesus Christ our Lord. **Amen.**

Sixth Sunday before Christmas collect – ASB

718

FOR UNITY

Heavenly Father, you have called us in the Body of your Son Jesus Christ to continue his work of reconciliation and reveal you to mankind. Forgive us the sins which tear us apart; give us the courage to overcome our fears and to seek that unity which is your gift and your will; through Jesus Christ our Lord. **Amen.**

For the Unity of the Church collect – ASB

719

GOING OUT FROM WORSHIP

Be with us, O God, as we go out in your name: may the lips that have sung your praises always speak the truth; may the ears which have heard your word listen only to what is good; and may our lives as well as our worship be always pleasing to you, for the glory of Jesus Christ our Lord. **Amen.**

adapted, Michael Botting

12 Following Jesus (Epiphany 2, 9 before Easter, Lent 1)/**Jesus' Teaching** (Epiphany 2–6, Easter 4)

720

DEDICATION

Father, we dedicate ourselves to serve you faithfully and to follow Christ, to face the future with him, seeking his special purpose for our lives. Send us out to work and witness freely, gratefully and hopefully, in the power of the Holy Spirit, and for the honour and glory of your Son, Jesus Christ our Lord. **Amen.**

from A Covenant Service – section 5
Patrick Goodland

13 The Life of Prayer (Lent themes, Pentecost 6, 19)/**Forgiveness** (7 before Easter, 8 before Christmas)

721

FOR PENITENCE

O God you made us and you love us; thank you for being so willing to forgive us: make us quick to own up to you whenever we do wrong, so that we may quickly be forgiven; then our day will not be spoilt by worry, and we shall live in your peace, through Jesus Christ our Lord. **Amen.**

after Dick Williams

722

ABOUT OUR TEMPTATION

Lord, we confess to you what we are we like the path of life to be easy; w like every step to be free from fear; w like the world to be at our feet. Lord, b all the grace of your forty desert day arm us against those temptations, ale us to their corruption, forgive us ou sins, and teach us to tread the way tha Jesus takes, for his sake. **Amen.**

14 Mothering Sunday/The Family (Christmas 2i, Lent 4, Pentecost 14)

723

FOR THOSE IN NEED

O God, we remember the ill and th unhappy: we ask you to be with thos who have no family, and those wh have few friends; we ask you to hea those who are ill and to comfort thos in pain: help them to trust you, an give them strength to get bette through the power of Jesus Christ ou Lord. **Amen.**

Michael Per

724

FOR MOTHERS*

Lord Jesus, you know the blessings a mother's care: your mother, Mary cared for you when you were a baby when you travelled about with you disciples, and when you hung on th

(*Written for use with young children)

cross. Thank you for our mothers, who are always busy caring for us; who laugh with us in our happy times, comfort us when we are sad, and are always there when we need them. Remind us how much we owe to our mothers. Help us to say 'Thank you' to them by doing all we can to help them; through Jesus Christ our Lord. **Amen.**

David Cavil†

725

ABOUT LOOKING AFTER CHILDREN

Almighty God, who has given to us the love and care of a mother, and has caused us to offer thanks this day: we pray for all who have the responsibility of looking after children; that, aware of their influence upon young lives, they may seek guidance and strength for their task, through Jesus Christ our Lord. **Amen.**

Michael Perry

726

FOR OUR FAMILIES

God our Father, whose Son Jesus Christ shared in the home at Nazareth: hear our prayer for every human family, and especially for each home represented here, that they may be blessed by his presence and united in his love. We ask this in his name. **Amen.**

after James M Todd

727

FOR OUR HOMES

Lord and Saviour Jesus Christ, who shared at Nazareth the life of an earthly home: reign in our homes as Lord and King; give us grace to serve others as you have served us, and grant that by deed and word we may be witnesses of your saving love to those among whom we live; for the sake of your holy name. **Amen.**

adapted from The Marriage Service – ASB

728

THANKSGIVING

We thank you for our family and our friends – for those who understand us better than we understand ourselves, for those who know us at our worst and still love us, for those who have forgiven us when we had no right to expect forgiveness. Help us to be true to our friends, as we would expect them to be to us; through Jesus Christ our Lord. **Amen.**

after William Barclay

15–16 Passiontide

729

FOR HUMILITY

Almighty Father, whose Son Jesus Christ has taught us that what we do for the least of our brothers and sisters we do also for him: give us the will to be the servant of others as he was the servant of all, who gave up his life and

Prayers to Match the Themes (725–729)

died for us, yet is alive and reigns with you and the Holy Spirit, one God, now and for ever. **Amen.**

Maundy Thursday collect – ASB

730

THANKSGIVING

Heavenly Father, we thank you for giving your Son to die on the cross that we may be forgiven: help us to understand what our sin has led to, and how great his love is; so that we may trust him as our saviour and serve him as our Lord, now and for ever. **Amen.**

from Michael Botting's collection

731

GOOD FRIDAY THANKSGIVING

Lord, it seems so strange to call a day like this Good Friday: so many lies, so much hate, so much pain. And yet through it all you went on loving; loving the liars, loving the haters, loving the people who gave you pain – with love so strong that nothing could overcome it. Thank you, Lord Jesus Christ. **Amen.**

Richard Hughes†

732

EASTER EVE INTERCESSION

We pray this day/*night* for all who look for the light of Christ, for all who have no hope in this world, for those who have rejected him, and those who have denied him: Lord, in your mercy,
hear our prayer.

(730–733) Prayers to Match the Themes

We pray this day/*night* for all who are tired or hungry, for all who are anxious or ill, for all who are in pain or in sorrow, for those who are afraid of dying, and for those who do not believe in the resurrection from the dead: Lord, in your mercy,
hear our prayer.

We pray this day/*night* for the baptized in Christ, for our families and friends, for all those across the world who will celebrate his rising, and for those who are persecuted for their faith: Lord, in your mercy,
hear our prayer.

Michael Perry

17 **Easter** (and Sundays after Easter)

733

EASTER DAY

Lord, we watch the news and sometimes it seems that evil and death always have the last word. There is so much fighting, so much pain, so many deaths. There seems so little we can do except stand and watch from afar like the disciples. But nothing could stop the power of Jesus' love – even on the cross he forgave his enemies; his love broke the power of evil and death, his love had the last word. On Easter Day the tomb is empty and he is risen. That's the best news of all. Thank you for it. **Amen.**

Richard Hughes

8 God's Creation (Rogation, before Christmas)

734

APPROACH TO WORSHIP

Lord, we want to worship you with our eyes, because they can see the wonderful world you have made; Lord, we want to worship you with our ears, because they can hear your words, and the sounds of your world; Lord, we want to worship you with our voices, because they can shout your praise; Lord, we want to worship you with our hands, because they can help other people; Lord, we want to worship you with everything, because you have made us your children; through Jesus Christ our Lord. **Amen.**   †

735

FOR FARMERS (COLLECT)

Almighty God, whose will it is that the earth should bear its fruit in their seasons; direct the labours of those who work on the land that they may employ the resources of nature to your glory, for our own well-being, and for the relief of those in need; through Jesus Christ our Lord. **Amen.**

Rogation Days collect – ASB

736

FOR FAITHFULNESS

Almighty God, Creator and Lord of all things, we thank you for the vast resources of the earth and the sea, and for the hidden forces of nature now brought within our grasp by scientific discovery: help us to use your gifts wisely and faithfully for the benefit of humanity, that all may rejoice in your goodness; through Jesus Christ our Lord. **Amen.**

from Contemporary Parish Prayers

737

FOR OUR RESPONSIBILITY

O God, our Father, thank you for the world in which we live. Thank you for all the beautiful things in it, for all the interesting things in it, for all the useful things in it. Help us never to do anything which would make the world uglier or sadder; help us always to add something to the world's beauty and to the world's joy: through Jesus Christ our Lord. **Amen.**

William Barclay

19 Jesus is Lord (Ascension, Sunday after Ascension)

738

FOR STRENGTH FROM GOD

Jesus said, 'When the Holy Spirit comes upon you, you will be filled with power, and you will be witnesses for me . . . to the ends of the earth':

We thank you, Lord Jesus, for your last words; we treasure them for the promise of your Holy Spirit to give us power: help us now to obey your command to be witnesses to the ends of the earth, starting from where we are now. In your name we pray. **Amen.**

Ian Bunting

Prayers to Match the Themes (734–738)

739

THANKSGIVING

We praise you, O God, because you have exalted your Son Jesus Christ to your right hand in glory, and given him the name above every name, that at the name of Jesus every knee should bow. So, our Father, accept our worship – our love and thanksgiving; and grant that we, with those of every tongue, may confess that Jesus Christ is Lord, to your glory and honour. **Amen.**

from Philippians 2

20 The Holy Spirit (Pentecost, Pentecost 8)

740

THEME PRAYER (COLLECT)

Almighty God, who on the day of Pentecost sent your Holy Spirit to the disciples with the wind from heaven and in tongues of flame, filling them with joy and boldness to preach the Gospel: send us out in the power of the same Spirit to witness to your truth and to draw all people to the fire of your love; through Jesus Christ our Lord. **Amen.**

Pentecost collect – ASB

741

FOR THE POWER OF THE HOLY SPIRIT

We praise you, O God, because you gave the Holy Spirit to the first Christians, making Jesus real to them, teaching them the truth and giving them the power to witness boldly: fill us with the same Spirit that we may know their experience and follow their example, in the service of your Son Jesus, our Lord and saviour. **Amen.**

from Michael Botting's collection

21 The Holiness and Majesty of God (Trinity Sunday)

742

ASCRIPTION

Blessing and honour, thanksgiving and praise, more than we can utter, more than we can conceive, be to your glorious name, O God, Father, Son and Holy Spirit, by all angels, all people, all creation, for ever and ever. **Amen.**

after Lancelot Andrewes

22 Sea Theme/Holidays (Sea Sunday, etc)

743

FOR SEAFARERS

O God, the sea is yours, and you made it; your hands prepared the dry land: grant that those who travel by sea and sail in deep waters may be aware of the works of their Creator, responsive to the moving of your Holy Spirit, and alert to the calling of him who once spoke across the waves, Jesus Christ our Lord. **Amen.**

Michael Perry

744

FOR SEAFARERS

O Lord our heavenly Father, we commend to your keeping all who sail the seas: enrich them with your presence, guard them in danger, protect them in temptation, sustain them in loneliness, and support them in sickness and anxiety. Bless those who minister to them, and guide us all to the haven of eternal life; through Jesus Christ our Lord. **Amen.**

Missions to Seamen†

745

FOR ALL WHO TRAVEL

O God, the giver of all things, we pray for those who travel by land, sea, or air this holiday time; that they may set out in peace and return in safety, refreshed in body, mind and spirit; and that seeing the glory of your works they may remember to give you their thanks and praise, for Jesus Christ's sake. **Amen.**

Christopher Idle

746

FOR OUR HOLIDAYS

Father God, thank you for holidays; for the excitement of preparing and packing, for interesting places to explore, for new people to meet, for time to be with our families and friends. Give rest to all who are tired or overworked and are not able to have a holiday away from home. Help us to use our holidays to make new friends and to learn new things, through Jesus Christ our Lord. **Amen.** †

23 God's Love to Us (Easter 2ii)

747

FOR THOSE WE LOVE

Heavenly Father, we bring to you in our prayers all whom we love, knowing that your love for them is so much greater than ours, and that your will for them is all that is for their good. So, guard them in your keeping, O Lord, and give them now and always your richest blessing; for Jesus Christ's sake. **Amen.**

Frank Colquhoun

748

FOR OUR FAMILIES

Thank you, Lord, for our homes and families; thank you for our health and happiness; thank you for the good times, and for helping us to cope with the times that are not so good. Thank you for life itself, and for your wonderful love in Jesus Christ our Lord. **Amen.**

Marjorie Hampson

24 Invitation to Faith (7 before Christmas, Easter 4, Pentecost 4, 5, 19)

749

WE ADORE GOD

Almighty Father, the source of all beauty, goodness and love: we come together to worship you; we are tiny people set in your vast and wonderful

Prayers to Match the Themes (744–749)

universe, too much absorbed by the transitory things of life; but today in this place we turn to you – to your eternity and greatness: widen our horizons, deepen our experience, and carry us out of ourselves: for in you alone is found joy, peace and salvation; through Jesus Christ our Lord. **Amen.**

from Companion to the Lectionary Volume 3†

25 The Missionary Church/The Worldwide Church (Advent 3, Pentecost 5, 11, 12; The Missionary Work of the Church)

750

FOR DEDICATION (COLLECT)

Almighty God, you have broken the tyranny of sin and have sent the Spirit of your Son into our hearts whereby we call you Father. Give us grace to dedicate our freedom to your service, that many may be brought to the glorious liberty of the children of God; through Jesus Christ our Lord. **Amen.**

after Pentecost 4 collect – ASB

751

FOR THOSE IN NEED

Our Father in heaven, help us, we pray, to give to all the peoples of the earth the food and warmth and clothing which they need; have mercy upon those who are cold and hungry, and give your people no rest until poverty and want have been driven from your world; in the name of our saviour, Jesus Christ. **Amen.**

C S Woodward†

(750–754) Prayers to Match the Themes

752

FOR COURAGE

Our heavenly Father, your Son left his glory for the sorrow of mankind: grant us the strength to leave behind our comfort and security, to take up the cross of our saviour and follow where he leads; for his name's sake. **Amen.**

Michael Perry

753

FOR RACIAL HARMONY

O Lord Jesus Christ, Prince of peace: break down the barriers which separate us from other people and from God; teach Christians to love each other across the walls of colour, class and culture; forgive us the excuses we make for our own prejudice; and make us all one in you, Jesus Christ our Lord. **Amen.**

St Michael-le-Belfrey, York

(See also numbers 756–757)

26 The Caring Church (Pentecost 7, 10, 12, 13, 16, 17; Social Responsibility)/**Healing** (8 before Easter)

754

FOR THOSE IN NEED

To your keeping, O Lord God, we commend all whose enjoyment of life has been impaired by sickness, by tragedy, or by human sin. May your love sustain them in their suffering, and may your people care for them in the name of Jesus Christ our Lord. **Amen.**

Roger Pickering

755

FOR HEALING

Merciful Father, help all who suffer pain of body or grief of heart, to find you their help; and, as Jesus suffered pain in his body and healed it in others, help them to find their peace and healing in him; for his sake. **Amen.**

St Michael-le-Belfrey, York

756

FOR RELIEF WORKERS

Bless, O God, all who dedicate their powers today to the making of peace in the world; bless all who give their training and experience to feed, clothe and house the destitute; bless all who lend their energies and skills to teach impoverished people to till their land, to water it, and harvest it. Give us all a lively concern for the underprivileged, and show us practical ways of helping; for Christ's sake. **Amen.**

Rita Snowden†

27 God's Gifts to the Church/ Renewal (Pentecost 2, 3, 8)

757

FOR THE CHURCH

Lord of the Church, enable your people to *be* the Church – a redeemed people,

a holy people, a united people, a missionary people, and in all things a people gladly submissive to the truth you have shown us in yourself, Jesus Christ our Lord. **Amen.**

Michael Saward

758

FOR CHURCH FAMILY LIFE

Look upon us, O Lord, and grant us the grace of your Holy Spirit: where there is weakness, give us strength; where there is disagreement, give us tolerance; where there is misunderstanding, give us patience, and where there is hurt, give us the courage to forgive and the grace to accept forgiveness; through Jesus Christ our Lord. **Amen.** †

759

FOR LOVE
We pray for the love of Christ:

O God, you are the Father from whom the whole family in heaven and on earth is named: bless us with the riches of your glory; make us inwardly strong, and powerful in your Spirit; let Christ live in our hearts by faith; that, rooted in love and founded on it, we may surely grasp with all your people how broad and long, how high and deep is his love. So may we know that love which passes knowledge, and be filled with all your fulness; through Jesus Christ our Lord. **Amen.** †

based on Ephesians 3

28 The Church Anniversary
(Festival of the Dedication or Consecration of a Church)/ **Giving** (Pentecost 11, 18, 22)

760

FOR THIS HOUSE OF PRAYER

O God, make the doorway of this house wide enough to receive all who need human love and fellowship; narrow enough to shut out all envy, pride and strife. Make its threshold smooth enough to be no stumbling-block to children, or barrier to the elderly and disabled. Let its door be rugged and strong to turn back the tempter's power, but open and inviting to those who are your guests: God, make this house the doorway to your eternal kingdom; through Jesus Christ our Lord. **Amen.**

from Contemporary Parish Prayers

(See also Act of Dedication, 784)

761

ABOUT OUR POSSESSIONS

O Lord, you told us not to store up possessions for ourselves on earth: help us to understand that anything we possess is a gift from you – you have given it to us to enjoy, but not to cling to. So help us to detach ourselves from our possessions, that we shall be free to use them in the way that you want, through Jesus Christ our Lord. **Amen.** †

29 Harvest (Harvest Thanksgiving)

762

THANKSGIVING FOR ALL GOD'S GIFTS

O heavenly Father, we thank you for the good things you so richly provide; we thank you for your wisdom given when we ask you; and we thank you for your love for us, unasked and undeserved. Give us ever thankful hearts, we pray, and always a sense of how much we owe you, that our lives may be faithful. Then shall we rejoice with all the saints in your eternal kingdom; through Jesus Christ our Lord. **Amen.**

Michael Perry

763

THANKSGIVING FOR THE HARVEST

We thank you, God, for the harvest of all good things: for making plants to grow in the earth; for giving farmers strength to work; for supplying the food we have each day. Teach us to use your gifts fairly and generously and to remember that you gave them to us; through Jesus Christ our Lord. **Amen.**

Christopher Idle

(See also numbers 735–737)

764

FOR STRENGTH

O Eternal God, help us always to remember the great unseen cloud of witnesses who are round about us. When in danger give us courage like theirs, and when in difficulty, perseverance like theirs; so that we too may be faithful. Then shall we rejoice with all the saints in your eternal kingdom; through Jesus Christ our Lord. **Amen.**

W A Hampson

765

FOR OUR HOMES AND FAMILIES

Heavenly Father, we thank you for our homes, our families and our fellowship; for our food and clothing, and for all the happiness we share together: we ask that your love will surround us, your care protect us, and that we shall know your peace at all times; for Jesus' sake. **Amen.**

St Michael-le-Belfrey

766

FOR CHILDREN AT SCHOOL

O God our Father, we pray for the children growing up in our schools: bless them in their work and play, now and as they prepare for their lives ahead; teach them wisdom as well as knowledge, to be strong in spirit and to do your will; through Jesus Christ our Lord. **Amen.**

Frank Colquhoun, adapted

(See also numbers 720–722)

31 Heaven (Pentecost 21, Last Sunday after Pentecost)/**God's Peace**

767

COMMEMORATION

God of the living, and Father of our risen Lord, we are glad in your presence today as we remember those who have gone before us believing in your promises and trusting in your mercy. Help us to follow them, as they have followed Christ, and with all your people on earth and in heaven to give you the glory and the praise that is your due; through Jesus Christ our Lord. **Amen.**

Christopher Idle

768

FOR THE COMING NIGHT

Be with us, merciful God, and protect us through the silent hours of this night, that we who are wearied by the changes and chances of this passing world, may rest in your eternal changelessness; through Jesus Christ our Lord. **Amen.**

from the Leonine Sacramentary

769

ASCRIPTION

And now to him who is able to keep us
from falling, and lift us from the dark
valley of despair to the bright mountain
of hope, from the midnight of despera-
tion to the daybreak of joy; to him be
power and authority, for ever and ever.
Amen.

Martin Luther King

32 Christ's Coming
(5 before Christmas, Advent 1, 3)

770

ADVENT SENTENCES

1
Now is the time to wake out of our
sleep: for now our salvation is nearer
than when we first believed.

Romans 13.11

2
Watch at all times, praying for strength
to stand with confidence before the Son
of Man. Luke 21.36

3
The kingdom of God is close at hand.
Repent, and believe the gospel.

Mark 1.15

4
When the Lord comes, he will bring to
light things now hidden in darkness,
and will disclose the purposes of the
heart. 1 Corinthians 4.5

5
Our Lord says, Surely I come quickly.
Even so: come, Lord Jesus!

Revelation 22.20

(769–772) Prayers to Match the Themes

6
The glory of the Lord shall be revealed:
and all mankind shall see it.

Isaiah 40.5

7
The virgin is with child and will soon
give birth to a son: and she will call him
Emmanuel, God-is-with-us.

Isaiah 7.14

8
In the morning you shall see the glory
of the Lord. Exodus 16.7

selected by the Alternative Service Book

771

ABOUT CHRIST'S COMING

O God, who has given us the sure
promise that Christ will come to judge
the earth: make us ready, we pray, for
his royal coming, that we may consider
daily what kind of people we ought to
be, and as faithful servants wait and
work for our Master's return; for his
name's sake. **Amen.**

Christopher Idle

772

FOR HELP IN BEING READY

Almighty God, our heavenly Father, as
we wait for the return of the Lord Jesus
Christ, help us to make the best use of
the gifts you have given us – our skills,
our time and our possessions; help us
to share our good things with those in
need as Jesus has taught us to do, and
help us to share our faith humbly with
those who are not following him, so
that they and we may be ready when he

pears. We ask these things in his ume. **Amen.**

St Simon and St Jude, Southsea

3 God's Word to Us
(Advent 2)

73

BEFORE WORSHIP

God, we have come to this house of ayer: help us to remember that you e here with us, to pray to you and ng your praise with all our hearts, and listen to your word with open ears; rough Jesus Christ our Lord. **Amen.**

after C S Woodward

74

OR UNDERSTANDING

od our Father, we praise and thank ou for the gift of words: the words we ear and read, the words we speak and rite. As we handle and use the Holy criptures, make us more sensitive to hat they say, more appreciative of the e and truth in these pages, and of the ve and courage of those who wrote em; and open our ears to your voice, d our lives to yourself; through Jesus hrist our Lord. **Amen.** †

75

OR THE ARTS AND THE MEDIA

reator God, we pray for all Christians ho work in the arts, or in the news edia – especially any among us here –

for all who design, all who write or compose, and all who direct or perform: help them to grow in their love for you, and let their work always reflect your truth as it is in Christ Jesus; for his sake. **Amen.**

St Michael-le-Belfrey, York

34 Christmas Prayers
(Advent 4, Christmas Eve, Christmas Day, Christmas 1)

776

CHRISTMAS EVE SENTENCE
(For a 'Midnight' service)

Let the heavens rejoice, and let the earth be glad before the Lord: for he comes!

1 Chronicles 16.31,33

777

CHRISTMAS SENTENCES

1
The people who walked in darkness have seen a great light: those who dwell in the land of deep darkness, on them has the light shone. *Isaiah 9.2*

2
I bring you news of great joy, a joy to be shared by the whole people: today in the town of David a Saviour has been born to you; he is Christ the Lord.
Luke 2.10

3
To us a child is born, to us a son is given: and his name will be called the Prince of Peace. *Isaiah 9.6*

Prayers to Match the Themes (773–777)

4

God's love for us was revealed when he sent his only Son into the world so that we could have life through him.

1 John 4.9

5

The Word became flesh. He came to dwell among us, and we saw his glory.

John 1.14

6

God has shone in our hearts to give the light of the knowledge of his glory in the face of Jesus Christ.

2 Corinthians 4.6

7

The grace of God has dawned on the world with healing for all mankind.

Titus 2.11

selected by the Alternative Service Book

778

GREETING

Welcome, everybody! At Christmas time we delight again to hear the story of the journey to Bethlehem, the song of the angels, the surprise of the shepherds, and their joy as they found Jesus in the manger. But lest we forget he was born to poverty, we remember at this season all who are hungry or cold. And lest we forget he became a refugee, we remember the stranger and the lonely among us. And lest we forget he felt the pain of life and death, we remember those who are ill, or anxious, or bereaved. And because we know he came for our salvation, let us in heart and mind go once again to Bethlehem, to hear the message of the angels and worship afresh the Son of God.

Michael Perry

779

FOR OUR WORLD

O God, we thank you for the message of peace that Christmas brings to our distracted world. Give peace among nations; peace in our land, peace in our homes, and peace in our hearts, as we remember the birth at Bethlehem of the Prince of peace, Jesus Christ our Lord. **Amen.**

from Worship Now

780

FOR THOSE WITHOUT FAITH

O Holy Spirit of Christ – teacher, helper, and friend: open the hearts and minds of many this Christmas-time to the good and saving news of Jesus Christ; that those who are insecure, or empty, or aimless, may find in the One from Bethlehem all that they need today, and much more besides; for his name's sake. **Amen.**

Christopher Idle

781

THE GREATEST PRESENT

O God our Father, we praise you for Christmas – our happiness and presents, our families and the friends we see again; and for this greatest present of all we thank you: for the gift of Jesus at Bethlehem to be our saviour and our king. **Amen.**

Michael Perry

(778–781) Prayers to Match the Themes

782

FOR HEARTS AND HOMES OPEN TO CHRIST

Loving Father, we thank you for the gift of your Son, whose birth at Bethlehem we now prepare to celebrate: make our hearts and our homes always open to him, that he may dwell with us for ever, and we may serve him gladly all our days, to the honour and glory of your name. **Amen.**

Roger Pickering

783

BLESSING

The joy of the angels, the wonder of the shepherds, and the peace of the Christ child, fill your hearts this Christmas time; and the blessing of God the Father, God the Son, and God the Holy Spirit, be with you now and always. **Amen.**

Michael Perry

(See also numbers 714–716)

Prayers to Match the Themes (782–783)

38 Full texts: Act of Dedication, Family Communion Prayer, ASB Canticles

784

ACT OF DEDICATION
(See sections 5 and 28. This act of dedication can be adapted for local use)

**A YOUTH GROUP
LEADER/MEMBER**
As members and leaders of the *youth group*, we dedicate ourselves to God's service and to the work of befriending young people in our neighbourhood, asking that through us he may bring many to a saving faith in Jesus Christ – this is our resolve.
May God be with you.

A SCOUT/GUIDE LEADER
As leaders and members of scouts, guides, cubs and brownies we offer our service to God, to our neighbour and to our Queen and Country; we shall try to ensure that as our members grow in skill they may also grow in wisdom and the knowledge of truth – this is our resolve.
May God be with you.

A TEACHER/SUNDAY SCHOOL TEACHER
As teachers/Sunday school teachers, we thank God for his gifts and for the responsibilities of our calling; and we determine by his strength to prepare ourselves well and bring to those we teach a fuller and clearer knowledge of his love and the blessing of his wisdom for their lives – this is our resolve.
May God be with you.

A BIBLE STUDY/PRAYER GROUP LEADER
As members of the *study groups*, we bring to God our intercession, and open our hearts to his word: in this way we purpose to encourage one another in faith, and seek his will for our lives – this is our resolve.
May God be with you.

A MUSICIAN/CHORISTER
As musicians of the church we offer to God our leadership, our service to the congregation and our desire to worship God in spirit and in truth – this is our resolve.
May God be with you.

A WOMEN'S GROUP LEADER
As members of the *women's group(s)*, we offer the service of our prayers for God's people, our practical help, and our concern for the integrity of family life and the honour of God's name – this is our resolve.
May God be with you.

AN ADULT ORGANISATION LEADER/A MEN'S GROUP LEADER
As members of the *adult organisation/men's group*, we seek God's blessing on our fellowship, and his strength to serve the wider church family and the local community – this is our resolve.
May God be with you.

A CHURCH OFFICER/COUNCIL MEMBER/ADMINISTRATOR/CHURCHWARDEN
As church officers we dedicate our stewardship of the church and our glad service of the congregation to the glory of God – this is our resolve.
May God be with you.

FLOWER-ARRANGER

s those who decorate the church with
)wers, we offer to God our gifts and
·rvice, for the beautifying of worship
ıd the glory of his name – this is our
solve.

ay God be with you.

BELL-RINGER

s bell-ringers, we dedicate our energy
ıd skill to God's glory, and determine
so to seek his presence in the worship
the congregation – this is our resolve.

ay God be with you.

MEMBER OF THE CHURCH
LEANING ROTA

s those who do the work of cleaning
.is house in which God is worshipped
ıd his voice heard, we offer to him our
re, our love, and our faithfulness in
·rving these who come here – this is
ır resolve.

ay God be with you.

A SIDESMAN/STEWARD

As *sidesmen/stewards*, we dedicate to
God our stewardship and ask for his
strength, that we may generously welcome all who enter this place, offering
friendship in the name of Christ and
careful assistance to the church's
worship – this is our resolve.

May God be with you.

MINISTER(S)

With all of you, *I/we* re-dedicate *my/our*
ministry to God; and offer *myself/*
ourselves as your servant(*s*) for Christ's
sake. To God be glory in the Church
and in Christ Jesus:

Yours, Lord, is the greatness,
the power, the glory,
the splendour, and the majesty;
for everything in heaven and on earth
**   is yours.**
All things come from you,
and of your own do we give you.   †

from 1 Chronicles 29
and page 129 – ASB

Act of Dedication (784)

785

FAMILY COMMUNION PRAYER
(Not authorised for use in Church of England services)

The Lord be with you:
and also with you.

Or

The Lord is here:
his Spirit is with us.

Lift up your hearts:
we lift them to the Lord.

Let us give thanks to the Lord our God:
it is right to give him thanks
and praise.

God our Father,
we give you the thanks we owe,
(at this season especially for . . .)
and we rejoice to praise you
through Jesus Christ our Lord.

Through him you made us;
through him you set us free
from sin and death.
Through him you gave us
your Holy Spirit,
and called us into one family.

So, Father, by the same Spirit,
let us who take this bread and wine,
receive the body and blood of Christ.

Or

So, Father, by the same Spirit,
make this bread and wine
which we bring before you
to be to us his body and blood.

For when the time came
for him to be lifted up to die
and so to enter his glory,
he gathered his disciples
and took bread
and gave thanks to you;
then he broke it
and gave it to them saying,
'Take, eat:
this is my body which is given for you
do this to remember me.'

After supper
he took the cup and gave thanks.
He gave it to them saying,
'Drink this, all of you:
this is my blood of the new covenant,
shed for you and for many,
that sins may be forgiven;
do this every time you drink it,
to remember me.'

Now as we look for his coming,
we celebrate with this bread and cup
his one perfect sacrifice,
proclaiming his death for our salvation
and rejoicing in the power
of his resurrection,
until we share with him
in the feast of his kingdom.

Either

Father,
accept the thanks and praise
of your children
in this sacred feast;
renew us by your Holy Spirit,
and make us one
in Christ Jesus our Lord. Amen.

Or

With the whole family
in heaven and on earth
we praise and adore you, saying:
Holy, holy, holy Lord,
God of power and might,
heaven and earth
are full of your glory.
Hosanna in the highest. Amen.

786

VENITE

1 O come let us sing | out · to the | Lord:
let us shout in triumph
to the | rock of | our sal|vation.

2 Let us come before his | face with | thanksgiving:
   **and cry | out to · him | joyfully ·
   in | psalms.**

3 For the Lord is a | great | God:
   and a great | king a·bove | all | gods.

4 In his hand are the | depths · of the | earth:
   **and the peaks of the | mountains ·
   are | his | also.**

†5 The sea is his and | he | made it:
   his hands | moulded | dry | land.

6 Come let us worship and | bow | down:
   **and kneel be|fore the | Lord
   our | maker.**

7 For he is the | Lord our | God:
   **we are his | people·
   and the | sheep of · his | pasture.**

8 If only you would hear his | voice to | day:
   for he | comes to | judge the | earth.

9 He shall judge the | world with | right-eousness:
   and the | peoples | with his | truth.

   **Glory to the Father and | to the | Son:
   and | to the | Holy | Spirit;
   as it was in the be|ginning is | now:
   and shall be for | ever. | A|men.**   †

   from Psalms 95, 98

787

JUBILATE

1 O shout to the Lord in triumph | all the | earth:
   **serve the Lord with gladness
   and come before his | face
   with | songs of | joy.**

2 Know that the Lord | he is | God:
   **it is he who has made us and we are his;
   we are his | people·
   and the | sheep of · his | pasture.**

3 Come into his gates with thanksgiving and into his | courts with | praise:
   **give thanks to him
   and | bless his | holy | name.**

4 For the Lord is good * his loving mercy | is for | ever:
   **his faithfulness
   through|out all | gener|ations.**

   **Glory to the Father and | to the | Son:
   and | to the | Holy | Spirit;
   as it was in the be|ginning is | now:
   and shall be for | ever. | A|men.**   †

   from Psalm 100

788

THE EASTER ANTHEMS

1 Christ our passover has been | sacri·ficed | for us:
   so let us | cele|brate the | feast,

2 not with the old leaven of cor | ruption · and | wickedness:
   **but with the unleavened | bread
   of · sin|cerity · and | truth.**

3 Christ once raised from the dead | dies no | more:
   **death has no | more do|minion |
   over him.**

4 In dying he died to sin | once for | all:
   in | living · he | lives to | God.

5 See yourselves therefore as | dead to | sin:
   **and alive to God
   in | Jesus | Christ our | Lord.**

6 Christ has been | raised · from the | dead:
   the | firstfruits · of | those who | sleep.

7 For as by | man came | death:
   **by man has come also
   the resur|rection | of the | dead;**

8 for as in | Adam · all | die:
   **even so
   in Christ shall | all be | made a|live.**

   **Glory to the Father and | to the | Son:
   and | to the | Holy | Spirit;
   as it was in the be|ginning is | now:
   and shall be for | ever. | A|men.**   †

   from 1 Corinthians 5, 15; Romans 6

ASB Canticles (787–788)

789

BENEDICTUS (The Song of Zechariah)

1 Blessed be the Lord the ǀ God of ǀ Israel:
**for he has come to his ǀ people ·
and ǀ set them ǀ free.**

2 He has raised up for us a ǀ mighty ǀ
saviour:
**born of the ǀ house · of his ǀ servant ǀ
David.**

3 Through his holy prophets he ǀ promised · of ǀ old:
**that he would save us
from our enemies
from the ǀ hands of ǀ all that ǀ hate us.**

4 He promised to show ǀ mercy · to our ǀ
fathers:
**and to re ǀ member ·
his ǀ holy ǀ covenant.**

5 This was the oath he swore to our ǀ
father ǀ Abraham:
**to set us ǀ free ·
from the ǀ hands of · our ǀ enemies,**

6 free to worship him with ǀ out ǀ fear:
**holy and righteous in his sight ǀ
all the ǀ days of · our ǀ life.**

7 You my child shall be called the prophet
of the ǀ Most ǀ High:
**for you will go before the ǀ Lord ·
to pre ǀ pare his ǀ way,**

8 to give his people knowledge ǀ of
sal ǀ vation:
by the for ǀ giveness · of ǀ all their ǀ sins.

9 In the tender compassion ǀ of our ǀ God:
**the dawn from on ǀ high
shall ǀ break up ǀ on us,**

10 to shine on those who dwell in darkness
and the ǀ shadow · of ǀ death:
**and to guide our feet ǀ into · the ǀ way
of ǀ peace.**

**Glory to the Father and ǀ to the ǀ Son:
and ǀ to the ǀ Holy ǀ Spirit;
as it was in the be ǀ ginning is ǀ now:
and shall be for ǀ ever. ǀ A ǀ men.**   †

from Luke 1

790

A SONG OF CREATION*

1 Bless the Lord all cre ǀ ated ǀ things:
**sing his ǀ praise · and ex ǀ alt him ·
for ǀ ever.**

2 Bless the ǀ Lord you ǀ heavens:
**sing his ǀ praise · and ex ǀ alt him ·
for ǀ ever.**

3 Bless the Lord you ǀ angels · of the ǀ Lord:
bless the ǀ Lord all ǀ you his ǀ hosts;

4 bless the Lord you waters a ǀ bove the ǀ
heavens:
**sing his ǀ praise · and ex ǀ alt him ·
for ǀ ever.**

5 Bless the Lord ǀ sun and ǀ moon:
bless the ǀ Lord you ǀ stars of ǀ heaven;

6 bless the Lord all ǀ rain and ǀ dew:
**sing his ǀ praise · and ex ǀ alt him ·
for ǀ ever.**

7 Bless the Lord all ǀ winds that ǀ blow:
bless the ǀ Lord you ǀ fire and ǀ heat;

8 bless the Lord scorching wind and ǀ
bitter ǀ cold:
**sing his ǀ praise · and ex ǀ alt him ·
for ǀ ever.**

9 Bless the Lord dews and ǀ falling ǀ snows:
bless the ǀ Lord you ǀ nights and ǀ days;

10 bless the Lord ǀ light and ǀ darkness:
**sing his ǀ praise · and ex ǀ alt him ·
for ǀ ever.**

11 Bless the Lord ǀ frost and ǀ cold:
bless the ǀ Lord you ǀ ice and ǀ snow;

12 bless the Lord ǀ lightnings · and ǀ clouds:
**sing his ǀ praise · and ex ǀ alt him ·
for ǀ ever.**

13 O let the earth ǀ bless the ǀ Lord:
**bless the ǀ Lord
you ǀ mountains · and ǀ hills;**

14 bless the Lord all that ǀ grows · in the ǀ
ground:
**sing his ǀ praise · and ex ǀ alt him ·
for ǀ ever.**

(*For a shorter version of this canticle verses
4–17 may be omitted.)

15 Bless the **|** Lord you **|** springs:
  bless the | Lord you | seas and | rivers;

16 bless the Lord you whales and all that **|** swim · in the **|** waters:
  **sing his | praise · and ex|alt him ·
      for | ever.**

17 Bless the Lord all **|** birds · of the **|** air:
  bless the | Lord you | beasts and | cattle;

18 bless the Lord all **|** men · on the **|** earth:
  **sing his | praise · and ex|alt him ·
      for | ever.**

19 O People of God **|** bless the **|** Lord:
  **bless the | Lord
      you | priests · of the | Lord;**

20 bless the Lord you **|** servants · of the **|** Lord:
  **sing his | praise · and ex|alt him ·
      for | ever.**

21 Bless the Lord all men of **|** upright **|** spirit:
  **bless the Lord
      you that are | holy · and | humble ·
          in | heart.**

  **Bless the Father the Son
  and the | Holy | Spirit:
  sing his | praise · and ex|alt him ·
      for | ever.**   †

from The Song of the Three Children

791

GREAT AND WONDERFUL

Great and wonderful are your deeds Lord **|** God · the Al**|**mighty:
**just and true are your | ways
O | King · of the | nations.**

Who shall not revere and praise your **|** name O **|** Lord?
for | you a|lone are | holy.

All nations shall come and worship **|** in your **|** presence:
**for your just | dealings ·
    have | been re|vealed.**

To him who sits on the throne **|** and · to the **|** Lamb:
**be praise and honour glory and might
for ever and | ever. | A|men.**   †

from Revelation 15

TE DEUM*

1 You are **|** God · and we **|** praise you:
  **you are the | Lord
  and | we ac|claim you;**

2 you are the e**|**ternal **|** Father:
  all cre|ation | worships | you.

3 To you all angels*all the **|** powers of **|** heaven:
  **cherubim and seraphim |
      sing in | endless | praise,**

4 Holy holy holy Lord*God of **|** power and **|** might:
  **heaven and | earth
      are | full of · your | glory.**

5 The glorious company of ap **|** ostles **|** praise you:
  **the noble fellowship of prophets
      praise you
  the white-robed | army · of | martyrs |
      praise you.**

6 Throughout the world the holy **|** Church ac**|**claims you:
  Father of | majes|ty un|bounded;

†7 your true and only Son*worthy of **|** all **|** worship:
  **and the Holy | Spirit |
      advocate · and | guide.**

8 You Christ are the **|** King of **|** glory:
  the e|ternal | Son · of the | Father.

9 When you became man to **|** set us **|** free:
  **you did not ab|hor
  the | Virgin's | womb.**

10 You overcame the **|** sting of **|** death:
  **and opened the kingdom of | heaven ·
  to | all be|lievers.**

11 You are seated at God's right **|** hand in **|** glory:
  **we believe that you will | come
  and | be our | judge.**

12 Come then Lord and **|** help your **|** people:
  **bought with the | price
  of | your own | blood;**

(*Verses *14–18* may be omitted.)

ASB Canticles (791–792)

13 and bring us ' with your ' saints:
   to ' glory ' ever'lasting.

14 Save your people Lord and ' bless · your
   in'heritance:
   **govern and up'hold them '
   now and ' always.**

15 Day by ' day we ' bless you:
   we ' praise your ' name for ' ever.

16 Keep us today Lord from ' all ' sin:
   have mercy ' on us ' Lord have ' mercy.

17 Lord show us your ' love and ' mercy:
   for we ' put our ' trust in ' you.

†18 In you Lord ' is our ' hope:
   **let us not be con'founded '
   at the ' last.**   †

793

GLORIA IN EXCELSIS

1 Glory to ' God · in the ' highest:
   and ⌐ peace · to his ' people · on ' earth.

2 Lord God ' heaven·ly ' King:
   al'mighty ' God and ' Father,

3 we worship you we ' give you ' thanks:
   we ' praise you ' for your ' glory.

4 Lord Jesus Christ only ' Son · of the '
   Father:
   Lord ' God ' Lamb of ' God,

5 you take away the ' sin · of the ' world:
   have ' mercy ' on ' us;

6 you are seated at the right hand ' of the '
   Father:
   re'ceive ' our ' prayer.

7 For you a'lone · are the ' Holy One:
   you a'lone ' are the ' Lord,

8 you alone are the Most High
   Jesus Christ with the ' Holy ' Spirit:
   **in the glory of God the ' Father. '
   A'men.**   †

794

SAVIOUR OF THE WORLD

1 Jesus saviour of the world * come to us ' i
   your ' mercy:
   we look to ⌐ you to ' save and ' help us.

2 By your cross and your life laid down yo
   set your ' people ' free:
   we look to ' you to ' save and ' help us.

3 When they were ready to perish you
   saved · your dis'ciples:
   we look to ' you to ' come to · our ' help.

4 In the greatness of your mercy loose u
   from our ' chains:
   forgive the ' sins of ' all your ' people.

5 Make yourself known as our saviour an
   mighty · de'liverer:
   **save and ' help us ·
   that ' we may ' praise you.**

6 Come now and dwell with us ' Lo
   Christ ' Jesus:
   **hear our ' prayer ·
   and be ' with us ' always.**

7 And when you ' come in · your ' glory:
   **make us to be one with you *
   and to ' share
      the ' life of · your ' kingdom.**

795

PSALM 134

1 Come bless the Lord all you ' servant
   of the ' Lord:
   **you that by night ' stand · in the ' hous
      of · our ' God.**

2 Lift up your hands toward the holy pl
   and ' bless the ' Lord:
   **may the Lord bless you from Zion
   the ' Lord who · made '
      heaven · and ' earth.**

   **Glory to the Father and ' to the ' Son:
   and ⌐ to the ' Holy ' Spirit;
   as it was in the be'ginning is ' now:
   and shall be for ' ever. ' A'men.**

796

O GLADSOME LIGHT

1 O gladsome light, O grace
   Of God the Father's face,
   The eternal splendour wearing;
   Celestial, holy, blessed,
   Our Saviour Jesus Christ,
   Joyful in thine appearing.

2 Now, ere day fadeth quite,
   We see the evening light,
   Our wonted hymn outpouring;
   Father of might unknown,
   Thee, his incarnate Son,
   And Holy Spirit adoring.

3 To thee of right belongs
   All praise of holy songs,
   O Son of God, lifegiver;
   Thee, therefore, O Most High,
   The world doth glorify,
   And shall exalt for ever.   †

797

MAGNIFICAT (The Song of Mary)

1 My soul proclaims the ׀ greatness · of
   the ׀ Lord:
   **my spirit re׀joices ·
   in ׀ God my ׀ saviour;**

2 for he has looked with favour on his ׀
   lowly ׀ servant:
   **from this day all gener׀ations ·
   will ׀ call me ׀ blessed;**

3 the Almighty has done ׀ great things ׀ for
   me:
   and ׀ holy ׀ is his ׀ name.

4 He has mercy on ׀ those who ׀ fear him:
   in ׀ every ׀ gener׀ation.

5 He has shown the ׀ strength · of his ׀
   arm:
   **he has scattered the ׀ proud
   in ׀ their con׀ceit.**

6 He has cast down the mighty ׀ from
   their ׀ thrones:
   and has ׀ lifted ׀ up the ׀ lowly.

7 He has filled the hungry with ׀ good ׀
   things:
   **and the rich
   he has ׀ sent a׀way ׀ empty.**

8 He has come to the help of his ׀ servant ׀
   Israel:
   **for he has re׀membered·
   his ׀ promise · of ׀ mercy,**

9 the promise he ׀ made · to our ׀ fathers:
   **to Abraham ׀ and his ׀ children ·
   for ׀ ever.**

   **Glory to the Father and ׀ to the ׀ Son:
   and ׀ to the ׀ Holy ׀ Spirit;
   as it was in the be׀ginning is ׀ now:
   and shall be for ׀ ever. ׀ A׀men.**   †

798

BLESS THE LORD

1 Bless the Lord the ׀ God of · our ׀ fathers:
   **sing his ׀ praise · and ex׀alt him ·
   for ׀ ever.**

2 Bless his holy and ׀ glori·ous ׀ name:
   **sing his ׀ praise · and ex׀alt him ·
   for ׀ ever.**

3 Bless him in his holy and ׀ glori·ous ׀
   temple:
   **sing his ׀ praise · and ex׀alt him ·
   for ׀ ever.**

4 Bless him who be׀holds the ׀ depths:
   **sing his ׀ praise · and ex׀alt him ·
   for ׀ ever.**

5 Bless him who sits be ׀ tween the ׀
   cherubim:
   **sing his ׀ praise · and ex׀alt him ·
   for ׀ ever.**

6 Bless him on the ׀ throne of · his ׀
   kingdom:
   **sing his ׀ praise · and ex׀alt him ·
   for ׀ ever.**

7 Bless him in the ׀ heights of ׀ heaven:
   **sing his ׀ praise · and ex׀alt him ·
   for ׀ ever.**

   **Bless the Father the Son
   and the ׀ Holy ׀ Spirit:
   sing his ׀ praise · and ex׀alt him ·
   for ׀ ever.**   †

799

NUNC DIMITTIS (The Song of Simeon)

1 Lord now you let your servant ǀ go in ǀ
peace:
your ǀ word has ǀ been ful ǀ filled.

2 My own eyes have ǀ seen the · sal ǀ vation:
which you have prepared
in the ǀ sight of ǀ every ǀ people;

†3 a light to re ǀ veal you · to the ǀ nations:
and the ǀ glory · of your ǀ people ǀ Israel.

Glory to the Father and ǀ to the ǀ Son:
and ǀ to the ǀ Holy ǀ Spirit;
as it was in the be ǀ ginning is ǀ now:
and shall be for ǀ ever. ǀ A ǀ men. †

800

THE SONG OF CHRIST'S GLORY

1 Christ Jesus was in the ǀ form of ǀ God:
but he did not ǀ cling · to e ǀ quality·
with ǀ God.

2 He emptied himself * taking the ǀ form · of
a ǀ servant:
and was ǀ born ·
in the ǀ likeness · of ǀ men.

3 Being found in human form he ǀ humbled ·
him ǀ self:
and became obedient unto death ǀ
even ǀ death · on a ǀ cross.

4 Therefore God has ǀ highly · ex ǀ alted him:
and bestowed on him
the ǀ name a·bove ǀ every ǀ name,

5 that at the name of Jesus every ǀ knee
should ǀ bow:
in heaven and on ǀ earth
and ǀ under · the ǀ earth;

6 and every tongue confess that Jesus ǀ
Christ is ǀ Lord:
to the ǀ glory · of ǀ God the ǀ Father.

Glory to the Father and ǀ to the ǀ Son:
and ǀ to the ǀ Holy ǀ Spirit;
as it was in the be ǀ ginning is ǀ now:
and shall be for ǀ ever. ǀ A ǀ men. †

801

GLORY AND HONOUR

1 Glory and ǀ honour · and ǀ power:
are yours by ǀ right O ǀ Lord our ǀ God;

2 for you cre ǀ ated ǀ all things:
and by your ǀ will
they ǀ have their ǀ being.

3 Glory and ǀ honour · and ǀ power:
are yours by ǀ right
O ǀ Lamb · who was ǀ slain;

4 for by your blood you ransomed ǀ men
for ǀ God:
from every race and language *
from ǀ every ǀ people · and ǀ nation,

5 to make them a ǀ kingdom · of ǀ priests:
to stand and ǀ serve be ǀ fore our ǀ God.

To him who sits on the throne ǀ and · to
the ǀ Lamb:
be praise and honour
glory and might *
for ever and ǀ ever. ǀ A ǀ men. †

CHANTING CANTICLES

(a) Breath is to be taken at asterisks, and at the end of lines except where the pointing clearly forbids it.

(b) The centred dot indicates how the syllables within a bar are to be divided, when there are more than two.

(c) The sign † indicates use of the second half of a double chant.

(d) A double space between verses indicates that a change of chant is appropriate.

9 Further Bible References

At the Thanksgiving and Blessing of a Child

The Birth of Samuel – 1 Samuel 1.20–28
Jesus' Presentation in the Temple –
Luke 2.21–35
Jesus Welcomes Children –
Mark 10.13–16
Foundation for Life – Matthew 7.24–27
Prayer for Growth – Ephesians 3.14–21
A Living Sacrifice – Romans 12.1,2
The Value of the Bible –
2 Timothy 3.14–17

At a Covenant Service

The Covenant under Nehemiah –
Nehemiah 10.28–39
Fulfilment in Christ – Luke 1.67–79
The Blood of Christ – Hebrews 9.11–15

(See also section 11 – 'The People of God')

At a Baptism/Thanksgiving for a Child

The Choice between Life and Death, Good
and Evil – Deuteronomy 30.15–20
Who will Serve the Lord? –
Joshua 24.14–24
Passing Through the Waters –
Isaiah 43.1–3a, 6b–7
God's Cleansing and His Spirit –
Ezekiel 36.25a, 26–28
Jesus' Baptism – Mark 1.1–11
What Baptism Means–
Romans 6.3–11; 8.11–17
Go–Baptise!–Matthew 28.16–20
Jesus Welcomes Children–Mark 10.13–16

At Holy Communion

The Covenant with Abraham –
Genesis 17.1–7
A New Covenant – Jeremiah 31.31–34
Sacrifice for Sin – Leviticus 9.5–7, 15–24

The Eternal Sacrifice – Hebrews 9.11–15
The Lamb of God – John 1.29–30, 35
The Bread of Life – John 6.25–40, 53–58

See also:
Psalm 43.3–5; 116.12–17; Isaiah 53.3–6;
Matthew 11.28–30; 27.32–54;
Luke 24.13–35; John 3.14–16; 19.17–30;
20.19–23; Romans 3.21–26; 5.1–11;
1 Corinthians 5.7,8; 10.16,17;
2 Corinthians 5.14–21; 1 Timothy 2.5,6;
Revelation 3.20

8 At Local Festivals/For the Peace of the World

Our Duties – Luke 20.19–26
The Promise of Peace – Psalm 85.8–13;
Isaiah 9.6,7
Peace by the Blood of Christ –
Ephesians 2.11–22

9 New Year/Thanksgiving for the Old Year

Joshua's Confidence in a Faithful God –
Joshua 23
Many Lessons of God's Guidance –
Psalm 37
A Warning – James 4.13–17
A Psalm of Praise – Psalm 103
Thanksgiving in Heaven – Revelation 5

10 The Wise Men/The Escape to Egypt/Epiphany

God's Call to a Young Man – 1 Samuel 3 or
1 Samuel 16.1–13
Simeon and Anna with Baby Jesus –
Luke 2.21–40
The Lord's Servant – Isaiah 49.1–7

EPIPHANY READINGS

PROCLAIMING THE SAVIOUR

Readings	Carols
1 The Light of the World – Isaiah 60.1–5a	104, 657
2 The King of the Jews – Matthew 2.1–2, 7–12	92–93, 99, 104
3 The Child of Destiny – Matthew 2.13–18	671

The Vine and the Branches –
John 15.1–17

31 Heaven/God's Peace

A Future and a Hope –
Jeremiah 29.4–14
Parable of the Ten Virgins –
Matthew 25.1–13
I Am the Resurrection – John 11.17–27
Creation Set Free – Romans 8.18–25

32 Christ's Coming

Salvation for Israel – Isaiah 51.4–16
Awake from Sleep! – Romans 13.8–14
Call to Righteousness – 1 John 2.28–3.3
First and Second Coming –
Hebrews 9.24–28

ADVENT READINGS

SET A: GOD'S PROMISE TO
HIS PEOPLE

SET B: THE HOPE OF
SALVATION

SET C: THE COMING LORD

33 God's Word to Us

Public Reading – Nehemiah 8
Expounding the Scriptures –
Luke 24.13–49
Requiring Action – James 1.22–25
Confidence in God's Word – Psalm 33

34–35 Christmas

The Word became Flesh – John 1.14–18
God's Unlikely Choice –
1 Corinthians 1.26–31
Sing and Give Thanks –
Ephesians 5.15–20
God Sent His Son – Galatians 4.1–7
The Grace of God Dawns –
Titus 2.11–14; 3.3–7
The Outworking of Love –
1 John 4.7–14

(Note: These Epiphany, Advent and Chris
mas readings in NIV are set out in full i
Carols for Today, ed. Perry and Iliff, Ho
der and Stoughton 1986.)

40 Notes for the use of Holy Communion Rite A

1 *Preparation* Careful devotional preparation before the service is recommended for every communicant.

2 *The President* The president (who, in accordance with the provisions of Canon B12 'Of the ministry of the Holy Communion', must have been episcopally ordained priest) presides over the whole service. He says the opening Greeting, the Collect, the Absolution, the Peace, and the Blessing; he himself must take the bread and the cup before replacing them on the holy table, say the Eucharistic Prayer, break the consecrated bread, and receive the sacrament on every occasion. The remaining parts of the service he may delegate to others. When necessity dictates, a deacon or lay person may preside over the Ministry of the Word. When the Bishop is present, it is appropriate that he should act as president. He may also delegate sections 32–49 to a priest.

Posture When a certain posture is particularly appropriate, it is indicated in the rubric. For the rest of the service local custom may be established and followed. The Eucharistic Prayer (sections 38, 39, 40, and 41) is a single prayer, the unity of which may be obscured by changes of posture in the course of it.

Seasonal Material The seasonal sentences and blessings are optional. Any other appropriate scriptural sentences may be read at sections 1 and 50 at the discretion of the president and 'Alleluia' may be added to any sentence from Easter Day until Pentecost.

Greetings (section 2 etc.) In addition to the points where greetings are provided, at other suitable points (e.g. before the Gospel and before the Blessing and Dismissal) the minister may say 'The Lord be with you'

and the congregation reply 'and also with you'.

6 *Prayers of Penitence* These are used either after section 4 or section 23.

7 *Kyrie eleison* (section 9) This may be used in English or Greek.

8 *Gloria in excelsis* (section 10) This canticle may be appropriately omitted during Advent and Lent, and on weekdays which are not Principal or Greater Holy Days. It may also be used at sections 1 and 16.

9 *The Collect* (section 11) The Collect may be introduced by the words 'Let us pray' and a brief bidding, after which silence may be kept.

10 *Readings* Where one of the three readings is to be omitted, provision for this is found in Table 3A of the Alternative Service Book 1980 pages 1049–60. See note 2 on ASB page 981.

11 *The Gospel in Holy Week* (section 17) From Palm Sunday to the Wednesday in Holy Week, and on Good Friday, the Passion Gospel may be introduced: 'The Passion of our Lord Jesus Christ according to N', and concluded: 'This is the Passion of the Lord'. No responses are used.

12 *The Sermon* (section 18) The sermon is an integral part of the Ministry of the Word. A sermon should normally be preached at all celebrations on Sundays and other Holy Days.

13 *Proper Prefaces* The Proper Prefaces are obligatory on certain days but may be used on other suitable occasions.

14 *Second Eucharistic Prayer* (section 39) The three paragraphs beginning 'For he is your living Word' and ending 'a people for your own possession' may be omitted if a Proper Preface is used.

15 *Acclamations* These are optional. They may be introduced by the president with the words 'Let us proclaim the mystery of faith' or with other suitable words or they may be used without introduction.

16 *Manual Acts* In addition to the taking of the bread and the cup at section 36 the

president may use traditional manual acts during the Eucharistic Prayers.

17 *Words of Invitation* (section 45) The words 'Draw near with faith . . . with thanksgiving' are to be used at least on Sundays and other Holy Days, and one of the other sentences provided in the text may be added. On other days one of the other sentences may be substituted for the words 'Draw near . . . with thanksgiving.'

18 *The Blessing* (section 54) In addition to the blessings provided here the president may at his discretion use others.

19 *Notices* Banns of marriage and other notices may be published after section ? section 19, or section 53.

20 *Hymns, Canticles, the Peace, the Collection and Presentation of the Offerings of the People and the Preparation of the Gifts of Bread and Wine* Points are indicated for these, but occasion requires they may occur elsewhere.

21 *Silence* After sections 6, 13, 15, 17, 18, 20 before sections 42 and 51, and after the biddings in section 21, silence may be kept.

11 Acknowledgements and Copyrights

ACKNOWLEDGEMENTS

We owe our thanks to all the many ministers and churches who contributed material for this publication, to the ministers' and clergy conferences and diocesan liturgical committees who gave us advice and effectively set the parameters of the book.

Our further thanks go to various consultants. Some of them may well not wish to be identified with every decision represented here, for they were not members of the committee. But they deserve our public thanks nevertheless: Tim Barlow, Tony Baker, Michael Botting, Colin Buchanan, Frank Colquhoun, Walter Davis, Timothy Dudley-Smith, Christopher Idle, Michael Perham, Philip Potter, Belinda Purkiss, Michael Saward, Owen Thomas, Diana Todd, the staff of Messrs. Hodder & Stoughton, and artist Deborah Noble.

We acknowledge our debt to the earlier work of the International Consultation on English Texts and the Church of England Liturgical Commission; and we express our appreciation for the use of their copyright material. We thank the copyright-holders of the New International Version of the Bible from which readings are drawn, and the copyright-holders of the Good News Bible for permission to make substantial quotation. Authors and copyright-holders of individual items are acknowledged either *ad loc* (in the case of hymns and songs) or otherwise in the numerical list below.

For the massive amount of copyright processing, painstaking checking, setting and computer programming, we thank Bunty Grundy and her team: Sylvia Bleasdale, Ann Darlington and Sally Solomon, Norman and Joan Gutteridge, Helen Perry.

Finally, we offer our thanks to the many Family Service congregations who have been guinea-pigs in the use of drafts of this material – especially to Bitterne Church Southampton, St Mary's Eversley, Emmanuel Church Northwood, All Souls Langham Place and Gorsley Baptist Church.

Michael Perry

Addresses from where copyrights are administered

American Catholic Press—1223 Rossell Avenue, Oak Park, Illinois 60302, USA

BBC Publications—35 Marylebone High Street, London W1M 4AA

Boosey & Hawkes Ltd—295 Regent Street, London W1R 8JH

Bourne Music Ltd—34–36 Maddox Street, London W1R 9PD

Cherry Lane Music Ltd—Grosvenor House, 18–20 Ridgway, London SW19 4QN

Church of Ireland—Church of Ireland House, Church Avenue, Rathmines, Dublin 6

Church of the Redeemer, Episcopal—4411 Dallas, Houston, Texas 77023, USA

Church Pastoral Aid Society—Falcon Court, 32 Fleet Street, London EC4Y 1DB

Collins, Publishers—8 Grafton Street, London W1X 3LA

David Higham Associates—5–8 Lower John Street, Golden Square, London W1R 3PE

Ears & Eyes Music—Kerygma House, Canal Road, Leeds LS12 2PL

Epworth Press—Room 195, 1 Central Buildings, Westminster, London SW1H 9NR

Faber Music Ltd—3 Queen Square, London WC1N 3AU

Franciscan Communications—1229 South Santee Street, Los Angeles, California 90015, USA

GIA Publications Incorporated—7404 South Mason Avenue, Chicago, Illinois, 60638 USA

High-Fye Music Ltd—c/o Campbell Connelly & Company Ltd, 78 Newman Street, London W1P 3LA

Hope Publishing Company—Carol Stream, Illinois 60188, USA

International Music Publications—Woodford Trading Estate, Southend Road, Woodford Green, Essex IG8 8HN

Josef Weinberger Ltd—12–14 Mortimer Street, London W1N 7RD

Jubilate Hymns Ltd—61 Chessel Avenue, Southampton SO2 4DY

Kingsway Publications Ltd—Lottbridge Drove, Eastbourne, E. Sussex BN23 6NT

Leosong Copyright Services Ltd—4a Newman Passage, London W1

Marshall Pickering Communications—3 Beggarwood Lane, Basingstoke RG23 7LP

Missions to Seamen—St Michael Paternoster Royal, College Hill, London EC4R 2RL

Moody Press—820 North Lasalle Drive, Chicago, Illinois 60610, USA

Mowbray, A R & Co Ltd—St Thomas House, Becket Street, Oxford OX1 1SJ

National Christian Education Council—Robert Denholm House, Nutfield, Redhill, Surrey RH1 4HW

New Song Ministries, PO Box 11662, Costa Mesa, California 92627, USA

Overseas Missionary Fellowship—Belmont, The Vine, Sevenoaks, Kent TN13 3TZ

Oxford University Press—(London) Ely House, 37 Dover Street, London W1X 4AH. (Oxford) Walton Street, Oxford OX2 6DP

Parish of Eastbourne Trust—PO Box 2257, Wellington, New Zealand

Prism Tree Music—PO Box 3194, Redding, California 96049, USA

SCM Press Ltd—26–30 Tottenham Road, London N1 4BZ

St Michael-le-Belfrey—St Cuthberts Centre, Peasholme Green, York YO1 2PW

Salvationist Publishing and Supplies Ltd—117–121 Judd Street, Kings Cross, London WC1H 9NN

Scripture Gift Mission—Radstock House, 3 Eccleston Street, London SW1W 9LZ

Scripture Union—130 City Road, London EC1V 2NJ

Society for Promoting Christian Knowledge—Holy Trinity Church, Marylebone Road, London NW1 4DU

Sound III Incorporated—Tempo Music Publication, 2712 West 104th Terrace, Leawood, Kansas 66206 USA

Stainer & Bell Ltd—82 High Road, London N2 9PW

Thankyou Music—PO Box 75, Eastbourne, Sussex BN23 6NW

The Saint Andrew Press—Church of Scotland, 121 George Street, Edinburgh EH2 4YN

Word of God Music—Box 8617, 840 Airport Boulevard, Ann Arbor, Michigan 48107, USA

Word Music (UK)—Northbridge Road, Berkhamsted, Herts HP4 1EH

World Student Christian Federation—27 ch. des crêts de pregny, 1218 Grand Saconnex, Switzerland

COPYRIGHTS

Additional Source and Copyright Information

hese notes correspond to numbered items in the book where the availability of further information is dicated by an obelisk †. The information here is supplementary to notices found beneath those items. rayers attributed 'Editor' are in most cases arrangements of scriptural and classical texts.

3   Editor
6   © 1981 Thankyou Music
7   Written in memory of Kristi, who died aged 4½ years
8   © 1974 Word of God Music
0   Author sought
3   Editor
6   Used by permission of Oxford University Press (London)
8   Adapted by the Editor
8   © 1984 Thankyou Music
    By permission of Stainer & Bell Limited
0   © 1981 Thankyou Music
2   Michael Perry
3   Reprinted with permission from *The Hymnbook: The Johannine Hymnal*, © 1967, 1970 by the American Catholic Press, all rights reserved
7   Patrick Goodland
8   Adapted by the Editor
9   By permission of Cherry Lane Music Limited
0   © 1978 administered by Word Music (UK)
5   Author sought
1   Editor
2   After Laurence Binyon (1869–1943), copyright-holder sought
7   © 1976 administered by Thankyou Music
8   © 1979 Thankyou Music
9   © 1973 by GIA Publications Inc. All rights reserved
0   ASB adapted
3   Michael Perry
4   From the *St Michael-le-Belfrey Worship Book*
5   Editor
4   Diocese of Sheffield, adapted
9   © 1981 Thankyou Music
0   Author sought
1   © 1981 Thankyou Music
2   Author sought
3   Editor
6   By permission of Oxford University Press (London)
7   Christopher Idle, adapted
4   Editor
0   By permission of the Parish of Eastbourne Trust Board, New Zealand
2   Editor
6   From *The Alternative Prayer Book 1984* published by Collins Liturgical Publications. Used with the permission of the General Synod of the Church of Ireland
7   Simon Baynes, adapted
2   Editor
7   © 1976 Sound III Inc. Used by permission. All rights reserved. International copyright reserved
8   © 1975 administered by Thankyou Music
9   © 1977 Thankyou Music
1   © 1982 Word Music (UK)
2   Editor
3   From *The Alternative Prayer Book 1984* published by Collins Liturgical Publications. Used with permission of the General Synod of the Church of Ireland
6   Editor
7   Editor
1   Editor
5   Editor
9   © 1976 copyright-holder sought
0   © 1976 administered by Word Music (UK)
2   © 1974 administered by Word Music (UK)

143   © 1985 Thankyou Music
144   © 1978 administered by Word Music (UK)
149   Editor
150   Author sought
153   Attributed to Richard of Chichester
156   From Michael Botting's collection
159   C S Woodward, adapted from *The Children's Service* published by the Society for Promoting Christian Knowledge
160   From *The Alternative Prayer Book 1984* published by Collins Liturgical Publications. Used with the permission of the General Synod of the Church of Ireland
162   From the *New Catholic Hymnal* © Faber Music Ltd
164   From the *New Catholic Hymnal* © Faber Music Ltd
165   © 1974/1975 administered by Thankyou Music
166   © 1971 Scripture Union
167   © 1982 Thankyou Music
168   © 1972 administered by Word Music (UK)
169   © 1981 administered by Word Music (UK)
170   Adapted from the ASB
175   From *Contemporary Parish Prayers*, used by permission of the editor
176   From *Prayers and Hymns for Junior Schools*, reproduced by permission of Oxford University Press (London)
177   From *Contemporary Parish Prayers*, used by permission of the editor
178   After St Boniface
184   Editor
188   Author sought
189   © administered by Marshall Pickering Communications
190   © 1972 administered by Word Music (UK)
191   © 1972 administered by Word Music (UK)
192   Editor
193   From *The Alternative Prayer Book 1984* published by Collins Liturgical Publications, used with the permission of the General Synod of the Church of Ireland
195   Used by permission of Oxford University Press (London)
196   Angela Needham
197   Editor
203   Editor
207   © 1978 Thankyou Music
208   By permission of Cherry Lane Music Limited
209   © 1975 administered by Thankyou Music
210   Used by permission of High-Fye Music Ltd
211   © 1978 administered by Word Music (UK)
212   Editor
216   Used by permission of Bishop Gordon Bates
220   Editor
224   © 1975 administered by Thankyou Music
225   Used by permission of Scripture Gift Mission
226   © 1974, 1979 administered by Thankyou Music
227   By permission of Kingsway Publications Ltd
228   By permission of Cherry Lane Music Limited
229   Editor
233   © 1984 Thankyou Music
234   Alan Warren, adapted
236   Editor
240   Frank Colquhoun
241   Frank Colquhoun, adapted
244   Editor
245   Based on a prayer from Michael Botting's collection
251   © 1983 Thankyou Music
252   © 1973 Word of God Music

xii/Copyrights

42 Legal Information

Hymns and Songs

Those seeking to reprint hymns in this book which are the property of Jubilee Hymns or associated authors (attributed '/Jubilate Hymns') may write to The Copyright Secretary, Jubilate Hymns Ltd., 61 Chessel Avenue, Southampton SO2 4DY. In the United States of America these copyrights and those of Timothy Dudley-Smith are administered by Hope Publishing Company, Carol Stream, Illinois 60188. Addresses of other copyright-holders can also be supplied.

Jubilate Hymns, Marshall Pickering Communications, Scripture Union, Thankyou Music, Word (UK) Ltd – along with other copyright-holders whose titles they administer (Celebration Services, Maranatha!, Word & Music etc.) have uniform concessions and rates. Details are available from the Copyright Secretary, Jubilate Hymns Ltd.

Most of these publishers also combine to offer a licensing scheme for limited term reproduction. Where this is felt to be an advantage, application should be made to the Christian Music Publishers' Association at PO Box 75, Eastbourne BN23 6NW, or at Northbridge Road, Berkhamsted, Herts HP4 1EH. Hymns copyrighted Stainer and Bell may not be reprinted or photocopied under any blanket licensing scheme, but should be cleared individually with Stainer & Bell Limited.

Prayers

Individual prayers in this book are not all subject to copyright control, but should not be reprinted without obtaining, where possible, the authors' permission. Prayers whose source is *Contemporary Parish Prayers* and *New Parish Prayers* are used by kind permission of the editor. Similarly, prayers indicated 'St Michael-le-Belfrey' are used by kind permission of St Michael-le-Belfrey, York.

The Alternative Service Book

The Alternative Service Book 1980 (ASB) is © the Central Board of Finance of the Church of England 1980.

The Congregational Services on pages 3 to 26 except the Covenant Service are drawn from alternative services authorised for use in the Church of England. The complete alternative services of Morning Prayer, Evening Prayer, The Order for Holy Communion Rite A, Baptism of Children, Thanksgiving for the Birth of a Child, Thanksgiving after Adoption and Renewal of Baptismal Vows on Various Occasions may be found in ASB. These services are authorised for use in the Church of England pursuant to Canon B2 of the Canons of the Church of England until 31st December 2000. Various collects and prayers have been reproduced from ASB. The copyright in ASB and in individual alternative services is held by the Central Board of Finance of the Church of England and they may not be reproduced without permission.

The text of the Apostles' Creed, as printed in Morning Prayer and Evening Prayer is copyright © 1970, 1971, 197? International Consultation on English Texts (ICET). The Lord's Prayer in its modern form is adapted from the ICET version.

Psalms printed within the services follow the text and pointing of the *Liturgical Psalter* first published as *The Psalms: a new translation for worship*

The sources of the canticles included in the services of Morning Prayer and Evening Prayer in *The Alternative Service Book 1980* are as follows. The Benedictus, Te Deum, Gloria in Excelsis, Magnificat, and Nunc Dimittis are © International Consulation on English Texts. The Easter Anthems and A Song of Creation are modern versions of Prayer Book texts. Great and Wonderful, Bless the Lord, and Glory and Honour which are canticles, and Saviour of the World, which is adapted from a nineteenth-century original, derive from Daily Office of the Joint Liturgical Group. Venite, Jubilate, and Psalm 134 are © Collins Liturgical Publications from the *Liturgical Psalter* (see above). The Song of Christ's Glory is © Church of the Province of South Africa. The hymn 'O Gladsome Light, O Grace' is a translation by Robert Bridges (1844–1930) from the *Yattendon Hymnal*.

Readings and Quotations

Bible text from the *New International Version* (copyright © 1973, 1978, 1984 by International Bible Society) is used with the permission of Hodder and Stoughton, 47 Bedford Square, London WC1B 3DP. Quotation from Today's English Version (*The Good News Bible*, copyright © 1966, 1971, 1976 American Bible Society, published by the Bible Societies and Collins) is by courtesy of The Bible Society Publishing Division, Stonehill Green, Westlea, Swindon SN5 7BG.

Recording and Broadcasting

Jubilate Hymns and associated authors, and Word & Music are members of the Mechanical Copyright and Performing Right Societies.

Artwork

Permission is hereby given for the reproduction of drawings in this volume for publicity and other purposes connected with services of worship at which copies of *Church Family Worship* are being used by the full congregation.

43   Bible Reference Index to Hymns, Psalm Versions, Songs and Prayers

Prayers are indicated by an asterisk *

OLD TESTAMENT

Genesis
1 – 279
1.2 – 350
1.3 – 416
3.16 – 664

Exodus
14.22 – 361*
16.4 – 129
20.3 – 127*

Numbers
6.24 – 5, 679*, 680, 690*
20.11 – 85

Deuteronomy
5.7 – 127*
6.4 – 685*

Joshua
1.9 – 542
3.14 – 129

1 Samuel
3.10 – 174

2 Samuel
6.14 – 472

1 Kings
8.23 – 505

2 Kings
22.13 – 603*

1 Chronicles
29.10 – 36*, 69*
29.11 – 502*

Nehemiah
2 & 4 – 492
9.5 – 265*

Job
38.10 – 350

Psalm
1 – 138
5 – 162
8 – 271

8.1 – 264*
13 – 222
17 – 124
18 – 248
22.3 – 334
23 – 27, 137, 560
24 – 204, 291, 584
24.7 – 587
33 – 558
34 – 576
34.8 – 28
36.5 – 370
36.9 – 299*
37 – 373
40 – 136, 392
46 – 77, 533
47 – 78, 332
48 – 313, 488
51.1 – 22*
51.10 – 312
65 – 512
65.9 – 514
66.1 – 462*
67 – 270, 527
67.1 – 600*
67.4 – 297
67.5 – 48*
68 – 534
68.32 – 285*
72.1 – 415
72.18 – 110
75.1 – 71*
80 – 161
80.14 – 155*
82.8 – 579*
83.18 – 579*
85 – 55
86.12 – 239*, 554*
87.3 – 183
89 – 354, 372
90 – 50
91 – 395
92.1 – 366*
93 – 333, 355
95 – 76, 115, 186, 205,
       393, 606, 786
95.1 – 181*
96 – 418
96.1 – 91*
96.9 – 92

97 – 290
98 – 249, 420, 583
98.1 – 348*, 664
99 – 289
100 – 96, 367, 443, 787
100.1 – 200*, 508*
103 – 89, 442, 459
103.1 – 80, 307*
103.2 – 376
104 – 311, 351
104.1 – 328*
105 – 114
105.1 – 413*
105.43 – 121
106.1 – 388
107 – 353*
107.1 – 1*
107.8 – 15*
108.13 – 540
111 – 605
113 – 4
113.1 – 132*
113.3 – 139
116 – 26
116.12 – 20*
117 – 97, 371, 419
117.1 – 437*, 528*
118 – 487
118.22 – 482
118.24 – 201, 319
119.129 – 607
122 – 53, 559
124 – 95
126 – 247
126.5 – 517
128 – 185
133 – 116
134 – 795
134.1 – 486
136 – 75
136.1 – 280
139 – 164, 394
139.7 – 357
143.6 – 312
147 – 467, 513
148 – 269, 284, 490,
       515
149 – 54, 535
150 – 54, 466, 468, 490
150.1 – 481*

44 Subject Index to Prayers

45 Lectionary Themes Index

(This is not a precisely equivalent list, but serves to indicate by numbers the major sections in which appropriate material may be found. *Italicised numbers* indicate items in the Minister's Section.)

46 Psalm and Canticle Index

With tunes to which metrical psalms and canticles may be sung

INDEX TO PSALMS

Psalm

1 Bless-ed is the man (To *Blessed is the man*) – 138

5 Lord, as I wake I turn to you (To *Daniel*) – 162

8 With wonder, Lord, we see your works (To *Almsgiving(Dykes)/Es ist kein Tag*) – 271

13 How long will you forget me, Lord? (To *St Hugh*) – 222

17 O Lord our guardian and our guide (To *Abridge*) – 124

18 I love you, O Lord, you alone (To *Jane*) – 248

23 My faithful shepherd is the Lord (To *Herongate*) – 560
The king of love my shepherd is (To *Dominus regit me/The Followers*) – 27
The Lord my shepherd rules my life (To *Brother James' Air/Crimond*) – 137

24 Fling wide the gates (To *Crucifer*) – 291
The earth is the Lord's – 204
This earth belongs to God (To *Trumpet Voluntary*) – 584

33 Sing joyfully to the Lord, you righteous – 558

34 Through all the changing scenes of life (To *Wiltshire*) – 576

36 Your love, O Lord reaches to the heavens – 370

37 The steadfast love of the Lord (To *The steadfast love of the Lord*) – 373

40 Happy are those who trust in God – 136
I waited patiently for the Lord – 392

46 God is our refuge and strength – 533
God is our strength and refuge (To *Dam Busters March*) – 77

47 Clap your hands, all you nations – 332
Take heart and praise our God (To *Christchurch/Gopsal/Harewood*) – 78

48 Great is the Lord; his praise is great (To *Great is the Lord/Truro*) – 488
How great is God almighty (To *Battle Hymn*) – 313

51 Create in me a pure heart, O God – 312

65 O God, it is right for us to praise you – 512
The earth is yours, O God (To *Franconia/St Michael/Venice*) – 514

67 God of mercy, God of grace (To *Heathlands*) – 527
May God be gracious to us and bless us – 270

68 Let God arise (To *Let God arise*) – 534

80 Hear us, O Shepherd of Israel – 161

85 When this land knew God's gracious love (To *Sine nomine*) – 55

89 Come, join to praise our God and king (To *Golden Sheaves*) – 354
Timeless love (To *All Saints/Timeless love*) – 372

90 O God, our help in ages past (To *St Anne*) – 50

91 Safe in the shadow of the Lord (To *Creator God/Lloyd*) – 395

93 Clothed in kingly majesty (To *Kingly majesty*) – 355
Sing we praise to God the king (To *Monkland/Savannah*) – 333

95 Come, let us sing to the Lord (To *Response Psalm*) – 393
Come, sing praises to the Lord above (To *Calypso Carol*) – 115
Come with all joy to sing to God (To *Fulda*) – 205
Come, worship God who is worthy (To *Epiphany Hymn/O quanta qualia*) – 606
Let us sing to the God of salvation (To *Give me joy*) – 186
O come let us sing out to the Lord – 786
O come, let us sing to the Lord (To *Weymouth Street*) – 76

96 Sing to the Lord a new song – 418

97 The Lord is king! Lift up your voice (To *Church Triumphant*) – 290

98 Sing a new song to the Lord (To *Littlebourne/Onslow Square*) – 420
Sing to God new songs of worship (To *Ode to joy*) – 249
Sing to the Lord a new song – 583

99 The Lord reigns: let the nations tremble – 289

100 All people that on earth do dwell (To *Old 100th*) – 367
Come, rejoice before your maker (To *Come, rejoice/Gott will's machen*) – 96
O be glad in the Lord and rejoice (To *Jane*) – 443
O shout to the Lord in triumph – 787

103 Praise, my soul, the king of heaven (To *Praise my soul*) – 459
Praise the Lord, my soul – 442
Praise to the Lord, the almighty (To *Lobe den Herren*) – 89

INDEX TO CANTICLES

Square brackets indicate prayers based on the text

MORNING CANTICLES

Venite (Psalm 95.1–7, Psalm 98.9)
Come, let us sing to the Lord (To *Response Psalm*) – 393
Come, sing praises to the Lord above (To *Calypso Carol*) – 115
Come with all joy to sing to God (To *Fulda*) – 205
Come, worship God who is worthy of honour (To *Epiphany Hymn/O quanta qualia*) – 606
Let us sing to the God of salvation (To *Give me joy*) – 186
O come let us sing out to the Lord – 786
O come let us sing to the Lord (To *Weymouth Street*) – 76

Jubilate (Psalm 100)
All people that on earth do dwell (To *Old 100th/Gott will's machen*) – 367
Come, rejoice before your maker (To *Come rejoice*) – 96
O be glad in the Lord, and rejoice (To *Jane*) – 443
O shout to the Lord in triumph all the earth – 787

The Easter Anthems (1 Corinthians 5.7–8; Romans 6.9–11; 1 Corinthians 15.20–22)
Christ our passover has been sacrificed for us – 788
Now lives the Lamb of God (To *Christchurch/Gopsal*) – 246

Benedictus (The Song of Zechariah – Luke 1.68–79)
Blessed be the Lord the God of Israel – 789
O bless the God of Israel (To *Morning Light/Thornbury*) – 585

A Song of Creation/Benedicite (The Song of the Three Children 35–64 – The Greek Old Testament)
Angels, praise him (To *Angels praise him/Little Barrington*) – 272
Bless the Lord all created things – 790
Bless the Lord, creation sings (To *Melling/University*) – 163

Great and wonderful (Revelation 15.3–4)
Great and wonderful are your deeds – 791
Great and wonderful your deeds (To *Württemberg*) – 335

Te Deum (A Christian hymn from the fourth century)
God of gods, we sound his praises (To *God of gods*) – 561
God, we praise you! God, we bless you (To *Lux Eoi*) – 536
[We believe in Christ the King of glory – Creed] – 298
[We believe in God the eternal Father – Creed] – 360
You are God and we praise you – 792

Gloria in excelsis (A Christian hymn from the fourth century – based on Luke 2.14)
Glory be to God in heaven (To *Abbott's Leigh/Ode to Joy*) – 24
Glory in the highest to the God of heaven (To *Land of hope*) – 25
Glory to God in the highest – 793

Saviour of the world (A free church hymn from the nineteenth century)
Jesus saviour of the world – 794
Jesus, saviour of the world (To *St Albinus*) – 356

EVENING CANTICLES

Psalm 134
Come bless the Lord all you servants of the Lord – 795
Come, praise the Lord, all you his servants (To *St Clement*) – 486

O gladsome light (A Christian hymn from the third century)
    Light of gladness, Lord of glory (To *Quem pastores laudavere*) – 154
    O gladsome light, O grace – 796

The Easter Anthems (1 Corinthians 5.7–8; Romans 6.9–11; 1 Corinthians 15.20–22)
    Christ our passover has been sacrificed for us – 788
    Now lives the Lamb of God (To *Christchurch/Gopsal*) – 246

Magnificat (The Song of Mary – Luke 1.46–55)
    Mary sang a song (To *Mary sang a song/Pavenham*) – 643
    My soul proclaims the greatness of the Lord – 797
    Tell out, my soul, the greatness of the Lord (To *Go forth/Woodlands*) – 187

Cantate Domino (Psalm 98)
    Sing a new song to the Lord (To *Littlebourne/Onslow Square*) – 420
    Sing to God new songs of worship (To *Ode to Joy*) – 249
    Sing to the Lord a new song – 583

Bless the Lord (The Song of the Three Children 29–32 – The Greek Old Testament)
    Bless the Lord the God of our fathers – 798
    Bless the Lord, our fathers' God (To *Orientis partibus*) – 56

Nunc Dimittis (The Song of Simeon – Luke 2.29–32)
    Faithful vigil ended (To *Faithful vigil*) – 562
    Lord, now let your servant go his way (To *Caswall*) – 98
    Lord now you let your servant go in peace – 799

Deus misereatur (Psalm 67)
    God of mercy, God of grace (To *Heathlands*) – 527
    May God be gracious to us and bless us – 270

The Song of Christ's Glory (Philippians 2.6–11)
    Before the heaven and earth (To *Narenza/Munden*) – 206
    Christ Jesus was in the form of God – 800
    God has exalted him (To *God has exalted him*) – 294
    [Though he was divine – Creed] – 212

Glory and honour (Revelation 4.11; 5.9,10,12,13)
    Come and see the shining hope (To *Marching through Georgia*) – 578
    Come, let us join our cheerful songs (To *Nativity*) – 555
    Glory and honour and power – 801
    Holy, holy, holy is the Lord (To *Holy, holy, holy is the Lord*) – 338
    [Our Lord and God – Ascription] – 552
    [We say together in faith – Creed] – 591
    [You are worthy, O Lord our God – Ascription] – 131, 435

Saviour of the world (A free church hymn from the nineteenth century)
    Jesus saviour of the world – 794
    Jesus, saviour of the world (To *St Albinus*) – 356

LITURGICAL HYMNS

Credal Hymns
    Firmly I believe and truly (To *Shipston*) – 145
    God the Father caused to be (To *Capetown*) – 320
    God the Father of creation (To *Love divine/Shipston*) – 277
    I believe in God the Father (To *All for Jesus*) – 404
    We believe in God Almighty (To *Irby/Unser Herrscher*) – 613

The Doxology
Praise God from whom all blessings flow (To *Come Together/Tallis' Canon*) – 70, 345

The Evening Collect (Lighten our darkness)
Lighten our darkness (To *Cloisters*) – 593

The Lord's Prayer
Father God in heaven (To *Kum ba yah*) – 171

The grace (2 Corinthians 13.14)
May the grace of Christ our saviour (To *Halton Holgate/Waltham*) – 504

Sources of Music

Most of the hymn settings are available in *Hymns for Today's Church*; most of the songs in *Jesus Praise, Songs of Fellowship* and *Mission Praise*; all the carols in *Carols for Today* and *Carol Praise*. Supplementary items will be found in *Spirit of Praise* and the *Church Family Worship Source Book*.

LIST OF ABBREVIATIONS
WITH PUBLISHERS

AHB	Anglican Hymn Book (Oxford University Press)
AMNS	Hymns Ancient & Modern (New Standard Edition)
AMR	Hymns Ancient & Modern (Revised)
BHB	Baptist Hymn Book (Novello)
CAP	Come And Praise (British Broadcasting Corporation)
CC	Carols for Choirs (Oxford University Press)
CFT	Carols for Today (Hodder & Stoughton)
CFW	Church Family Worship (Hodder & Stoughton)
CFW Source Book	
	Church Family Worship Source Book (Church Pastoral Aid Society)
CGC	Carol Gaily Carol (A&C Black)
CH	Cry Hosanna! (Hodder & Stoughton)
CP	Christian Praise (Inter-Varsity Press)
CPr	Carol Praise (Marshall Pickering Communications)
CSSM	Children's Special Service Mission chorus book (Scripture Union)
EH	English Hymnal (The Canterbury Press)
FS	Fresh Sounds (Hodder & Stoughton)
GKSB	Graham Kendrick Song Book (Kingsway Publications)
HF	Hymns of Faith (Scripture Union)
HP	Hymns and Psalms (Methodist Publishing House)
HTC	Hymns for Today's Church (Hodder & Stoughton)
JP	Jesus Praise (Scripture Union)
JrP	Junior Praise (Marshall Pickering Communications)
MP	Mission Praise (Marshall Pickering Communications)
MTB	Merrily To Bethlehem (A&C Black)
NCP	New Church Praise (The Saint Andrew Press)
PGT	Praise God Together (Scripture Union)
PiP	Partners in Praise (Stainer & Bell)
PP	Psalm Praise (Kingsway Publications)
SF	Songs of Fellowship (Kingsway Publications)
SG	Songifts (Hodder & Stoughton)
SLW	Sound of Living Waters (Hodder & Stoughton)
SOP	Songs of Praise (Oxford University Press)
SoW	Songs of Worship (Scripture Union)
SpP	Spirit of Praise (Word Music (UK))
STG	Sing To God (Scripture Union)
WOV	With One Voice (Collins Liturgical Publications)
YP	Youth Praise (Kingsway Publications)

47 Index to Hymns, Psalm Versions, Songs and Canticles

FIRST LINES AND SOURCES OF MUSIC

Indicates musical items suitable for services of praise and celebration. Liturgical Canticles are listed
the separate Psalm and Canticle Index at Section 46. The *words* set within the books represented
low are not necessarily the same as those in Church Family Worship. Italics indicate traditional first
es, and relate them to new versions.)

new commandment
See: The new commandment – 445
bba, Father – 399
  Abba Father: JP 54, JrP 2, MP 1, SF1 1, SpP 2
l creation join to say
See: Love's redeeming work – 259
l creatures of our God and King* – 283
  Easter Song (Lasst uns erfreuen): AHB 251,
  AMNS 105, AMR 172, BHB 1, CP 4, EH 519, HF 26,
  HP 329, HTC 13, SOP 157, WOV 3
l glory, praise and honour* – 202
  St Theodulph: AHB 166, AMNS 328, AMR 98,
  BHB 114, CP 49, EH 622, HF 10, HP 160, HTC 120,
  SOP 135, WOV 250
l people that on earth do dwell* – 367
  Old 100th: AHB 236, AMNS 100, AMR 166, BHB 2,
  CP 2, EH 365, HF 20, HP 1, HTC 14, SOP 443,
  WOV 10
l Scriptures are given – 608
  All Scriptures are given: JP 152, SoW 89, YP 87
l the way, all the way – 207
  All the way: JP 65
l things bright and beautiful – 266
  All things bright (or Royal Oak): AHB 233,
  AMNS 116 (ii), AMR 442, BHB 472, EH 587, HF 606,
  HP 330, HTC 283, SOP 444, WOV 70(ii)
eluia, alleluia, give thanks* – 252
  Alleluia, give thanks: HTC s3, JP 2, JrP 3, MP 9,
  PGT 1, SF2 161, SLW 1, SoW 47, SpP 5
eluia, alleluia! he is Lord* – 292
  Alleluia, alleluia! he is lord: CH 7, JP 3, SG 135
eluia, my Father – 224
  Alleluia, my father: FS 6, JP 55, MP 66, SF2 202,
  SpP 50
azing grace – 158
  Amazing grace: AHB 3A, HF 50, HP 215, HTC 28,
  MP 10, SLW 5, WOV 56
d can it be that I should gain* – 389
  Sagina: BHB 426, CP 235 (ii), HF 348, HP 216,
  HTC 452, MO 11, WOV 138(ii)
gels from the realms of glory – 661
  Iris: AHB 93, AMNS 39, BHB 89, CC1 7, CFT 86,
  CP 38, HTC 77, SOP 71, WOV 235
gels, praise him* – 272
  Angels, praise him: HTC (2nd Edn) s32, PP 11
with gladness – 104
  Dix: AHB 126, AMNS 51, AMR 79, BHB 90,
  CFT 146, CP 44, EH 39, HF 160, HP 121, HTC 99,
  SOP 83, WOV 239
the name of Jesus* – 305
  Camberwell: CAP 58, HF 115, HTC 172, MP 15(ii),

SpP 15, WOV 170(ii). **Evelyns:** AHB 254,
AMNS 148, AMR 225, BHB 199(ii), CP 93, HF 115,
HP 74, HTC 172(ii), SpP 15(ii)
At your feet we fall* – 251
  At your feet: SF2 167, SpP 16
Away in a manger – 651
  Cradle Song: AHB 95, BHB 734, CC1 2, CFT 57,
  HP 94, HTC 72, JrP 12, SOP 353, WOV 242

Be bold, be strong – 542
  Be bold, be strong: JrP 14, SpP2 215
Be thou my guardian and my guide
See: O Lord, our guardian – 124
Because he died and is risen* – 568
  Because he died and is risen: JrP 81
Because your love is better than life* – 79
  Because your love: MP 19, SF2 169, SpP2 216
Before the heaven and earth – 206
  Munden: CFT 171. **Narenza:** AHB 605, AMNS 150,
  AMR 229, BHB 197, CFT 172, CP 312, EH 518,
  HF 492, HP 248, WOV 474
Behold, I tell you a mystery – 563
  Behold, I tell you: SF3 339
Bethlehem, what greater city – 93
  Stuttgart: AHB 127, AMNS 48, AMR 76, BHB 78,
  CFT 134, CP 42, EH 40, HF 139, HP 122, HTC 8,
  SOP 84, WOV 216
Bind us together, Lord – 119
  Bind us together: HTC s4, JP 133, JrP 17, MP 21,
  SF 6, SpP 23
Bless the Lord, creation sings – 163
  Melling: BHB 394, CP 256, EH 373, HF 403,
  HP 470(ii), HTC 566, SOP 463. **University:**
  AMNS 110, AMR 178, BHB 212, CP 247(ii), EH 93,
  HF 503, HP 43, HTC 408, SOP 653, WOV 141
Bless the Lord, O my soul* – 80
  Bless the Lord: MP 26, SF3 341
Bless the Lord, our fathers' God* – 56
  Orientis Partibus: AHB 601(ii), AMNS 302,
  AMR 524, BHB 48, CP 177, EH 129, HP 168,
  HTC 472, SOP 153, WOV 149
Bless-ed is the man – 138
  Blessed is the man: PP 62, YP 160
Break now the bread of life – 614
  Gottlieb: BHB 243, HF 453. **Lathbury (Bread of
  life:** CP 140(ii), HF 260, JP 154, WOV 334
Break thou the bread of life
See: Break now the bread – 614
Breathe on me, breath of God – 326
  Carlisle: AHB 27, AMNS 157, AMR 362,
  BHB 523/592(ii), CP 1, EH 190, HF 3, HP 513,

HTC 226, SOP 458, WOV 383. **Dominica:** AHB 68,
AMNS 21, AMR 42, CP 370, HF 81, HTC 380.
Trentham: HF 179, HP 280, MP 25

Bring to the Lord a glad new song* – 54
Jerusalem: AMNS 294, AMR 578, EH 656A,
HTC 336, SOP 446, SoW 38

Broken for me, broken for you – 40
Broken for me, broken for you: CH 68, HTC s6,
JP 134, SpP 25

Caring, sharing – 448
Living the Jesus way: SG 153

Child in the manger – 652
Bunessan: AHB 96, AMNS 415, BHB 92, CFT 45,
CP 395, HF 161, HP 350, HTC 51, SOP 30, SoW 7, 8,
WOV 241

Children of the heavenly king – 556
Innocents: AHB 552, AMNS 249, AMR 191,
BHB 739, EH 37, HF 403, HP 738, HTC 566,
SOP 366

Christ, from whom all blessings flow – 463
Culbach: AHB 417, AMR 73, BHB 327, CP 23,
EH 286, HF 574, HP 625, HTC 258, SOP 1, WOV 62

Christ in me is to live* – 140
Christ in me: JP 174, SpP 27

Christ is born within a stable – 666
Russian Air: CFT 114

Christ is made the sure foundation – 483
Westminster Abbey: AHB 660(ii), AMNS 332,
AMR 574, BHB 372, HF 516, HP 485, HTC 559,
MP 27, WOV 343(ii)

Christ is our corner-stone – 482
Darwall's 148th: AHB 24, AMNS 198, AMR 371,
BHB 36, CP 19, EH 517, HF 23, HP 20, HTC 171,
SOP 701, WOV 26. **Harewood:** AHB 456, AMR 243,
BHB 267, CP 107, HF 168, HP 384, HTC 564,
SOP 464(ii), WOV 344

Christ is surely coming – 598
Land of hope: CFW Source Book

Christ the Lord is risen again – 258
Württemberg: AHB 179, AMNS 79, AMR 136,
BHB 167, EH app12, HF 192, HP 192, HTC 153,
WOV 282(ii)

Christ the Lord is risen today
  See: Love's redeeming work – 259

Christ triumphant* – 300
Angel voices: AHB 234, AMNS 163, AMR 246,
BHB 4, CP 17, HP 377, HF 61, HTC 307. **Christ
triumphant:** HTC 173, MP 28, SoW 31, JrP 25.
Guiting Power: HTC 173(ii)

Christ whose glory fills the skies* – 134
Ratisbon: AHB 36, AMNS 4, AMR 7, BHB 673,
CP 126, EH 282, HF 114, HP 457(ii), HTC 266,
SOP 24, WOV 140(ii)

Christian soldiers, onward go! – 530
University College: AHB 584, AMNS 210,
AMR 291, BHB 524, CP 297, EH 467, HF 369,
HP 715, HTC 524, SOP 619

Christians, join in celebration – 458
Regent Square: AHB 172, AMNS 185, AMR 279,
BHB 377, CP 63, EH 431, HF 51, HP 80, HTC 30,
SoW 54, WOV 84

Church of God, elect and glorious – 444
Lux Eoi: AHB 178, AMNS 80, AMR 137, BHB 17,
CP 66, HF 25, HTC 504

City of God, Jerusalem – 595
Benson: AHB 315, AMR 271, BHB 371, EH app63
HF 221, HP 769, HTC 187

Cleanse me from my sin, Lord – 225
Cleanse me: JP 175, JrP 27, MP 30, SpP2 227

Clothed in kingly majesty – 355
Kingly majesty: PP 110

Come and go with me – 564
Come and go: JP 136

Come and hear the joyful singing – 662
Nos Galan: CC2 7, CFT 106, CPr

Come and join the celebration – 669
Celebrations: CPr, SoW 12

Come and praise the Lord our king – 188
Michael, row the boat: HTC s8, JP 66, JrP 34
SoW 15, YP 2

Come and see the shining hope – 578
Marching through Georgia: HTC 188, MP 33

Come and sing the Christmas story – 638
All through the night: AMNS 12, AMR 26
BHB 590(ii), CFT 101, EH 268, HP 641, HTC 8:
SOP 46, SoW 78

Come down, O love divine! – 308
Down Ampney: AHB 214, AMNS 156, BHB 22:
CP 118, EH 152, HF 241, HP 281, HTC 23'
SOP 177, SoW 24, WOV 310

Come, join to praise our God* – 354
Golden Sheaves: AHB 653, AMNS 291, AMR 48
BHB 731, EH app17, HF 577, HTC 291

Come let us join our cheerful songs* – 555
Nativity: AHB 16, AMNS 144, AMR 221, BHB 20
CP 98, EH app48, HF 2, HP 810, HTC 20
WOV 133

Come, let us sing to the Lord – 393
Response Psalm: CFW Source Book

Come, most Holy Spirit, come – 327
Veni Sancte Spiritus: AHB 225, AMNS 9
AMR 156, BHB 228, CP 134, EH 155(ii), HP 28
HTC 227, SOP 180(ii), WOV 326

Come, praise the Lord* – 486
St Clement: AHB 52(ii), AMNS 16, AMR 3:
BHB 706, CP 364, EH app16, HF 572, HP 64
HTC 280, WOV 388

Come, rejoice before your maker* – 96
Come, Rejoice: HTC 17, PP 17, SoW 135

Come, sing praises to the Lord* – 115
Calypso Carol: HP 118, HTC 91, JP 14, MTB 9
SLW 118, SoW 10

Come sing the praise of Jesus* – 250
Battle Hymn: HP 242, HTC 208, SOP 578, SoW 4
WOV 205(ii)

Come, thou Holy Spirit, come
  See: Come, most Holy Spirit – 327

Come with all joy to sing to God* – 205
Fulda: AHB 504, AMNS 431, BHB 680, CP 2
HF 74, HP 316, HTC 16, SoW 66, WOV 137

Come, worship God* – 606
Epiphany Hymn ('Epiphany'): AHB 1:
AMNS 47(ii), BHB 91, CP 43, EH app9, HP 700(
HTC 338, SoW 27. **O quanta qualia:** AMNS 1:
AMR 281, HF 608, HTC 18, PP 42, SoW 4

Come, you thankful people, come – 526
St George's, Windsor: AMNS 289, AMR 131(
BHB 724, CP 377, EH 289, HF 576, HP 3!
HTC 284, SOP 9, WOV 290

Cradle rocking, cattle lowing – 649
  Cradle rocking, cattle lowing: CH 140, CPr

Crown him with many crowns* – 198
  Diademata: AHB 209, AMNS 147, AMR 224, BHB 182, CP 72, HF 111, HP 255, HTC 174, WOV 163

Ding-dong! Merrily on high – 667
  Branle de l'Official: CC1 10, CFT 99, CPr, JrP 38

Earth has many a noble city
  See: Bethlehem, what greater – 93

Emmanuel, Emmanuel – 642
  Emmanuel, Emmanuel: JP 68, PGT 5, SF2 177, SpP2 235

Eternal Father, strong to save – 350
  Melita: AHB 408, AMNS 292, AMR 487, BHB 665, CP 226, EH 540, HF 104, HP 379, HTC 285, WOV 74

Every nation, praise the Lord* – 97
  Llanfair: AHB 203(ii), AMNS 87, AMR 147, BHB 154, EH 143, HF 193, HP 14, HTC 345, SOP 149

Faithful Shepherd, feed me – 571
  Pastor pastorum: AHB 7, AMNS 453, AMR 415, CP 209(ii), HF 601, HTC 29

Faithful vigil ended – 562
  Faithful vigil: HTC 55, PP 30, SoW 87, YP 170

Falling, falling, gently falling – 315
  Rain Song: CH 106

Father God in heaven – 171
  Kum ba yah: HP 525, HTC 358, NCP 49

Father, hear the prayer we offer – 85
  Gott will's machen: AHB 579, AMNS 251, AMR 364, BHB 467(ii), EH 253, HP 436, HTC 360, SOP 487. **Marching:** AHB 414, AMNS 113, AMR 182, BHB 559, CP 272, EH 503, HF 519, HP 441, HTC 466, SOP 678, WOV 110. **Sussex:** AMNS 509, BHB 467, EH 239, HF 373, HP 436(ii), MP 43, SOP 321, WOV 304

Father, in your presence kneeling – 10
  Quem pastores laudavere: AHB 263, AMNS 54, AMR 456, BHB 617, CP 388, EH 543, HF 162, HP 607, HTC 96, SOP 540, WOV 177

Father, let us dedicate – 73
  Dedication: AHB 657, BHB 713, CP 373, HF 582, HTC 257

Father, now behold us – 11
  North Coates: AHB 353, AMNS 248, AMR 360, BHB 453, HF 86, HTC 384, WOV 521(ii)

Father of mercies, in your word – 601
  Abergele: BHB 245. **Southwell (Irons):** AHB 300, AMNS 187, AMR 282, BHB 76, HF 257, HP 475, HTC 247

Father, we adore you* – 191
  Father, we adore you: HTC s5, JP 15, JrP 44, MP 44, SF3 360, SG 29, SLW 26

Father, we love you* – 336
  Father, we love you: JrP 45, MP 46, PGT 6, SF 22, SpP 41

Fear not, rejoice and be glad – 516
  Fear not, rejoice: MP 47, SLW 59, SoW 41

Fierce raged the tempest – 362
  St Aëlred: AHB 553(ii), AMNS 225, AMR 313, BHB 117, CP 276, EH app62, HF 402, HP 144

Fight the good fight – 546
  Duke Street: AHB 577(ii), AMNS 220, AMR 268, BHB 289, CP 293(ii), EH 167, HF 384, HP 26, HTC 526, SOP 298, SoW 24

Fill your hearts with joy* – 513
  Cwm Rhondda: AHB 555(ii), AMNS 214(ii), AMR 296, BHB 541, CP 283(ii), HF 410, HP 437, HTC 528, MP 63, WOV 478. **Regent Square:** AHB 172, AMNS 185, AMR 279, BHB 377, CP 63, EH 431, HF 51, HP 80, HTC 30, SoW 54, WOV 84

Firmly I believe and truly – 145
  Shipston: AHB 348, BHB 726, CP 252, EH 390, HF 598, HP 344, HTC 282, SOP 364, WOV 94

Fling wide the gates* – 291
  Crucifer: AMNS 72, AMR 633, HP 170, HTC 508, MP 139, WOV 271

For all the saints – 550
  Sine nomine: AHB 460, AMNS 305, BHB 7, CP 147, EH 641, HF 506, HP 814, HTC 567, SOP 202, WOV 384

For God so loved the world – 402
  Londonderry Air: AHB 262, BHB 183, CP 87, HF 547, HP 238, HTC 194, MP 83, SOP 230, SoW 11

For I'm building a people of power* – 469
  For I'm building: JrP 47, MP 50, SF 25, SpP 42

For the beauty of the earth* – 182
  England's Lane: AHB 18, AMNS 450, BHB 8, EH 309, HF 29, HP 333(ii), HTC 298, SOP 494

For the bread which you have broken – 46
  Cross of Jesus: AHB 86, AMNS 31, AMR 54, BHB 227, CP 85, HF 270, HP 230, HTC 403, SoW 35, WOV 72(ii)

For the fruits of his creation – 522
  All through the night: AMNS 12, AMR 26, BHB 590(ii), EH 268, HP 641, HTC 81, SOP 46, SoW 78. **East Acklam:** AMNS 457, HP 342, HTC 286, MP 52

For this purpose Christ was revealed* – 255
  For this purpose: SF3 364, SpP2 244

For your mercy and your grace – 72
  Culbach: AHB 417, AMR 73, BHB 327/714, CP 23, EH 286, HF 574, HP 625, HTC 258, SOP 1, WOV 62

From all who live beneath the skies* – 419
  Deus tuorum militum: AHB 35, AMNS 303, AMR 516, BHB 238, CP 291, EH 181, HF 186, HP 433(ii), HTC 580, SOP 633, WOV 31. **Truro:** AHB 39, AMNS 483, AMR 220, BHB 645, CP 294, EH 420, HF 233, HP 190, HTC 516, MP 123, SOP 545, WOV 33

From heaven you came* – 449
  From heaven you came: GKSB 6, SF3 368, SpP2 247

From the rising of the sun* – 139
  From the rising: JrP 49, MP 54, SF2 191

Girls and boys, leave your toys – 668
  Zither Carol: CC1 12, CFT 115, CGC 12

Give me joy in my heart* – 446
  Give me joy: CAP 43, HTC s11, JP 111, MP 58, SLW 4, SoW 85, YP 120

Glorious things of you are spoken – 183
  Abbot's Leigh: AHB 424, AMNS 356, BHB 17, CP 143, HF 515, HP 774, HTC 494, WOV 93. **Austria:** AHB 29, AMNS 195, AMR 257, BHB 257, CP 20, EH 393, HF 515, HP 222, HTC 494, MP 59, SOP 500, WOV 577

Glory be to God in heaven* – 24
Abbot's Leigh: AHB 424, AMNS 356, BHB 17, CP 143, HF 515, HP 774, HTC 494, WOV 93. **Ode to Joy:** HTC 352, PP 27

Glory in the highest* – 25
Land of hope: CFW Source Book

Go forth and tell – 506
Go forth: HTC 42, MP 215, SoW 69, YP 132. **Woodlands:** AHB 474, AMNS 241, BHB 366, CP 16, HP 86, HTC 42, MP 215(ii), SOP 299, SoW 108(ii), WOV 109. **Yanworth:** HTC 505, MP 61

Go, tell it on the mountain – 424
Go, tell it on the mountain: CFT 78, HP 135, JP 181, JrP 65, SLW 121, SoW 109, YP 150

God forgave my sin – 293
Freely, freely: FS 101, HTC s12, JP 182, JrP 54, MP 60, SF3 369, SpP 45

God has exalted him* – 294
God has exalted him: SF3 371

God has spoken to his people – 611
God has spoken: JP 183, HTC s13, SLW 95

God is good – we sing and shout it* – 377
God is good: JrP 55, SF3 372, SG 8

God is love – his the care* – 368
Personent hodie: AMNS 484, CFT 128, HP 83, HTC 311, SOP 502, SoW 18

God is love: let heaven adore him – 386
Blaenwern: AHB 612, AMNS 464, BHB 595, CP 271, HF 76, HP 267, HTC 217, MP 149, WOV 165(ii)

God is our strength and refuge* – 77
Dam Busters March: HTC 527, SoW 127

God is so good – 396
God is so good: JP 56, SpP2 251

God of glory, we exalt your name* – 337
God of glory: SF2 197, SG 9, SpP 46

God of gods, we sound his praises* – 561
God of gods: HTC 340, PP 6

God of light and life's creation – 505
All Saints: AHB 301, AMNS 323, AMR 570, BHB 214, CP 110, EH 204, HF 234, HP 60(ii), HTC 561(ii), SOP 210

God of mercy, God of grace – 527
Heathlands: AHB 46, AMNS 179, AMR 264, BHB 373, CP 169, EH 395, HF 487, HP 457, HTC 293, SOP 170, WOV 399

God save our gracious Queen – 68
National Anthem: AHB 664, AMNS 293, AMR 577, BHB 641, EH 560, HF 589, HP back cover, HTC 592, SOP 318, WOV 578

God the Father caused to be – 320
Capetown: AHB 230, AMNS 154(ii), AMR 163, BHB 47, CP 129, EH 501, HF 636, HP 301(ii), HTC 12, SOP 507

God the Father of creation – 277
Love divine: AHB 625, AMNS 131, AMR 205, HF 76, HP 267(ii), HTC 217(ii), WOV 148. **Shipston:** AHB 348, BHB 726, CP 252, EH 390, HF 598, HP 344, HTC 282, SOP 364, WOV 94

God, we praise you – 536
Lux Eoi: AHB 178, AMNS 80, AMR 137, CP 66, HF 25, HTC 504

God, whose almighty word – 416
Moscow: AHB 333, AMNS 180, AMR 266, BHB 46, CP 164, EH 553, HF 102, HP 29, HTC 506, SOP 303, WOV 61

God's Spirit is in my heart – 422
Go tell everyone: SLW 93, SoW 110

Gracious Spirit, Holy Ghost
See: Holy Spirit, gracious guest – 476

Great and wonderful your deeds* – 335
Württemberg (Nassau): AHB 179, AMNS 79, AMR 136, BHB 167, EH App12, HF 192, HP 192, HTC 150, WOV 282(ii)

Great is the Lord, his praise is great* – 488
Great is the Lord: PP 93. **Truro:** AHB 39, AMNS 483, AMR 220, BHB 645, CP 294, EH 420, HF 233, HP 190, HTC 516, MP 123, SOP 545, WOV 33

Great is your faithfulness* – 523
Great is thy faithfulness: BHB 576, HF 49, HP 66, HTC 260, JrP 64, MP 62

Guide me, O my great Redeemer – 129
Cwm Rhondda: AHB 555(ii), AMNS 214(ii), AMR 296, BHB 541, CP 283(ii), HF 410, HP 437, HTC 528, WOV 478

Happy are they, they who love God – 125
Binchester: AHB 532, AMNS 176, AMR 261, BHB 496, CP 286, EH 398, HF 517, HP 711, HTC 473, SOP 509

Happy Christmas, everybody – 639
Jubilate everybody: JP 25, PP 20, SoW 134

Hark the glad sound – 217, 580
Bristol: AHB 74, AMNS 30, AMR 53, BHB 81, CFT 14, CP 34, EH 6, HF 463, HP 82, HTC 193, SOP 62, WOV 197

Hark! the herald angels sing – 660
Mendelssohn: AHB 112, AMNS 35, AMR 60, BHB 98, CC1 14, CFT 84, CP 39, EH 24, HF 155, HP 106, HTC 59, SOP 74, WOV 227

He gave his life in selfless love – 34
Christmas Carol: AHB 122, BHB 105, CFT 40, CP 392, HF 152, HTC 88, 498, SOP 79(ii). **Selfless Love:** HTC 405, SoW 58

He is Lord (one or two verses)* – 295, 586
He is Lord: HTC s7, JP 70, JrP 75, MP 69, SF 3, SG 137, SpP 51

He's got the whole world – 189
He's got the whole world: CAP 19, JP 70, JrP 78, PiP 25, STG 4

Help us, O Lord, to learn – 615
Sandys: AHB 102, AMNS 240, AMR 337, BHB 3, CP 311, EH 485, HF 336, HP 474, HTC 49, SOP 652, WOV 458. **St Michael:** AHB 29, AMNS 84, AMR 142, BHB 363, CP 219, EH 2, HF 342, HP 591, SOP 702, WOV 300

Help us to help each other, Lord – 439
Dunfermline: AHB 304, AMNS 374, AMR 20, BHB 501, CP 31, EH 64, HF 258, HP 6, HTC 54, SOP 517, WOV 365. **St Hugh:** AHB 609, AMNS 22, AMR 317, BHB 325, CP 263, EH 606, HF 46, HP 679, HTC 367, SOP 371

Here from all nations* – 577
Epiphany Hymn: AHB 125, AMNS 47(ii), BHB 9, CP 43, HP 700(ii), HTC 338, SoW 27. **O quanta qualia:** AMNS 186, AMR 281, HF 608, HTC 1, PP 42, SoW 4

Here he comes robed in majesty – 57
Here he comes: CH 134

His name is higher than any other* – 640
His name is higher: JP 74, MP 71, SF 37, SpP2 262

ove divine, all loves excelling* – 387
Blaenwern: AHB 612, AMNS 464, BHB 595, CP 271, HF 76, HP 267, HTC 217, JP 273, MP 149, WOV 165(ii). Love divine: AHB 625, AMNS 131, AMR 205, HF 76, HP 267(ii), HTC 217(ii), WOV 148

ove's redeeming work is done – 259
Savannah: AMNS 83, AMR 141, EH 135, HP 546(ii), HTC 150(ii), SOP 160, WOV 520. Württemberg: AHB 13, AMNS 79, AMR 136, BHB 167, EH app12, HF 192, HP 192, HTC 153, WOV 282(ii)

oving Shepherd of your sheep – 147
Buckland: AHB 337, AMNS 134, AMR 444, BHB 287, EH app67, HF 645, HP 287, HTC 305

Majesty, worship his majesty* – 339
Majesty: JrP 160, MP 151, SF2 257, SpP 127

Make me a channel of your peace – 470
St Francis: FS 97, HTC s19, JP 161, JrP 161, MP 153, SoW 111, SpP2 320

Make way, make way for Christ* – 587
Make Way: CFW Source Book

Man of Sorrows – 237
Man of sorrows (Gethsemane): AHB 159, BHB 186, CP 62, HP 228, HTC 130, MP 154

Mary had a baby – 650
Mary had a baby: CFT 49, CGC 21, PGT 63, PiP 38

Mary sang a song, a song of love – 643
Mary sang a song: JP 28, PP 25. Pavenham: CFW Source Book, CPr

May the grace of Christ our saviour – 504
Halton Holgate (Sharon): AHB 198, AMNS 118, BHB 284, HF 190, HP 655, HTC 370, WOV 78. Waltham: AHB 21, AMNS 181, AMR 636, BHB 449, CP 144, HF 591, WOV 373

May the mind of Christ my saviour – 452
St Leonard's: AHB 634, BHB 596, CP 348, HF 480, HP 739(ii), HTC 550, JrP 165, MP 157, WOV 537

Morning has broken* – 279
Bunessan: AHB 96, AMNS 415, BHB 92, CP 395, HF 161, HP 350, HTC 265, SOP 30, SoW 8, WOV 241

My faithful shepherd is the Lord – 560
Herongate: AHB 400, AMNS 70, BHB 142, CP 53, EH 597, HF 302, HP 224, HTC 131, SOP 602, WOV 413

My God, how wonderful you are – 341
Westminster: AHB 10, AMNS 102, AMR 169, BHB 64, CP 6, EH 441, HF 11, HP 51, HTC 369, SOP 581, WOV 71

My God is so big/great – 82
My God is so big: JP 62, JrP 169

My Lord, he is a-coming soon – 588
My Lord, he is coming: CH 138, JP 94

My Lord of light – 342
Barbara Allen: HTC 4, SoW 43

My song is love unknown – 215
Love unknown: AHB 155, AMNS 63, AMR 102, BHB 143, CP 46, HF 169, HP 173, HTC 136, SOP 127, WOV 257

Name of all majesty* – 306
Majestas: HTC 218

No weight of gold or silver – 223
Ewing: AHB 432, AMNS 184, AMR 278, BHB 295,

HF 371, HTC 573, SOP 198, WOV 346. Passion Chorale: AHB 158, AMNS 68, AMR 111, BHB 145, CP 52, EH 102, HF 182, HP 176, HTC 139, SOP 128, SoW 56, WOV 255

Not the grandeur of the mountains – 382
Everton: AHB 178(ii), AMNS 132, AMR 207, BHB 379, CP 170, EH app27, HF 544, HP 303, HTC 102

Nothing but the love of Jesus – 398
Nothing but the love: JP 96

Now evening comes to close the day – 461
Charnwood: CFW Source Book. Stracathro: AHB 147, AMNS 383, BHB 70, CP 124, EH 445, HF 450, HP 392(ii), HTC 144, SOP 438, WOV 168

Now let us learn of Christ – 148
Ibstone: AHB 631, AMR 356, BHB 317, CP 274, HF 404, HP 730, HTC 250. Quam dilecta: AHB 13, AMNS 160, AMR 242, CP 157, EH 508, HF 63, HTC 558

Now lives the Lamb of God – 246
Christchurch: AHB 202, AMNS 402, AMR 280, BHB 716, CP 108, EH 411(Stegall), HF 106, HP 203, HTC 565, SOP 197(ii), WOV 37. Gopsal: AHB 210, AMNS 139, AMR 216, BHB 190, CP 80, EH 476, HF 216, HP 243, HTC 180, SOP 632, WOV 147

Now thank we all our God* – 199
Gracias: BHB 18, HP5 66(iii), HTC 33(ii). Nun danket: AHB 22, AMNS 205, AMR 379, BHB 18(ii), CP 26, EH 533, HF 38, HP 566, HTC 33, SOP 350, WOV 14

O be glad in the Lord and rejoice* – 443
Jane: HTC 475

O bless the God of Israel – 585
Morning Light: AHB 586, AMNS 221, AMR 307, BHB 556, CP 296, EH 581, HF 388, HP 721, HTC 535, MP 211, SOP 646(ii), WOV 509. Thornbury: AHB 426, AMNS 171, AMR 256, BHB 264, CP 336, EH 545, HF 518, HP 784, HTC 521, MP 247, SOP 255(iii), WOV 389

O Breath of life – 464
Spiritus vitae: AHB 298, CP 133, HF 254, HTC 237, MP 164, WOV 322

O come, all ye faithful – 672
Adeste fideles: AHB 106, AMNS 34, AMR 59, BHB 104, CC1 26, CFT 102/103, CP 40, EH 28, HF 154, HP 110, HTC 65, SOP 78, WOV 228

O come, let us sing to the Lord* – 76
Weymouth Street: CFW Source Book

O give thanks to the Lord* – 493
O give thanks to the Lord: MP 182, SF1 97

O God beyond all praising* – 47
Thaxted: AMNS 295, AMR 579, BHB 642, HTC 36, SOP 319

O God, our help in ages past – 50
St Anne: AHB 244, AMNS 99, AMR 165, BHB 71, CP 27, EH 450, HF 41, HP 358, HTC 37, SOP 598, WOV 46

O Holy Spirit breathe on me – 316
O Holy Spirit: JP 125, MP 170

O Holy Spirit, come to bless – 475
St Stephen: AHB 339, AMNS 29, AMR 52, HP 245, HTC 483(ii), SOP 250. St Timothy: AHB 41, AMNS 3, AMR 5, BHB 252, HF 559, HTC 269

O how good is the Lord* – 376
O how good: JP 30, SLW 6

O let the Church rejoice* – 467
Christchurch: AHB 202, AMNS 402, AMR 280, BHB 716, CP 108, EH 411(Steggall), HF 106, HP 203, HTC 565, SOP 197(ii), WOV 37

O little town of Bethlehem – 647
Christmas Carol: AHB 122(ii), BHB 105, CFT 40, CP 392, HF 152, HTC 88, 498. **Forest Green:** AHB 122, AMNS 40, AMR 65, BHB 718, CC 27, CFT 39, CP 202, EH 15, HF 152, HP 113, HTC 88, SOP 79, WOV 240

O Lord of heaven and earth and sea – 498
Almsgiving (Dykes): AHB 599(ii), AMNS 287, AMR 480, BHB 68, CP 258, HF 31, HP 337, HTC 287

O Lord our guardian and our guide – 124
Abridge: AHB 146, AMNS 217, AMR 300, BHB 600, CP 225, EH 369, HF 72, HP 602, HTC 363, SOP 100, SoW 114, WOV 476

O praise ye the Lord
See: Sing praise to the Lord – 490

O taste and see that the Lord is good* – 28
O taste and see that the Lord: SF3 461

O what a gift, what a wonderful gift – 33
Canticle of the Gift: JP 99, MP 176, SLW 2, SoW 21

O worship the King* – 351
Hanover: AHB 248, AMNS 101, AMR 167, BHB 22, CP 25, EH 466, HF 8, HP 28, HTC 24, SOP 618, WOV 67

O worship the Lord* – 92
Was lebet: AHB 11, AMNS 49, AMR 77, BHB 35, CFT 150, EH 42, HF 15, HP 505, HTC 344, SOP 470, WOV 104

Oft in danger, oft in woe
See: Christian soldiers – 530

On Calvary's tree – 227
On Calvary's tree: JP 100, JrP 183

On Jordan's bank the Baptist's cry – 581
Winchester New: AHB 79, AMNS 27, AMR 2, BHB 86, CFT 160, CP 76, EH 9, HF 291, HP 84, HTC 119, SOP 137, WOV 45

Once in royal David's city – 646
Irby: AHB 107, AMNS 46, AMR 432, BHB 106, CC1 30, CFT 41, CP 41, EH 605, HF 156, HP 114, HTC 67, SOP 368, WOV 237

One must water, one must weed – 471
One must water: CH 103

One shall tell another – 30
One shall tell another: SF2 274, SG 53

Onward, Christian soldiers – 551
St Gertrude: AHB 562, AMNS 333, AMR 629, BHB 520, EH 643, HF 379, HP 718, HTC 532, SoW 28

Open our eyes, Lord – 612
Open our eyes: JP 164, MP 181, SF2 275, SpP 150

Praise God from whom* – 70, 345
Come Together: HTC 585, JP 33, MP 185, SF3 466. **Tallis' Canon** or **Canon:** AHB 37, AMNS 10, AMR 23, BHB 694, CP 358, EH 267, HF 561, HP 642, HTC 586, SOP 45, WOV 357

Praise God today* – 180
Crucifer: AMNS 72, AMR 72, HP 170, HTC 508, WOV 271

Praise him on the trumpet* – 468
Praise him on the trumpet: JPr 200, SF2 280

Praise him, praise him, everybody* – 379

Praise him, praise him: BHB 753, HP 565, HTC s21, JrP 201

Praise him, praise him – Jesus* – 304
Ludgrove: HF 130, JrP 203, MP 186

Praise, my soul, the king of heaven* – 459
Praise my soul: AHB 247, AMNS 192, AMR 365, BHB 23, CP 8, EH 470, HF 9, HP 13, HTC 38, MP 187, SOP 623, WOV 68

Praise the Lord our God* – 515
Kum ba yah: HP 525, HTC 358, NCP 49

Praise the Lord, you heavens* – 284
Austria: AHB 29, AMNS 195, AMR 257, BHB 24, CP 20, EH 393, HF 515, HP 222, HTC 494, SOP 500, WOV 577

Praise the name of Jesus* – 401
Praise the name: MP 189, SF2 283, SpP 154

Praise to the Lord, the almighty* – 89
Lobe den Herren: AHB 246, AMNS 207, BHB 25, CP 24, EH 536, HF 33, HP 16, HTC 40, MP 192, SOP 626, WOV 28

Put on the sword of the Spirit – 541
Put on the sword of the Spirit: CFW Source Book

Reign in me, sovereign God – 403
Reign in me: SpP2 351

Rejoice! rejoice! Christ is in you* – 538
Rejoice! rejoice!: SF3 478, SG 100, SpP2 352

Rejoice, the Lord is king* – 301
Gopsal: AHB 210, AMNS 139, AMR 216, BHB 190, CP 80, EH 476, HF 216, HP 243, HTC 180, SOP 632, WOV 147

Restore, O Lord, the honour – 589
Restore O Lord: MP 196, SF2 286, SpP 158

Revive your church, O Lord – 479
Carlisle: AHB 27, AMNS 201, AMR 362, BHB 523, CP 1, EH 190, HF 3, HP 513, HTC 515, SOP 458, WOV 390. **Venice:** AHB 139(ii), AMNS 301, AMR 510, CP 178, HF 27, HP 156, HTC 34, WOV 317

Ride on, ride on in majesty – 218
St Drostane: AHB 167, AMNS 61, AMR 99, BHB 128, CP 50, HF 171. **Winchester New:** AHB 79, AMNS 27, AMR 2, BHB 86, CP 76, EH 9, HF 291, HP 84, HTC 119, SOP 137, WOV 45

Ring out the bells – 665
Past three a clock: CC1 31, CFT 129

Safe in the shadow of the Lord – 395
Creator God: HTC 445, PP 108. **Lloyd:** HF 50

Salvation is found in no-one else – 397
Salvation: CFW Source Book

Saviour, again to your dear name – 553
Ellers: AHB 63, AMNS 15, AMR 31, BHB 702, CP 212, EH app38, HF 280, HP 643, HTC 281

See him lying on a bed of straw – 656
Calypso Carol: CFT 110/111, HP 118, HTC 91, JP 103, JrP 214, MTB 24, SLW 118, SoW 10

See the feast our God prepares – 17
Orientis Partibus: AHB 601(ii), AMNS 302, AMR 524, BHB 48, CP 177, EH 129, HP 168, HTC 472, SOP 153, WOV 149

Seek ye first the kingdom of God – 168
Seek ye first: HP 138, JP 204, JrP 215, MP 201, SF2 290, SLW 58, SpP 161

FIRST LINES

(Italics indicate traditional first lines and relate them to new versions.)

new commandment
See: The new commandment – 445
bba, Father – 399
l creation join to say
See: Love's redeeming work – 259
ll creatures of our God and King – 283
ll glory, praise and honour – 202
ll people that on earth do dwell – 367
ll Scriptures are given – 608
ll the way, all the way – 207
ll things bright and beautiful – 266
lleluia, alleluia, give thanks – 252
lleluia, alleluia! he is Lord – 292
lleluia, my Father – 224
mazing grace – 158
nd can it be that I should gain – 389
ngels from the realms of glory – 661
ngels, praise him – 272
s with gladness – 104
t the name of Jesus – 305
t your feet we fall – 251
way in a manger – 651

e bold, be strong – 542
e thou my guardian and my guide
See: O Lord, our guardian – 124
ecause he died and is risen – 568
ecause your love is better than life – 79
efore the heaven and earth – 206
ehold, I tell you a mystery – 563
ethlehem, what greater city – 93
ind us together, Lord – 119
less the Lord, creation sings – 163
less the Lord, O my soul – 80
less the Lord, our fathers' God – 56
less-ed is the man – 138
reak now the bread of life – 614
reak thou the bread of life
See: Break now the bread – 614
reathe on me, breath of God – 326
ring to the Lord a glad new song – 54
roken for me, broken for you – 40

aring, sharing – 448
hild in the manger – 652
hildren of the heavenly king – 556
hrist, from whom all blessings flow – 463
hrist in me is to live – 140

Christ is born within a stable – 666
Christ is made the sure foundation – 483
Christ is our corner-stone – 482
Christ is surely coming – 598
Christ the Lord is risen again – 258
Christ the Lord is risen today
See: Love's redeeming work – 259
Christ triumphant – 300
Christ whose glory fills the skies – 134
Christian soldiers, onward go! – 530
Christians, join in celebration – 458
Church of God, elect and glorious – 444
City of God, Jerusalem – 595
Cleanse me from my sin, Lord – 225
Clothed in kingly majesty – 355
Come and go with me – 564
Come and hear the joyful singing – 662
Come and join the celebration – 669
Come and praise the Lord our king – 188
Come and see the shining hope – 578
Come and sing the Christmas story – 638
Come down, O love divine! – 308
Come, join to praise our God – 354
Come let us join our cheerful songs – 555
Come, let us sing to the Lord – 393
Come, most Holy Spirit, come – 327
Come, praise the Lord – 486
Come, rejoice before your maker – 96
Come, sing praises to the Lord – 115
Come sing the praise of Jesus – 250
Come, thou Holy Spirit, come
See: Come, most holy Spirit – 327
Come with all joy to sing to God – 205
Come, worship God – 606
Come, you thankful people, come – 526
Cradle rocking, cattle lowing – 649
Crown him with many crowns – 198

Ding-dong! Merrily on high – 667

Earth has many a noble city
See: Bethlehem, what greater – 93
Emmanuel, Emmanuel – 642
Eternal Father, strong to save – 350
Every nation, praise the Lord – 97

Faithful Shepherd, feed me – 571
Faithful vigil ended – 562

Falling, falling, gently falling – 315
Father God in heaven – 171
Father, hear the prayer we offer – 85
Father, in your presence kneeling – 10
Father, let us dedicate – 73
Father, now behold us – 11
Father of mercies, in your word – 601
Father, we adore you – 191
Father, we love you – 336
Fear not, rejoice and be glad – 516
Fierce raged the tempest – 362
Fight the good fight – 546
Fill your hearts with joy – 513
Firmly I believe and truly – 145
Fling wide the gates – 291
For all the saints – 550
For God so loved the world – 402
For I'm building a people of power – 469
For the beauty of the earth – 182
For the bread which you have broken – 46
For the fruits of his creation – 522
For this purpose Christ was revealed – 255
For your mercy and your grace – 72
From all who live beneath the skies – 419
From heaven you came – 449
From the rising of the sun – 139

Girls and boys, leave your toys – 668
Give me joy in my heart – 446
Glorious things of you are spoken – 183
Glory be to God in heaven – 24
Glory in the highest – 25
Go forth and tell – 506
Go, tell it on the mountain – 424
God forgave my sin – 293
God has exalted him – 294
God has spoken to his people – 611
God is good – we sing and shout it – 377
God is love – his the care – 368
God is love: let heaven adore him – 386
God is our strength and refuge – 77
God is so good – 396
God of glory, we exalt your name – 337
God of gods, we sound his praises – 561
God of light and life's creation – 505
God of mercy, God of grace – 527
God save our gracious Queen – 68
God the Father caused to be – 320
God the Father of creation – 277
God, we praise you – 536
God, whose almighty word – 416
God's Spirit is in my heart – 422

Gracious Spirit, Holy Ghost
  See: Holy Spirit, gracious guest – 476
Great and wonderful your deeds – 335
Great is the Lord, his praise is great – 488
Great is your faithfulness – 523
Guide me, O my great Redeemer – 129

Happy are they, they who love God – 125
Happy Christmas, everybody – 639
Hark the glad sound – 217, 580
Hark! the herald angels sing – 660
He gave his life in selfless love – 34
He is Lord (one or two verses) – 295, 586
He's got the whole world – 189
Help us, O Lord, to learn – 615
Help us to help each other, Lord – 439
Here from all nations – 577
Here he comes robed in majesty – 57
His name is higher than any other – 640
Holy child, how still you lie – 653
Holy, holy, holy is the Lord – 338
Holy, holy, holy, Lord God almighty – 32
Holy Spirit, gracious guest – 476
Holy Spirit, hear us – 602
Holy Spirit, truth divine – 322
How good a thing it is – 116
How good is the God we adore – 84
How great is God almighty – 313
How long will you forget me, Lord? – 222
How lovely on the mountains – 421

I am a new creation – 359
I am trusting you, Lord Jesus – 406
I believe in God the Father – 404
I come with joy to meet my Lord – 16
I love to think, though I am young – 194
I love you, O Lord, you alone – 248
I want to walk with Jesus Christ – 141
I was glad when they said to me – 559
I will sing about your love – 81
I will sing, I will sing a song – 517
I'm going to say my prayers – 167
If I were a butterfly – 273
If you want to be great – 142
Immortal, invisible, God only wise – 267
In Christ there is no east or west – 429
In my life, Lord, be glorified – 495
In the cross of Christ I glory – 231
In the presence of your people – 334
It is a thing most wonderful – 232

Jesus Christ is risen today – 242